It's All of Our Business

Communicating Competently in the Workplace

FIRST EDITION

J. DAN ROTHWELL

CABRILLO COLLEGE, CALIFORNIA

MICHELLE WATERS

CABRILLO COLLEGE, CALIFORNIA

OXFORD

UNIVERSITY PRESS

OXFORD
UNIVERSITY PRESS

Oxford University Press is a department of the University of Oxford.
It furthers the University's objective of excellence in research, scholarship,
and education by publishing worldwide. Oxford is a registered trademark
of Oxford University Press in the UK and certain other countries.

Published in the United States of America by Oxford University Press
198 Madison Avenue, New York, NY 10016, United States of America.

Library of Congress Cataloging in Publication Data

Names: Rothwell, J. Dan, author. | Waters, Michelle (Communication
    consultant), author.
Title: It's all of our business : communicating competently in the
    workplace / J. Dan Rothwell, Michelle Waters.
Description: First edition. | New York : Oxford University Press, [2023] |
    Includes bibliographical references and index. | Summary: "It's All of
    Our Business: Communicating in the Workplace is a brief, inexpensive,
    conversational and comprehensive text that balances practical skills and
    competence with scholarly insight. The text will address several topics
    often ignored or given only glancing coverage in competing texts
    including connecting bids, dialectics and conflict, anger management,
    difficult group members, virtual groups, cognitive dissonance,
    persuasion, power, and culture"—Provided by publisher.
Identifiers: LCCN 2022027291 (print) | LCCN 2022027292 (ebook) |
    ISBN 9780190078188 (paperback) | ISBN 9780190078195 (epub)
Subjects: LCSH: Business communication. | Communication in organizations.
Classification: LCC HF5718 .R6748 2023 (print) | LCC HF5718 (ebook) | DDC
    650.01/4—dc23/eng/20220818
LC record available at https://lccn.loc.gov/2022027291
LC ebook record available at https://lccn.loc.gov/2022027292

9 8 7 6 5 4 3 2 1
Printed by Sheridan Books, Inc., United States of America

To my family:
MARCY, HILARY, GEOFF, BARRETT, AND CLARE

—Dan

For
Brendan

—Michelle

Brief Contents

Contents

CHAPTER 9 The Nature of Groups: Working with Others   143

CHAPTER 10   Competent Leadership: A Process More Than a Person   165

CHAPTER 11   Work Teams: A Special Type of Group   185

CHAPTER 12   Meetings: A Perpetual Challenge   203

CHAPTER 13 Business Writing: Representing Yourself with Words 221

CHAPTER 16   Visual Aids and Delivery 273

Preface

It's All of Our Business: Communicating Competently in the Workplace is intended for an introductory business communication course. It is a comprehensive text, covering the standard topics with several important novel twists. There is no shortage of books and articles on business communication, especially in the trade book market, that provide extensive and often contradictory recipes for improving communication in the workplace. Most authors of these works offer no theoretical rationale for their advice other than "It worked for me"; and they often present only anecdotal evidence to support their recipes. This raises the justifiable critique that the advice seems to be mere personal opinion and individual taste, generically applied as universal wisdom. Those who uncritically accept such generic advice reveal the "naïve belief that if a particular course of action helped other companies to succeed, it ought to help theirs" (Christensen & Raynor, 2003). In contrast, we provide a theoretical rationale, thoroughly developed, by taking a **communication competence perspective** that informs our analysis and advice. **Communication competence** *is engaging in communication with others that is perceived to be both appropriate and effective in a given context* (Spitzberg, 2015). We are not the first to reference the communication competence perspective for business and the workplace, but we believe that we are by far the most comprehensive in its development and application.

Noteworthy Features

1. **Affordability**. The cost of textbooks has become a national issue shared by students and faculty alike. An Oxford University Press national survey of 327 professors who teach at U.S. universities and community colleges revealed that almost 75% of respondents viewed price as an "extremely or very important" feature of a text. Maximum effort has been exerted to make *It's All of Our Business* an attractive but affordable alternative to other much more expensive choices. **Oxford University Press is a** *not-for-profit publishing company*, so this alone provides considerable price advantage of between 25% and 35% discounts for students surviving on tight budgets. The lean size of *It's All of Our Business* also helps reduce the price. Depth of treatment, however, is not sacrificed to brevity. Coverage is consistently substantial. Also, **the e-book version provides a very affordable option for students while providing an extensive package of ancillaries not likely found in OERs (open educational resources)**.

2. **Unique Coverage**. *It's All of Our Business* addresses several topics often ignored or given only glancing coverage in competing texts. For example

   a. The strong focus on **power** is a major attribute. Two substantial chapters plus additional applications in other chapters are required to cover this essential topic and provide needed context for analysis and application to workplace communication. Important topics, such as sexual harassment, gender bias, and bullying at work, are best analyzed for their causes and prevention in terms of power dynamics. The fact that *competing texts barely address power, or give it only peripheral consideration*, is an enormous oversight. As social psychologist Dacher Keltner (2016a) explains, "Power defines the waking life of every human being, . . . emerges instantaneously when humans interact," and "shapes our every interaction, from those between parent and children to those between work colleagues." As we note in Chapter 3, "power is everywhere" (Battilana & Casciaro, 2021). *You cannot communicate with others without power operating as a blatantly obvious or sometimes subtle dynamic because it permeates every aspect of business*. To ignore or give only cursory treatment to power is strikingly inadequate. From our viewpoint, the topic requires extensive analysis and applications for a text to be truly relevant to the contemporary workplace.

b. **Communication climate** is given prominent coverage in a full chapter, far more comprehensive than in most texts and trade books. Studies show conclusively that a negative workplace environment is a leading cause of quitting jobs or avoiding employment even at leading companies.

c. Although some competing business communication texts include a separate chapter on **culture**, *we instead infuse multiple chapters with cultural context*. This has the advantage of not treating culture as a separate topic but one that permeates the contemporary business environment. Too often, leadership theory and practice, for example, are discussed only in the context of the United States. There is important and interesting research, however, that questions the universality of leadership theory applied to all cultures.

d. With the advent and continuation of the COVID pandemic, **virtual groups and teams** have become ubiquitous. Consequently, a unique focus on virtuality in the business arena has been included throughout the text.

e. Business and workplace meetings have always been a source of complaint and considerable concern. The pervasiveness of virtual meetings has added to the many challenges associated with conducting productive meetings. Consequently, **virtual meetings** have been addressed extensively.

3. **Readability**. The wisdom of Samuel Johnson seems apt on the subject of readability: "What is written without effort is in general read without pleasure." Maximum effort has been devoted to writing a textbook that might ignite the interest of student readers, not induce a coma. Textbooks are not meant to read like spy thrillers, but they need not read like an audit report. We strive to give our writing style a personality.

Therefore, the style is slightly edgy and conversational. First-person singular is more engaging than impersonal references such as "the author experienced" or "a student in the author's class," which makes us sound professorial and detached. We identify each other by our first name when a personal narrative is used as an illustration or attention strategy. We like to talk directly to you, our readers, by employing second-person pronoun references to "you." Students that do not read their text because the style is impersonal, dull, stuffy, overly academic, and uninspiring can never profit from the sophisticated advice discovered from decades of research and study.

Lastly, a more abbreviated text compared to standard-sized competitors makes the task of reading seem less intimidating for students. Relatively short chapters provide students with a sense of accomplishment as each chapter is rapidly completed.

4. **Scholarship**. Melding substantial research and a high-level of scholarship into a relatively brief text is a supreme challenge for any author. Abundant research is cited in a free-flowing writing style. Hundreds of references are cited throughout our text. Yes, student readers do not necessarily appreciate such citations, but we think it extremely important to document our claims and advice with the most credible available evidence. This is a college textbook and should meet appropriate expectations and standards.

5. **Visual Illustrations**. Competing texts tend to be light on photos, and those that are included often rarely venture from the mundane. This is understandable. Choosing interesting photos for a business

communication book is challenging, a task we explored and often found quite frustrating. A maximum effort has been undertaken, admittedly not always successfully, to offer an abundance of interesting photos to attract the student reader. *Captions have been added for each photo that make an important point, offer evidence, add humor, and/or explain a concept*. In addition, although the work of a few recognizable cartoonists is used, **most cartoons are custom efforts** by Marcy Wieland, who has provided terrific cartoons for other published textbooks. The advantage of working with Marcy is that we suggested ideas and she then rendered them in her own creative way under our guidance. This provides a very unique quality to *It's All of Our Business*.

6. **Available Formats.** To reduce the price, *It's All of Our Business* will be available as a relatively inexpensive e-book, bound copy rental, or, for those who do not have easy access to a computer, a loose-leaf version.

Pedagogy

Many recent business communication texts have become heavy with pedagogical tools to help readers understand material presented (usually presented in boxed asides). Although in theory these are probably useful to students, they increase the price of each text, and students are likely to skip such aids, especially if chapters are lengthy and boxed asides are plentiful. *It's All of Our Business* includes only a few, carefully chosen boxed self-assessment instruments, tables, and graphs. Plentiful practical advice *supported by research* is included in the main text, not in boxed asides. Pedagogical aids are placed on a website for easy access without driving up the price of the text or interrupting the flow of the chapter.

Here is a list of pedagogical tools available as ancillaries for *It's All of Our Business*:

1. **Enhanced e-book version.** The e-book version of *It's All of Our Business* will incorporate short video clips in every chapter that illustrate points and can provide opportunities for thoughtful analysis.

2. **Film School Case Studies.** Carefully selected films provide optimum opportunities for illustration and analysis of key chapter points.

3. **TED Talks** and **YouTube video** links at the end of each chapter provide visual illustrations and elaborations of key points.

4. An **Instructor's Manual** contains dozens of unique activities and exercises, as well as a wide variety of video resources.

5. A **Test Bank** provides a multitude of questions from which to choose for construction of exams.

6. A **glossary** of important terms will appear at the end of the text. All **boldfaced** terms in the text will be defined when the term first appears and will be included in the glossary.

7. **PowerPoint lecture slides** that are often more than mere "grocery lists" of bullet points are available.

8. The **Oxford Learning Link** provides students with the following:
   a. Key term *flashcards*
   b. Videos for in-class discussion

9. **Course cartridges** for a variety of Learning Management Systems, including Blackboard, Canvas, Moodle, and D2L, allow instructors to create their own course websites integrating student and instructor resources available on the Oxford Learning Link. Contact your Oxford University Press representative for access or for more information about these supplements or customized options.

Acknowledgments

Our sincere thanks are extended to reviewers of this text. They include the following:

Lisa Barley
Eastern Michigan University

Dana Bible
Sam Houston State University

Lynda Fuller
Wilmington University

Laura Hammel
John Carroll University

Erin Harrison
UNC Greensboro

Heidi Huntington
West Texas A&M University

Tatia Jacobson Jordan
The University of Texas of Arlington

Barbara Looney
Black Hills State University

Gregory Morin
University of Nebraska–Omaha

Teeanna Rizkallah
CSU Fullerton

Andre Albert Favors
Lamar University

Rita Rahoi-Gilchhrest
Winona State University

Paul T.M. Hemenway
Lamar University

Teresa Filipowicz
Pima Community College

Karley Goen
Tarleton State University

Felicia Stewart
Morehouse College

Kari Cameron
Rochester Institute of Technology

Sean C. Flannery
Immaculata University

Bryan-Mitchell Young
Ivy Tech Community College

Creshema Murray
University of Houston-Downtown

We also want to thank the many professionals at Oxford University Press who worked to bring *It's All of Our Business* to the marketplace. They include former executive editor, Steve Helba, and Alyssa Quinones, associate editor.

I (Dan) personally want to offer a special thanks to my wife, Marcy, for the wonderful *custom cartoons*. I gave her ideas and she produced beautiful, animated renderings. Artist, singer, writer, musician, computer program analyst—her talents seem boundless. I also want to thank the voters of my Santa Cruz county district for electing me to the Cabrillo College Board of Trustees by an overwhelming margin. The practical experience campaigning for public office was invaluable, and tantamount to a three-month migraine.

I (Michelle) want to thank all the people who helped me make this book a reality! First, to my co-author, Dan—Thank you for letting me be a part of this phenomenal project. We did it! You led the way, encouraged my contributions, and always believed in me—even when I didn't. I am grateful. Next, I owe a debt of gratitude to my family members who cheered me on: Brian Waters, Sandy Printer, Carol Williams, Leslie Gandy, Shannon Niland, Hoshi Printer, and my two kiddos, Macy and Brendan. Thank you, thank you. You make my world a happy place.

About the Authors

J. Dan Rothwell is the former chair of the Communication Studies Department at Cabrillo College. I have a BA in American history from the University of Portland (Oregon), an MA in rhetoric and public address, and a PhD in communication theory and social influence, both from the University of Oregon. I have authored five other books in addition to *It's All of Our Business*. They are *In Mixed Company: Communicating in Small Groups and Teams* (Oxford University Press), *In the Company of Others: An Introduction to Communication* (Oxford University Press), *Practically Speaking* (Oxford University Press), *Telling It Like It Isn't: Language Misuse and Malpractice* (Prentice Hall), and *Interpersonal Communication: Influences and Alternatives* (with James Costigan and published by Charles-Merrill).

I deeply appreciate receiving more than two dozen teaching awards during my lengthy academic career, including, among others, the "Ernest L. Boyer International Award for Excellence in Teaching, Learning, and Technology"; the Cabrillo College "Innovative Teacher of the Year"; the National Communication Association "Community College Educator of the Year" award; an official "Excellence in Teaching" resolution by the California State Senate; and the Western States Communication Association "Master Teacher" award. Having never achieved one of my early life goals—to be a Hall of Fame major league baseball pitcher—these teaching awards, as much as I truly value them, will have to compensate for this one lifelong disappointment.

Michelle Waters, MA in Communication Studies, San Jose State University, is a high-energy communication consultant and executive coach with more than 25 years of teaching experience. I taught for the communication departments of Jose State University and Cabrillo College for a total of 20 years. Concurrently, I paired academic instruction with corporate training, enabling competent communication at all levels of an organization, from top-level leaders to entry-level employees. In 2016, I left academia and made training my full-time career. I absolutely love what I do! I get the privilege of sharing communication techniques and research with others so they can make waves of positive impact on their teams and throughout their organizations. My greatest professional joy extends beyond the training room—it's from hearing about the transference and application of concepts that take place after the training experience. What happens in my classes—the content delivered onsite or virtually—better not stay in my classes; otherwise, I've just wasted everyone's time. I strive for high-participation experiences with high-impact results.

I've successfully partnered with organizations in the financial, health, agriculture, and government sectors, teaching classes with an emphasis on leadership, customer service, and presentation skills. Multiple times, I've facilitated leadership programs for Driscoll's in Spain, Australia, and the Netherlands. This gave me a deeper understanding of cultural communication differences. Though this is my first textbook, it is not my first book. I was diagnosed with leukemia during my last semester of graduate school, and while traversing the complexities of the disease, I wrote Dancing with the Diagnosis, a communication guide for those newly diagnosed with cancer. It was published in 2004.

I am an avid runner who lives by the beach in Santa Cruz, CA, with my husband, son, and two rescue dogs.

After successful completion of this chapter you should be able to

1. Build a strong case for the importance of competent communication in the workplace.

2. Debunk common myths about communication.

3. Describe the many facets of communication through examination of the transactional model of communication.

Communication: How It Works

On April 9, 2017, Dr. David Dao, a 69-year-old passenger on United Airlines flight 3411, was forcibly removed from the plane by Chicago Department of Aviation officers. Dao had purchased a ticket for the flight and was not causing any disruption. A computer randomly picked him to disembark because the flight was overbooked, and not enough passengers accepted an offer of $800 and a hotel stay to leave the flight. Dao insisted that he could not "volunteer" to leave the overbooked flight because he had patients to see the next morning. The next available flight was in the afternoon the next day. Dao refused to comply with the officers demands that he leave the airplane, so they dragged him from his seat, inflicting numerous injuries, including a severe concussion, broken nose, and the loss of two front teeth.

Cellphone video by another passenger of this astonishing event went viral. The response from the Twitterverse was swift. One person tweeted, "United: You may be asked to vacate or be taken off the plane by force, but for $49.99 you can upgrade to trial by combat." Another tweeted,

CHAPTER OUTLINE

- Communication Myths
- Defining Communication

4. Identify several challenges of finding shared meaning in verbal and nonverbal messages, particularly in a cultural context.

"In the unlikely event of an overbooking, please assume the crash position whilst we hunt down volunteers." Yet another individual offered this sardonic take on the event—"United: Putting the hospital in hospitality."

United CEO Oscar Munoz's initial response was viewed as tone deaf by almost every news commentator, public figure, and contributor on social media. He apologized for "having to re-accommodate" passengers because of overbooking the flight, making no direct mention that a human being had been brutally dragged by his arms and legs off a plane. Chastened by the overwhelming public outrage, Munoz, to his credit, profusely apologized and

took responsibility for the inappropriate reaction to a booked passenger's refusal to leave his flight.

This entire incident is a dramatic lesson in the centrality of communication in the world of business and organizations. This was not merely a public relations disaster. It was a complete communication debacle from top to bottom even if the incident had never gone viral. As Dao noted in his first interview in 2019 about the incident, the onboard airline employees could have explained "nicely" and "reasonably" their justification for wanting to remove him from the flight. Passengers who observed this event close up reported that Dao was "very polite" when asked to leave. Aviation officers were called to

The United Airlines fiasco involving Dr. David Dao is an astonishing lesson in the centrality of communication in the world of business and organizations. This was not merely a public relations disaster, even though this protest by Jesse Jackson and others certainly attests to that being true. More importantly for our purposes, it was a complete communication calamity from top to bottom.

remove Dao from the plane with little attempt to find an alternative, such as increasing the compensation and travel vouchers to encourage someone else to volunteer. Initially, the officers tried to convince Dao to deplane, but suddenly treated Dao as you would a criminal, demanding he leave and then inflicting injurious force (Jacobs & Harrison, 2019). No euphemistic "re-accommodation" can camouflage the communication in-competence that was exhibited at every stage of this unfortunate event.

Communication is mostly what we humans do, but as the United Airlines fiasco illustrates, we often do it poorly. As one expert notes, "That communi-cation problems are omnipresent in companies or organizations is simply an understatement" (Odine, 2015). A survey of almost 1,400 respondents from 80 countries revealed that 98% of self-identified global leaders of **vir-tual teams**—groups whose members are connected by electronic technol-ogy—viewed themselves as exhibiting effective intercultural leadership, but only 19% of team members agreed (Solomon, 2016). *Ironically, it is the poorest communicators who inflate their self-assessments the most.* It is called the **Dunning-Kruger effect**—incompetence prevents accurate self-awareness of one's limitations (Dunning, 2017). One survey of a thousand U.S. employees conducted by Dynamic Signal warned businesses: "Repair the way we com-municate with employees at work or risk crippling financial consequences" (Hannah, 2019). Yet another study found that 86% of corporate execu-tives, employees, and educators say that poor communication is a key reason for workplace failures (Sanders, 2020).

Communication is the lifeblood of any business or workplace. A survey by the Graduate Management Admission Council (2017) of almost a thousand employers from 628 companies in 51 countries concluded that four of the top five skills deemed most desirable for employees to possess, way ahead of technical or administrative skills, were oral communication as the top choice, followed by listening skills, written communication, and presentation skills. An extensive study by LinkedIn of 100 metropolitan areas in the United States found that communication is "the #1 skill in demand in all 100 metros we analyzed" (Barrett, 2018; see also Bauer-Wolf, 2019). Students essen-tially agree with employers, ranking communication skills (both oral and written) among the top three "career readiness competencies" ("2018 Stu-dent Survey Report," 2019).

This is not a one-and-done process. It is a lifelong enterprise that requires constant updating as our world changes. Just con-template the enormous, unexpected communication challenges and often clumsy attempts to adapt initially that emerged as a result of the COVID-19 pandemic! Even negotiating the "mute" option on Zoom became a constant source of conversational interruptions and annoyance. More significantly, companies and small businesses have had to adapt to radically chang-ing circumstances. They have had to be flexible or not survive. As the authors of *Out of Office* explain, flexibility "means reconceiving what sorts of tasks and collaborations need to be synchronous [occurring in person] and what can actually be done asynchronously [virtually], and how many days we'd like people to be in an office, and for how long, and for what purpose" (Warzel & Petersen, 2021).

So, are you sufficiently convinced that communication is an essential component of business success? If not, then realize that this entire book is a testament to the centrality of communication to your success in the world of work, whether a laborer, executive, or any occupation that requires working with people. More narrowly at this point, *the primary purpose of this chapter is to describe and explain the nature of the communication process so essential to success in business at all levels*. Toward this end, chapter objectives are as follows: (1) identify common communication myths, (2) define communication generally, and (3) describe the many challenges posed by both verbal and nonverbal meaning, especially in a cultural context.

Communication Myths

Before defining communication, we address three major misconceptions about this activity that dominates our lives. As American humorist Will Rogers reputedly remarked, "It isn't what we don't know that gives us trouble; it's what we know that ain't so." As you read this book, note that what passes in the popular media for knowledge and insight about communication in the world of business is often pure

myth—a belief contradicted by fact. How do we know? Because abundant research says so.

Myth 1: More Communication Equals Better Communication

"One of our culture's most cherished ideas is that when it comes to communication in relationships, more is better" (Swann et al., 2003). As research shows, this is a myth (Hung & Lin, 2013). Communication quantity does not automatically equal communication quality. Technology entrepreneur Mitchell Kapor once noted, "Getting information off the Internet is like taking a drink from a fire hydrant."

The rise of social media has connected coworkers in unprecedented ways, but not always beneficially. One study found that the average "knowledge worker" checks emails and instant messaging every 6 minutes (MacKay, 2018). *It can take a group as much as 5 minutes to refocus its attention after just a 30-second interruption* (Spira, 2011). Employees at all levels of an organization spend more than 90 minutes a day, on average, recovering from email interruptions and returning to their normal tasks (Rosen et al., 2019). *Another study found that constant emailing and text messaging decreases mental capacity by an average of 10 IQ points*, like missing a night's sleep (D. Rock, 2009).

Social media are prime contributors to at-work distractions. One survey of Gen Z respondents ages 19–25 in 2020 ranked social media platforms in this order of usage: Instagram, TikTok, Snapchat, Facebook, and YouTube ("Gen Z," 2020). Preferences are sure to change as we all just try to keep up with the never-ending, frenetic world of technological innovation and obtrusive social connectivity. "The avalanche of demands for input or advice, access to resources, or sometimes just presence in a meeting causes performance to suffer. Employees take assignments home, and soon burnout and turnover become real risks" (Cross et al, 2016).

Combatting this problem requires putting yourself on a social media diet, switching off your smartphone for lengthy periods of time to enhance concentration on tasks, setting priorities so you can separate what you need to know from what there is to know *and* thus finding

Resist multitasking. Despite what you may think, research shows that you are no good at it (Cherry, 2021). Ironically, as Stanford psychologist Clifford Nass notes, "It turns out multitaskers are terrible at every aspect of multitasking" ("Interview: Clifford Nass," 2010). Your communication with coworkers, bosses, and customers becomes fragmented, unfocused, and in many cases simply chaotic when attempting to juggle too many tasks at once.

the few gold nuggets among the pile of iron pyrite, and *definitely stopping multitasking* that splits your attention and produces bad decision making (Schmidt, 2020). As comedian Doug Benson "explains," "Just the other day I was walking down the street, I was putting eyedrops in my eyes, I was talking on my cellphone, and I was getting hit by a car."

In addition to overload challenges, additional quantitative communication problems include abundant criticism, verbal abuse, dishonesty, and rumor dissemination, all of which hardly improve our work-a-day world by increasing their amount. *More communication is not always desirable. More competent communication is.*

Myth 2: 93% of Message Meaning Is Conveyed Nonverbally

How important nonverbal communication is to the communication process in general has been wildly overstated. Some communication texts and innumerable Internet sites misinterpret research by Albert Mehrabian (see Lapakko, 2007; Konstantinova & Astakhova, 2018, for detailed critiques). Marketing consultant Ian Brodie (2021) notes, "I've lost track of the number of times I've heard this [93% statistic] in sales training sessions or read it in books, articles and blogs." Joshua Uebergang (2020), director of Digital Darts and business consultant, claims this statistic that will not die "is a close contender for the greatest communication myth."

Mehrabian (1971) never drew such a broad statistical conclusion from his research. In fact, he repudiated it directly. In 2009, BBC reporter Tim Harford asked Mehrabian if 93% of communication meaning is nonverbal. He responded: "Absolutely not, and whenever I hear that misquote or misrepresentation of my findings I cringe because it should be so obvious to anybody who would use any amount of common sense that that's not the correct statement" (quoted by Lovett, 2016). Why bother learning a language, a difficult undertaking, if only a minuscule 7% of meaning is derived from verbal communication? Turn off the sound when watching a movie scene of two characters quarreling and see if you can ascertain 93% of the meaning of their argument. Yes, you can know they are quarreling and even ascertain emotion (anger), but can you discern specific claims being made, examples used to support claims, and issues unresolved? Travel to China without understanding the language and observe people in casual conversation. Can you understand more than a hint of the meaning in their transaction?

There is no specific number that indicates the importance of nonverbal communication generally. Its importance varies widely depending on the situation.

Myth 3: Communication Is a Cure-All

Communication is an enormously important tool for success in the workplace. When employed skillfully, communication can help solve numerous problems. *Communication, however, is a means to an end, not an end in itself.* It is not the basis of all problems you may encounter. For example, despite its importance to your employment future, improving your interviewing skills may not be sufficient to land a job. Your chances of landing a high-skills managerial or technical position without sufficient education and experience are about the same as a snail's safe passage across a busy freeway.

Research also reveals that some problems between individuals are not solvable regardless of your communication proficiency (Fulwiler, 2018). Your coworker may never develop a sunny disposition and a less cynical view of the

Why does Japanese superstar baseball player Shohei Ohtani ("Sho Time") require an interpreter (in the middle) during interviews even after years in the major leagues if only minimal communication meaning is derived from language? The truth is, learning a language is challenging, but it permits communicating highly specific and complex, even abstract, concepts and ideas that nonverbal communication cannot begin to reproduce.

Some problems, such as an arrogant, imperious, bullying boss, may not be improved even if you communicate competently. Does this person even look approachable much less interested in possibly improving his communication competence? Looks can be deceiving, but they also can either invite or repel others from confronting communication difficulties. Communication is a significant tool, but not a cure for every problem you might encounter at work.

a transactional process of sharing meaning with others. This seemingly simple definition requires explanation. Be thankful that we are not going to explain the OED's definition.

Communication Is Transactional: Beyond Information Exchange

To understand the ways in which communication is transactional, some basic elements need brief explanation. When you give a training presentation to a group of your coworkers, you are the *sender* who *encodes* your ideas by organizing and expressing them in a spoken language. The *message* is composed of the ideas you wish to express, such as ways to improve listening skills. Every message has two dimensions (Watzlawick et al., 1967). The *content dimension* refers to what is actually said and done. The *relationship dimension* refers to how that message defines or redefines the association between individuals. "Please edit this report; thank you" and "Edit this report" both have the same essential content about carefully checking a report for errors, but the first message communicates respect and politeness; the second is a command. There is likely a different power relationship exhibited in the two messages. A *channel* is the medium used to share a message, such as presenting in person or remotely by social media. The *receivers* are your coworkers who *decode* your message by interpreting your spoken words.

Defining communication as a **transactional process** means that the speaker is both a sender and a receiver, not merely a sender or a receiver. (Listeners are likewise sender–receivers). As you give a presentation at work, you receive *feedback* or responses, mostly nonverbal, from listeners. When audience members are doing face plants onto tabletops from mind-numbing boredom or they are perusing their smartphones during a Zoom meeting, that is

world. Your boss may never be more than an imperious, narcissistic, inconsiderate tyrant. Your marketing instructor may never change her position on late assignments despite your "valid excuse." Competent communication can help you cope with recurring disagreements and challenges, but it may not alter the results. Also, a dysfunctional organizational system characterized by unclear roles and responsibilities and poorly designed decision-making processes may be the root cause of poor communication. Training to improve communication in such circumstances is likely to prove futile without systemic changes (Baker, 2015).

Defining Communication

The *Oxford English Dictionary* (OED) takes about 1,200 words to define communication. Communication scholars have contributed more than a hundred different definitions of their own. There is no ideal, or sacred, definition of communication. Authors, scholars, and students of human communication offer definitions suitable to their perspectives on this complex subject. We define **communication** as

feedback that should inform you that you need to step up the dynamism of your delivery and invigorate your listeners with humor or other attention strategies.

Then there is *noise*, or any interference with effective transmission and reception of your message. This might be a loud or obnoxious cellphone ringtone disturbing your presentation, coworkers arriving late to a meeting, an applicant for a professional job appearing before an interviewing panel dressed in plaid shorts and a T-shirt with an image of a rock band (it happens), words that trigger a strong reaction (e.g., racist epithets), or prejudice of any kind. (See Chapter 6 for a more comprehensive discussion of noise.)

Next, *fields of experience* or your frames of reference include your cultural background, ethnicity, geographic location, education, extent of travel, and general personal experiences accumulated over the course of a lifetime. You carry these fields of experience with you to every communication event. Fields of experience between individuals may be poorly matched and consequently produce misunderstanding. The more experiences we have in common, the more likely it is that misunderstandings can be avoided.

Finally, communication transactions occur within a *context*. The context consists of who (sender) communicates what (message), to whom (receiver), why (purpose) the sender does it, where (setting) it occurs, when (time),

and how (method) it is done. Change any aspect of the context and the results can be enormously different. For example, saying disparaging remarks about your boss to gain favor with like-minded coworkers is far different than saying the very same things to your boss's face.

Cultural differences especially highlight the importance of context. Individuals are expected, for example, to initiate job searches and engage in personal promotion, called **self-enhancement**, to land employment in the United States. In most Asian countries, however, **self-effacement**, which downplays one's performance and exhibits modest talk and self-deprecating messages, is preferred (Ting-Toomey & Dorjee, 2018). Typical self-enhancement communication is likely to offend employers who value self-effacement, and self-effacing communication is likely to seem unimpressive to employers who expect self-enhancement if it does not become over-the-top boasting. Context largely determines expectations and goal achievement.

Communication Is a Process: The Continuous Flow

Communication is a process of adapting to the inevitable changes that affect any relationship. The process view recognizes communication as dynamic, ever-changing, and continuous. In any relationship, "nothing never happens" (Johnson et al., 1974), or as the bumper sticker

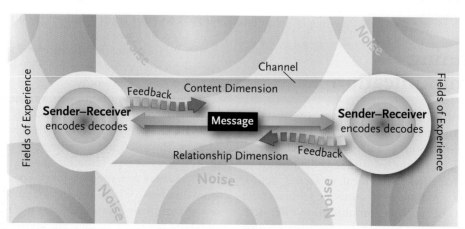

FIGURE 1-1   Transactional Model of Communication

In the United States, self-promotion is encouraged, even expected when interviewing for a job. Such self-enhancement, however, is not typically viewed as appropriate in the context of many cultures that prefer self-effacement.

says, "Change is inevitable, except from a vending machine."

If you wanted to understand the ocean, you would not just take a picture of a single wave or scoop up a cupful of water. The ocean can be understood only in terms of its entirety—the tides and currents, waves, plant and animal life, and so forth. Likewise, to understand communication, you need to focus not on single words, sentences, or gestures but on how currents of thoughts and feelings are expressed by both verbal and nonverbal means in the context of change.

Relationships at work cannot be frozen in time, though your memories may be. Every conversation with a coworker, boss, client, or customer is a foothold on your next conversation; and you bring your accumulated experiences to each new conversation. Communication is an ongoing process, and each new experience influences future transactions.

Communication Is Sharing Meaning: Making Sense

The term *communication* is derived from the Latin word *communicare*, which denotes "to share." Sharing from this perspective does not mean merely exchanging information like one would exchange gifts. Communication is not merely transferring "stuff" from one person to another. This is not simply FedEx delivering packages or DoorDash delivering dinner. You are not merely posting Instagram photos with no feedback expected. You attempt, and often achieve, something deeper when you communicate with other humans. You attempt to share **meaning**, which is "the conscious pattern humans create out of their interpretation of experience" (R. Anderson & Ross, 1994). You construct meaning by making connections and patterns in your mind that "make sense" of your world. You then attempt to share this constructed meaning with others, who in turn reconstruct your message to try to understand your meaning as constructed in your mind.

There is never a perfect "meeting of the minds" regarding meaning. The meaning another person has for an experience, idea, relationship, concept, or symbol *approximates* the meaning you have for the same thing. *The closest you come to shared meaning is when there are overlapping interpretations between individuals*. For example, when you view a relationship with a coworker as a friendship and the other person sees it likewise, there is an overlap, and meaning is shared, approximately. The depth of that friendship, or even what constitutes friendship, however, is not identical between two people. There are always subtle differences. Those subtle differences can be quite meaningful, as when one party views the friendship as potentially romantic but the other party does not. Welcome to the world of the awkward! We all attempt to share meaning both verbally and nonverbally. This, however, is an imperfect process.

Verbal Sharing: Telling It Like It Isn't Sometimes meaning does not get shared verbally, even though words are transmitted from one person to another in a common language. **Language** is a structured system of symbols for sharing meaning. Symbols are representations of *referents*—whatever the symbol refers to. Because symbols represent referents but are not the objects, ideas, events, or relationships represented, symbols have no meaning apart from us. Meaning is in the mind of the beholder. *Words are symbols, so meaning is not contained in words*. We are not "telling it like it is" (identifying objective reality); we are telling others what our subjective perception of the world is.

The meaning and usage of words depend on common agreement. As a speech community, English speakers tacitly agree to certain meanings and appropriate usages for words, even if this sometimes seems odd. For example, comedian Steven Wright asks, "Why is it that when you transport something by car it's called a shipment but when you transport something by ship it's called cargo?" The simple answer is that when decoding words we give them agreed-upon meanings.

This decoding process is no small challenge given the multiple meanings of most words, as Groucho Marx once illustrated with his famous quip, "Time flies like an arrow; fruit flies like a banana." Consider actual newspaper headlines reported by the *Columbia Journalism Review*: "Prostitutes Appeal to Pope"; "Kids Make Nutritious Snacks"; and "City Manager Tapes Head to District Attorney." Imagine a nonnative speaker of English trying to decode this sentence: "The woman was present to present the present to her boss, presently." Lexicographer Peter Gilliver calculated that the seemingly simple word *run* has 645 separate meanings, the most of any word in the English language. You can have your 2-mile run, a trial run, a run of bad luck, a run in a card game, or a run on the banks, to provide just a few examples (Liao, 2017). Can you think of others? Then there is the challenge of decoding words that can have contradictory meanings, called **contranyms**, such as *sanction* (permit or forbid), *fast* (move quickly or stick firmly), and *blunt* (dull instrument or sharp, pointed remark). Also, there are seeming opposites with the same meaning. For example, *fat chance* and *slim chance* both mean highly unlikely; and *couldn't care less* and *could care less* both mean not at all interested.

Misunderstandings using language in work environments are likely to be more prevalent as "the first generation of true digital natives is entering the workforce, and a pandemic has forced us into virtual offices. Workplace communication is undergoing a major shift, with some huge potential pitfalls" (Morgan, 2020). A shared lexicon or "business speak" that previously has functioned as a sign of "professionalism" is clashing with a more relaxed, casual use of language

Common agreement among language users determines the meaning of words, even though at times, literal meaning would seem odd at best. For example, our feet can smell but our noses can run. Misunderstandings, especially cross-culturally, can easily occur because common agreement also has to be understood for language to function effectively. Coworkers who speak English as a second language may struggle with deciphering common understanding of word choices.

A survey of 2,070 airline pilots found that "words, phrases, and sentences with more than one meaning" was "the biggest communication issue" with ground control (V. Wilson, 2016). Ambiguous verbal communication between cockpit crews and ground control have caused near disasters and actual catastrophes (Howard, 2008). Seemingly simple messages can produce potentially deadly incidents when multiple meanings for words create misunderstandings.

among Generation Z employees. Older generations, even Millennials, are more accustomed to **code switching**—adjusting one's language to the professional work environment—but Gen Z workers tend to use more casual language, even slang (Morgan, 2020). *Code switching is also a challenge for ethnic groups, especially African American employees.* Expected to "blend in" among a predominately white workplace environment to be accepted and gain promotions, black employees can feel a necessity to use language that hides their ethnicity and sounds "more white." Such code switching, however, is viewed as inauthentic, and research shows that it can diminish performance and increase job burnout (McCluney et al., 2019).

"Organizations can and should play a pivotal role in creating environments where code-switching is not necessary for success, particularly by cultivating spaces that value inclusion and differences" (McCluney et al., 2019). The influence of Gen Z employees will

likely make such environments inevitable. Nicky Thompson, a business psychologist with a background in linguistics, claims that forced code switching to a shared lexicon (vocabulary) is unsustainable. "Gen Z won't put up with it anymore" (Morgan, 2020). Language can be relaxed somewhat, especially when a work occasion is clearly not a formal affair. With the rapid and pervasive move to virtual and casual workspaces from home offices during the COVID-19 pandemic, the pressure to loosen language use expectations is further increased.

Sharing meaning between cultures poses its own unique problems because of the nuances of language. Electrolux, a Scandinavian manufacturer, discovered this when trying to sell its vacuum cleaners in the United States with the slogan "Nothing sucks like an Electrolux." In preparation for the 2008 Beijing Olympic Games, David Tool, a retired army colonel living in the Chinese capital, was hired to correct notoriously poor English on signs throughout the city. "Deformed Man Toilet" was thankfully replaced with "Disabled Person Toilet," and "Beijing Anus Hospital" was replaced with "Beijing Proctology Hospital" (Boudreau, 2007). Consider further nuances of languages. For example, an email from the leader of a multicultural business team says that the team project "is fine." Should that be interpreted as damning with faint praise or as giving a genuine thumbs up for a job well done? In addition, "maybe" to an American means possibly yes, but to a Japanese, "maybe" typically means a polite no, potentially producing misunderstanding during business negotiations (Kameda, 2014).

Increasingly, multicultural workplaces make even the choice of English as the predominant language of American businesses of considerable importance (Weedmark, 2019). "Those who share a mother-tongue have a linguistic bond that differs from those who speak the same language as a second language" (Victor, 2007). If English is chosen as the preferred language of business, an in-group/out-group dynamic can develop between those who speak it easily and those who do not. The choice of language to conduct business can strongly influence teamwork and continuing business relationships for good or ill (Chen et al., 2006; Tenzer et al., 2017). When the predominant language employed in an organization is not well understood by all its members, those excluded from conversations because of difficulties fully comprehending the language used may feel socially ostracized. This *linguistic divide* can reduce group productivity (Dotan-Eliaz et al., 2009).

The rise of global virtual teams has also posed a linguistic challenge. Increasingly, virtual teams in the realm of international business are composed of members from diverse cultures, many of whom speak English as a second language. English is the dominant language of the Internet ("Internet World Users by Language," 2020). Inevitably, problems of interpretation and even translation, especially for global virtual teams, occur. A study of virtual teams showed that 75% of respondents found language difficulties challenging (C. Solomon, 2016).

Even when "sharing" a common language across cultures, problems can arise. For example, there are a number of British business phrases that Americans would likely find confusing ("12 UK Phrases," 2017). For example:

- "We have to set prices on *wash its face basis*" (An action will pay for itself);

- "I'm going to *look under the bonnet* on that" (You look under the hood of a car—analyze a situation);

- "I think I'll modify *the strategic staircase*" ("I think I'll modify the business plan").

George Bernard Shaw once remarked that England and America are two countries separated by the same language.

Nonverbal Sharing: Wordless Challenges   We share meaning nonverbally as well as verbally. **Nonverbal communication** is wordless communication. Nonverbal cues can be at least as challenging to decode as language. For example, while giving a presentation to a work project group you notice that almost everyone is looking down, and not at, you. Does this mean they are bored, uncomfortable with your message, daydreaming, carefully considering your message, or devising a plan to exit the meeting at the earliest opportunity? When your boss frowns, is he or she showing confusion, taking offense, disagreeing, or suddenly remembering the dog was left alone in the house with no exit for using the outdoors as a toilet?

One of the difficulties with communicating in virtual groups is the absence of nonverbal cues, in whole or in part, that accompany verbal, face-to-face messages (Z. Yang et al., 2018). One study of virtual teams revealed that "lack of face-to-face contact" was identified by 89% of respondents as a significant problem (C. Solomon, 2016). Ghosting—ignoring texts or emails—is especially problematic because it implies indifference or rancor in this age of immediate response expectations. What may appear to be ghosting, however, may simply be a lengthy nonresponse because the email or text message got lost in a jumble of daily digital communications. Failure to confirm reception of an email, especially with important attachments, can be a source of ambiguity and frustration. Misunderstandings easily emerge in our digital world.

"The loss of nonverbal body cues is among the most overlooked reasons why employees feel so disengaged from others," acclaimed international business consultant Erica Dhawan (2021a) argues. Emojis help, but are still limited. Individuals may also be hesitant to use them in business communication for fear of appearing too informal and unprofessional, but the increasing prevalence of virtual group work has encouraged some researchers to advocate their wider use in workplace environments (Meluso et al., 2020). One study, however, found that smiley emojis, "contrary to actual smiles … do not increase perceptions of warmth and actually decrease perceptions of competence" (Glikson et al., 2017). Videoconferencing through platforms such as Zoom can add a nonverbal element to business meetings, but it has its own limitations, discussed in detail later.

Sharing meaning nonverbally between cultures can also pose unique problems (Cotton, 2013; Manolaki, 2016). For example, the "A-OK" gesture that forms a circle with the index finger and the thumb is obscene in Brazil; and it means "worthless" in France and "money" in Japan; and recently has become a white power sign in the United States. Raising the index finger to signify "one," as Americans often do to signify "We're number one," means "two" in Italy; so the gesture becomes "We're number two," a less satisfying source of celebratory pride. In Japan, however, the upright thumb means "five" (counting begins with the index finger, and the thumb is the last digit). Nodding the head up and down means "yes" in the United States, and shaking it side to side means "no." In Bulgaria, Turkey, Iran, and Bengal, however, it is the reverse. In Greece, tipping the head back abruptly means "no," but the same gesture in India means "yes."

Gestures, such as the thumbs up, do not necessarily have universal meaning. In some cultures, thumbs up is obscene, even when done with a big smile. In a very simple way, this highlights the challenges you face when teams are composed of members from very diverse cultures.

(Nod your head if you understand all of this.) You can imagine the potential for misunderstandings and even international incidences when gestures are misinterpreted during intercultural business transactions.

Nonverbal communication, despite efforts to quantify and exaggerate its importance, often does play a predominant part in some communication with others (Knapp et al., 2014). For example, the strength of your handshake can communicate degree of confidence. The intensity of your anger is exhibited mostly nonverbally (e.g., tone of voice, facial expressions, gestures, and posture). Anxiety is chiefly communicated nonverbally. Touch can be a source of comfort and compassion or a key indicator of sexual harassment in the workplace. A smile can communicate a host of differing messages (e.g., approval, affection, sarcasm, contempt, discomfort). The top nonverbal mistake candidates make when interviewing is failure to make direct eye contact (L. N. Hayes, 2018). If nonverbal communication were merely incidental to verbal messages, few would pay it notice.

Mixed messages also show the impact of nonverbal cues and their potential for misunderstanding. A **mixed message** occurs when there is positive verbal and negative nonverbal communication, or vice versa. A project group member may verbally endorse the group's decision but nonverbally exhibit disagreement, even contempt. Attempting to wipe an opinion off your face is challenging. The "Customer Rage Study" found that the number one most annoying catchphrase when calling to complain about a company's service is "Your call is important to us, please continue to hold" (Murcott, 2016). The mixed message is the verbal affirmation of claimed concern but the nonverbal contradiction when being forced to wait an often ridiculous period of time before talking to a customer service representative, assuming one is ever reached. So, both verbal and nonverbal communication pose significant challenges associated with shared meaning, underlining the monumental complexity of the human communication process.

SUMMARY

Human communication is a transactional process of sharing meaning with others. Although it may seem like just common sense, voluminous evidence shows that in the world of business, miscommunication is commonplace. More communication also does not necessarily mean better communication, and even textbook-perfect communication will not resolve all problems and challenges that emerge in the business world. Both verbal and nonverbal communication present myriad challenges, especially when experienced in multicultural and multiethnic work environments. What should be obvious, even from this brief, initial discussion of the nature of communication, is that this ubiquitous human activity is no easy task.

Film School Case Studies

This activity section, *found in every chapter*, presents select films for you to analyze. A movie rating (PG-13, R, etc.) is included to assist you in deciding which films are appropriate. A specific question or issue is raised that is relevant to each film listed. You are asked to explore this question or issue using chapter material for your analysis.

The Founder (2016). Biographical drama. PG-13

This is the story of Ray Kroc, founder of McDonald's. Examine the importance of social connections, or lack thereof, in his success as a businessman, but strained family relationships.

TED Talks and YouTube Videos

This ancillary activity, *added to each chapter*, provides video presentations and segments that both illustrate key communication concepts and provide opportunities for specific analysis, discussion, disagreement, and application of text material. *These TED Talks and YouTube videos can be accessed by going to the Oxford Learning Link for It's All of Our Business or by typing the title of the video into a Google search window.*

"Adam Ruins Everything – The Dunning-Kruger Effect/Tru TV"

"Communication in the 21st Century: Is It What You Say, Not How You Say It?"

"It's How You Say It—The Science of Emotions"

"The Power of Nonverbal Communication" Joe Navarro

"Why Language Is Humanity's Greatest Invention"

After successful completion of this chapter, you should be able to

1. Diagnose business communication problems through the lens of the communication competence model.

2. Distinguish between appropriate and effective communication in business and cultural contexts.

3. Identify the implicit and explicit rules that permeate every communication context.

CHAPTER 2

Communication Competence: A Model for Success

THERE IS A PERMANENCE to communication that often is not fully appreciated. Try remarking to a coworker, "You've gained a little weight." Be prepared for an angry response: "Are you calling me fat?" "No, no, forget I even said anything." Too late! You cannot simply delete the message from a receiver's memory. *The permanence of communication is one of the challenges posed in business by the ready accessibility of email and social media*. For example, emails from Steve Jobs, even after his death, have been used for and against Apple in various lawsuits. Similarly, emails by Bill Gates have been offered as key evidence in antitrust lawsuits against Microsoft (Price, 2017). Apparently, Adidas forgot about the deadly 2013 terror attack at the Boston Marathon when, in 2018, it sent this unfortunate email to customers it knew who had completed the race: "Congrats, you survived the Boston Marathon" (Griffith, 2018). Ouch! You can delete the email abruptly, but you cannot erase the memory. You cannot simply say "Never mind" and wash away the indelible stain left by the message. Even posting a heartfelt apology, as Adidas did, only

CHAPTER OUTLINE

- Communication Competence Model
- Culture and Communication Competence

4. Prioritize the We-orientation of effective business communication.

5. Use five ways to enhance your own communication competence in any situation.

6. Appreciate the differences between individualist and collectivist cultures, as well as the impact of a culture on communication competence.

limits the damage but does not entirely erase it. How often have you seen coworkers post embarrassing, even offensive comments or compromising photos on social media, then get verbally shelled or ridiculed, provoking quick removal too late because the damage has been done? As a Chinese proverb notes, "A harsh word dropped from the tongue cannot be brought back by a coach and six horses." Recognizing the permanence of communication should provide added appreciation for how critical communicating competently is to your success at all levels in the world of business.

Consequently, *the primary purpose of this chapter is to define communication competence as a blueprint for successful business and organizational communication.* Toward this end, chapter objectives are as follows: (1) define communication competence, (2) apply the communication competence model to the business arena, and (3) expand the application of the model to the intercultural business realm.

Communication Competence Model

There are numerous books and articles on business communication that provide often superficial, even contradictory recipes for improving communication in the workplace. Most authors of these works, especially in the popular trade book market, offer no theoretical rationale for their advice, other than "It worked for me," and they often present only anecdotal evidence to support their recipes. There is a significant reason that academics typically advocate for a theoretical foundation supported by credible and abundant research to inform their analysis and advice. We want to move beyond mere personal opinion and individual taste, generically applied as universal wisdom based on narrow, highly suspect personal experience. Consequently, we provide a theoretical rationale by taking a communication competence perspective, based on abundant research, that imbues every chapter. **Communication competence** *is engaging in communication with others that is perceived to be both appropriate and effective in a given context* (Spitzberg, 2015). The next few sections explain this theoretical and important perspective.

Appropriateness: Communication Is Audience Centered

The two key elements of communication competence are appropriateness and effectiveness. We address appropriateness first. **Appropriateness** *is behavior that meets expectations dictated by the rules of a particular context.* This means that appropriateness is audience centered. You strive to fit the form and content of your messages to the expectations of your receivers. This requires understanding the rules of every communication context.

Rules: Explicit and Implicit   *There are rules for every communication context,* whether they are apparent or unobtrusive. A **rule** "is a prescription that indicates what behavior is obligated, prohibited, or preferred in a given context" (Shimanoff, 2009). Some rules are *explicit* (directly expressed), such as "No smoking in the conference room," or "Do not drink beverages at your computer station." Then there is the "Disney point" rule. Employees in the Disney parks are instructed never to point with a single index finger to provide directions for visitors. The rule is to use two fingers, partly because in Middle Eastern cultures and elsewhere, pointing with only the index finger is viewed as singling out someone for ridicule (McCusker, 2020).

Most rules, however, are merely *implied* (indirectly indicated) by patterns of behavior. You do not have to be told directly what to do, or not do. For example, when you encounter a coworker who asks, "How ya doing?" you know better

The COVID-19 pandemic resulted in explicit rules requiring masks, protective gloves, and plastic shields in most workplaces.

than to respond with a long-winded appraisal of your current disposition. Normally, you just say, "I'm fine, how are you?" even if your dog died and your computer crashed. Cultural greeting rules dictate that the question should not be interpreted literally. Consequently, the greeting becomes ritualistic, even mindless, which is why you may have, as we both have done, caught yourself on more than one occasion asking, "How are you?" and receiving the response from the other person, "I'm fine, how are you?" whereupon you give the slightly embarrassing response, "I'm fine, how are you?" (Oops, already asked that—trapped in a feedback loop.)

A violation of an implicit rule often leads to an explicit statement of the rule, and even its means of enforcement. For example, as professional and personal lives blend, many businesses have found it necessary to issue direct rules that prohibit the use of company technology to do personal business and surf political websites and social media. This **cyberloafing**—using the Internet and social media for purposes unrelated to work—costs businesses in the United States an estimated $85 billion annually (Hofherr, 2016).

Rule Violations: Consequential Effects   There is an expectation that rules will be followed, but when rules are violated, the consequences can be significant. One study asked college

professors to assess an email message from a student that read "R U Able to Meat Me?" Professors especially disliked the casual "R U" acronym for "are you" and expressed strong dislike for using "meat" for "meet." Messages such as the above made professors "like the student less, view them as less credible, have a lesser opinion of the message quality, and made them less willing to comply with students' simple email requests" (Stephens et al., 2009). There are expected rules of formality and careful attention to grammar and spelling attached to professor-student communication, as there typically are in employer-employee communication.

This study underlines the importance of proofreading all written business communication, remembering the inherent permanence of messages. It is not that misspelled messages cannot be deciphered. For example, read this edited version found on the Internet:

> Aoccdrnig to stdees at an Amrcan uinervtisy, ltteer oredr in a wrod is uniprmeotnt. Olny the frist and lsat lttr msut be in the crrocet pclae. The rset of the wrod can be a cmolpete mses. Tihs is bcuseae we raed words as a wolhe, not by idndvidaul ltters.

Undoubtedly, you were able to decipher the message without much difficulty despite the disastrous spelling. Have you ever received an email or text message that resembled this jumbled mess? We have. Imagine the impression you leave if you send such an error-filled missive to a client, customer, or boss.

Even a casual email to a coworker can invite ridicule prompted by a simple grammatical miscue, such as, "Let's eat Fred" instead of "Let's eat, Fred." Then there is autocorrect, the dubiously helpful technological aid. Autocorrect is notorious for changes to text messages that make you seem moronic or weird if you do not catch the sometimes ludicrous "corrections." Instagram has accounts dedicated to them, Buzzfeed does

With the advent of the COVID-19 pandemic, rules regarding social contact had to be changed. Such rule changes were not always greeted with enthusiasm.

year-end roundups, and websites are devoted to cringeworthy autocorrected messages.

Autocorrect errors can seem amusing, but your credibility can be significantly diminished when your emails, text messages, LinkedIn resumes and the like have careless errors that reveal little concern for standard rules for messaging, or at the very least, little time for actual proofreading.

Some rules, however, may need to be altered. One study of cyberloafing found that there can be significant benefits to occasional and moderate amounts of off-task Internet and social media browsing at work (Sao et al., 2020). Absolute bans with harsh, punitive enforcement against such workplace browsing may be counterproductive because browsing benefits include regenerating attention spans, taking brief rests to rejuvenate energy and motivation, skill building, and even improved job performance. Surprisingly, a study of almost 7,000 people concluded that watching cat videos on YouTube at work reduces stress and can enhance employee performance and productivity if done occasionally (L. Smith, 2018).

Effectiveness: Achieving Goals

Effectiveness is the second principal element of the communication competence definition. **Effectiveness** *is the degree to which you have progressed toward the achievement of your goals*. Effectiveness is not the sole determinant of communication competence because goals are not always achievable. Your lack of effectiveness may be due to forces beyond your control. A person can exhibit exemplary, perfectly appropriate communication and still have relationships with bosses, coworkers, clients, and customers fail (personality clashes; sheer orneriness, perhaps). Nevertheless, communication that often fails to achieve goals suggests possible deficiencies.

Degrees of Effectiveness: From Deficiency to Proficiency You may be proficient at establishing strong relationships with most coworkers, but you may feel awkward in large gatherings of strangers at business mixers after work. You may relish the challenge of delivering a speech to a large audience of businesspeople, while some coworkers would rather be dipped in molasses and strapped to an anthill than give such a presentation. Communication competence can vary by degrees from highly proficient to severely deficient depending on the circumstances. Labeling someone a "competent communicator" makes a judgment of that individual's degree of proficiency *in a particular context*, but it does not identify an immutable characteristic of that person. ***Being a competent communicator is also not an idyllic state of perfection***. Even the best leaders occasionally err and cause problems for their groups and organizations.

We-Orientation: Audience Centeredness

Because communication is transactional, competence comes from focusing on "We" (what makes relationships and groups successful), not "Me" (what makes the *individual* successful at the expense of the group or organization). Psychologist Dacher Keltner (2016a) concludes, based on voluminous scientific studies, that ***constructive power and influence in business and organizations depend on putting "the focus on others,"*** not on oneself. Research by the Gallup organization found that 60% of government workers are miserable because of "horrible bosses" who exhibit less interest in the welfare of employees than in nailing a good tee time on the golf links. How about you? Have you ever suffered the demoralizing experience of working for a horrible boss? Are you working for one now? If so, you have our empathy. As Dr. Travis Bradberry (2019), president of TalentSmart, when commenting on the Gallup research, says "Bad bosses contaminate the workplace [and] cause irrevocable damage to their companies and employees by hindering performance and creating unnecessary stress." If you plan to open a small business such as a gym or online reselling shop, or you already have done so, you are the boss. As a boss now

or in the future, put the welfare of your employees ahead of your own desires. ***Be audience centered not self-centered.*** To do otherwise is to damage your business success and potentially the success of others. Dealing with a bad boss is addressed comprehensively in Chapter 8.

Achieving Communication Competence: Five Ways

Effectiveness and appropriateness are the two key elements of communication competence, but how do you achieve both? There are five general ways, each expanded throughout this text: knowledge, skill, sensitivity, commitment, and ethics. In this section, these five ways are discussed as an overview.

Knowledge: Learning the Rules Knowledge provides an understanding of what is required to be an effective communicator. We cannot determine what is appropriate and effective without knowing the rules operating in a given situation. When first hired, for example, there is a period of adjustment where you learn to navigate in your new job based on the rules that become apparent. What authority do you have to influence decision making? How should you address your boss—formally or casually? What information technologies are you permitted to access at work? How should you dress? These and many more rules may operate at your workplace given your position.

Consider how implicit rules operate regarding how to relate to LGBTQ employees. Canela Lopez and Marquerite Ward (2020), writing for *Business Insider*, identify 12 things to avoid saying to LGBTQ coworkers. Among these are: (1) never offer a "compliment" by saying "You don't strike me as gay"; (2) do not keep mentioning your one gay family member; and (3) avoid saying, "I would never have guessed you were transgender." Workplace rules are changing as gender fluidity has become a more transparent issue.

Skill: Showing, Not Just Knowing Skill puts your knowledge into practice. ***Knowledge without skill means you know how, but you cannot show how to communicate competently.***

A **communication skill** is the ability to perform a communication behavior effectively and repeatedly. Clearly, fluently, concisely, eloquently, and confidently communicating a message is an example. Knowledge about communication without communication skill will not produce competence. Knowing what you should do to nail an interview, for example, does not automatically translate into a skillful performance. Knowing the "right answers" to interview questions but loading your responses with dozens of vocal disfluencies such as "um," "ah," "like," "you know," and myriad other disrupters can destroy your credibility. You can read stacks of books about making effective business presentations, but there is no substitute for skill gained by practice and experience speaking in front of multiple audiences.

Conversely, *skill without knowledge is equally unproductive*. Learning to "express your feelings honestly" can be an important communication skill in many situations. Expressing your honest feelings indiscriminately, however, no matter what the likely consequences, mimics the act of an innocent child, not a mature adult. One glaring danger of social media use in the workplace is revealing information that is overly personal, even controversial, which can go viral and reflect badly on the company or organization. A Career Builder survey found that 34% of employers have reprimanded or fired employees for inappropriate online content (L. N. Hayes, 2018). To an intimate partner or close friend, a message may be appropriate. To a colleague or manager, the same message could be embarrassing or worse. Remember the permanence of communication. Consider not just your immediate audience (e.g., a friend or coworker) but the potential wider audience (e.g., the entire organization or even beyond that).

The importance of both communication knowledge and skill was apparently off many employers' radar when the COVID-19 pandemic smacked the United States with the force of a hurricane (Senior, 2020). By July 2020, almost 50 million Americans either were laid off or fired because measures to blunt the spread of the virus produced a major economic crash (Thorbecke & Mitropoulos, 2020). How

businesses broke the news to employees that they were being furloughed or fired too often exhibited communication incompetence. For example, Bird, the Santa Monica, California, based scooter rental company, informed 406 employees that they were fired by posting a slide on a Zoom "COVID-19 webinar" with a female voiceover announcing the bad news (Senior, 2020). WW International, formerly Weight Watchers, fired thousands of its employees by having a manager read from a script on a 3-minute Zoom announcement while placing every employee on mute (Schmidt, 2020). Telling employees that they no longer have a job warrants knowing that empathy and compassion are required plus exhibiting those skills when doing the deed. You certainly do not just post the news impersonally on a Zoom slide with a disembodied voiceover, or have a manager read from a short script with no opportunity for questions or feedback. Employees at WW International were outraged by how the company handled their firings (Schmidt, 2020). As one fired employee remarked, "I cried for about 24 hours because a company that I respected and valued, devoted my life to, felt I and countless others deserved to be permanently fired with a cold mass script" (quoted by Digital, 2020).

Sensitivity: Receptive Accuracy Knowing what constitutes appropriate communication in a specific context and having the skill to communicate appropriately are great, but what if you do not have your antenna extended to pick up and understand signals coming from others? How will you know which rules apply and how you should communicate?

Sensitivity means receptive accuracy—the ability to detect, decode, and comprehend signals from others (Bernieri, 2001). This includes the ability to decipher the needs and emotions of others and respond appropriately. Can you tell when a coworker is uncomfortable, encouraging, angry, or just friendly but nothing more than that? Sensitivity is even more important than the general intelligence of group members. Google conducted a huge study called Project Aristotle and found that members of effective work teams had high scores on

Dr. Louisa Parks of the Brain Health Center at California Pacific Medical Center notes that people are spending so much time on social networking devices instead of face-to-face interactions that "the ability to recognize things like sarcasm, humor, or even the emotions on a human face" are on the wane (quoted in D. Brown, 2013). Our receptive accuracy is suffering from the ubiquity of the digital universe.

sensitivity; members of ineffective teams had low scores (Duhigg, 2016).

Fortunately, sensitivity can be learned (Hall & Bernieri, 2001). A major aspect of sensitivity is being mindful, not mindless, about your communication with others. We exhibit **mindfulness** when "we think about our communication and continually work at changing what we do in order to become more effective" (Griffin et al., 2019). Put down the electronic gadgets, view your surroundings, engage others face to face in your classes or workplaces, and be mindful. We exhibit **mindlessness** when we pay little attention to our communication with others, and we put little or no effort into improving it. One of the functions of this text is to help you become more sensitive to your audience by mindfully identifying patterns of communication that cause problems in the workplace and then committing yourself to improve.

Commitment: A Passion for Excellence Abundant potential to be successful in business goes unrealized without a **commitment**, that passion for excellence, to gain knowledge and hone your skills by hard work. *Attitude, however, is as important as aptitude.* Even if you have the necessary knowledge, skills, and sensitivity to be successful at work, embracing an "I don't care" attitude about performing optimally will act as an anchor that drags down your team. The predominant motivation of the competent communicator is the desire to avoid previous mistakes and to find better ways of communicating with coworkers. Someone who makes the same mistakes repeatedly and shows little interest in altering their behavior can be a deadweight who can sink a group.

Ethics: The Right and Wrong of Communication
Competent communicators are concerned with more than just what works (effectiveness). As humans, we care about right and wrong behavior (appropriateness). It is one of the characteristics that separates humans from the beasts-as-feasts daily killing field that occurs on the African Serengeti. **Ethics** is a system for judging moral correctness by using a set of standards

to determine what constitutes right and wrong behavior. The Edward Lowe Foundation states pointedly, "Good ethics make good business sense" ("Why You Need Good Business Ethics," 2020). The Credo of the **National** Communication Association identifies five ethical standards to guide our communication (see also Knights, 2017).

1. *Honesty/Integrity* "There is no more fundamental ethical value than honesty" (Josephson, 2002). Honesty is a cultural expectation. A survey of 23,000 young people (ages 13–19+) revealed that 95% agreed with the statement "In business and the workplace, trust and honesty are essential" ("2012 Report Card," 2012). Most businesses have a formal written code of ethics that incorporates honesty and integrity. For example, Coca-Cola "reveals a clear, unifying theme: integrity" (Munim, 2017). Intel's "Code of Conduct" pledges to "conduct business with uncompromising integrity" ("Intel Code of Conduct," 2020).

Unfortunately, the demand for honesty often exceeds the supply. "Indeed, lying is so commonplace in corporations that it often passes without comment" (Jenkins & Delbridge, 2016). Honesty, however, requires more than refraining from deceit. It necessitates "coming clean" when you know that you are wrong.

2. *Respect* A study of 600 employees ranked respect as the most important contributor to job satisfaction (C. Lee, 2014). Showing respect is not only ethical practice, it is pragmatic. Bruce Weinstein (2020), writing for *Forbes* on the WW International mass firings in 2020, commented: "Group Zoom firings are a perfect example of how to disrespect loyal employees … Ethical leadership means treating all employees, especially loyal ones, with respect. WW blew it." Companies do acknowledge the importance of exhibiting respect despite not always showing it in practice. Starbucks included in its code of ethics these statements: "We treat our customers as we treat one another, with respect and dignity" and "We respect diversity in each other, our customers and suppliers and all others with whom we interact" (quoted by Munim,

2017). Apple aims to establish "a safe and respectful workplace for everyone" ("People and Environment," 2022).

3. *Fairness* Fairness requires equal treatment. Millennials (born between 1982 and 1997) consider fairness in the workplace as more important than even recognition or opportunity (Knights, 2017). Research of Generation Z members (born between 1997 and 2013) reveals that "perceived fairness of procedures and how one is treated" is significant and affects their performance, satisfaction, commitment, trust, and self-esteem (Schroth, 2019). "Management-by-fairness approach motivates employees to work collaboratively for the long-term good of the organization and its members" (Blader, 2018).

4. *Choice* Our communication should strive to allow people to make their own choices free of coercion, whenever practical (Jaksa & Pritchard, 1994). Persuasion allows free choice among available options. Coercion forces choice without permitting individuals to think or act freely for themselves. Bullying, violence, blackmail, firing, and threats of dismissal are all examples of coercion. Coercion may be ethical in some instances, such as when an employee behaves unethically and must be fired. Encouraging free choice is a strong ethical guideline, but it is not an ethical commandment.

5. *Responsibility* "Ethical responsibility means maintaining—even improving—your bottom line, while setting a high bar for making a positive contribution to society" (Sarokin, 2019). Responsibility means that ethical communication requires a We-orientation, a concern for others.

In the abstract, these five ethical standards may seem straightforward and uncontroversial, but almost nothing in human communication is absolute and clear-cut. Consider **ethnocentrism**—exalting one's own culture while disparaging other cultures. This is prejudice on a grand scale. Unfortunately, *all cultures are ethnocentric to some degree* (Triandis, 2009). Generally, you should embrace cultural diversity and repudiate ethnocentrism (cultural prejudice). Not all cultures, however, treat women with respect in the workplace, for example, or even allow them to hold certain jobs. To respect a culture's beliefs in this or similar cases of unacceptable practices clashes with showing respect for others and celebrating fairness and choice. Prejudice that degrades and dehumanizes others cannot be accepted with the justification, "That's just the way they do things in their culture." Despite such difficulties, however, all five ethical standards—*honesty*, *respect*, *fairness*, *choice*, and *responsibility*—are strong values in our culture, and they closely parallel the United Nations Universal Declaration of Human Rights (Harrison, 2000). Ethical standards serve as important guidelines for our workplace communication behavior.

In review, *being agile and adaptable to changing contexts in the workplace is essential to effective and appropriate communication*. Learn about rules that operate in diverse situations. Hone your skills by abundant practice. Sharpen your sensitivity by being mindful of nonverbal cues that exhibit various emotions, kindle your commitment to be the most competent communicator possible, and practice ethical communication behavior.

FIGURE 2-1
Communication Competence
Model

Culture and Communication Competence

So far, we have provided some cultural references and examples as illustrations of key concepts. Here we take a deeper look at culture and its application to the communication competence model with its emphasis on appropriateness and effectiveness. In the increasingly diverse world of business imbued with cultural differences and challenges, no discussion of communication competence would suffice without addressing cultural applications more than as a mere sidenote.

Culture is a learned set of enduring values, beliefs, and practices that are shared by an identifiable, large group of people with a common history. To explain this definition, a **value** is the most deeply felt, generally shared view of what is deemed good, right, or worthwhile thinking or behavior. Values constitute a shared conception, not of what is, but of what ought to be. A **belief** is what a person thinks is or probable. Two individuals may *value* human life, for example; but one may *believe* that capital punishment preserves life by deterring homicides, while the other may believe the contrary. Finally, a **co-culture** is any group that is part of a dominant culture yet often has a common history and shares some differences in values, beliefs, and practices from the dominant culture. African Americans, Asian Americans, Native Americans, and Mexican Americans are some obvious examples of co-cultures within the United States. The LGBTQ community is also a co-culture, as is the deaf community and a variety of other groups.

Rules of appropriateness vary widely among cultures and co-cultures, sometimes surprisingly so. Knowing cultural rules can be critical. Consider, for example, when traveling on business to different cultures, the common practice of tipping after a meal at a restaurant. In cultures such as China, Japan, South Korea, New Zealand, and Costa Rica, there is no tipping; and Americans who do are perceived to be disrespectful. Even if you are intending a magnanimous gesture by picking up the lunch check for your business team while traveling abroad and you add a healthy tip, you are communicating the insulting message that the waitperson must be bribed to provide decent service ("Tipping," 2022). Taking a business card in Japan and immediately placing it in your pocket is insulting. The card should be received with both hands, carefully examined, then held throughout the remaining conversation. Finally, arriving on time in China is interpreted as arriving late. It is expected that you arrive at least 15 minutes before a business appointment (Bruk, 2017).

These common practices are visible *surface differences* among cultures, and they can change, sometimes swiftly. Core values of a culture, however, are resistant to change (Hofstede & Hofstede, 2010). **Value dimensions**—varying degrees of importance placed on those deeply felt views of what is right, good, and worthwhile—are the *deep structure* that serves as the bedrock of a culture. When they clash cross-culturally, they can provoke serious conflict in the multicultural world of business, as discussed in this next section.

Individualism–Collectivism: The Prime Directive

The individualism–collectivism dimension is thought to be the most important of all deep structural, value dimensions that distinguish cultures. It clearly has received the most voluminous supportive research and interest (Santos et al., 2017).

General Description: The Me-We Dimension

An **individualist culture** has a "me" consciousness. Individuals see themselves as loosely linked to each other and largely independent of group identification (Hofstede & Hofstede, 2010). They are chiefly motivated by their own preferences, needs, and goals. Personal achievement and initiative are stressed. People communicate as individuals and pay little heed to a person's group memberships. Decision making is based on what is best for the individual, sometimes even if this sacrifices the group welfare. Words such as "independence," "self," "privacy," and "rights" permeate cultural conversations.

A **collectivist culture** has a "we" consciousness. Individuals see themselves as closely linked to one or more groups. Commitment to valued groups (family, organization) is paramount (Hofstede & Hofstede, 2010). People take notice of a person's place in the hierarchy of a group. Individuals often downplay personal goals in favor of advancing the goals of a valued group. Competitive self-enhancement can incite envy, jealousy, and friction within groups; and it is thought to divert energies away from the welfare of the group. Words such as "loyalty," "responsibility," and "community" permeate collectivist cultural conversations.

All cultures vary in their emphasis on individualism and collectivism, and no culture is entirely one way or the other. Even some

Rules for eye contact vary widely among cultures. In the United States, direct eye contact shows interest, even respect. Wandering eyes while your boss is talking to you will likely invite reproach. In many Asian cultures and a host of other countries, however, averting your eyes is a sign of respect, especially when communicating with a higher-status person (Samovar et al., 2021).

individuals within a culture may disagree with the prevailing cultural values. Sociologist Geert Hofstede, however, ranked cultures based on the relative importance placed on individualist or collectivist values. In general, North American, Western European, and European-influenced cultures such as Australia, New Zealand, and South Africa are individualist, with the United States ranking number one among them. The United States is progressively becoming even more individualistic (Twenge et al., 2017). East Asian, North African, and most Latin American cultures are collectivist. *Approximately 70% of the world's population live in collectivist cultures* (Hofstede & Hofstede, 2010); but here too, individualism seems to be slowly increasing across much of the globe. Despite this increase, "cultural differences remain sizable" (Santos et al., 2017), and "relative country rankings tend to be rather

stable" (Beugelsdijk & Wetzel, 2018). Very little has changed in the rankings on the individualism–collectivism dimension since Hofstede's original research, as depicted in Figure 2.2 (Beugelsdijk et al., 2015).

The highly combustible issue of whether to wear masks and social distance during the COVID-19 pandemic graphically illustrates cultural differences between individualist and collectivist cultures. Collectivist cultures, generally, were more inclined to wear masks and engage in social distancing than individualist cultures such as the United States that exhibited relatively strong pushback on such practices, especially when businesses mandated mask wearing (Biddlestone et al., 2020; Hyun, 2020). Wearing a mask or refusing to wear one often communicated political messages that spilled over into nasty confrontations in businesses of great variety.

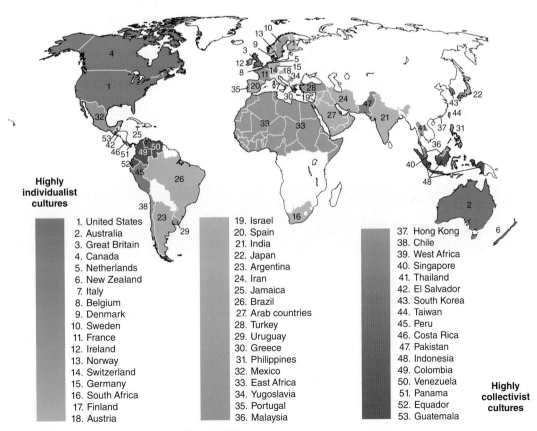

Highly individualist cultures		
1. United States	19. Israel	37. Hong Kong
2. Australia	20. Spain	38. Chile
3. Great Britain	21. India	39. West Africa
4. Canada	22. Japan	40. Singapore
5. Netherlands	23. Argentina	41. Thailand
6. New Zealand	24. Iran	42. El Salvador
7. Italy	25. Jamaica	43. South Korea
8. Belgium	26. Brazil	44. Taiwan
9. Denmark	27. Arab countries	45. Peru
10. Sweden	28. Turkey	46. Costa Rica
11. France	29. Uruguay	47. Pakistan
12. Ireland	30. Greece	48. Indonesia
13. Norway	31. Philippines	49. Colombia
14. Switzerland	32. Mexico	50. Venezuela
15. Germany	33. East Africa	51. Panama
16. South Africa	34. Yugoslavia	52. Ecuador
17. Finland	35. Portugal	53. Guatemala
18. Austria	36. Malaysia	Highly collectivist cultures

FIGURE 2-2   Map of Individualist and Collectivist Cultures

Communication Differences: Direct Versus Indirect Styles   Edward Hall (1981) was the first to identify a specific difference in communication styles between individualist and collectivist cultures. *Individualist cultures typically use a low-context style, and collectivist cultures typically use a high-context style* (Ting-Toomey & Dorjee, 2018). A **low-context communication style** is verbally precise, direct, assertive, self-enhancing, and explicit. There is little assumption that others will be able to discern what you mean without precise verbal explanation. Self-expression and speaking ability are highly valued. Points of view are openly expressed, and persuasion is an accepted goal of speech (Ting-Toomey & Dorjee, 2018).

In collectivist cultures, context is paramount, not the explicit message. A **high-context communication style** uses indirect verbal expression. You are expected to "read between the lines." Significant information must be derived from contextual cues, such as the relationship, situation, setting, and time. Talk is tactful and self-effacing (Ting-Toomey & Dorjee, 2018), as discussed in Chapter 1.

The contrast between the high- and low-context communication styles is aptly illustrated by a seemingly confusing English message written by a Japanese manager: "Our office has moved to Kawasaki. I'm going to buy a Honda." To Americans, this likely seems to be two unrelated sentences. To the Japanese, the meaning is clear: "Our office has moved to Kawasaki. It's too far from the station to walk, so I'll have to buy a car. I'm going to buy a Honda." "Japanese do not specify things down to the last detail. … They merely sketch the outlines and expect their listeners to be able to 'fill in the gaps.'" (Kameda, 2014)

Harmony is highly regarded in collectivist cultures, and verbal messages tend to be vague to avoid causing offense. According to Dr. Mona Chung, when a Chinese businessperson says "yes" when queried whether an agreement has been reached "there's about a 20 percent chance yes means they agree" (quoted by Gettler, 2016). The way that "yes" is said, the cadence, and the sound may indicate "Yes, because I don't want to say no and I'll figure that out later on." Wow! Even Yes can mean No! The emphasis on harmony and indirectness can be frustrating to Americans who expect, with some exceptions, that everyone, no matter the cultural influence, will speak openly and straightforwardly. Americans tend to view public agreement but private disagreement as deceptive or manipulative. Conversely, imagine how American directness and in-your-face communication are perceived by cultures that value harmony. The potential for intercultural miscommunication based on individualism and collectivism differences is great.

SELF-ASSESSMENT:
Be Ye Individualist or Collectivist?

How closely do you personally reflect individualist or collectivist values of your culture or co-culture? Consider the following statements, and using a scale from 1 (strongly disagree) to 9 (strongly agree), indicate in the blanks your degree of agreement or disagreement with each statement.*

1. I prefer to be direct and forthright when I talk with people.   ◯

2. I would do what would please my family, even if I detested that activity.   ◯

3. I enjoy being unique and different from others in many ways.   ◯

4. I usually sacrifice my self-interest for the benefit of my group.   ◯

5. I like my privacy.   ◯

6. Children should be taught to place duty before pleasure.   ◯

7. I like to demonstrate my abilities to others.   ◯

8. I hate to disagree with others in my group.   ◯

9. When I succeed, it is usually because of my abilities.   ◯

10. Before taking a major trip, I consult with most members of my family and many friends.   ◯

Total your score for all odd-numbered statements (1, 3, etc.), then total your score for even-numbered statements (2, 4, etc.). All odd-numbered statements reflect individualism, and all even-numbered statements reflect collectivism. Which are you?

*For the entire 63-statement measuring instrument, see Triandis (1995).

Differences in cultural values can lead to misperceptions. For example, when brainstorming ideas in diverse face to face or global virtual groups, team members from more individualist cultures such as the United States and Australia tend to voice unfiltered ideas and opinions during brainstorming sessions. Members from more collectivist cultures such as China, Korea, and Taiwan, however, are far more reluctant to contribute, fearful that they will appear superficial or foolish, and consequently lose face (Toegel & Barsouz, 2016). From the perspective of these Asian cultures, this lopsided difference in brainstorming participation rates can lead to misperceptions that Americans are domineering, rude, and arrogant bullies instead of eager participants. Conversely, Americans can misperceive these Asian participants as docile, timid, and uncreative. Doing a quick "whip-around" in which each team member is given an opportunity to speak in turn before opening the brainstorming to more of a free-for-all markedly improves brainstorming participation rates among members of collectivist cultures (Aritz & Walker, 2014).

Cross-Cultural Guidelines: Quick Tips

Expecting you to memorize dozens, even hundreds, of contradictory rules that operate in diverse cultures around the globe is impractical. Formal training may be necessary to delve into complex intercultural rule variations, especially if you need to reside for business reasons in a distinctly different culture for several months or years. At this juncture, however, we offer a short list of guidelines in addition to the simple, specific advice already provided, which should promote both appropriateness and effectiveness across even highly diverse multicultural workplaces.

1. *Embrace diversity*. As Henry David Thoreau once said, "It's never too late to give up your prejudices." Even surface differences between cultures can trigger prejudice. For example, Dan, this text's coauthor, has visited Great Britain a half-dozen times. Early visits revealed a frustrating lack of showers in his accommodations. He is not a bath person unless left with no alternative. Sitting in a tub of hot water mingled with his own residual dirt after washing ("Dan soup," as his son refers to it) is unappealing to him. His initial reaction to the shower scarcity was "What a goofy culture." He has since embraced diversity and accepted the difference-is-not-deficiency perspective (and lately, finding showers in Great Britain is easy). Diversity is part of the colorful tapestry of humankind. Be open to new

experiences and views of others because business has become increasingly global.

2. *Reduce uncertainty*. According to **uncertainty reduction theory**, when strangers first meet, the principal goal is to reduce uncertainty and increase predictability (Rahmani, 2017). Uncertainty often produces anxiety. This is especially true in highly diverse small groups, or when you might be the lone member from an individualist culture in an otherwise collectivist-oriented work group. We fear embarrassing ourselves or causing offense if we say or do the wrong thing in unfamiliar intercultural situations. Uncertainty reduction can improve the effectiveness of your intercultural communication (Neuliep, 2014). Engaging others in conversation is an important way to reduce uncertainty by getting to know others. Ask questions. Explore coworkers' cultural stories. Make friends with coworkers from different cultural backgrounds. Be accessible. Demonstrate true interest in another person's culture.

3. *Listen and learn*. "Listen" is an anagram for "silent" (same letters, different words). Too often we are more interested in hearing ourselves talk than in remaining silent, the first step in the listening process. *No one ever insulted individuals from another culture by actively listening to them*. Think about that! It is when we open our mouths, or act in inappropriate ways, that trouble can emerge. (Listening is explored in great detail in Chapter 6.)

4. *Avoid stereotyping*. Allow for individual differences. Describing cultures as primarily individualist or collectivist is a generalization that does not accurately reflect every member of a specific culture.

5. *Employ the Platinum Rule*. The Golden Rule is to treat others as *you* want to be treated. This is a nice sentiment. Not everyone, however, wants to be treated the same, especially when cultures clash. "That doesn't bother me; why should it bother you?" and "That wouldn't offend me" are comments that reveal the problem with this rule applied interculturally. The **Platinum Rule** is more useful: treat others as *they* want to be treated (Alessandra, 2020).

   In Japan, for example, you demonstrate respect by bowing in ritual greetings. To Americans, bowing is usually seen as subservience ("lowering yourself"). An accommodation from both cultural views can be made, as witnessed when Barack Obama greeted Japanese Emperor Akihito in 2009. Obama bowed and Akihito shook Obama's hand simultaneously. They both employed the Platinum Rule.

6. *Learn to style shift.* When working in multicultural environments, use a low-context communication style with individuals or

Although often awkward for Americans, the Japanese cultural rules regarding bowing as a greeting between businesspeople are important. When greeting a person of superior status, the rule is that you bow lower and longer and your eyes should be respectfully cast downward (Axtell, 1998). Failure to follow these rules can produce problematic perceptions of disrespect. Employing the Platinum Rule avoids engendering disrespectful nonverbal communication.

groups whose cultural background is individualist. Use a more high-context communication style, one that respects a desire for harmony and face-saving, with individuals or groups whose cultural background is collectivist. Dial down the direct, no-frills communication that can seem harsh, even rude. Do not insist on everyone else adapting to your accustomed way of communicating. Be flexible, as individuals from collectivist cultural backgrounds must be to adapt when working in the predominant individualist American culture.

SUMMARY

Communication competence, a recurring theme throughout this book, is communicating effectively and appropriately in a given context. For this exposition, the context occurs in workplace situations that are ever more frequently multicultural experiences. Communicating competently in the workplace is no easy matter, especially when addressing key differences between primarily collectivist and individualist cultures. There are enormous, pervasive challenges that occur in the world of business. Generally, it requires knowledge, skills, sensitivity, commitment, and ethics to achieve. Remaining chapters will explore in detail this most important and complex foundation of business success or failure.

Film School Case Studies

Becoming Warren Buffett (2017). Documentary; PG

This is the story of a one-of-a-kind billionaire with a strong moral core. Note his awkwardness in social situations and difficulties making human connections. Examine his ethical perspective.

Mr. Baseball (1992). Comedy/Romance; PG-13

Jack Elliot (Tom Selleck), a professional baseball player whose skills are waning, is forced to play in Japan. Identify examples of the clash between his individualistic ways of communicating and the more collectivist ways of the Japanese he encounters.

Up in the Air (2009); Comedy/Drama; R

George Clooney plays a corporate downsizing expert who travels around the country firing people. Analyze his communication competence as he fires employees of companies being downsized.

Wolf of Wall Street (2013). Drama; R

Stockbroker Jordan Belfort (Leonardo DiCaprio) claws his way to the top of the financial food chain until he tumbles as the result of crime and corruption. Examine the ethical issues depicted graphically by applying the five standards of ethical business communication behavior.

TED Talks and YouTube Videos

These TED Talks and YouTube videos can be accessed by going to the Oxford Learning Link for It's All of Our Business or by typing the title of the video into a Google search window.

"Don't Lose Your Accent/Learning Accents" Trevor Noah

"How American and Chinese Values Shaped the Coronavirus Response"

"The Lies Our Culture Tells Us About What Matters—and a Better Way to Live"

After successful completion of this chapter, you should be able to

1. Explain how power permeates every aspect of business communication.

2. Define power and distinguish among three forms as they relate to the workplace: dominance, prevention, and empowerment.

3. Identify verbal and nonverbal indicators of power in the workplace.

Power: The Inescapable Dynamic

ACCESS TO BATHROOMS on the job rarely poses a problem for white-collar workers. Lawyers, business executives, and college professors do not need to ask for permission to relieve themselves, nor do they have their bathroom activities monitored. Because of their positions, they have the power to relieve themselves at will. This observation may strike you as too obvious to bother mentioning, but less powerful workers in factories, telephone-calling centers, food-processing plants, and construction sites can be refused permission when they request a bathroom break. They also can be timed with stopwatches while they are in the restroom, can be chastised and disciplined for frequent restroom visits, and can even be hunted like quarry by supervisors if they remain in the stalls too long (Clawson, 2014).

The courts have ruled that these common practices by supervisors are not necessarily illegal ("What Are the OSHA Restroom Break Laws?" 2021). Consequently, workers have in some instances taken to wearing adult diapers while toil-

CHAPTER OUTLINE

- The Nature of Power
- Consequences of Power Imbalances
- Power-Distance: Cultural Variation

4. Recognize deleterious consequences that stem from power imbalances.

5. Spot power differences in virtual and cultural communication that complicate business exchanges.

ing on assembly lines because bathroom breaks are not permitted often enough (Galimberti, 2018).

Power is inescapable in human communication transactions. Organizations and institutions are typically structured as hierarchies, with the powerful at the top issuing orders—such as rules for bathroom breaks—and the more abundant workers experiencing diminishing levels of power below. As social psychologist Dacher Keltner (2016a) explains, "Power defines the waking life of every human being, . . . emerges instantaneously when humans interact," and "shapes our every interaction, from those between parent and children to those between work colleagues." In short, "power is everywhere" (Battilana & Casciaro, 2021).*You cannot communicate with others without power operating as a blatantly obvious or sometimes subtle dynamic.* The moment that you enter the work force, power becomes an ever-present dynamic.

The COVID-19 pandemic and the prospect of some future pandemic spotlighted power as an inescapable dynamic in workplaces globally. Are masks required to be worn, and who gets to create and communicate the rules? Must social distancing be mandated and maintained? Are vaccinations mandatory for all employees?

An Oxfam America report titled "No Relief" (2016), based on extensive research on the four largest poultry companies that control 60% of the market, found widespread abuse of workers' bathroom rights. "What would be shocking in most workplaces happens far too often in poultry plants: workers relieving themselves [wearing diapers] while standing at their work station." Power dynamics at work can play out in unusual, even disturbing ways

Who gets to make such decisions and how will these decisions be presented to workers? How will such decisions be enforced, or will they? *To ignore or give only cursory treatment of power would be strikingly inadequate when exploring communication competence in the workplace. Power permeates every aspect of business communication*. Power is a central underlying element in conflict management and negotiation, developing teamwork, engaging in group decision making and problem solving, creating normative behavior, designating formal roles, conducting effective meetings, creating a positive communication climate, exercising leadership, text messaging, emailing colleagues and supervisors, and using social media at work, just to name some of the relevant topics. Power as a concept inextricably relevant to communication competence in the workplace requires extensive analysis and applications carefully explored throughout this text.

Power, however, often has negative connotations. References to "power plays," "power struggles," or "power politics" do not engender warm, fuzzy feelings of pleasant transactions. English historian Lord Acton reputedly observed, "Power tends to corrupt, and absolute power corrupts absolutely." This is a popular perspective unless, of course, we are the ones with the power. Then, as former Secretary of the Navy John Lehman once quipped, "Power corrupts. Absolute power is kind of neat." It is commonplace to think of power as coercive, illegitimate, or even evil.

Research on the communication behavior of high-power individuals does not help diminish this negative viewpoint. As Berkeley psychology professor Dacher Keltner (2007) notes, there is a "wealth of evidence that having power makes people more likely to act like sociopaths. High-power individuals are more likely to interrupt others, to speak out of turn, and to fail to look at others who are speaking." More unsettling, as Keltner continues, "Surveys of organizations find that most rude behaviors—shouting, profanities, bald critiques—emanate from the offices and cubicles of individuals in positions of power." (See also Fancher, 2016.) Research also reveals that high-power individuals, exuding a misplaced confidence in their own self-efficacy, are inclined to ignore advice from lower-power individuals who may even be experts on relevant subjects of discussion. Power doesn't just corrupt, it can result in flawed judgment and decision making (Tost et al., 2012).

There is no virtue, however, in exercising little power (Aubin et al., 2016). As the opening examples regarding restrictions on bathroom breaks vividly illustrate, relative powerlessness constrains choices and can produce negative outcomes. Feeling powerless creates apathy, shrivels the desire to perform at work, and strains personal relationships with coworkers. It also inhibits the direct expression of ideas, stokes fear of making mistakes and appearing foolish, triggers stress, ignites destructive conflict, and encourages withdrawal from communicating with colleagues (Keltner, 2017; Laslo-Roth & Schmidt-Barad, 2020). The choice is not between using or not using power. "We only have options about whether to use power destructively or productively for ourselves and relationships" (Wilmot & Hocker, 20121.

The primary purpose of this chapter is to discuss the inescapable and critical role power plays in our workplace communication. Toward this end, chapter objectives include (1) define power in its three basic forms, (2) describe verbal and nonverbal indicators of power, (3) identify and explore power resources and their applications to the workplace, (4) explore serious consequences that emanate from power imbalances, and (5) provide an explanation of the power-distance dimension of cultural communication that complicates business transactions. *Communication strategies used to address power imbalances are discussed in Chapter 4.*

The Nature of Power

Power *is the ability to influence the attainment of goals sought by you or others.* Power is not a characteristic of any individual but is contextual. It is determined by your communication transactions with others in different settings. For example, you can be a powerful executive at work who is lionized by subordinates as an outstanding leader but perceived as a bumbling mess at home with your family, branded as irredeemably ineffectual, especially by teenage children.

No one, however, is all-powerful or completely powerless. Have you ever seen a child pitch a fit in a grocery store, demanding some desired sweet from a parent, and observe the parent cave to the demand just to stop the obnoxious din? Who is running the show in this case, the parent or the child? If each person at work has some degree of power, the appropriate question is not "Is Person A powerful or powerless?" The apt question is "How much power does Person A exercise compared to Person B?" It is not an all-or-nothing proposition but a matter of relative influence. *Power is not the sole prerogative of leaders and managers in the world of business. To think thusly is to view power far too narrowly, constricting important insights that could be gained from a far more expansive view.* Forms of power and their interaction also matter.

Forms of Power: Dominance, Prevention, and Empowerment

A Captain spots a light in the distance, directly in the path of his ship. He orders the following message be sent: "Turn 10 degrees south." A message is transmitted back to the ship: "*You need to turn 10 degrees north.*" Irritated, the captain orders a second message transmitted: "I am this ship's captain, and I order you to turn 10 degrees south." An immediate reply ensued, "I am a seaman second class, and I am telling you to turn 10 degrees north." Outraged that his authority to issue a clear order is being ignored by a lowly seaman second class, the captain responds: "This is a battleship coming right at you; turn 10 degrees south." This prompts a quick reply: "This is a lighthouse; turn 10 degrees north."

The captain and the seaman are engaged in a power struggle. The captain expects his commands to be obeyed because of rank. Seamen do not usually get to order captains to change course, but the seaman with lesser power asserts himself to avoid calamity. Fighting over who has the legitimate power in a transaction can end up with a battleship on top of a lighthouse.

Such power struggles are the way we too often see power playing out in the world of work, but there are three forms of power (see Box 3.1) and they are considerably different from each other (Hollander & Offerman,

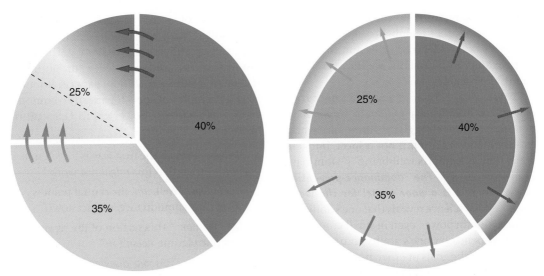

FIGURE 3-1 and 3-2 Depicted in these pie graphs, dominance-prevention power struggles (left image) are based on seeing the power pie as a fixed, zero-sum contest. The more powerful try to poach power from the less powerful, and the less powerful try to prevent the poaching. Empowerment (right image), conversely, sees the power pie as expandable. Every person may have the same proportion of power relative to others; but when the power pie grows larger, everyone gains more pie.

1990). **Dominance** is the communication of power over others. A boss can walk into an employee's office unannounced and interrupt without asking permission, expostulate mind-numbingly about the wonders of the video replay rule in football, for example, while the employee must endure her boss's boring blather. Employees are not accorded the privilege of doing the same to their bosses.

Prevention is power used to thwart those with greater influence. It is a communicated reaction to dominance. The willingness to say

"no" can be formidable in the face of dominating attempts, but it also comes with consequences, as detailed later.

Empowerment is power derived from enhancing the capabilities, choices, and influence of individuals and groups. It is power communicated proactively and constructively. Empowered individuals exude capability and effectiveness because they perform well, not because they seize power from another person. *Those who seek to empower themselves and others see power as expandable.* On a project

BOX 3.1 Forms of Power

Type	Definition	Description
Dominance	Power over	Active
Prevention	Power from	Reactive
Empowerment	Power to	Proactive

team, for example, your success is aided by the success of other members. Improving each member's knowledge and skills and their ability to exhibit both can enhance the overall success of their team.

Those who harbor a negative concept of power are usually responding to dominance-prevention power struggles. "Dominance works as a tool to gain power, if not respect, but generally douses a group's well-being" ("Dominant Leaders," 2018). *The dominance-prevention power struggle is a poor model for the workplace.* "Social science reveals that one's ability to get or maintain power, even in small group situations, depends on one's ability to understand and advance the goals of other group members" (Keltner, 2007). Dominance-prevention cycles will not end, but empowerment can gain a wider audience and become more broadly applied.

Communication Indicators of Power

Indicators of power are the ways in which relative degrees of power are communicated. To understand the centrality of power in your transactions with everyone in the workplace you must recognize its inherent presence. This recognition can occur by understanding three communication types of power indicators: general, verbal, and nonverbal.

General Indicators: Defining, Following, and Inhibiting There are several general indicators of power. First, *those who can define others exercise power.* Bosses can define employees (e.g., hard worker; sluggard). Legal entities can define businesspeople as criminals. A second general indicator of power is *whose decisions are followed.* Employees follow the directives of managers, not vice versa. Finally, *communication inhibition* is a general indicator of power (Cho & Keltner, 2020). The less powerful are more passive, withdrawn, and taciturn, especially if expressing ideas might challenge more powerful individuals. Conversely, more powerful individuals are usually more assertive or aggressive in pushing their ideas and opinions.

Verbal Indicators: Language Choices The way we speak indicates degrees of power.

The speech of a less powerful person is often flooded with self-doubt, approval seeking, overqualification, hesitancy, personal diminishment, and deference to authority (Hosman & Siltanen, 2006; Leaper & Robnett, 2011). Examples of speech patterns commonly viewed as relatively powerless in U.S. culture include the following:

Hedges: "*Perhaps* the best way is . . ." "I'm a *little* worried that this *might* not work."

Hesitations: "Well, *um,* the central point is . . ." "Gosh, *uh,* shouldn't we, *um,* act now?"

Tag Question: "This section of the report seems irrelevant, *doesn't it?*"

Disclaimers: "You *may disagree* with me, but . . ." "This idea is *probably silly,* but . . ."

Excessive Politeness: "I'm *extremely sorry* to interrupt, but . . ."

"Powerless" language advertises a person's subordinate status and creates the impression of low self-confidence (Dhawan, 2021).

Powerless forms of speech, however, are not necessarily inappropriate or ineffective. Members of a work team, for example, may view a fellow member who uses "powerless" forms of language as exuding warmth and a willingness to collaborate (Fragale, 2006). If you are a new and inexperienced member of such a team, using "powerless" forms of speech initially can invite group acceptance.

Unlike "powerless" language, powerful speech is direct, fluent, declarative, commanding, and prone to interrupt or overlap the speech of others. It advertises superior status, dynamism, and credibility (Moran, 2021). "Prepare this presentation by Friday"; "Do not ignore the conclusions of this report"; and "This is clearly the best offer we have received" are examples of powerful speech.

The appropriateness and effectiveness of powerful forms of speech are complicated. Incivility, or verbal abuse, can seem powerful, but they are inappropriate victimizations of the less powerful by those with greater power (MacLennan, 2015). Sometimes deferential language is a sign of respect and politeness (Marsh, 2019). Japanese, for example, use expressions such as "I think," "perhaps,"

Exaggerating to make the point, would you even bother listening to the ensuing message after hearing such excessive politeness and these disclaimers and hesitations that scream "I'm not worthy"? Such powerless language communicates lack of self-confidence.

and "probably" with great frequency during disagreements because they strive to preserve harmony. Americans, however, typically view such indirect language as weak and ineffectual (Kameda, 2007; Samovar et al., 2021).

In the United States, verbal indicators of power also show several gender differences. Despite persistent stereotypes, voluminous evidence shows that men, not women, are typically more talkative in mixed-sex groups and business meetings (A. Grant, 2021; Tannen, 2017). Men in general also are more verbally aggressive, direct, opinionated, and judgmental than women (Ferenczi et al., 2017). Women tend to use tag questions, hedges, and disclaimers more than men, but this may reflect greater interpersonal sensitivity (Leaper & Robnett, 2011).

Nonverbal Indicators: Silent Exercise of Power

There are numerous nonverbal indicators of power (Moore et al., 2014). *Clothing*, for example, is a strong indicator of power. As Mark Twain once remarked, "Naked people have little or no influence on society." Most people typically associate uniforms with power and authority and business suits with status involving financial success and position within an organization. Complicating the relationship between clothing and power in the workplace, however, is that "We live in a time in which our moguls dress in hoodies and t-shirts, and in which more and more workers are telecommuting—working not just from home, but from PJs" (Garber, 2016). This was amplified by the COVID-19 pandemic. "Shelter in place" and "work from home" became a first line of defense against the disease, resulting in much greater acceptance of casual dress when Zooming meetings. *We tend not to groom for the Zoom with the same attention to formality as when interacting in person.*

Touch is another important nonverbal power indicator. *The more powerful person can usually touch the less powerful person more frequently*, and with fewer restrictions (Moore et al., 2014). A pat on the shoulder intending to denote good work, for example, would more likely be seen from a boss to an employee than vice-versa. Sexual harassment laws recognize this difference and try to protect subordinates from tactile abuse.

Eye contact also indicates a power difference. Staring is done more freely by the more powerful person (Moore et al., 2014). *Less powerful individuals must monitor their eye contact more carefully*. A boss can show lack of attentiveness during conversations by looking away from subordinates, even ignoring them while texting, but a subordinate doing the same to a boss may invite a reprimand. Strong eye contact shows interest, or at least respect; poor eye contact exhibits indifference.

Space is a clear nonverbal indicator of power—*the more powerful usually have more of it.* Executives usually have reserved parking spaces closer to an office building. Lesser employees' parking permits become hunting licenses for too few spaces often located somewhere in the next time zone. The higher up in the corporate hierarchy that you travel, typically the bigger is your office space. Lower-level employees are not so fortunate. White collar workers are familiar with open-plan offices dubbed "warehousing" in which large numbers of employees are clustered at desks separated only by insubstantial partitions that provide merely the illusion of privacy, and certainly little protection from infectious diseases as glaringly obvious with the recent pandemic. Workers in meat processing plants, for example, stood shoulder-to-shoulder, often with little protection from the COVID-19 virus.

Research clearly shows that workers highly value **autonomy**—the ability to control their own workspace by decorating as they please without being monitored by supervisors—and such autonomy increases workers' productivity (Haslam & Knight, 2010; "Workplace Effectiveness," 2020). *So, if you are, or will be, in a leadership position at work or when starting your own small business, provide as much spatial autonomy for employees as is practical.*

Status Cues: Virtual Groups *Power differences may be less obvious in virtual groups.* Rank is less apparent when emailing group members than it is when communicating face to face. Even videoconferencing can minimize status differences. As professor of psychology Comila Shahani-Denning explains, "When we communicate via Zoom, participants are often presented side by side on the computer screen, with it being difficult to tell status and power, as all images are equal size except for the person speaking at the moment" (quoted by Lashbrook, 2020). When everyone is working from home, the formality of one's workspace often becomes more informal. Even the most

Executives typically do not work shoulder-to-shoulder with lower-level employees, but they have private offices. The less powerful are usually not accorded much private space, if any at all. Social distancing during the pandemic made such arrangements extremely risky, leading to work-at-home requirements, but some executives could continue to work and shelter in place in their semi-protected private offices.

powerful individuals on the planet appear less formidable when conducting a Zoom team meeting with a backdrop of a mere bookshelf or a wall with family pictures. Also, "Seeing your boss interact with children and pets, or seeing their own (possibly messy) office space humanizes them, which can erode hierarchical differences between employer and employee" (Lashbrook, 2020). Similarly, status cues such as the size of a person's office space are typically hidden. Conducting a videoconference in a large room can just create an echo effect and make the speaker appear diminutive, swallowed up by the extraneous space. In addition, micromanaging by supervisors can be diminished.

This **status equalization effect**, however, is probably more prominent in text-only communication (Carr, 2017). *There are two types of status characteristics that are hidden from text-only communication:* (a) physical characteristics such as ethnicity, gender, and age; and (b) communication cues such as rapid speaking rate, fluency of speech (few pauses or disfluencies such as "ums" and "ahs"), emphatic tone of voice, strong eye contact when speaking, and head of the table seating location (Driskell et al., 2003). Email-only screens these status markers that are immediately available in face-to-face communication.

Audioconferencing screens out some of these status markers, although age, gender, ethnicity, and even physical attributes can often be discerned from voice-only communication (Krauss et al., 2002). *Even videoconferencing is not a perfect parallel to in-person group discussion in which nonverbal status cues are plentiful.* For example, during Zoom group meetings, eye contact is unfocused as members stare at computer screens. "We lose the ability to observe others observing us, since we often don't know where their gaze is directed" (E. Keating, 2020). Are we taken seriously when we can't determine whether anyone is observing us? When team members stare at their computer screens, are they focusing on you as you speak or are they peering at other members?

Who are these Zoom participants looking at? You can't turn your head to face someone on either side of you. Everyone is staring at a screen. Direct eye contact can be very difficult to discern, making status differences hard to detect. How do you know who is paying attention to whom (dark glasses don't help)?

Note, however, that this status equalization effect might be only temporary—experienced during the initial development of a virtual group. *More mature groups typically develop status markers even when restricted to text-only communication*, such as waiting a long time to respond to messages from less powerful group members, answering questions with curt responses, and using "powerful" language (e.g., "Get this done by noon tomorrow"; Boughton, 2011).

Power Resources: Raw Materials of Influence

Thus far, power has been defined, types of power have been described, and indicators of power have been explained to sensitize you to the pervasive, unavoidable role that power plays in your workplace communication transactions. But how does power influence our transactions with supervisors, coworkers, customers, and clients in an ongoing basis? To begin this discussion, understanding what power resources are available and how they might be used is important.

A **power resource** is anything that enables individuals to achieve their goals, assists others to achieve their goals, or interferes with the goal attainment of others. The range of power resources is broad. This section lays out the primary resources from which power is most extensively derived.

Information: Good and Plenty   A report titled "2020 Vision: The Future of Business Information" (2016) notes that "the power of information resources to create competitive advantage" has never been greater. The challenge, however, is how to manage the tsunami of information, some critical and much that is pointless drivel, available at the touch of a few keystrokes on a computer ("Data Creation," 2021). Author and former CEO John Bell (2015) explains, "There comes a point where the insatiable thirst for information does not bring power. Pass this point and data overload starts to work against you, reducing the power that

Information is so readily available and seems to inundate us from everywhere that information overload has become noise that can impair your power to make competent decisions and solve problems.

you were working so hard to achieve in the first place." As noted in Chapter 1, more communication is not necessarily better communication.

Expertise: Information Plus Know-How Information and expertise are closely related, but a person can have critical information without being an expert. You might possess a valuable technical report without being able to decipher any of the information. A corporate lawyer presumably knows the law but may not practice it skillfully in the courtroom. Expertise is more than just having information. *An expert understands the information and knows how to use it wisely and skillfully in various contexts*. No business could ever hope to function effectively without at some time requiring the services of experts.

One study found that expert power used by the leader of a group to be the most influential among power resources. The authors note that "the most convincing way to display expert power is by solving important problems, making good decisions, providing sound advice, and successfully completing challenging but high visibility projects" (Meng et al., 2014). You do not have to be the designated leader of a group, however, to achieve any or all of these to exercise power.

Interculturally, however, recognizing who are actual experts within a group can be confusing. One study discovered that communication indicators of expertise can produce misattributions in which nonexperts can be mistaken for actual experts and vice versa. For example, "conversational control" exhibited by behaviors such as "speaks frequently," "tends to come on strong," and "likes to determine the directions of our group conversation" showed "a huge variation in expertise evaluation of a given person" when comparing Chinese and non-Asian group participants. In addition, the communication of confidence "is a culturally shared cue for expertise judgment" even though such confidence may be undeserved (Yuan et al., 2019).

Expertise recently has become devalued as a power resource, according to Tom Nichols (2017), in his thoughtful book with the somewhat overstated title, *The Death of Expertise*. He argues persuasively that "a Google-fueled,

Wikipedia-based, blog-sodden collapse of any division between professionals and laypeople, students and teachers, knowers and wonderers—in other words, between those of any achievement in an area and those with none at all" underlines the need to recognize the difference between mere access to information and understanding and ability to offer intelligent advice on subjects of critical importance. *The quality of decision making is diminished when expertise is undervalued*.

Legitimate Authority: When to Comply and When to Defy In a series of famous studies by social psychologist Stanley Milgram (1974), participants were told to deliver increasingly painful electric shocks to an innocent victim for every wrong answer on a word-association test. Two-thirds of the participants in some of the studies obeyed the experimenter and delivered the maximum shock to the victim, who in some cases screamed in agony. No shocks, however, were delivered. The experiments were made to seem real, though, and none of the participants suspected trickery. In all, 19 variations of these obedience-to-authority studies were conducted. One replication required participants to shock a cute, fluffy puppy. The shocks in this case were real, not faked, but surreptitiously reduced in intensity. Three-quarters of the participants, all college students, were obedient to the end (Sheridan & King, 1972). More recent studies suggest that nothing much has changed since the original Milgram studies (Bocchiaro & Zimbardo, 2017; Burger, 2009).

Participants in the Milgram studies followed orders, not because they were evil or sadistic, but because they could not resist *legitimate authority* (Milgram, 1974). A **legitimate authority** is someone perceived to have a right to direct others' behavior because of his or her position, title, role, experience, or knowledge. The experimenter was the legitimate authority. He issued a series of increasingly direct orders that participants continue to deliver progressively higher levels of electric shock to the victims.

Obedience to authority is an ever-present reality in the workplace. Distinguishing between appropriate and inappropriate use of authority, either as an employee or a boss, is an intrinsic part of the world of business. Even CEOs are beholden to boards of directors. Any supervisor who orders subordinates to engage in unethical behavior is acting inappropriately. Blindly obeying unethical commands from supervisors, however, is also inappropriate. *Ethical criteria—respect, honesty, fairness, choice, and responsibility—are guidelines for choosing when to defy and when to comply: not always an easy choice.*

Rewards and Punishments: What Works Best?   Distributing rewards and punishments can be an important source of power. Salaries, bonuses, work schedules, perks, hirings, and firings are typical job-related rewards and punishments.

The power potential of punishment depends on the degree of certainty that the punishment will be administered. Verbal threats without follow-through become impotent bluster. Punishment can be used positively to change behavior from antisocial to prosocial, but it also is coercive and reinforces dominance. Consequently, *it easily triggers backlash.* Individuals on the receiving end of punishment typically rebel. We do not normally like our tormenters.

A reward can be an effective power resource, but there is a difference between intrinsic and extrinsic rewards. An **intrinsic reward** is enjoying what one does for its own sake and because it gives you pleasure, such as doing your job because it is intellectually stimulating and fulfilling. An **extrinsic reward** is an external inducement, such as money, recognition, praise, awards, or prestige.

One study of more than 500 organizations and 200,000 employees found that money was way down the list of what motivates employees to excel at their jobs. An "intrinsic desire to do a good job" came in second just behind "peer camaraderie" ("The 7 Trends," 2020). Creating a workplace communication climate that promotes intrinsic rewards and motivates productivity is discussed in Chapter 5.

Personal Qualities: A Powerful Persona   Some individuals exhibit personal qualities that draw people to them, often referred to as **charisma**. Some individuals have no more charisma than driftwood; others have an abundance. Being charismatic is strongly associated with likability (Tousley, 2017). Likable people receive more job offers and promotions and are perceived as more credible (Vozza, 2015). Also, good looks, an attractive personality, dynamism, persuasive skills, warmth, and charm are some of the personal qualities that make an individual charismatic. *There is no precise formula for*

Charisma is not determined objectively. Dwayne "The Rock" Johnson is an international celebrity, but Bill Gates is a "rock star" celebrity in his own sphere of influence. What in the world do they have in common? Even their glasses do not match.

determining charisma, however. What is attractive to you may be unattractive to others (Haslam & Reicher, 2012).

Before leaving this section on power resources, we should note that *a person does not possess power; a person is granted power by communication with others*. A reward that nobody wants will influence no one. Information that is irrelevant to the needs of individuals or groups has no power potential. Charisma means little in a job interview if a hiring committee prefers diligence, expertise, and efficiency. In this case, charisma might look like flash without follow-through (Rast et al., 2016). Prevailing research shows that *leaders who exhibit personal qualities of humility and persistence, and nurture the talent of other group members, were more likely to produce high-performing teams than charismatic leaders* (Chamorro-Premuzic, 2019).

Consequences of Power Imbalances

Despite many examples of truly compassionate, caring, and admirably ethical business leaders at all levels of organizations, workers are too often abused by those with more power. Power can be seductive and tempt anyone to use it unethically. In this section, main consequences of power imbalances at work are explored.

Sexual Harassment: When "Flirting" Is Hurting

Sexual harassment in the workplace has been a persistent pathology that, like many diseases, remains chronic. More than half of women in the workplace have experienced sexual harassment (Zetlin, 2018), although research shows that the great majority of men do not engage in sexual harassment (Patel et al., 2017). As pervasive as sexual harassment against women is in the workplace, *sexual harassment against males, however, is not an insignificant problem*. The U.S. Equal Employment Opportunity Commission reports that men file almost 17% of all sexual harassment complaints ("Charges

Alleging," 2021). Female supervisors are not immune to abusing their power by harassing male subordinates. Also, a UCLA study reports that a quarter of LGBTQ employees experience sexual harassment at work ("LGBT People's Experience," 2021). Women also harass other women and men likewise harass other men, although far less frequently.

Sexual harassment is generally defined as "verbal, visual, nonverbal or physical conduct of a sexual nature or based on someone's sex that is severe or pervasive and affects working conditions" ("Sexual Harassment at Work," 2019). *Sexual harassment is toxic communication*. The law defines two principal types of sexual harassment: quid pro quo (you give something to get something) and hostile environment. **Quid pro quo harassment** occurs when the more powerful person requires sexual favors from the less powerful person in exchange for keeping a job, landing an employment promotion, or job perks, and avoiding punishment (e.g., firing or demotion) for rejection of sexual advances. **Hostile environment harassment** is employment discrimination based on unwelcomed sexual conduct that creates an intimidating, hostile, or offensive work environment characterized by such offensive communication as sexual comments, jokes, and discussions about sex (Berlin, 2017). To meet the criteria established by the courts for violations, a pattern of offensive conduct must be established, unless a single, unusually egregious incident of such harassment is shown.

Aside from fear of losing one's job, the consequences to the victims of sexual harassment, both male and female, have been well documented: psychological distress, depression, shame, embarrassment, diminished job performance, and even post-traumatic stress syndrome ("Sexual Harassment in the Workplace," 2016). *Almost half of the women who have been victims of sexual harassment leave their jobs or switch careers* (Beras, 2018).

Sexual harassment is a difficult issue to address because men and women are not always offended by the same communication behaviors. What may be perceived by men as flirting may be received by women as hurting. Nevertheless, the courts have decided that the standard for determining instances of sexual harassment is the *reasonable person rule*. What would a reasonable person find offensive, not what would any individual, regardless of where they perceive themselves to be on the gender spectrum, find offensive.

Sexual harassment is fundamentally an abuse of power. Quid pro quo harassment is a clear instance of dominance by perpetrators against less powerful victims. Dealing with this kind of sexual harassment is extremely difficult because the harasser has legitimate authority and can punish the victim for openly complaining. Most women who are harassed never file a formal complaint with the Human Resources department for fear of losing their job, harming their career, not being believed, or because of embarrassment or shame associated with being harassed (Shaw et al., 2018).

Sexual harassment is a systemic problem that requires systemic solutions. Laws forbidding such behavior, policies that explicitly punish such harassment, and enforcement of laws and policies are all helpful in combating quid pro quo harassment. Power imbalances also promote hostile environment sexual harassment. Combating it is also difficult. A firm, clearly defined policy staunchly supported by those in power positions goes a long way toward diminishing sexual harassment. Policies, however, must be more than window dressing purporting to take sexual harassment seriously but serving instead to protect companies from lawsuits by at least claiming that a policy exists, even though it is not enforced (Morelli, 2017).

Despite the challenge of combating sexual harassment in the workplace, individual communication behaviors can also help combat this problem. *Firm, unequivocal verbal rejection of such harassment by the target of an unwanted sexual advance is an important communication approach*: "I'll file a formal complaint if you ever ask me again for sex and threaten to terminate me if I refuse." Such assertiveness, discussed extensively in Chapter 4 as a source of personal power, should not be underestimated as a means of short-circuiting sexual harassment the moment it emerges. In most companies, sexual harassment complaints are taken to the Human Resources department that provides steps for making an official complaint if assertiveness fails to stem the egregious behavior by harassers and requires formal action.

Bias Against Women and Ethnic Minorities: Leadership Gap

Although more than half of all professional and management positions in the United States are held by women, they hold just 8% of Fortune 500 CEO positions, actually a record in 2021 (Ammerman & Groysberg, 2021). At the current pace, America will have established a fully functioning human colony on Mars before gender equity in corporate power positions is a reality.

So, do these statistics prove gender bias exists? Perhaps not as many women are qualified for high-level positions. Not true. Women earn the majority of college degrees at every level, and this has been consistent since 1981 (Tanzi, 2018). There are more women than men in the U.S. workforce who have a college degree (Fry, 2019). Consistently, studies show that women outscore men on leadership capabilities tested, suggesting that they make "better leaders for the 21st century" (Young, 2016; see also Andersen, 2018).

So why do numerous well-qualified women not rise to the top of corporate America? As previously noted, almost half of women who experience *sexual harassment* quit their jobs or change careers. That diminishes their chain of experience to compete for top-level positions. Also, unlike men, *women with children are perceived to be less reliable and committed to their jobs, a myth that persists but is refuted by substantial research* (Ammerman & Groysberg, 2021; Padavic et al., 2019).

Even when women tough it out in the sometimes corporate Hunger Games, however, quite *often gender stereotyping thwarts female job advancement*. "Archetypal leadership characteristics such as authoritativeness, decisiveness, and directness are typically coded as masculine, which means that women who demonstrate them appear to be violating gender expectations and are often characterized as difficult to work with or temperamental" (Ammerman & Groysberg, 2021). Thus, according to a comprehensive study, viewing women in this way means they are "more likely to be shunted into support roles rather than landing the core positions that lead to executive jobs" (R. E. Silverman, 2015).

Additionally, *the male dominated work culture often stifles female communication. The New York Times* columnist Susan Chira (2017) observes, "Academic studies and countless anecdotes make it clear that being interrupted, talked over, shut down or penalized for speaking out is nearly a universal experience for women when they are outnumbered by men." As organizational psychologist Adam Grant (2021) also notes, "It's usually men who won't shut up. Especially powerful men." He cites numerous studies to support the prevalence of "manologues," the tendency of men

in groups of five members to dominant the discussion. When a woman is alone in such groups, she averages 40% less speaking time than *each* of the four male group members. *Only when four women outnumbered the one male participant does speaking time for each female member equal airtime individually for the one male.*

Finally, 16% of the female respondents "experienced repeated, small slights at work, compared to only 5% of male respondents" (Bailey, 2017). These **microaggressions**—seemingly innocuous comments that are subtle put-downs not always intended as such—can create a negative group climate and marginalize women in the workplace (Williams, 2020). A man conversing with a female colleague referring to their female boss as "hysterical," remarking

In 2017, a term was coined for the propensity of men to dismiss or derogate women's contributions in meetings but then later to repeat the exact same ideas as their own brilliant contribution. It was termed *hepeating*.

on the difficulty pronouncing a female supervisor's "ethnic or foreign sounding" name, an older male colleague commenting to a younger female colleague "You look so young" or "You look like an intern" are just a few examples of microaggressions (M. Ward & Premack, 2021).

The dismal statistics on gender inequity and bad male behavior at work are depressing enough, but *for both women and men of color the picture is even worse* (Somvichian-Clausen, 2020). The number of African American CEOs, including *both male and female*, at Fortune 500 companies hit its zenith at 7 in 2007; and, for Hispanic/Latino/a it peaked at 13 in 2008. African American women held *zero* positions as CEOs of Fortune 500 companies, and only *five* African American men held such positions at the end of 2020 (Wahba, 2020). According to the Hispanic Association on Corporate Responsibility, fewer than 2% of Fortune 500 CEOs were Hispanic at the end of 2020 ("Only 9 Hispanic CEOs," 2020).

The answer to gender and ethnic bias is extremely complicated and is systemic, requiring concerted efforts to provide greater opportunities for advancement for women and ethnic minorities (Revenga & Boudet, 2017). Including "voluntary diversity training as opposed to forced sessions, getting managers on board through college recruitment programs targeted to women and people of color, and formal mentoring for underrepresented groups" is part of the solution (Clouse, 2018). Also, in general, "individuals are more likely to pursue leadership when they receive feedback suggesting that they might be good at it" (Bear et al., 2017). Thus, encouragement can go a long way toward nurturing leadership emergence among women and ethnic minorities.

Communication improvements can also help (see especially Chapter 4 discussion of enhancing personal power resources). According to one report, women get less access to leaders

This "Fortune Most Powerful Women Summit" celebrated strides made by women to rise to positions of power, but it also underlined the significant challenges that remain for women, especially women of color, to attain true equality at the highest levels in the hierarchical workplace.

in organizations; ask for feedback from managers as often as men but receive far less; and when they negotiate for promotion or higher compensation, they are 30% more likely than men to receive feedback that they are "bossy," "too aggressive," or "intimidating" (A. Grant, 2021; "Women in the Workplace,"2021). Men especially who are in positions of power, until greater gender and ethnic equity are achieved, need to assist women and minorities by providing requested feedback that especially highlights a person's strengths, increase access to managers, and resist viewing women and minorities negatively who negotiate for promotions and compensation in the same ways as most white men (Young, 2016).

In addition, hepeating and manologues can be addressed by **amplification**—"echoing and supporting one another's [women's] points and publicly giving one another credit" ("3 Ways," 2021). Leaders, both male and female, can engage in amplification by outwardly noting a point or contribution made by a female participant, acknowledging its usefulness, and thereby short-circuiting the manologues. Balance the participation.

Workplace Bullying: Verbal and Nonverbal Aggression

Workplace bullying is defined by the Workplace Bullying Institute as "repeated mistreatment of an employee by one or more employees, abusive conduct that is threatening, humiliating, or intimidating; work sabotage or verbal abuse" (Bortz, 2021). It is unethical behavior, egregiously disrespectful, and irresponsible action against others.

One survey found almost 61 million workers affected by bullying ("Work Shouldn't Hurt," 2021). *Workplace bullying is especially problematic for LGBTQ workers, with 56% reporting being repeatedly bullied at their job, higher than any other group in the workplace* (Nauen, 2017). More than two in five LGBTQ workers leave their job as a result (Whaley, 2017). Online bullying, dubbed **cyberbullying**, is also a widespread problem in the workplace (Kowalski et al., 2018). Women are disproportionately targets of such online abuse

(Felmlee et al., 2019). Damage from workplace bullying increases depression, anxiety, absenteeism, sick days, and turnover rates as well as decreases in productivity—not only from the targets, but also from witnesses to the bullying (J. Rock, 2017).

Workplace bullying is fundamentally a dominance-prevention power struggle. Bullying persists primarily because most transgressors (legitimate authorities) are in more powerful positions than victims. Toxic bosses not only create significant group and organizational harm (Kim et al., 2021), but "the primary intent of toxic leaders is to conceal lack of relevant competence and maintain a position of control" (Milosevic et al., 2019). Their rage and abuse is typically a cover for their own inadequacies as leaders. Even the far less frequent instances of bullying by coworkers, a bit more prevalent in the case of LGBTQ workers because of ugly prejudice, exhibit an attempt to dominate the more reticent or vulnerable individuals. Higher-ups who could address the problem constructively often ignore bullying.

Ultimately, *prevention is far more effective than filing formal complaints*. First, *developing a constructive communication climate is essential and a significant way to address workplace bullying* (Keashly & Neuman, 2009). Creating an organizational culture that discourages social dominance is imperative (Moss, 2016). Enlightened leadership can create a group culture that discourages such social dominance (Khan et al., 2016). *If and when you are in a position of leadership, it becomes your responsibility to snuff out the first signs of bullying group members* (see Chapter 5 for a thorough discussion).

Second, a *zero-tolerance policy* in organizations for any acts of bullying is an important step. Addressing directly the first signs of bullying behavior and providing communication training for bullies to change their ways is important. When clear policies exist and are enforced to discourage bullying, the fear of losing one's job if a complaint is filed can dissipate. Mediation from a neutral person trained in conflict resolution can be effective if instituted early when bullying first occurs (Lempp et al., 2020).

Power-Distance: Cultural Variation

Cultures vary widely in their attitudes concerning the appropriateness of power imbalances. These variations in the acceptability of unequal distribution of power are called the **power-distance dimension** (Hofstede & Hofstede, 2010). *The extent to which members of a culture endorse the society's overall level of inequality determines its place on the power-distance dimension* (hereafter referred to as PD; Hofstede, 2012).

General Description: Horizontal and Vertical Cultures

All cultures are **stratified**—divided into various levels of power that put distance between the haves and the have-nots. *The difference on the PD dimension lies in whether the culture tends to accept or reject stratification, even though it is a fact of life.* A national survey by the Stanford University Rock Center for Corporate Governance found that 74% of respondents believe CEOs are vastly overpaid. Only 16% believe otherwise (Larcker et al., 2016).

The United States is a **low-PD culture** (see Figure 3.3), or what Triandis (2012) calls a *horizontal culture*. A low-PD culture values relatively equal power sharing and discourages attention to status differences and ranking in society. Challenging authority, flattening organizational hierarchies to reduce status differences between management and employees, and using power legitimately are encouraged in a low-PD culture. *Low-PD cultures do not expect power disparities to be eliminated.* Whether your first job following your graduation from college is

Comparing piggy banks as a metaphor, vast pay disparities, even in the low-PD United States, are common, but it can create a huge power imbalance and become a source of worker dissatisfaction and conflict. The 2022 AFL-CIO study of executive pay in the United States found that the average CEO for a major U.S. corporation was paid 324 times the average annual compensation of workers.

at Google, Amazon, Fitbit, or some other recognized or startup company, you undoubtedly will start at the lower rungs of the stratified organization unless, perhaps, you risk establishing your own business with you as the CEO. Nevertheless, in low-PD cultures such as the United States, Great Britain, Sweden, Denmark, Austria, Israel, and New Zealand, norms that minimize power distinctions act as guides for appropriate behavior.

High-PD cultures, or what Triandis (2012) calls *vertical cultures*, have a relatively strong emphasis on maintaining power differences. The norms of cultures such as Malaysia, Guatemala, the Philippines, Mexico, India, Singapore, and Hong Kong encourage power distinctions. Authorities are rarely challenged, the most powerful are thought to have a legitimate right to exercise their power, and organizational and social hierarchies are nurtured.

Communication Differences: With Whom May You Communicate?

Communication in low-PD cultures reflects the minimization of power disparities. Workers may disagree with their supervisors; in fact, some bosses may encourage disagreement. Socializing outside the work environment and communication on a first-name basis between workers and bosses is not unusual. Communication in high-PD cultures, however, reflects the desire to maintain power disparities. Workers typically avoid disagreeing with their bosses. Supervisors give orders and expect prompt obedience from workers. Friendship between a worker and a boss would appear inappropriate (Hofstede & Hofstede, 2010). Grabbing a brew at the local pub with your boss would not even occur to employees as an option.

Cultural differences on this dimension do not mean that high-PD cultures never experience

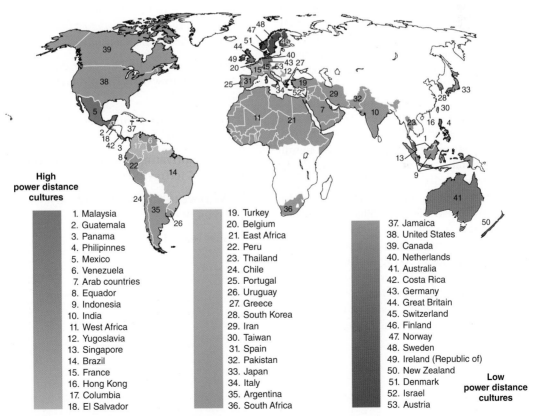

High power distance cultures

1. Malaysia
2. Guatemala
3. Panama
4. Philipinnes
5. Mexico
6. Venezuela
7. Arab countries
8. Equador
9. Indonesia
10. India
11. West Africa
12. Yugoslavia
13. Singapore
14. Brazil
15. France
16. Hong Kong
17. Columbia
18. El Salvador

19. Turkey
20. Belgium
21. East Africa
22. Peru
23. Thailand
24. Chile
25. Portugal
26. Uruguay
27. Greece
28. South Korea
29. Iran
30. Taiwan
31. Spain
32. Pakistan
33. Japan
34. Italy
35. Argentina
36. South Africa

37. Jamaica
38. United States
39. Canada
40. Netherlands
41. Australia
42. Costa Rica
43. Germany
44. Great Britain
45. Switzerland
46. Finland
47. Norway
48. Sweden
49. Ireland (Republic of)
50. New Zealand
51. Denmark
52. Israel
53. Austria

Low power distance cultures

FIGURE 3-3   Power distance and cultural comparison (Hofstede & Hofstede, 2010)

conflict and aggression arising from power imbalances. Members of low-PD cultures, however, are more likely to respond to power imbalances with frustration, anger, and hostility than members of high-PD cultures. This occurs because low-PD cultures subscribe to power balance even though the reality of everyday life may reflect significant power disparities, especially for historically disadvantaged groups such as African Americans, Mexican Americans, Native Americans, and others. Cultures do not handle power disparities uniformly.

SUMMARY

Power is the ability to influence the attainment of goals sought by yourself and others. Power is not a property of any individual. It is the product of transactions between individuals. There are three types of power: dominance, prevention, and empowerment. Information, expertise, rewards and punishments, legitimate authority, and personal qualities are primary power resources. Groups must endorse these resources before they have power potential. You can approximate the distribution of power in the workplace by observing certain general patterns of communication, plus verbal and nonverbal indicators.

Workplace power imbalances produce serious negative consequences. These include sexual harassment, bullying, and gender bias. The root cause of all three lies in the significant inequitable distribution of power in the American workplace. There are cultural differences, however, in the acceptance of inequitable power distribution. Collectivist cultures are far more accepting of power imbalances than individualist cultures such as the United States. This makes working multiculturally an especially challenging enterprise. In Chapter 4, communication behaviors that both exacerbate and diminish problems associated with power imbalances are discussed in greater depth.

Film School Case Studies

Horrible Bosses (2011). Dark comedy; R

Three friends decide to murder their horrible bosses. Beware the vulgarity. Examine the depiction of horrible bosses from the perspective of bullying and its consequences.

Miss Sloane (2016). Drama; R

Jessica Chastain's job is that of a political power broker in Washington, DC. Examine what power resources emerge and what type of power is predominant.

TED Talks and YouTube Videos

These TED Talks and YouTube videos can be accessed by going to the Oxford Learning Link for It's All of Our Business or by typing the title of the video into a Google search window.

Dacher Keltner, Ph.D.—"The Power Paradox: How We Gain and Lose Influence"

"Why Ordinary People Need to Understand Power" Eric Liu

"Why Cultivating Power Is the Secret to Success" Jeffrey Pfeffer

"We Have to Stop Calling Women Girls" Mayim Bialik

"Boss Made Her . . ."

After successful completion of this chapter, you should be able to

1. Develop competent communication strategies to balance power in your interactions with others at work.

2. Explain the benefits and drawbacks of the common reactions to power imbalances, along with ways to combat incompetent communication.

3. Strengthen your own empowered communication by developing your assertiveness skills.

CHAPTER 4

Balancing Power: Communication Strategies Good and Bad

YEARS AGO, Dan (yes, coauthor of this text) worked in quality control at a can factory to pay for college. In a less-than-commendable effort to avoid the horrid press department, he kept ducking out of sight at the start of the morning shift to avoid the supervisor, who regularly selected a worker in quality control to replace someone who had quit the press department, an almost daily occurrence. One day the supervisor spotted dodging Dan and sent him to the press department. He went reluctantly, planning to make just enough nuisance of himself that he would be returned to quality control.

CHAPTER OUTLINE

- Dominance-Prevention Power Struggles
- Empowerment Enhancement

The job involved stacking and packing can lids pumped rapidly from a machine. The trick was to keep up with the machine and not spill any lids onto the greasy floor to avoid having to discard them. By the end of the shift, Dan had spilled thousands of lids onto the factory floor and shut the machine down four times. This halted the entire production line, incensed the machinist who had to spend 20 minutes starting up the machine each time it was shut down, and forced his supervisor to call in two workers to clean up his mess. Despite Dan's relative powerlessness, his purposeful sabotage infuriated but perplexed those in charge.

The next day, Dan returned to his previous job, pretending not to know that no one ever returned to quality control once assigned to the press department. He hid out behind huge stacks of cans yet to be inspected for defects, watched his supervisor pick another young employee to take the press job, and spent the rest of the summer free from press department duties. Inexplicably, he even received a promotion a month later. Ironically, Dan ended up in the press department the next summer, however; and with a change of attitude, he managed to master the job with little difficulty, although he continued to "rage against the machine."

No one is entirely powerless, as Dan demonstrated. What he chose to do was not admirable, and *the main point of this chapter is not to teach you how to emulate his disruptive behavior*, but his experience is instructive. Resistance is not always futile, and power imbalances do not necessarily produce ugly consequences such as bullying, gender and ethnic bias, or sexual harassment. Power imbalances often play out in the workplace in more innocuous circumstances, and communication strategies to balance power are not always justified or without backlash. Thus, *the purpose of this chapter is to explore communication strategies, both beneficial and counterproductive, that attempt to balance power in workplace situations*. Toward that end, this chapter has the following objectives: (1) explain the myriad communication reactions that result from dominance-prevention power struggles, and (2) examine how empowerment can be encouraged and developed to provide constructive alternatives to dominance-prevention clashes.

Dominance-Prevention Power Struggles

Dominance-prevention power struggles produce two principal methods for balancing power: *defiance* and *resistance*. Although neither of these methods inherently produces incompetent communication, each often produces negative outcomes and must be addressed.

Defiance: Digging in Your Heels

Low-power persons sometimes overtly defy higher-power persons. **Defiance** is unambiguous, purposeful noncompliance. It is a refusal to give in to those with greater power. Defiance is the prevention form of power where one stands against those who attempt to dominate.

Defiance can be contagious. Those in authority are anxious to halt defiance before it spreads, especially with the ready availability of social media to raise awareness of such acts. The very nature of defiance is disagreeable to those who want compliance, and they normally are the most powerful. *Usually, defiance should be considered an option of last resort because the potential negative consequences can be significant, especially to the less powerful*. You can be socially ostracized and branded a social leper, or you can be severely punished. Supervisors may simply brand your defiance as "insubordination," using this as justification for demotion or termination of your employment.

Defiance also can be unjustified. It may simply be an irresponsible reaction to disliking one's job, lackluster motivation, or poor interpersonal skills. Confronting the defiance directly and immediately, and providing positive solutions to claims of injustice or poor treatment, combat defiance of this nature. *What is truly critical, however, is the creation of a positive communication climate in the workplace* (discussed extensively in Chapter 5) that provides no substantive justification for actual defiance.

Nevertheless, *defiance may be the ethical choice in some workplace situations characterized by toxic communication climates*. As psychologists Piero Bocchiaro and Philip Zimbardo (2017) note, "We should encourage obedience to just authority, while promoting defiant disobedience against all forms of unjust authority." They further claim that "any organization can benefit from 'intelligent disobedience,' a behavior typical of individuals who have the courage to speak up when they realize that certain positions are wrong or that obedience would produce harm." When is intelligent disobedience most likely to occur? When the workplace environment established by organizational leaders encourages candor, and when those who defy unjust authority are listened to by those with power who are not the actual perpetrators of unethical conduct, intelligent disobedience will occur in appropriate situations. This requires servant leadership, sometimes referred to as ethical leadership, a topic for full discussion in Chapter 10.

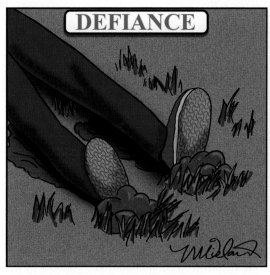

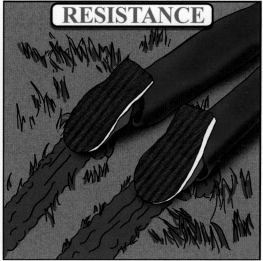

Resistance: Dragging Your Feet

Although defiance is chosen in some instances, and may be a moral imperative in certain circumstances, *resistance is far more often the choice of the less powerful to prevent dominance from others*. Resistance is also a far more complex strategy for workers than defiance. While defiance is overt, unambiguous noncompliance, **resistance** is covert, ambiguous noncompliance. Truly successful resistance leaves people wondering if resistance even occurred. Defiance, however, leaves no one scratching their heads wondering whether an employee is being defiant. It is obvious. When faced with a more powerful person or group, resistance is usually safer to use as an indirect means of noncompliance than direct confrontation. Those who are defiant dig in their heels and openly cause trouble, but those who resist merely drag their feet.

Resistance strategies are sometimes referred to as *passive aggression*. The passive part is a seeming willingness to comply with an authority's dictates, often to avoid uncomfortable conflict. The aggressive part is the undermining of an authority's power to require obedience. Passive aggression is generally a disruptive influence in the workplace (Cherry & Morin, 2020). Its covert nature may occasionally be used as the only perceived "safe" approach to a toxic work environment, but generally it is a poor long-term strategy for promoting a constructive workplace. In most instances, *there are better ways to prevent dominance* than by employing passive-aggressive strategies, as you will see later when we discuss communication climate (Chapter 5) and conflict management (Chapter 8). As a leader at any level of an organization, or even a fellow team member working on a project, you likely will need to address passive-aggressive strategies in the workplace when they interfere with workplace performance. *Our purpose here is not to encourage the use of resistance strategies, or to teach you how to employ them effectively*. Instead, readily recognizing such strategies and understanding how to address them competently is our focus.

Minimum Effort: How Slow Can You Go?   Some individuals use the minimum effort resistance strategy. They choose to decrease productivity by slowing down work. It isn't that they refuse to complete tasks, especially those deemed tedious or onerous. They just take a grindingly slow pace to complete the work. If the frustration experienced by supervisors becomes palpable because tasks are not being completed in a timely fashion, other more productive and compliant employees may be given the tasks, thus freeing the passive aggressor from unwanted responsibilities.

Strategic Stupidity: Smart People Acting Dumb
This is the "playing stupid" strategy. Strategic stupidity works exceedingly well when the low-power person claims "not to know how," is forced to attempt the task anyway, and then performs it ineptly. The poor performance becomes "proof" that the stupidity was real. The passive aggressor can assert, "I told you I didn't know how to do this." *The strategic stupidity strategy in the workplace is particularly prevalent in the technological realm*. Technology changes so rapidly and can be enormously complex. It can seem quite reasonable, at least initially, for workers to exhibit difficulty mastering computer systems and the like when they just do not want to be forced to assume certain tasks that they perceive are not in their job description.

Loss of Motor Function: Conscious Carelessness
This resistance strategy is an effective companion to strategic stupidity. The resister does not act stupid, just incredibly clumsy, often resulting in costly damage. There is a mixed message here of resistance on one hand but apparent effort on the other.

Dan's can factory resistance employed this trifecta of passive-aggressive strategies addressed so far. He clearly utilized the minimum effort strategy. Dan was intent on packing and stacking lids just slowly enough to be occasionally unsuccessful. He also used loss of motor function by spilling lids onto the grimy floor. Finally, he employed the strategic stupidity strategy when he returned to his former job in quality control, knowing that no one ever returned after being assigned to the press department. As sneakily effective as the first three strategies used by Dan can be, there are still other strategies that resisters sometimes use.

The Misunderstanding Mirage: Confusion Illusion   This is the "I thought you meant" or the "I could have sworn you said" strategy. The resistance is expressed with great sincerity. A deadline is "misunderstood" as a mere "target to shoot for," not a critical timetable to complete a project. As project requirements become more complex, this strategy can be employed more easily. The implied message is that since this is a simple misunderstanding, penalizing the employee would be unfair.

Selective Amnesia: Fake Forgetfulness   Have you ever noticed that some people are particularly forgetful about those things that they clearly do not want to do? This temporary amnesia is highly selective when used as a resistance strategy because selective amnesiacs rarely forget what is most important to them. No outward signs of resistance are manifested. Resisters agree to perform the task—but conveniently let it slip their minds. "Forgetting" important documents for a critical meeting is one way of striking back at perceived disrespect or indifference shown by managers.

In a sophisticated version of this strategy, a person, who considers it demeaning to "run errands," shops for office supplies and purchases all but two key items. Hey, no one's perfect. He or she remembered almost everything. The group project cannot be completed, but whatever!

Tactical Tardiness: Late by Design   When you really do not want to attend an office meeting, you can show contempt by arriving late. Tactical tardiness irritates and frustrates those who value the event. It can hold an entire group hostage while everyone waits for the late person to arrive. *With the pervasiveness of virtual work groups, tactical tardiness has become easier to employ.* Assembling group members can be a daunting task in the best of circumstances. It is especially challenging to do so when work groups are virtual. Being late or missing a virtual meeting entirely can easily be excused by arguing scheduling issues across time zones or technical difficulties joining a virtual meeting.

Purposeful Procrastination: Deliberate Delays   Most people put off doing what they dislike, but there is nothing "purposeful" about simple procrastination. Purposeful procrastinators, however, pretend that they will pursue a task "soon." While promising imminent results, they deliberately refuse to commit to a specific time or date for task completion. They delay the completion of tasks on purpose. Trying to pin down a purposeful procrastinator is like trying to nail Jell-O to a wall—it will not stick. Really clever resisters can provide an almost endless stream of plausible excuses for not meeting deadlines. If those waiting for the task to be completed express exasperation, they can appear to be excessively compulsive about time constraints.

Dependence on electronic speed-of-light technology ironically can be excruciatingly slow even without users intending to be passive aggressive procrastinators. Emails to group members with attachments that need to be reviewed are unlikely to receive quick attention in the best of circumstances. If virtual group members are in different countries, time zones interfere with prompt responses because some group members will be asleep when the email or text message arrives. Think how easy it is, however, to feign attempts to reply "as soon as possible" but "a computer glitch occurred" or cellphones lost their charge. The procrastination may be on purpose, but it can be challenging to prove it.

All seven of these resistance strategies result primarily from power imbalances, although in some instances these strategies are incompetent communication employed by those seeking to avoid work responsibilities or tedious tasks. It is difficult to know for sure when any of these strategies is being used. A single occurrence

Passive aggression is one way to combat power imbalances, and they should be recognized frequently as a sign of a toxic work environment. Constructing a positive, supportive work environment (see Chapter 5) and confronting passive aggressive strategies constructively, not encouraging their use, however, should be the focus.

of forgetfulness or tardiness, for example, does not necessarily indicate resistance, even though resistance may be occurring. If the behavior becomes repetitive, however, it is safe to conclude that resistance strategies are being used, unless a worker truly is incapable of completing tasks because of limited abilities or training.

There are three principal ways to combat passive-aggressive resistance strategies: confrontation, clarity, and consequences. Again, it is a mistake to view this *exclusively as a top-down process of management disciplining employees*. For example, an entire project group may need to address passive-aggressive strategies being used by one or more members without the intervention of management at all. With this in mind, addressing passive aggression whether individually or as a group includes the following communication steps:

1. *Confront the strategy directly*. Be assertive (see detailed discussion later in this chapter). Describe in detail what behaviors you have observed that lead to a conclusion that passive aggression is occurring. Ask why the strategy has been used, and work cooperatively with the resister to find an equitable solution so that resistance strategies are not used.

2. *Be very clear*. Instructions regarding tasks and performance expectations must be precise and easy to understand. If there are several steps necessary to complete tasks, make sure that the steps are clearly outlined and explained. The misunderstanding mirage can operate effectively as a resistance strategy only if task instructions are murky.

3. *Produce consequences for resistance*. When individuals or groups continue to wait for

the tactically tardy, the behavior is encouraged. If, when frustrated by purposeful procrastination, other employees perform the tasks or they are assigned to more pliable and responsible workers because it is just easier than cage fighting with a passive aggressor, the resistance is enabled and such strategies are likely to persist.

You thwart the enabling process by making sure consequences result from resistance. If employees are persistently late for meetings, continue without them, and do not interrupt the meeting to fill them in on missed information. Encourage them to be punctual. Continued tardiness may necessitate expulsion from the group. Refrain from rescuing those who use strategic stupidity or loss of motor function. Compensation for damage caused by such resistance strategies typically should be the responsibility of the resister. *Allow for human failing*, however. Sometimes a person just makes a mistake. Look for a pattern of behavior before assessing that it is passive aggression.

Despite the negative aspects of resistance strategies, *the primary focus should be on how to reduce power imbalances and dominance-submissiveness transactions that foster a desire to resist*. A constructive communication environment, discussed in Chapter 5, provides a systemic approach to passive aggression and can markedly diminish any desire to resist.

Empowerment Enhancement

Empowerment is a constructive form of power. As Dacher Keltner (2016b) concludes based on vast research, "Your power expands as you empower others." Advancing the interests of others increases your influence with them. *Individuals become empowered by learning to communicate competently*. Acquiring communication knowledge and developing a broad range of communication skills can give you the confidence to adapt your communication appropriately in the workplace. In this section,

several ways to empower less powerful workers are explained. When first embarking on your career or professional path, learning empowerment is extremely useful.

Developing Assertiveness: Confidence and Skill

The terms *assertive* and *aggressive* are often confused (Scott, 2020). **Assertiveness** is "the ability to communicate the full range of your thoughts and emotions with confidence and skill" (R. Adler, 1977). Those who confuse assertiveness with aggressiveness tend to ignore the last part of this definition. Assertiveness is not merely imposing your thoughts and emotions on others. Too often abrasive behavior is excused as "simply being assertive." Assertiveness requires competent communication of thoughts and feelings, not some infantile, cathartic rant dressed up in a clown suit and modeled under the pretense of assertiveness.

Assertiveness falls between the extremes of aggressiveness and passivity, and it is distinctly different from both. Aggressiveness puts one's own needs first; you wipe your shoes on other people. Passivity underemphasizes one's needs; you are a doormat in a world of muddy shoes. *Assertiveness considers both your needs and the needs of others*.

Although assertiveness can be used to defy others, it is primarily an empowering skill. Assertive individuals try to enhance their significance in the eyes of others, not alienate anyone. When passive, reticent individuals learn assertiveness, they become more productive contributors at work. When aggressive individuals learn to be assertive, they are more likely to receive a fair hearing and cause less turmoil.

Assertiveness requires practice, and it involves five key communication steps (Bower & Bower, 1976):

1. *Describe your needs, rights, and desires or the basis of your conflict with others*. "We need to work more energetically on this presentation."

2. *Express how you feel*. "I feel anxious when our team appears to be falling behind

Communicating confidence, determination, and skill is the essence of assertiveness: a willingness to stand your ground when challenged. Assertiveness, however, is not "constructive aggression" as some have "asserted." Aggression is defined as "behavior that is intended to harm another person" (Allen & Anderson, 2017). That is not "constructive." You can be determined, yet respectful, toward others. You can be firm without being rude.

schedule to complete this project." Understand, however, that there is no magic in beginning a statement with "I feel." For example, "I feel that you are an imperious, pathetic jerk" or "I feel that you are a terrible boss" is not being assertive. It is an aggressive attack.

3. *Specify the behavior or objective you are seeking*. "Let's commit to meeting from noon to 3:00 twice a week on Mondays and Wednesdays for the next 3 weeks, if that works for everyone's schedule."

4. *Identify consequences*. The emphasis should be on positive, not negative, consequences. "Finishing this project on time after concerted effort will make us all proud of our accomplishment." This is a better statement than "If we don't finish on time and make

a concerted effort to produce a quality proposal, then we'll all have hell to pay."

5. *Remain respectful*. You can remain firm and direct and still be unwaveringly polite and respectful. Tone of voice is especially important. A weak, quavering voice communicates passivity, and a loud voice can seem aggressive. Find the balance in between the two. You can ask for feedback from others to find that balance. (See Box 4.1).

Being assertive is particularly challenging when using social media. Written messages without companion nonverbal cues (e.g., facial expressions, tone of voice, gestures, and eye contact) can easily be perceived as aggressive. "I need this document to be changed immediately" can seem pushy and demanding when intended to be merely direct and firm. Soften the tone: "Please make the required changes

BOX 4.1
Stand Up, Sit Down: An Exercise in Assertiveness

Studies reveal that most individuals do not accurately perceive how they come across to others in the workplace: too passive, aggressive, or appropriately assertive (Ames & Wazlawek, 2014). We have used an instructive exercise in dozens of classroom and boardroom presentations to demonstrate this very point. It requires the following steps:

1. The group is divided into pairs, and these dyads indicate by simple agreement who will be person A and who will be person B.
2. Person A is instructed to say "Stand up" to person B, *using absolutely no other words*.
3. Person B is told to physically stand up only if he/she feels that person A has said it assertively. If it seems like an order (aggressive) or a plea (passive), then person B remains seated but provides feedback (e.g., "Too aggressive"; "Too passive"). Once successful, person A says "Sit down" with the same instructions. Partners switch roles after several successful attempts and following the same steps.
4. Participants then break into groups of 6–9 members. Each member, in turn, makes the statement "Stand up" to the group. Each group member is told to make an independent judgment whether the statement is said assertively, aggressively, or passively. Group members obey only when the statement is deemed assertive. Sometimes all group members obey simultaneously, and sometimes compliance is sporadic. Each member must get every group member to stand up before making the statement "sit down." Individuals remain standing until every group member has risen.

When every group member rises or sits in unison, this occurs when all nonverbal cues seem to communicate assertiveness. The more typical mixed reactions, however, occur because nonverbal cues are mixed. This underlines a key point that *assertiveness is mostly nonverbal in nature*. The statements "Stand up" and "Sit down" seem to be inherently commands and therefore aggressive. Yet this exercise clearly demonstrates that the verbal "command" can be communicated in an exceedingly passive way through hesitant or questioning tone of voice, lack of eye contact, soft-spokenness, nervous twitches, frozen facial expressions, and so forth. Thus, *what you say is often not as important as how you say it when you are trying to be assertive*. Depending on which nonverbal cues each group member focuses on can result in split-member reactions. If you are sitting beside the person issuing the statement, for example, you cannot use eye contact or facial expressions as nonverbal cues for determining assertiveness, aggressiveness, or passivity. Tone of voice thus becomes more salient.

This is a surprisingly difficult exercise for most people. We have witnessed CEOs of organizations large and small appear baffled and increasingly frustrated that other people perceive aggressiveness when they are convinced that they have toned down the statements to be assertive, even passive. In some cases, the opposite occurs. Individuals up and down the status hierarchy of an organization come off as passive when they think they are being obviously aggressive.

to this document by tomorrow. Thank you." This version is polite but firm, and it avoids the undertone of a demand. Using emoticons or emojis can sometimes convey a softer tone as well.

Assertiveness is an important skill to learn, and recognizing how you are perceived by others allows you to adjust to your audience and the context. Despite its empowering nature, however, *it is not always appropriate to be assertive*, especially if harm may come to you or others (e.g., your boss will fire you). Research clearly shows that being assertive in the workplace is more challenging for women than men because of gender stereotypes, and assertiveness must be employed judiciously (Lease, 2018). Consequently, women are often not assertive in the workplace (Amanatullah & Morris, 2019).

Also, as noted previously, *collectivist cultures are accustomed to high-context communication, and individuals from such cultures typically do not respond well to assertiveness because it is direct and unambiguous.* Conversely, aggressiveness, although generally an undesirable communication pattern, is sometimes appropriate and effective (e.g., sexual harassers who will not back off deserve to suffer the harm of losing their job). Occasionally, passivity is the appropriate choice if it avoids negative consequences (e.g., when personal security might be in jeopardy). The competent communicator analyzes the context to determine the appropriate use of assertiveness. Sometimes you have to pick your spots to be assertive, weighing any potential

backlash that may occur against the perceived benefits.

Forming Coalitions: Gaining Allies

Sometimes we just need help in balancing power in the workplace. Bullying and abuse at work can be decreased if coworkers also object to such behavior, even if they are not the target, but merely witnesses (Shavin, 2014). They become allies of the abused. *To address gender bias, it can be especially helpful to gain male coworkers as allies who support gender and ethnic equity in the workplace.* Research by sociologist Tsedale Melaku "shows that Black women who progressed at their law firms typically had trusting relationships with certain white male partners who took a genuine interest in their careers" (Melaku et al., 2020). As Greg Young (2016), in his white paper titled "Women, Naturally Better Leaders for the 21st Century," observes, "Clearly,

Acquiring a mentor at work can be a great aid especially for women just starting in a new job.

men play a big part in women getting the real power in companies." This is especially true for senior leadership in organizations (Melaku et al., 2020). Gaining a **mentor**—someone knowledgeable and experienced who can help you advance your career—is a key way to enhance personal power. A report by the Rockefeller Foundation found that *two-thirds of women believe it is critical to have female mentors in leadership positions.* Powerful female leaders can help other women change sexist policies, encourage a diverse workplace by affecting hiring practices and promotional decisions, and by fighting the wage gap that favors men ("Women in Leadership," 2016). There is strength in numbers. Gaining allies can be extremely helpful in balancing power at work.

Women can proactively solicit mentorship. *Choosing a mentor and proactively developing an ally for your personal advancement involves several steps* (D'Angelo, 2018).

1. Decide what gaps in your knowledge exist and *what you most hope to learn from a mentor.*

2. You are not looking for an intense friendship. *The mentor–mentee relationship can be professional, but casual.*

3. *A mentor does not have to be a manager or higher-status person.* You might choose a peer, a coworker who knows the ropes much better than you, especially if you are just embarking on your career or job. A mentor does not have to work in the same department necessarily, or even at the same company or organization. Sometimes someone from the outside can provide important perspective and wisdom.

4. *Build an interpersonal relationship with your potential mentor.* Meet for coffee or lunch, converse casually about work or outside activities. Once you feel comfortable with this person, you can ease into asking him or her to mentor you.

5. *You do not have to schedule formal meetings with your mentor, but you should plan to meet occasionally.* In some instances, social media contacts in which you seek specific advice on a project or proposal, exchange relevant articles or research, or simply check-in with your mentor works well.

Mentors are your allies. Becoming empowered requires assistance from others.

Increasing Personal Power Resources: Expanding Choices

We previously identified five power resources that can be exploited to balance power: information, expertise, rewards and punishments, legitimate authority, and personal qualities. Information and expertise are especially useful for empowering oneself. Learning computer skills can make you an important asset in a group or organization. When coworkers or even managers get snagged by gaps in computer knowledge, being able to assist them, at least on problems that do not require real experts to solve, increases your power. You may even become the informal "computer whiz," the "go-to" person when minor technological problems emerge.

Developing expertise that can be communicated to those with greater power can be enormously empowering. Receiving education or training to expand your capabilities makes you a more valuable employee, especially if that expansion moves you beyond your standard job description. As Maureen Habel (2015) observes about nurse–physician power relationships, "encouraging nurses to obtain more nursing education and specialty certification is an important way to support nurses in becoming intellectual peers with physicians." Beyond this, "nurses can continue to expand their clinical expertise through participation in continuing education programs." Nurses then have "separate but equal" complementary knowledge and skills with physicians.

Leaders perceived to be *highly* transformational are sometimes referred to as charismatic leaders (Judge & Piccolo, 2004).

Collaborating as mutual mentors, ignoring hierarchical titles, and just working together to expand knowledge and skills, is empowering. Gen Z employees may have superior technical knowledge to share that even supervisors from an older generation may not have. That knowledge can be a potent power resource if exploited.

Charismatic leaders capitalize on personal qualities as a power resource. They exhibit a constellation of attributes that others find attractive. They have a significant impact on group members' lives, and they provoke fierce loyalty, commitment, and devotion from followers. If group members identify with the leader, and the leader is successful in advancing key group goals, members will likely perceive the leader as charismatic (Steffens et al., 2013). As previously noted, however, charisma is a power resource, but it does not necessarily equate to effective leadership.

Then there is mentorship. Despite the traditional view that mentorship is a one-way process in which more powerful leaders and long-time employees help newcomers adapt to new jobs, consultant Jonah Stillman explains that "We have a generation entering the workforce that innately knows more about operating in the modern world than any other generation. Typically, Gen Z employees have a stronger grasp of technology than older generations. This idea of two-way mentorship is about aligning older and younger generations" (quoted by Morgan, 2020). *Empowerment can be a bottom-up, not just a top-down process*. We can learn from each other without this educational effort being hierarchical.

Developing public speaking and interpersonal skills also is empowering. This text extensively addresses both (see Chapters 14, 15, and 16) because such skill development is critical for those desiring advancement and success in the workplace. Such skills open new horizons, new capabilities, and unforeseen options.

SUMMARY

When power is unequally distributed in the workplace, efforts to balance power often occur. Some of these efforts are constructive and often effective, and others not so much. Defiance is direct and unambiguous; but as a power balancing communication strategy, it is fraught with risk. Resistance, or passive aggressive strategies, are less risky but ethically questionable. Neither defiance nor resistance strategies are likely if power is relatively evenly distributed in the workplace. Finally, empowerment strategies are a constructive alternative to more typical dominance-prevention power struggles. Alliances develop as a power equalizer when power distribution is unbalanced. Acquiring a mentor and developing important, relevant skills are useful strategies for developing empowerment.

TED Talks and YouTube Videos

These TED Talks and YouTube videos can be accessed by going to the Oxford Learning Link for It's All of Our Business or by typing the title of the video into a Google search window.

"How to Speak Up for Yourself"
Adam Galinsky

"How to Disagree with Someone More Powerful: The Harvard Business Review Guide"

Film School Case Studies

Morning Glory (2010). Comedy/Drama; PG-13

Workaholic Becky Fuller, played by Rachel McAdams, is the executive producer of a failing early morning network TV show called "Daybreak." Desperate to raise the pathetic ratings of the show, she hires, under protest, egomaniacal news reporter Mike Pomeroy (Harrison Ford) to cohost the show. Pomeroy views the job as distasteful and beneath him. Identify and analyze resistance strategies used by Pomeroy.

The Intern (2015). Comedy/Drama; PG-13

Seventy-year-old widower Ben Whittaker (Robert De Niro) comes out of retirement by becoming a senior intern at an online fashion site, founded and run by Jules Ostin (Anne Hathaway). Analyze the De Niro character regarding the dimension spanning from aggressiveness to assertiveness and to passivity. Does De Niro exhibit all three, only assertiveness, or only passivity? What ways does he engage in mentoring his Millennial coworkers?

After successful completion of this chapter, you should be able to

1. Define communication climate and understand the critical role it plays in the business arena.

2. Denote key differences in positive and negative communication climates.

3. Assess your reactions to supportive and defensive communication instances at work.

CHAPTER 5

Communication Climate: Positively Critical

On April 24, 1997, the board of directors for Delta Air Lines announced the unanimous decision not to renew the contract of Delta's chairman, Ronald Allen. He was forced out because, as one board member put it, there was "an accumulation of abrasions over time." So, what were these "abrasions" that led the board to replace him? Allen had a caustic management style that concentrated on the financial "bottom line" at the expense of relationships with workers. He developed a reputation for berating employees in front of other workers. He was known as autocratic, intolerant, and harsh. Employees were extremely upset with his cost-cutting measures and the heavy-handed way in which it was done. Allen acknowledged that workers were upset, but his glib response was "so be it." Soon, buttons reading "So Be It" began appearing on the chests of pilots, flight attendants, and mechanics. Worker morale plunged. An exodus of senior managers began. Many experienced workers were laid off or quit. Delta service, once the envy of the airline industry, rapidly deteriorated. Dirty planes and

CHAPTER OUTLINE

- Creating Positive Communication Climates
- Developing Trust: Tough to Gain, Easy to Lose

4. Prioritize building trust in work teams.

frustrated flight attendants became the norm. On-time performance of flights sank from the top to the bottom of the industry. Passengers began joking that Delta stood for "**D**oesn't **E**ver **L**eave **T**he **A**irport" (Brannigan, 1997). Tough measures were necessary to save Delta financially when Allen took over, but under Allen's direction, "What the airline embarked on was nothing less than a suicidal mission" ("Plane Business Ron Allen," 2008).

Delta filed for bankruptcy protection and reorganization in 2005. Richard Anderson became CEO of Delta. "After the bankruptcy, Delta spent millions to rebuild morale, flying in many of its 47,000 employees for a series of events that were equal parts team-building and tent revival. Delta also convinced creditors to cede 15% ownership to employees" (Foust, 2009). Anderson established the practice of flying in a Delta cockpit jump seat once a month to garner suggestions for improving the company from pilots in flight, and he spent a 2-day stretch soliciting suggestions from 2,000 employees. Delta posted its first profit since bankruptcy, $500 million, in 2007. The company made an aggregate profit of $3.2 billion between 2010 and 2013 with Anderson at the helm, surviving the "Great Recession" that hit hard in 2008 (Caulderwood, 2013). In 2015, $1.5 billion was disseminated to employees under its profit-sharing plan. Delta returned as an industry leader in on-time performance. In 2014, Anderson was named one of the World's Best CEOs by *Barron's* magazine. Delta was named Airline of the Year by Air Transport World magazine in the same year. Anderson retired in 2016 (Mouawad, 2016).

The Delta experience provides a historical example necessary to gain a long view that spans initial calamity to eventual resurrection and exhibits the centrality of the communication climate that pervades a workplace. A **communication climate** is the emotional atmosphere, the enveloping tone that is created by the way we communicate in the workplace. Its importance is readily documented. For example, *a large LinkedIn study of full-time professional workers found that 70% would avoid working even at a leading company if they had to endure a negative workplace environment. These same employees would also choose to accept lower pay and forego a fancy title instead of tolerating a bad workplace culture* (McQueen, 2018). A study by Dynamic Signal found that 63% of employees have contemplated quitting "because ineffective communication interfered with their ability to do their job" (Hannah, 2019). A more recent survey found that the most annoying coworker behaviors are interrupting, taking credit for another person's work, and oversharing. A troubling 57% of workers have considered quitting their jobs because of annoying coworkers that create a negative communication climate (M. Smith, 2022). Whether you are an intern, a struggling newbie at work, or a manager at any level, virtually everyone prefers a positive, constructive communication climate at work instead of a Lord of the Flies environment. *It is not an exaggeration when we say that workplace climate "is all of our business."* Everyone from the bottom to the top of a business contributes to creating a positive communication climate.

The purpose, therefore, of this chapter is to identify and explain communication patterns that produce either positive or negative communication climates and offer constructive advice to improve workplace environment. Toward this end, chapter objectives are (1) distinguishing positive from negative communication climates, their benefits and drawbacks; (2) understanding how positive and negative communication climates are created; and (3) exploring ways to build trust in the workplace.

Creating Positive Communication Climates

A **positive communication climate** exists when individuals perceive that they are valued, supported, and treated well by the group. In one study, 90% of employees reported that "good company communication" is critical to establishing a positive workplace environment (Hannah, 2019). A **negative communication climate** exists when employees do not feel valued, supported, and respected; when trust is minimal; and when workers perceive that they are not treated well.

The importance of establishing a positive communication climate in all workplaces and the damage that a negative climate can produce is indisputable. As one study of a large Malaysian oil and gas company concludes, "Communication climate is of paramount importance in an organization as it contributes to the effectiveness and success of an organization." The authors of this study further explain, "In organizations with defensive climates, employees have the tendency to abstain from communicating their needs, as they become very cautious in making statements." In a high-risk work environment apparent in this particular industry studied, defensive climates "could lead to fatal consequences." Conversely, "organizations with supportive environments encourage active participation, healthy exchange of information and constructive conflict resolution" (Nordin et al., 2014). Developing a positive workplace climate through "good company communication" is a complicated and challenging task, as explained in this next section.

The Negativity Bias: A Major Impediment

If a new coworker were described to you as "outgoing, intelligent, fun-loving, articulate, and deceitful," what would be your impression of this person? Would the single negative quality cause you to pause despite the four very positive qualities? On the other hand, if a new coworker were described to you as "abrasive, rude, domineering, closed-minded, and smart," would the one positive quality even make a dent in the negative initial impression created by the first four qualities? Would you want to work with this person?

These examples illustrate the human phenomenon called the **negativity bias**—our strong tendency to be influenced more heavily by negative than by positive information. One negative quality can neutralize a bunch of positive qualities, but one positive quality is unlikely to override several negative qualities. *This negativity bias is built into the human brain* (C. Moore, 2021). As comedian Stephen Colbert once observed, "Mother Nature is on your side, keeping fear alive." Your amygdala, "the alarm bell of your brain," uses about two-thirds of its neurons to search for bad news. Why? Because negative information is potentially threatening to human well-being, but positive information is merely pleasant, with little likely risk to human survival (Hanson, 2016). Even though most negative information ("deceitful") is not usually an immediate threat to a person's survival, your brain does not make that nuanced assessment. Hesitation when faced with a real threat could prove fatal. It is best to be constantly on guard.

The negativity bias can be particularly strong during job interviews (Tierney & Baumeister, 2020). In fact, negative information, especially if it is received early in the interview, is likely to lead to a candidate's rejection even when the total quantity of information about the candidate is overwhelmingly positive. In a hypercompetitive job market where differences in quality between candidates can be hard to discern, one poorly chosen phrase or inappropriate remark during an interview can negate very positive letters of recommendation and an impressive overall resume.

Sometimes the negative information, however, should outweigh the positive. Our previous discussion of sexual harassment, bullying, and gender bias underlines this point. Movie mogul Harvey Weinstein was instrumental in advancing the careers of many actors and producing numerous highly regarded and successful films for several decades, and he gave millions of dollars to social causes, but he also proved to be a sexual harasser and predatory lecher who preyed on women in the industry. The one outweighs the many in this instance.

Emphasizing the Positive: The "Magic Ratio"

Depending on how powerful or relatively inconsequential the negative quality or information might be, presenting an abundance of positive information can sometimes overcome negativity bias generally (Tierney & Baumeister, 2020). In an analysis of almost 300 scientific studies that incorporated more than 275,000 subjects, the power of positivity was strongly supported (Lyubomirsky et al., 2005). What this research showed was that *frequent positive*

Most people won't sit on a rock watching crashing waves because their brains alert them to potential danger (being swept into the sea). This is the negativity bias at work. The negativity bias is built into your brain as a survival mechanism, as an alarm to warn against potential disaster, even though at times it may go unheeded. Sometimes, as in this case, the negative (risk) should outweigh the positive. Nevertheless, the bias is difficult to overcome in groups where risk is minimal or no threat to personal well-being is relevant, but your brain wants to insist that you be ever vigilant.

communication both verbally ("We're making progress"; "I hadn't thought of that") and nonverbally (giving gifts on a coworker's birthday; sharing lunch with coworkers) can create a climate for success manifested by greater satisfaction at work, higher salaries, and greater productivity, among other life-affirming benefits. More specifically, a study conducted by the University of Michigan found that the best-performing work teams made about six times as many positive comments ("I agree"; "terrific idea") as negative ones ("I disagree"; "Don't consider doing that"). *The worst performing teams, on average, made three negative comments for every positive one* (Ko, 2013). Additionally, research by the Corporate Leadership Council found that employee performance declined 27% when managers focused on workers' weaknesses but improved by 36% when managers focused on employees' strengths (McQuaid, 2015).

POSITIVE COMMUNICATION	NEGATIVE COMMUNICATION
"Clear, concise writing style"	"Too many grammatical errors"
"Thanks for meeting our deadline"	"Late reports are unacceptable"
"Let's organize an office party to recognize how hard everyone has been working lately"	"Too much socializing at work has reduced productivity"
"This is a great team"	"We're not working well as a team"
"Your time off is well deserved"	"We're way behind schedule, so expect to work longer hours until project completion"

Must you be positive all the time to reap these benefits, cheerfully greeting your coworkers each day at work, or never uttering a discouraging word to anyone at any time during your workday? That would be unrealistic, and probably somewhat irritating. As psychologist Barbara Fredrickson (2010) notes, "To experience 100-percent positivity defies and denies the humanness of life." Studying several sets of data, however, she has concluded that there is a clear ratio of positive to negative communication that leads to important benefits. *This "tipping point" occurs when there is at least a 3-to-1 positive to negative ratio in how we communicate with others* (see also Tierney & Baumeister, 2020). An even higher "magic ratio" of 5-to-1 positive-to-negative communication for optimum results has research support (Benson, 2017). Notice that the ratio is not 5-to-0. Even if your life is a bed of roses, there are thorns that can sometimes prick personal positivity.

Offering Praise and Recognition: The Essential Building Blocks

A key element of establishing a positive communication climate is offering recognition and praise for workers at all levels of an organization ("The Power of Praise and Recognition," 2014). Millennials in particular value praise and recognition, with 92% in a recent survey claiming that it is "important to be recognized and appreciated by their colleagues for their hard work" ("54 Workplace Statistics," 2021). Praise is highly desired but often absent. Surveys consistently reveal that scant praise and limited recognition for quality performance produce job dissatisfaction and a desire to leave (Nink & Robison, 2021). The *praise does not necessarily have to be a top-down process.* Even if you are a mere worker bee at the bottom of the organizational hierarchy, praise from you of your team leader, bosses, and coworkers can be meaningful.

Understand, however, that praising inauthentically or indiscriminately produces no benefits, and it may poison the workplace climate. You do not want to be perceived as a phony or a manipulator (e.g., offering praise to achieve a possible promotion). This is not a daily checklist: "Positive comment made to my assistant—check!"

Nevertheless, following a few clear steps for praising others can produce meaningful workplace benefits. First, *praise specific behavior not general personal qualities*. "You handled that customer complaint very adroitly by keeping calm and on task" is preferable to "You are a good worker." Vague praise does not identify particular behavior that can be repeated. Second, *praise improvement*. Do not wait until excellence has necessarily been achieved. Use praise to motivate positive steps toward ultimate excellence. Third, *praise occasionally*. Abundant praise can diminish the impact. Offering praise for every little thing someone does can become meaningless. Praise effort that leads to meaningful accomplishments. Finally, *do not wait to praise until something goes wrong*. There is a debate regarding whether a **criticism sandwich**—praise-criticize-praise—is the preferred way of delivering negative feedback in performance reviews. Psychologist Clifford Nass (2010), however, argues that the human brain forgets the praise when the more impactful negative criticism follows. While praise occurs initially, people tend to wait for the "but," expecting criticism to follow the praise. Nass suggests beginning with the negative, then following that with plentiful praise. (We discuss how to defuse criticism later).

We have mixed feelings about both approaches. *Our preference is that meaningful praise be offered in other contexts separate from a performance review or a coworker's meeting about a problem*. This approach develops an atmosphere of trust and allows an employee to view any negative descriptive feedback to be perceived as constructive. Praise that is deserved certainly can be offered during a performance review, but do not relegate praise just to these anxiety-producing events.

Cultivating Collaboration: Working Together

Developing a positive group climate is more likely when collaboration is cultivated in the workplace instead of competition. **Collaboration** is the cooperative process by all parties involved in decision making and problem solving of working together to achieve a common goal. Reviews of more than 1,200 research studies clearly show that collaboration is more likely to produce higher levels of group achievement and performance on a wide variety of tasks than competition (C. Johnson, 2009; D. W. Johnson et al., 2014). Also, a review of more than 180 studies concluded that collaborative communication promoted significantly greater liking, support, acceptance of group members, and cohesiveness—all elements of a positive group climate—than did competitive communication (Johnson, 2003). *How to cultivate collaboration specifically is a very complex process that we discuss extensively in Chapters 8 (conflict), 9 (groups), and 11 (teams).*

Despite the clear advantages of collaboration, in our individualist culture, competition is pervasive. Maintaining a positive climate while competing instead of collaborating with coworkers, teammates, or task group members is very challenging. The principal difficulty is that *attempting to achieve excellence and trying to beat others are different, often conflicting goals*. A series of studies conducted at a business school at Cambridge University makes the point. Teams composed of members with high IQ scores performed worse on a challenging task than teams whose members had more ordinary IQ scores. (The groups did not compete against each other but were merely compared on the basis of results.) Why did the high-IQ groups perform relatively poorly? High-IQ members spent a great deal of time in hypercompetitive debate, attempting to outshine each other. They became immersed in a negative group climate of adversarial egocentrism that focused more on individual accomplishment than group achievement. Moderate-IQ members, however, collaborated as a team, uninterested in competing with each other for intellectual star status (Belbin, 1996). Trying to beat other group members diverts attention from achieving group excellence.

Collaborating means working together to reach a common goal. Despite all of these cheerful faces, collaborating can be an extremely challenging process.

Defensive and Supportive Communication: Shaping Climates

Jack Gibb (1961), in a classic 8-year study of groups, identified specific communication patterns that both increase and lessen **defensiveness**—a reaction to a perceived attack on our self-concept and self-esteem. Workers feel personally diminished by communication patterns that ignite defensiveness. Defensive communication patterns lead to worker burnout and turnover (Becker et al., 2005). These results occur because *defensive communication patterns heighten negativity. Conversely, supportive communication patterns heighten positivity*. The differences between the two patterns are explored in this next section. As each of these communication patterns (with some modification from Gibb's list) is discussed, see if you recognize any of them in your own experience with small groups and teams (see also Box 5.1 for a self-assessment test).

Criticism Versus Description   Criticism can be traumatic, especially when it is harsh and you feel blindsided, but one study found that even rather mild criticism ("Make your emails less flowery or soft") still packs a punch felt long after the delivery (Grenny, 2019). A disturbing study regarding *who gets criticized most often in the workplace found an astounding gender difference*. Negative personal criticism, such as "Watch your tone," "Stop being so judgmental," and "You come across as abrasive," appeared twice in 83 performance reviews (2.4%) received by men but in 71 of 94 reviews (75.5%) received by women. There was no gender difference, however, in who wrote these performance reviews, men or women (Snyder, 2014).

Criticism immediately puts people on the defensive for two reasons: (1) it requires submission—copping to mistakes, and (2) it devalues a person (Stosny, 2014). Typical protective responses to criticism include denying the validity of the criticism, counterattacking (not

SELF-ASSESSMENT

Reactions to Defensive and Supportive Communication

Project yourself into each situation below and imagine how you would react. Choose a number for each situation that reflects how much you would like or dislike the statements presented.

1. At work, you forgot to clean your dishes in the break room twice this week. One of your colleagues says to you, "Do your dishes. I'm tired of cleaning up your mess."

STRONGLY DISLIKE			STRONGLY LIKE	
5	4	3	2	1

2. You're working with your team on a group project. One member says to the group, "I'm feeling very concerned that we will not finish our project in time. We're about halfway and we only have 2 days before our presentation. What do the rest of you think?"

STRONGLY DISLIKE			STRONGLY LIKE	
5	4	3	2	1

3. You are a member of your company's softball team. Your coach says to you in front of the team, "You blew the game last week. Are you prepared to do better this game?"

STRONGLY DISLIKE			STRONGLY LIKE	
5	4	3	2	1

4. At work, you tripped and badly bruised your shoulder. Your boss says to you, "I heard that you injured yourself yesterday. Do you need time off? That must really hurt. Can I do anything to make you more comfortable while you work in your office?"

STRONGLY DISLIKE			STRONGLY LIKE	
5	4	3	2	1

5. Your support group meets once a week to share experiences and solve personal problems. The group facilitator announces to the group, "We haven't got time to hear from (your name). We have more important things to consider."

STRONGLY DISLIKE			STRONGLY LIKE	
5	4	3	2	1

6. During a group problem-solving session, one member says to the group, "I have a suggestion that might solve our problem. Perhaps this will move us forward."

STRONGLY DISLIKE			STRONGLY LIKE	
5	4	3	2	1

7. During a discussion on a controversial problem at work, the CEO says to the group, "We're obviously divided on this issue. Because I'm in charge of this company, I'll make the final decision."

STRONGLY DISLIKE			STRONGLY LIKE	
5	4	3	2	1

8. During a business meeting, one participant says to the group, "I know we all have strong feelings on this issue, but let's put our heads together and see if we can find a solution everyone can support. Does anyone have ideas they wish to share with the group?"

STRONGLY DISLIKE			STRONGLY LIKE	
5	4	3	2	1

9. During a heated group discussion with fellow colleagues, one individual says, "I know I'm right and there's no way any of you will convince me that I'm wrong."

STRONGLY DISLIKE			STRONGLY LIKE	
5	4	3	2	1

10. Your project group approaches your teacher and proposes an idea that your teacher initially dislikes. She says to your group, "I can see that you really like this idea, but it doesn't satisfy the requirements of the project. I suggest that you keep brainstorming."

STRONGLY DISLIKE			STRONGLY LIKE	
5	4	3	2	1

11. You're a member of a hiring panel. During a break from an interviewing session, one member of the panel takes you aside and says, "Look, I want you to support my candidate. We've been friends a long time. This is important to me. Whaddaya say? Can I count on you to back me up?"

STRONGLY DISLIKE			STRONGLY LIKE	
5	4	3	2	1

12. You've been asked to participate on a committee to solve the parking problem at work. The chair addresses the committee: "It is my hope that this committee can come to a consensus on solutions to this parking problem. Despite the fact that this committee is composed of individuals with titles reflecting various levels in our corporate hierarchy, let me emphasize that every vote on any final solution will have equal weight."

STRONGLY DISLIKE			STRONGLY LIKE	
5	4	3	2	1

13. An individual addresses his work team: "I'm sick of you losers constantly pushing your political stupid agenda. You're all pathetic."

STRONGLY DISLIKE			STRONGLY LIKE	
5	4	3	2	1

14. "Please, let's all disagree without being disagreeable, OK?"

STRONGLY DISLIKE			STRONGLY LIKE	
5	4	3	2	1

Answers 1, 3, 5, 7, 9, 11, and 13 = **defensive** communication (control, evaluation, indifference, superiority, certainty, manipulation, and incivility—in that order); 2, 4, 6, 8, 10, 12, and 14 = **supportive communication** (description, empathy, provisionalism, problem orientation, assertiveness, equality, and civility—in that order). Find your average score for each set (divide by 7 both the sum of the odd-numbered items and the sum of the even-numbered items). Which do you like best (lower average score)—defensive or supportive communication?

particularly fruitful if it is your boss), or withdrawing (quitting your job).

Despite the negative effects of criticism, a criticism-free workplace is a fairy tale. As Aristotle noted, "There is only one way to avoid criticism: do nothing, say nothing, and be nothing." When individuals are not pulling their weight, performing in ways that are dangerous, or creating dissension among coworkers, criticism is warranted and necessary. Criticism, however, does not have to be delivered with a sledgehammer, pounding people into submission, and it should not be offered in a public setting. *How you deliver the message is critical.*

Description is necessary feedback delivered in ways that can minimize defensiveness. Description is composed of the following steps: (Stosny, 2014):

1. *Make suggestions as I-statements.* Here's an example of an *I-statement*: "I feel good about this report, but I have just a couple of

Sometimes aggressive, hurtful remarks about a coworker are excused as merely "constructive criticism." Although criticism is not always avoidable, it can be demoralizing or trigger anger. Describing behaviors instead of alleged character flaws is less likely to ignite defensiveness. Also, remember the 5:1 "magic ratio" of positive-to-negative communication

suggestions." This statement avoids pointing the finger of blame and offers to help, not tear down a person (Ryan, 2020). Focus on improvement, not on what's wrong.

A *You-statement* of negative evaluation, on the other hand, places the focus on someone who is an object of attack. "You haven't helped your work team finish on time" is a statement that blames. Assigning blame may be necessary eventually if improvements do not materialize, but avoid it when possible. Expect *denial* when a person is blamed for inadequate results ("No I haven't") or a *counterattack* ("I've worked a lot harder than the rest of these simpletons"). Any statement that begins with "You didn't …" or "You shouldn't …" or "You haven't …" can instantly put the recipient on guard because it can seem like an accusation will follow.

2. *Describe specific behaviors, not character flaws*. "You're lazy" or "You're irresponsible" or "You're abrasive" identifies perceived character flaws. Constructive feedback describes what behavioral change is desired. "Arriving late to work impacts your team as they must wait for you to lead them. Is there anything I can do to help?" seeks a specific behavior that can fix the problem collaboratively.

So, how should you *respond to criticism* that you view as undeserved or overly abrasive and unconstructive? Your boss or teammates may not exhibit competent communication skills when giving negative feedback, so you will need to adapt. Here are several suggestions:

1. *Resist defensiveness; ask for clarification*. Your first reaction likely will be to defend yourself by denying the correctness of the criticism, or counterattacking. Instead, pause momentarily, then request elaboration if the criticism is too vague or is focused on an alleged character flaw and not specific objectionable behavior. Seek to focus on behaviors not personal qualities.

2. *Listen carefully*. Even if you disagree with the criticism, it is best that you at least understand what exactly bothers those who criticize you.

3. *Agree if the criticism is factual*. If you have been late or absent from work, cop to it without offering lame excuses. Just say, "You're right. I'll take steps to correct this immediately," then enjoy the surprised looks when you offer no resistance and accept responsibility.

4. *Disagree without becoming disagreeable*. You do not have to accept the criticism if it is not factual. Nevertheless, stay calm and provide credible information dispassionately to counter factually incorrect criticism.

5. *Seek a solution*. You may be able to find a compromise or a mutually acceptable solution if you pursue one. "Perhaps a more flexible work schedule would meet your expectations and help me avoid tardiness and absences. What do you think?"

Control Versus Problem Orientation   English poet Samuel Butler once said, "He who agrees against his will, is of the same opinion still." Issuing orders and demanding obedience is controlling communication (dominance form of power). Jack Brehm (1972) developed a theory of psychological reactance to explain our resistance to efforts aimed at controlling our behavior. Simply put, **psychological reactance** means the more someone tries to control us by telling us what to do, the more we are inclined to resist such efforts or even to do the opposite. Controlling strategies challenge our sense of personal freedom to choose (S. Moore, 2019). The COVID-19 mask-wearing debate illustrates this in a stark way. The following bit of popular wisdom captures psychological reactance well: "There are three ways to make sure something gets done—do it yourself; hire someone to do it; *forbid* your kids to do it."

Consider a common scenario. Imagine while returning to your car in the company's congested parking lot, another car follows you and then waits for your space. Are you inclined to leave faster or slower? What if your parking stalker honks at you to encourage a faster exit? One study found that most people slow their exit, especially if honked (Ruback & Juieng, 1997). When we have posed this exact scenario to dozens of audiences, there usually is a split result when the car is just waiting. When the driver honks, however, we usually hear uniformly negative responses, such as "I'd get out of my car and walk away" (accompanied by an obscene gesture), or "I'd sit there and browse my smartphone until the jerk left." Such is the typical reaction to perceived controlling strategies.

You help prevent psychological reactance from emerging when the orientation is on the problem and how best to solve it, not on how best to control other people's behavior. Polite requests usually work better than demands, especially when the power distribution is unequal. All controlling communication cannot be eliminated, but it can be kept to a minimum. Ownership of a solution to a problem comes not from mandating it ("This is what I've decided, so do it"), but from collaborating as a group and brainstorming possible solutions.

When communication seems to be an order, not a request, psychological reactance can easily emerge, even when individuals might be inclined to act like lemmings. Both individualist and collectivist cultures typically experience reactance; but in individualist cultures such as the United States, not restricting one's personal freedom is highly significant, whereas in collectivist cultures, "it is more important that their group's freedom is not restricted" (Sittenthaler et al., 2015).

Manipulation Versus Assertiveness We do not like feeling manipulated. A study of 6,000 team members in 600 organizations found that playing politics, an especially cutthroat version of manipulative communication, destroys social relationships and team effectiveness (LaFasto & Larson, 2001). **Hidden agendas**—personal goals of group members that are not revealed openly and that can interfere with group accomplishment—can create a defensive atmosphere. When you suspect that a team member is complimenting your performance merely to gain an ally against other members in a dispute, this hidden agenda will likely ignite defensiveness.

Assertiveness is the alternative to manipulation. Assertiveness is that honest, open, and direct, but nonaggressive, communication previously discussed in Chapter 4. It is the opposite of game playing and strategic manipulation. Assertiveness is also a communication skill that can defuse the defensiveness of others because it is nonaggressive and nonjudgmental. So, when you perceive that someone is trying to manipulate you, try being assertive and bring it out into the open: "I feel I'm being manipulated, and it is making me uncomfortable."

Indifference Versus Empathy We like being acknowledged when we are present in a group. We dislike being treated like a piece of furniture, sitting alone in a corner. Indifference from coworkers and team members makes us defensive. Making little or no effort to listen exhibits indifference and treats the communicator as a nonperson. When your online team members do not respond to your phone calls, emails, text messages, or postings on social media, this apparent indifference can be a frustrating experience and a huge impediment to team success. Research shows that responding indifferently to others damages an interpersonal relationship as much as outright rejection (Ury, 2019).

You counter indifference with empathy. William Howell (1982) defines **empathy** as "thinking and feeling what you perceive another to be thinking and feeling." Empathy is built on concern for others. It requires that we try to see from the perspective of the other person, perceiving the needs, desires, and feelings of workers because that is what we would want others to do for us (Chamorro-Premuzic & Akhtar, 2021). "How would you like it if I ignored you?" is a plea for empathy from others.

A study by Businessolver found that 96% of employees view empathy as important for their employers to demonstrate, but 92% do not believe employers value its importance enough (Higginbottom, 2018). A cross-cultural study of almost 7,000 managers in 38 countries found a positive correlation between empathy and job performance (Gentry et al., 2016).

Active listening, as explored in Chapter 6, *is a principal way to increase empathy in the workplace.* One study shows that "active-empathic listening" by supervisors at work has a positive effect on employees' perceptions of their working conditions and quality of life. Supervisors who have lower levels of such empathy produce an opposite effect (Kristinsson et al., 2019). Even if others do not listen actively, your active listening can improve the overall climate and, by modeling such behavior, you may encourage others to follow suit.

Superiority Versus Equality *Communicating superiority sends the message that one is me-deep in self-importance.* It is often called arrogance. It can be a tremendous turnoff for most people. Business leaders who exhibit superiority undermine their credibility and influence (S. B. Silverman et al., 2012). As consultant Peter Barron Stark (2016) notes, "Arrogance is leadership kryptonite." Treating people like they are IRS agents at the award ceremony for the state lottery winner will invite enmity and retaliation. Whatever the differences in our abilities, talents, intellect, and the like, treating

Texting during a team meeting can communicate indifference, as in "I find a personal message more important than this meeting."

people with respect and politeness—as equals on a personal level—encourages harmony and productivity. Delta CEO Richard Anderson (chapter opening case study) was particularly adept at doing exactly that when he sought feedback from all employees in the company and he traveled in a jump seat on Delta flights, not in first class accommodations, in his effort to garner feedback from pilots and crew.

Equality does not mean we all have the same abilities. Equality from the standpoint of workplace climate means that *you give all employees an equal opportunity to succeed and exhibit whatever potential they possess, and to share their wisdom where appropriate regardless of status*. You recognize that everyone has faults and limitations. In fact, one way of demonstrating equality as a means of minimizing defensiveness is to share your own shortcomings with group members (Hornsey et al., 2008). A national study by Lynn Taylor Consulting found that 91% of employee respondents said that admitting mistakes as a manager was a significant factor in promoting employee job satisfaction (M. Ward et al., 2020). **Self-deprecating humor** that makes fun of yourself can also be an effective means of communicating equality, not superiority (Greengross & Miller, 2008). For example, "So, last night, my partner gave me some good advice about this presentation. She said, 'Whatever you do don't try to be too charming, witty, or intellectual … just be yourself!'" (Elsesser, 2019). One study compared a leader's self-deprecating humor to "aggressive" humor. At the end of a leader's introduction of a new employee named Pat, the leader says, "I am so glad that Pat took this job despite knowing all about me" (self-deprecating humor) in one condition; and in another condition says, "I am so glad Pat took this job despite knowing all about you [other employees]" (aggressive humor). Admittedly, neither is thigh-slappingly funny, but perhaps mildly amusing to those familiar with the leader. More importantly, despite no differences in ratings of how funny each statement was, the self-deprecating leader received significantly higher positive ratings on trustworthiness and leadership ability than the leader who used aggressive humor (Hoption et al., 2013).

Poking fun at yourself just makes you seem more human and likable if it is done occasionally. It is the antithesis of ego. *If done too frequently, however, it could diminish your credibility*. During a job interview in which you are attempting to enhance your status and credibility in the minds of the interviewing panelists, self-deprecating humor is inadvisable unless your interviewing panel is composed of colleagues who already know you well and might appreciate some light humor.

Certainty Versus Provisionalism   There are very few things in this world that are certain—death, taxes, your clothes dryer will eat your socks, your toast will fall buttered-side down, and your technological devices will fail at the most inopportune times are a few that come to our minds. Communicating certainty to coworkers or bosses is asking for trouble.

Certainty is reflected in terms such as *never, always, impossible, can't*, and *won't*. "We'll never finish this project on time" and "We always procrastinate" are two examples. These terms of certainty may provoke defensiveness, shut down discussion, and kill motivation to succeed (Wright, 2022.

Provisionalism   counters   certainty. **Provisionalism** means you qualify statements, avoiding absolutes. Provisionalism is reflected in the use of qualifying terms such as *possibly, probably, perhaps, occasionally, may, might,* and *sometimes*. "We may have difficulty finishing this project on time unless we organize our effort" is a provisional statement. This is the language of precision, not fence-straddling. Problems are approached as interesting issues to be investigated and discussed, not defensive power struggles regarding who is right or wrong. *When others use the language of certainty, note it out loud and rephrase the issue in provisional terms*: "I know that it seems that the team is always late and disorganized, but to be fair, that occurs only occasionally, but let's all try to improve."

Incivility Versus Civility   Commonplace acts of rudeness and disrespect communicated both verbally and nonverbally are called **incivility**. Most organizations recognize incivility is pervasive, but few take action to discourage it (Ross, 2017). Bullying, by comparison, is far more intense, malicious, continuous, and damaging. Nevertheless, Christine Porath (2016), author of *Mastering Civility: A Manifesto for the Workplace*, found in a poll she conducted that 80% of respondents reported losing time on the job worrying about even mild indignities, while 78% were less committed to their employer, and half reduced their effort because of on-the-job incivility. A worldwide survey found that 47% of Millennials and 44% of Gen Z respondents believe that incivility is growing ("The Deloitte Global Millennial Survey," 2020). Social media was considered a major cause.

Additional research shows that name-calling and vulgarity are perceived to be the most egregious forms of incivility, and that there tend to be different norms for women and men. Women "have heightened sensitivity to uncivil comments" and they are "less willing themselves to engage in such discourse" than men (Kenski et al., 2020).

Civility is treating people with respect. As Porath notes, "Civility is smart, it's savvy, it's human. By being civil, you get to be a nice person, and you get ahead. People are more likely to support you and work harder for you" (quoted by Ross, 2017). Improving workplace civility can reduce employee burnout (Leiter & Maslach, 2015). Even brief exposure to civil discourse can create a positive communication environment (Antoci et al., 2018). *Creating a civil workplace environment is everyone's responsibility*, but workplace leaders must set the tone by example. Incivility is contagious, and when managers exhibit incivility toward employees, it encourages employees to do likewise to those of equal or less power. Nevertheless, you do not have to follow suit when others display incivility. Incivility times incivility equals incivility squared. KABOOM! Resist the desire to retaliate in kind, especially if you are a new employee or in a relatively powerless position. *Remaining unconditionally civil and encouraging others to choose civil discourse can alter the tone and tenor of disputes*.

The seven defensive communication patterns create a dysfunctional workplace filled with negativity. The seven corresponding supportive communication patterns provide a safe, constructive workplace characterized by a relentlessly positive environment conducive to worker productivity and satisfaction. One final

Box 5.1
Defensive Versus Supportive Communication

DEFENSIVE	SUPPORTIVE
Criticism	Description
Control	Problem Orientation
Manipulation	Assertiveness
Indifference	Empathy
Superiority	Equality
Certainty	Provisionalism
Incivility	Civility

topic that flows from this discussion of positivity versus negativity at work is trust, our final segment.

Developing Trust: Tough to Gain, Easy to Lose

Warren Buffett observes, "Trust is like the air we breathe—when it's present, nobody really notices; when it's absent, everybody notices." Trust is often viewed as a soft skill that does not impact business results. Now we see it as an essential predictor of corporate success (Lamptey, 2021). Research supports the clear benefits of creating a trusting communication climate. "Compared with low-trust companies, people at high-trust companies report: 74% less stress, 106% more energy at work, 50% higher productivity, 13% fewer sick days, 76% more engagement, 29% more satisfaction with their lives, 40% less burnout" (Zak, 2017). So, would you rather work for an organization that magnifies your stress, makes you sick and depressed, makes being productive a daily struggle, and encourages you to quit from burnout; or would you rather work for an organization that produces the opposite? Tough decision?

As a corporate trainer, Michelle leads many workshops on creating a climate of trust. *When she asks participants to brainstorm signs of a low-trust work environment, lists include gossip, micromanaging, high degree of turnover, working in silos instead of matrices, rumors, and secrecy. Additional trust-breaking behaviors commonly seen in the workplace include* acting inconsistently (saying one thing and doing another), taking credit for other's work, jumping to conclusions, not following through on commitments, and micromanaging. Regarding the latter, Muriel Maignan Wilkins, managing partner of Paravis Partners, an executive coaching and leadership development firm, says, "Micromanaging dents your team's morale by establishing a tone of mistrust—and it limits your team's capacity to grow" (quoted by Knight, 2015). Bosses who are always looking over employees' shoulders

and double-checking their work (controlling strategies) communicate lack of trust. This is a major complaint revealed in a study of MBA students and graduates (Allen, 2018). *One does not even have to be a boss to micromanage others*. As a team member, an individual might be overly concerned that other teammates are not sufficiently committed to completing a project and producing superior results. Constantly checking whether others are living up to their responsibilities to advance a group's task can be perceived as micromanaging.

One company we know of took mistrust to a new level. The manager installed GPS on each of the outside salespersons' cars and constantly monitored where they were. If parked in any one spot for longer than the manager saw necessary, the suspected salesperson would get a call questioning why they were not moving along with their route. Instead of motivating

Micromanaging can destroy trust. It can also be beyond annoying, even intimidating. Helicopter managing is almost universally disdained by employees (Petrone, 2018). Who wants a supervisor hovering while constantly blowing up dust when an error is perceived?

the sales team to move quickly, this mistrust inspired them to purposefully stop at random places to keep the manager guessing.

In contrast, *when asked for a list of qualities in a high-trust environment, descriptors include collaboration, ease, increased productivity, sharing of ideas and information, innovation, creativity, and loyalty.* Lamptey (2021) adds that leaders should value employees and treat them fairly by acknowledging their efforts, rewarding accomplishments, exhibiting empathy, and creating opportunities for growth. **Psychological safety**—the communication climate that encourages open expression of ideas and opinions, and fosters the freedom to make mistakes, ask questions, and take risks without reprisals or concerns about job security—is required for any of this to occur (Dhawan, 2021b).

You build trust based on both who you are and what you do. For example, you might be trusted because you do quality work and deliver results on time (competence). On the other hand, you might be trusted because you are honest in meetings about the strengths and weaknesses of a proposal (character). Attention to both character and competence are equally important (Covey, 2008).

SUMMARY

There is a vast difference between positive and negative communication climates in the workplace. Counteracting the negativity bias is challenging. Defensive communication patterns of criticism, control, manipulation, indifference, superiority, certainty, and incivility nurture negative work climates. Supportive communication patterns of description, problem orientation, assertiveness, empathy, equality, provisionalism, and civility nurture positive work climates. The latter produces substantial benefits while the former produces significant detriments. Building trust is also important to the establishment of a positive,

Film School Case Studies

Wall Street (1987); Drama; R

Oliver Stone directed this blistering critique of the damage done by ruthlessness and greed on Wall Street. Michael Douglas utters the memorable line, "Greed is good." Analyze defensive communication patterns heavily exhibited throughout the movie and all of the factors contributing to the destruction of trust.

The Devil Wears Prada (2006), Comedy/Drama; PG-13

The Meryl Streep character, Miranda Priestly, treats her Ann Hathaway assistant, Andy Sachs, in ways that clearly provoke defensive communication. Identify the numerous examples and analyze especially Priestly's arrogance and its implications. Also, note the rare display of praise and the frequent use of blame and its consequences.

productive workplace climate. Character and competence are critical elements of the trust equation.

TED Talks and YouTube Videos

These TED Talks and YouTube videos can be accessed by going to the Oxford Learning Link for It's All of Our Business or by typing the title of the video into a Google search window.

Hardwiring Happiness: Dr. Rick Hanson at TEDxMarin 2013

Praise Effort, Not Intelligence

Why Trust Is Worth It

After successful completion of this chapter,
you should be able to

1. Clearly define the listening process and all its components.

2. Distinguish different types of listening and prevent problems unique to each kind, particularly in business settings.

3. Identify barriers to effective listening and explore strategies to remove them.

CHAPTER 6

Listening: More Than Meets the Ear

WHEN FRANKLIN ROOSEVELT WAS president, he once decided to test whether people that he greeted in a receiving line actually listened to him. As he received each person, Roosevelt remarked, "I murdered my grandmother this morning." Listeners typically responded, "Thank you," "How kind of you," and the like. Many people passed in the receiving line pretending to listen before someone actually listened to the president and retorted, "I'm sure she had it coming to her" (Fadiman, 1985).

Effective listening is a critical communication skill (M. Cole, 2016; Yavuz & Celik, 2017). Research claims and observations confirm that people spend more time listening than in any other communication activity (Janusik, 2019). One study of almost 2,200 hiring managers, human resource professionals, and current and former college students showed that *skillful listening is the most in-demand "soft skill" in business* (Bauer-Wolf, 2019). Listening is a crucial though often overlooked tool for coaching, setting goals,

CHAPTER OUTLINE

- The Listening Process
- Types of Listening
- Listening Problems and Solutions

managing conflict, and building trust at work (Daimler, 2016).

In college and corporate classrooms, we often ask learners to boast about their communication strengths. Repeatedly, most people report to us that they are "good listeners." When asked to model their good listening skills, they immediately demonstrate making eye contact, leaning in, and nodding. Sadly, just as pretending to be famous does not make us so, merely modeling the appropriate visuals on request does not make a master listener. It is a much more complex process. Multiple studies confirm the worst: we think we are much better listeners than we are. For example, research of more than 3,600 professionals at all levels from 30 countries concluded that those who self-report their excellent listening skills are the same ones who also confess to multitasking and "tuning out" during conference calls (S. Cole, 2015). Another study of students from first to 12th grade confirmed that not only were participants poor listeners, but their listening skills declined as their ages increased (Sullivan & Thompson, 2013). Considering that those in the workforce are typically past the age of 18, you can see we are headed for trouble. Accepting that listening skills decrease with age, it is interesting that most college degrees require proof of competence in oral communication, but few prioritize the completion (let alone the offering) of listening courses. As opportunities to connect and practice our listening skills diminish in our digital age, conversation and a chance for genuine connection are often replaced with brief texts or emoji (Murphy, 2020). Soon the only one listening might be Amazon's Alexa. The conclusion is clear: *even though we need to be good listeners, we are not.*

The average listener can think at a rate of about 400–500 words per minute, but a normal conversational speaking pace ranges between 125 and 180 wpm (McCoy et al., 2005; Sullivan & Thompson, 2013). Like a restless puppy seeking adventure, our curious brains seek stimulation, and that is not always satisfied merely by listening to another. Nevertheless, the general thrust of this chapter can be summed up in the slogan of the Sperry Corporation (now part of UNISYS): "Nothing new ever entered the mind through an open mouth." Because listening is one of the most valuable communication skills you can hone, *the purpose of this chapter is to explore the process of effective listening in the business arena.* Toward that end, this chapter has four objectives: (1) define the listening process, (2) differentiate the five types of listening, (3) explain listening problems that arise, and (4) offer solutions to address listening problems.

The Listening Process

Listening, according to the International Listening Association, is "the process of receiving, constructing meaning from and responding to spoken and/or nonverbal messages"

(Bodie et al. 2008). Listening is a remarkably complex process. Judi Brownell (2019) developed the **HURIER model**, which is an acronym for the six stages of the listening process. This section briefly describes each stage.

Hearing: Receiving Raw Data

Hearing and listening are not synonymous. Hearing is the physiological process of registering sound waves as they hit the eardrum. The sounds have no meaning until we construct meaning for them. Hearing acuity, of course, presents a serious challenge for listeners if their hearing diminishes or is already compromised ("Age-Related Hearing Loss," 2018). The sounds of a language that we hear, called **phonemes**, constitute the raw material from which meaning can be extricated. In the workplace, we can increase our ability to hear messages by reducing the urge to multitask; eliminating other sounds vying for our attention such as loud music or machinery; and by positioning ourselves in a place where it is easy to hear, such as sitting toward the front in a large meeting room.

Understanding: Shared Meaning

Hearing sounds is simply noise until meaning is shared. When workers do not share a common language as can occur often in a global marketplace, understanding messages is thwarted. Similarly, technical language and jargon unfamiliar to coworkers can be confusing. Bryan Garner (2013), author of *HBR Guide to Better Business Writing*, offers this jargon loaded example of what not to do: "Leading-edge leveraging of your plain-English set will ensure that your actionable items synergize future-proof assets with your global-knowledge repository." To anyone in the business community unfamiliar with this bushel basket of buzz words, this probably sounds more like Dothraki or Klingon than any language suitable for sharing meaningful messages with clients or even coworkers. Asking for clarification on unfamiliar terms and restating what you think you heard will aid understanding.

Remembering: Not an Easy Task

Memory is essential to the listening process. Otherwise, why bother tuning into the study guide review session before an upcoming exam? If you listen to a business presentation and retain none of the information, of what value was it to you? Naturally, our minds do not retain every morsel of information as we listen to someone. An analysis of 14 memory studies with 69 conditions concludes that "forgetting varies widely." *Retaining information depends on many conditions*, such as the complexity of the information, one's interest in the subject matter, the learners' motivation to learn, the effectiveness of the methods used to present the information, and whether the information is crammed overnight or learned along the way over weeks or months (Thalheimer, 2010). Applying this listening lens to the world around us, it is no wonder we might retain a simple toll-free number that is set to music in an often-played commercial about donating your "cars for kids," but cannot seem to hold onto the quadratic formula long past the dismissal of Algebra 1. Robert Kraft, professor of cognitive psychology at Otterbein University, says that "the broadest reason we forget is … that we focus on understanding the world, not remembering it" (Kraft, 2017).

Sometimes we just do not pay attention. Suppose you are introduced to new coworkers, and you are concerned with what kind of impression you are making on them. Their names skip off the surface of your memory. You are forced to say, "I'm sorry, but I've forgotten your name." You heard their name. You understood their name. But you did not remember their name. Another example is dubbed digital amnesia or the "Google effect." The ready accessibility of the Internet and Google searches primes our memory for where to find information but lowers our ability to recall the information itself (Sparrow et al., 2011). The information is stored on the Internet, so why bother to store it in our brains? Why memorize mom's telephone number when we can press one button (instead of 10 digits) on our smartphones or simply ask Siri, Alexa, or other forms of artificial intelligence to call her?

Thanks to the "Google Effect" we are less inclined to remember information we can easily access online. Looking things up on the Internet does not permit memory to serve the retention process. You can't look up everything on the Internet (e.g., "What did my boss just tell me to do to improve my report?").

making a visual connection with the words, and associating ideas with things you already know are other effective ways to strengthen your memory (Cherry, 2019 Lickermann, 2009).

Interpreting: Message Perception

"Nice job!" That's a simple message. No chance of misinterpreting the meaning, right? What if this message was meant to be sarcastic? Recall that sensitivity (see Chapter 2) is receptive accuracy—the ability to detect, decode, and comprehend accurately messages from others. Can you decipher from facial expressions, tone of voice, and myriad other nonverbal cues the emotional content of verbal messages? Interpreting messages accurately is a transactional process between senders and receivers (listeners).

In 2020, when wearing masks that covered your nose and mouth was recommended by the Centers for Disease Control, hearing-impaired people were particularly challenged. Not only could they no longer interpret messages through lipreading, but they also could

Whether listening in the classroom or boardroom, taking effective notes, however, reviewing them for just 10 minutes within 24 hours of learning the information, then reviewing your notes for 5 minutes a week later will vastly improve retention (Hoffman, 2014). *Using information immediately also enhances retention*. When a coworker says his or her name, repeat it immediately. For example: "Hi! I'm Victoria." "Hello, Victoria. It's great to meet you. I'm Manuel." If you immediately apply what you have learned, your retention will improve markedly and last longer. The adage "use it or lose it," applies here. *Becoming interested in what you are hearing,*

not infer meaning from facial expressions such as frowns or smiles. When asked about the new communication barrier, Jenna Giesey, who is deaf and prefers communicating with American Sign Language and reading lips, likened masks to "looking at a wall with eyes" (as quoted in Lehr, 2020). The fact that some masks muffle sound, coupled with the six-feet apart COVID-19 social distancing recommendation, made it even harder to hear and thus accurately interpret messages. Using face shields or masks that have clear windows helps those who can read lips, but not all who are hard of hearing can do so. Learning several ASL phrases, being

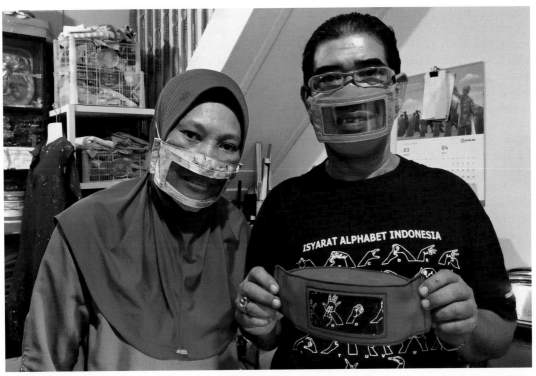

Indonesian couple Faizah Badaruddin and Imam Sarosos, both deaf, designed face masks with a transparent window that allows people to read lips. They sold hundreds of masks, averaging 20 a day, throughout Indonesia, during the height of the COVID-19 pandemic.

patient, and being kind top the list for improving message interpretation when communicating with those whose hearing is challenged (Holohan, 2020).

Evaluating: Separating Fact from Fiction

Listening involves more than accurately understanding the messages of others. We are not simply sponges passively absorbing information. Once we understand the message, we often need to evaluate it, typically by assessing the sender's intention, credibility, and expectations. With a critical ear, we put personal bias aside and aim to distinguish emotional appeals from evidence and logic. We hear a dizzying variety of claims every day. As critical listeners, you need to know the difference between prime rib and baloney, between fact and fiction. While we address critical listening much more extensively in this and ensuing

chapters, to immediately improve your evaluative skills, listen to the entire message before responding and aim to put your own biases aside (Brownell, 2008).

Responding: Giving Feedback

Speakers look for responses from listeners to determine whether a message is being processed or ignored. Without a clear response from the listener, you have no way of knowing whether listening actually occurs. These responses can be both verbal and nonverbal. As listeners, we indicate confusion by frowning or by asking a question for clarification. If listeners are staring out a window, doing a face plant onto the desktop, doodling, talking to the person next to them, or texting when you are talking, then listening to you probably is not a top priority.

When listening, helpful nonverbal responses include head nodding, deliberate eye contact, smiling, and leaning forward during conversation. Helpful verbal behaviors include asking questions, paraphrasing, and perception checking, all discussed later in this chapter. In the process of providing helpful responses while listening to a speaker, you are likely to create what is called **immediacy**—the perception of closeness and involvement with others. A few examples of immediacy when listening include giving the speaker your undivided attention, smiling, and encouraging elaboration of ideas. A connection between speaker and listener develops. In the superior-subordinate relationship of a manager and employee, managers who create immediacy are seen as more interested and concerned in the employee.

These six stages—hearing, understanding, recalling, interpreting, evaluating, and responding (HURIER)—equal six nuanced opportunities for success or missteps. Knowing that listening is a transactional process, and your co-communicator must traverse these same stages while listening to you, illuminates why listening is hardly as simple as it sounds.

Types of Listening

Just as you would not use the same tone for every email or the same vocabulary for every conversation, we need to adjust the way we listen to match the situation. For the purposes of listening in the workplace, it is helpful to be familiar with five specific types of listening that flow from the six listening stages.

Discriminative Listening: Deciphering Speech Sounds

Discriminative listening is the ability to distinguish sound and is the basis for all other types of listening. Discriminative listening does not isolate the underlying meaning of communication. It addresses only what we hear. When using our discriminative ears, we hear the sound structure and we may also notice things such as change of pitch, a wavering voice, or the pace of communication. Honing discriminative listening skills is most appropriate in the workplace when relating to people with different accents. Hopping in an overseas

ride share recently, the heavily accented English-speaking driver asked the monolingual American passenger if she wanted "Are-Cone." The rider did not know what Are-Cone was, so she replied quizzically, "Pardon?" The driver repeated: "Are Cone?" to which the passenger said again, "What?" Once more, but louder, as if volume were the barrier, the frustrated driver said, "ARE CONE?" Unfamiliar with his accent, it was nearly impossible for the passenger to discern that the driver was kindly asking if she would like the *air-con (air conditioning)* on. Looking back, it sounds crystal clear now. Had the passenger been more familiar with the cadence of the driver's mother tongue in which a soft "o" sound does not exist, she likely would have been more effective in this short exchange. To further complicate this base step, discriminative listening is difficult even when accents are not particularly different from one's own (Ockey et al., 2016).

Sloppy speech patterns can also make discriminative listening challenging. Ordinary conversational speech is typically full of sloppy pronunciations, hesitations, and mumbled words, making comprehension difficult. Men tend to mumble far more than women (Weinrich & Simpson, 2014). The reasons for the gender difference are still being studied (Wienrich et al., 2014). Mispronouncing words and poor articulation are also common issues. Proper **articulation,** or speaking words clearly and distinctly, and **pronunciation**, or saying words correctly as indicated in any dictionary based on Standard English rules, are important remedies to discriminative listening difficulties. The *YourDictionary* website identifies the 100 most often mispronounced words and phrases in English, which are primarily the result of simply not hearing the words properly articulated. For example, when you want to stop something at its source, like a flowering bloom at its base, "nip it in the bud" is correct not the oft misused "nip it in the butt." You do not "take for granite" but instead you "take for granted," and you *"should have"* known the difference" not "should of." Many people come by such mistakes honestly. They merely repeat what they think they heard. Still, professionalism in the workplace is diminished when such simple mistakes are made.

Comprehensive Listening: Understanding Messages

Listening to understand the message being communicated requires not only hearing what is said but an ability to interpret the nonverbal cues such as tone and expression that accompany a message. Comprehensive listening requires (a) paying attention to the message (mindfulness), (b) processing the info (discriminative listening), (c) asking clarifying questions to confirm your comprehension, and (d) remembering what you heard (The "R" in the HURIER model). Clarification includes questions and probes of fact that help us understand what we have heard. Examples include

> *I am not sure what _____ means. Can you give me an example?*
>
> *Let me see if I understand this …*
>
> *Is this correct?*
>
> *Which specifically? When?*
>
> *So, you're saying …*

People in a low-context environment, as described in Chapter 2, **are likely less apt to ask clarifying questions because they fill in meaning for themselves.**

Informational Listening: Learning

When one engages in informational listening, they steer clear of critique and evaluation and instead simply *listen to learn*. This type of listening is the type most associated with lecture presentations and business reports. **Informational listening** is geared toward learning something new. You move beyond merely understanding the verbal and nonverbal messages. You listen to expand your intellectual horizons. Taking notes, asking questions, and using memory cues such as creating a mental outline aid informational listening effectiveness.

Critical Listening: Analysis Not Criticism

Critical listening is the rational process of analyzing and evaluating others' claims (see Chapter 15 on supporting materials for additional discussion). In this case, the word *critical* does not imply criticism or looking for flaws, but instead *it denotes careful examination of reasoning and evidence presented*. Critical listening is particularly appropriate at work when we are on the receiving end of persuasive presentations or proposals. Because analysis precedes evaluation, we avoid jumping to conclusions.

Skepticism is the essence of critical listening. **Skepticism** is a process of listening to claims, evaluating evidence and reasoning supporting those claims, and drawing conclusions based on probabilities. Skeptics may seem to be annoying nags, always asking for evidence and challenging people's beliefs. The term *skeptic*, however, is derived from the Greek *skeptikos*, which means thoughtful or inquiring, not doubtful and dismissive. People generally do not give themselves a chance to spot faulty claims while listening because they listen only for information that supports their beliefs, and they ignore contrary information. This is called **confirmation bias** (Lilienfeld et al., 2009). Competent critical listeners must be prepared to say to themselves consistently, "So why would some people disagree with this speaker/person?" and "What am I not hearing?" Steer clear of confirmation bias particularly on either side of a job interview. When interviewing a favored candidate, for instance, be sure not to ignore red flags that make the interviewee less than desirable. On the flip side, if in the position of interviewing for a promising job, aim to hear those things you might not want to hear, whether they be about the office culture, the management, or corporate values, for example. Do not let bias interfere with good judgment.

In his classic work *Rhetoric*, Aristotle isolated the three modes of persuasion: ethos, pathos, and logos. **Ethos** refers to speaker credibility, **logos** is the reasoning and evidence involved, and **pathos** is the emotional appeal. Upon analyzing these components, a listener can then decide to believe or dismiss what he or she is hearing (evaluate). When striving to be heard, we benefit by considering our own character and reputation (ethos), the amount of emotion that comes through in our messages (usually in the form of the examples we give or in our nonverbal reinforcement of a message), and the soundness of our arguments (logos). *A more detailed explication of these modes of persuasion are discussed in later chapters*.

Empathic Listening: Caring and Sharing

Empathic listening is specifically based on seeking emotional comprehension of a message and it is commonly used in interpersonal situations. As defined earlier, **empathy** is "thinking and feeling what you perceive another to be thinking and feeling." It is the ability to identify and understand another's situation, feelings, and motives and to communicate that back to them. *Empathy is most appropriate in the workplace for coaching and conflict management* and brings the benefits of connections, trust, and loyalty. Shift into empathic listening in the workplace when (a) you genuinely care about the person involved, (b) you have time to listen, and (c) a person is expressing particularly

negative (or sometimes positive) feelings about something.

Marshall Rosenberg, developer of Nonviolent Communication, places empathy at listening's core. **Self-empathy** reflects a deep awareness of one's own experience when communicating. When engaged in this type of empathy, we acknowledge our tendencies to judge and stereotype and choose a more empowered filter of compassion. **Empathy for others** is demonstrated through listening to others' needs and feelings and reflecting them to the speaker for verification and understanding (Rosenberg, 2015).

Goleman (2013) distinguishes three types of empathy: Cognitive, emotional and compassionate. We will apply each to a scenario in which a co-worker comes to you, distraught because they were denied the raise they requested.

Cognitive empathy (know) is the ability to understand how a person feels and what they might be thinking. We access our cognitive empathy through awareness, curiosity, humility,

Empathic listening requires an emotional understanding of what others are experiencing, and often a reaching out to provide assistance where possible.

and guessing. When our co-worker discusses their disappointment about not getting a raise, we notice that they are near tears, their brow is furrowed, and they are speaking at a quick rate, with increased volume. We conclude that they are very upset, perhaps about the rejection of their request, the perception they are not valued, or the impact of the missed opportunity for a financial boost. We respond by paraphrasing and checking for accuracy. We might say, "I can see you're really upset about this. I understand why."

Emotional empathy (share) is the ability to share the feelings of another person. This type of empathy helps you build emotional connections with others. With your co-worker, you internally reflect on a time you've been disappointed in a somewhat similar situation. Maybe you have never been denied a raise, but surely you have experienced situations in which you felt you deserved something you did not get, or perhaps you were on the receiving end of a similar rejection. Ask yourself, when have I felt something similar or been through something like this? A tip is when relating your own experiences, tap into the feeling, not the event.

Compassionate empathy (do) takes cognitive and emotional empathy to the next level: it actually moves us to take action, to help however we can. Building on emotional empathy, we ask ourselves, "when I experienced something similar, what helped me? What can help them?" We might respond by saying, "I've been through something similar and I know how upsetting it can be. I'm sorry you're going through this. Would you like to get some fresh air and go for a walk with me? I'd love to listen and see how I can help."

To demonstrate empathic listening, paraphrase, ask good questions, and monitor your co-communicator's nonverbal cues. **Paraphrasing** involves restating in your own words the concise essence of a message that you heard. *Paraphrase for content* (the words that were spoken) or *paraphrase for feeling* (the emotion lying beneath the words). Paraphrasing allows you to check what you heard (or interpreted) with what the speaker said (or intended to say). You can paraphrase by using questions or statement form (*that sounds tough* … or . . . *Do*

you mean you're quitting?). Whichever you employ, steer clear of slipping into a therapeutic or mechanical sounding delivery style.

Since much of any message received is gleaned through nonverbal cues—both the speaker's and your own—they should be monitored closely. Look for confirming clues and possible discrepancies in tone of voice, eye contact, facial expressions, posture, and movement. Monitor your nonverbal communication as well. What messages is your face expressing? Is your brow furrowed? Is your jaw clenched? Check your tone. Does it reflect the emotion you seek to convey such as confidence or concern? If you are not sure, seek feedback from your peers as to how you are coming across. A favored feedback technique is to say, "I am looking to improve my listening skills. Can you tell me one thing I do well when listening and one thing I could do to improve?"

As with comprehensive listening, both **open-ended questions** (those that prompt the speaker to expand with examples, lists, and stories) and **closed-ended questions** (those that limit a speaker's answers to a narrow choice of right/wrong or yes/no, for instance) come in handy when practicing empathic listening. *Questions that clarify terms* ("What do you mean by that?"), elicit more information ("Could you give me an example?"), encourage further exploration through comparison ("When is it worst? When is it best?"), and *queries that help find resolution or open new doors* ("Ideally, how do you see this turning out?" or "What positive things could come out of this?") all help you gain empathy for a co-worker's situation and ultimately help the speaker feel heard. When listening empathically, avoid leading questions that are intended to sway a speaker's response by slyly implying your preferred answer. "You agreed with what I said in the meeting, didn't you?" and "You don't like her either, right?" are examples of leading questions.

Of course, we do not engage in empathic listening with everyone all the time. The relationship matters and so does the time we are willing to invest. Use empathic listening primarily to build relationships at work, especially when those relationships are perceived to be important.

Listening Problems and Solutions

By now you should realize that listening is not a simple process. In this section, we will tackle common listening problems and offer solutions.

Noise: Four Types

In Chapter 1, the concept of communication noise—any interference with effective transmission and reception of your message—was presented. The four types of noise, however, were merely hinted at without elaboration or indication that each type is an impediment to effective listening.

Physical noise, or external, environmental distractions, such as startling sounds, poorly heated rooms, or the unfortunate periodic reappearance of neon clothes, is the most obvious type of noise that disrupts effective listening.

Physiological noise, or biological influences, such as sweaty palms, pounding heart, and butterflies in the stomach induced by speech anxiety while giving a business presentation, or feeling sick or exhausted at work, can produce dramatic interference on both senders and receivers of messages.

Psychological noise, in the form of preconceptions, biases, and assumptions, also interferes with effective message transmission and reception. If a coworker comes to you with the secret of youth but you have the preconceived belief that they are an incompetent blowhard, the message might be lost. Such preconceived, dangerous biases, particularly around ethnicity and religion, make effective transmission and reception of messages in a global economy extremely difficult.

Finally, **semantic noise** as reflected in word choice that is confusing, incomprehensible, or distracting also creates interference. Looping back to discriminative listening, the mere mispronunciation of a phrase can get in the way

Differing values can be one of the loudest forms of psychological noise, especially political values conflicts such as Democrats (Donkey) and Republicans (Elephant).

of message reception. When speaking to others, one way to improve your listener's comprehension is to avoid the preponderance of acronyms. Unless you are 100% positive that the acronym you would like to use is known by every person in your audience, do not use it! At a recent meeting, a business manager said he needed to talk to the GLT about LE and LYT. *(WTH?)* Using the abbreviations may have saved him some time by cutting out a few syllables, it might have made him feel smart or inclusive, but it is TMA (Too Many Abbreviations). It certainly frustrated and excluded one listener who did not know what the manager was talking about. (So as not to leave you in suspense, he needed to talk to the Global Leadership Team about the Leadership Essentials and Leading Your Team training programs.)

Consider another example. Is the preferred term "African American," "black" or "Black" (capitalized in written form) when referring to the relevant ethnic group? In print, the Associated Press decided to use Black, while the New York Times and Washington Post are still

undecided about the proper labeling (Eligon, 2020). Should you use "Native American," "indigenous," or "Indian"? "Hispanic," "Latino," or "Latinx"? *Different groups, even individuals within a group, prefer different terms.* For example, a Pew Research survey found that only a scant 3% of Hispanic/Latino/a respondents preferred the term "Latinx," but 61% preferred "Hispanic" and 29% preferred "Latino" (Noe-Bustamante et al., 2020). Choosing the "wrong" term can derail your message by drawing attention to terminology disputes while drowning the content of your intended message. Analyze your audience to know what terminology is appropriate and preferred. When in doubt, ask respectfully.

Unfocused Listening: Mindlessness and Multitasking

A prominent informational listening problem is called glazing over. **Glazing over** occurs when listeners' attention wanders and daydreaming occurs. The lights are on, but no one's

Beware the stare: Though some research links daydreaming to creativity, it is best not to glaze over when listening at work.

home. One caught in this state is easily startled when called back into the conversation.

Multitasking and distractions also give way to unfocused listening. One study showed that the mere possibility that one's cell phone might ring reduces a person's ability to pay attention to messages by 20% (Sullivan & Thompson, 2013). The typical college student plays with a digital device (smartphone, laptop, tablet) an average of 11 times a day during classes for non-class purposes, and more than 80% admit that their use of these distracting devices interferes with learning (Reed, 2013). As previously noted in Chapter 1 despite the common belief that you can multitask effectively (texting and listening simultaneously), research debunks this belief.

Illustrated by the discrepancy in speaking rates and listening ability, we can listen faster than we can speak. This leaves plenty of opportunity for absorbing and reflecting on a speaker's message but also for daydreaming and glazing over. Listeners may benefit from a faster speaking rate. Listeners' comprehension of speech does not decline markedly until the speaker's rate exceeds 250 words-per-minute (wpm; Foulke, 2006). A lethargic speaking rate may put listeners to sleep. Linguist Deborah Tannen (2003) also notes that a very slow speaking rate (fewer than 100 wpm) is stereotyped as slow-witted and unintelligent in every culture studied. If the pace is slow, ***listeners should try to put the differential between the rate of speaking and thinking to good use***. Think about the speaker's message. Apply the message to your life experience. In contrast to unfocused listening, we listen actively with presence and participation. We are mindful not mindless.

Mentioned in Chapter 2, **mindfulness** *is the practiced ability to be present in order to be as effective and appropriate as possible*. You eliminate noise. You are aware of what is going on around you and what is happening inside of you (Alidina, 2018). When you are actively mindful in conversation, you put your own agenda and perspectives on hold and listen fully to another person, trying to hear them without imposing your own thoughts and feelings. As with so many competent communication strategies,

mindfulness is easier read than done. The first step, however, is to gently nudge your mind back to the present moment—in this case, the speaker and their message—whenever it wanders off. ***Mindfulness benefits you because you get a chance for connection and clarity.*** It illuminates communication choices instead of slipping into autopilot responses. This type of focus also gives energy and amplification to a conversation (Knight, 2020). ***Mindfulness benefits the recipient because when you give your full attention to others, they are more likely to express themselves with depth and honesty.*** Consider it from your own perspective: When someone does not pay attention while you talk, do you feel like continuing the conversation? Typically, a listener's failure to focus erodes the quality of what we choose to say, in turn causing us to suppress, forget, or deflate our message (Knight, 2020).

Pseudolistening: Faking It

Pseudolistening is pretending to listen. It is slightly different from glazing over. When listeners glaze over, they are not even pretending to listen. Staring blankly while another person is speaking shows no effort to disguise inattention to the message. Pseudolisteners attempt to disguise inattention to the message. Responding with "Mmm-hmm," "really," and "uh-huh" as someone speaks gives the illusion of attention if one's mind is not focused on the speaker's message. Pseudolistening typically is easier to enact over the phone, where visual cues are unavailable.

People pretend to listen for many reasons. Often we engage in pseudolistening because we do not want to be accused of not listening, or it is too awkward to admit we did not understand. Such an accusation from a boss, for example, would not only be embarrassing, it could get you into trouble, even if the boss is mind-numbingly boring or rambles on and on and on. So, you nod your head to indicate listening, when all the time your mind is light years away.

Focusing attention is the responsibility of both speakers and listeners. ***Speakers should make their points meaningful to listeners.***

That which is meaningless, mere trivia, rarely is remembered. As a speaker, answer the question for listeners, "Why should they care?" *When speaking with someone who is known to be a poor listener, you should adapt your message accordingly.* For example, is the message recipient more visual or verbal? Do they prefer email or meetings? Do they appreciate the bottom line or details? (Knight, 2017). Can you avoid rambling and get to the point? Beginning an impromptu conversation at work with, "Is this a good time to talk?" is appreciated. If you notice someone is distracted, you can gently bring it to their awareness by checking your perceptions. Say something like, "I see you're checking your phone a lot and I'm wondering if I've caught you at a bad time. Should we continue this conversation later?" *Listeners should focus their attention on what is being said by speakers.* This means coming prepared to listen (mindfulness) and by bringing a notepad or laptop computer to take notes. Instead of looking like a detective logging details of a crime, let your speaker know you plan on taking notes to make sure you remember the details. If that seems out of place, lock the message in by mentally reviewing key points. This is especially critical for developing competent informational listening, although this also relates to critical and empathic listening previously reviewed. Being a great listener takes commitment, time, and presence. When you are short on time or attention, be prepared to communicate openly and respectfully by saying something like, "I'd like to listen to you and I only have 5 minutes right now ... can we make a plan to meet later when I can give you my full attention?"

Shift Response: Conversational Narcissism

When we vie for attention during a group discussion, our listening becomes competitive and can turn into **conversational narcissism**—the tendency of listeners "to turn the topics of ordinary conversations to themselves without showing sustained interest in others' topics" (Derber, 1979; McKay & McKay, 2021). "Well, I've been talking long enough about me, so what do you think of me" typifies the conversational narcissist (Aune et al., 2000). Conversational narcissists are perceived to be socially unattractive and inept communicators (Vangelisti et al., 1990).

Conversational narcissists use an attention-*getting* initiative called the **shift response** where the listener attempts to shift the focus of attention from others to oneself by changing the topic of discussion. The shift response is self-centered and therefore Me-oriented. In the workplace, we call this "spotlight speaking." Visualize a stage spotlight that encircles whoever is speaking—people who use shift response make sure the spotlight is on them at all times.

The **support response,** in contrast, is an attention-*giving* effort by the listener to focus attention on the other person, not on oneself (Derber, 1979; Vangelisti et al., 1990). The listener shows interest, allowing the spotlight to be on the speaker. The support response fosters positivity into group discussions. We like being shown respect by others listening to us, and in turn are more likely to expand on our thoughts (Knight, 2020).

Consider examples that highlight differences between shift and support responses:

> **Maria:** I'm feeling frustrated by our group's lack of progress toward our goal.
>
> **Declan:** I was more frustrated by Jerry's awful attitude during yesterday's meeting (*shift response*).

Notice that Declan does not respond to Maria's frustration. Instead, he shifts the focus to his own frustration about another issue, in this case, Jerry's attitude. Compare the shift response with this support response:

> **Maria:** I'm feeling very frustrated by our group's lack of progress toward our goal.
>
> **Declan:** I hear you. I have some concerns as well. First, what do you think we should do about our progress? (*support response*)

Here, the response from Declan keeps the focus on the speaker and encourages Maria to explore the topic she initiated. Declan can discuss his feelings about Jerry's attitude when they have fully mined Maria's concerns.

A shift response can easily provoke shift responses from other group members in a hyper-competitive battle for attention, such as in the following example:

Jamie: I think we've gone off-track on this project. I'm worried that we'll embarrass ourselves.

Alex: The information that the Marketing team gave us is a mess. It's as if they're speaking a different language. (*Shift response*)

Annu: I think they were quite clear. It's the actual presentation before the executive team that concerns me. (*Shift response*)

Jamie: But what about our written summary on this project? I still don't think we've configured a coherent report and we will look incompetent. (*Shift response* to refocus attention on the initial topic)

Alex: I need help. Remind me what the heck CRM means? (*Shift response*)

Although the shift response may be appropriate in some instances where individuals drift from the main topic of conversation and need to be refocused, *competent communicators emphasize support responses and use shift responses infrequently. Background acknowledgment* ("really," "uh-huh"), a *supportive assertion* ("That's great," "Nicely done"), and a *supportive question* ("How do you think we should proceed?") are the types of supportive responses that encourage cooperative discussion, not competitive struggles for attention. As for the example above, any one of the conversation participants could aim to narrow the discussion by offering a summary and redirect. For example, Jamie could say, "It sounds like we all have several concerns, including the target, the content, and the presentation. Let's take each one by one and see how we can get back on track."

Competitive Interrupting: Seizing the Floor

Nathan Miller asserted that "conversation in the United States is a competitive exercise in which the first person to draw a breath is

Aim to share the spotlight, thus avoiding the shift response, by putting the focus back on the speaker.

declared the listener" (quoted by Bolton, 1979). Competitive interrupting is closely related to the shift response. It differs, however, in one key way. *Listeners who use the shift response usually observe the "one speaker at a time" rule of conversation. Competitive interrupters do not.* Interrupting becomes competitive when the listener attempts to seize the floor from the speaker and dominate the conversation. In a healthcare study, physicians interrupted patients within 11 seconds of the patient beginning to speak in 67% of encounters. The study's authors conclude, "Eliciting patient concerns and listening carefully to them contributes to patient-centered care. Yet, clinicians often fail to elicit the patient's agenda and, when they do, they interrupt the patient's discourse" (Ospina et al., 2019).

Not all interrupting, of course, is competitive. Sometimes group members interrupt to express support ("I agree with Joe") or enthusiasm ("Great idea"), seek clarification ("I'm confused. Could you explain that again before we move on?"), warn of danger ("Look out. You're falling over backward") or cut short a nonstop monologue that stymies group participation. A listener's role is far more than sitting silently while another speaks.

Competitive interrupting is Me-oriented. The focus is on individual needs, not group needs. Competitive interrupting creates antagonism, rivalry, hostility, and in some cases withdrawal from group discussion by frustrated members. Group members often mirror the interrupting patterns of others. If one member interrupts to seize the floor, another member will likely interrupt to seize it back. If members rarely interrupt, and when they do, primarily offer support, others will likely follow suit and keep the conversation supportive and cooperative. The bottom line is, when hoping for competent communication with others, it pays to model the supportive way.

Ambushing: Preparing Rebuttals

When a group member is ready to pounce on a point made by a speaker, this is called **ambushing**. That member is listening with a bias.

The bias is to attack the speaker verbally, not try to understand the speaker's point of view. Ambushers aim to defeat a speaker in a verbal jousting match. Preparing a rebuttal while a speaker is still explaining their point shows little interest in comprehending a message except to find flaws. In competitive debates, message distortion is a common problem. The focus is on winning the argument, not discerning a message accurately. In the workplace, ambushing most often appears when siloed departments perceive scarce resources such as budget, materials, or staff, and thus they engage in unhealthy competition.

Debating ideas is a useful and important process in a democratic society. Ambushing, however, promotes negativity into group discussion. Defeating an opponent becomes the driving force for ambushers. During group discussion, try to understand messages clearly and accurately *before* evaluating them.

Probing and paraphrasing can short-circuit ambushing. **Probing** means seeking additional information from a speaker by asking questions. Probing includes *clarifying questions* ("Can you give me an example of an important goal for the group?"), *exploratory questions* ("Can you think of any other approach to this problem?"), and *encouraging questions* ("Who can blame us for making a good effort to try a new approach?").

Paraphrasing should be concise and precise. For example

> **Gabriela:** I'm sick and tired of working on this budget. We have so little to show for it. If we'd started earlier, we would be done by now.
>
> **Frank:** You seem frustrated and unhappy with the team's effort.
>
> **Gabriela:** Frustrated? Yes! Unhappy with the group effort? No! We all just have impossible schedules to coordinate.

Paraphrasing can reveal misunderstanding. Ambushing merely assumes a message is understood without checking. Noncompetitive listening is a useful communication skill that nurtures a positive group climate.

SUMMARY

Regardless of your role, effective listening is imperative in today's workplace. Listening to the needs, ideas, and concerns of our peers, leaders, and the public alike builds trust and relationships. When reviewing the complexity of listening, including the HURIER stages and the five types of listening, keep in mind that as indicated in the introduction, the perception of good listening is subjective, and is owned by the speaker. Whether or not we think we are good listeners is less important than if others think we are. Strategies to improve your listening skills include being mindful, asking good questions, paraphrasing, interrupting purposefully, and eliminating noise, to name a few. When in doubt, seek feedback about the way you listen.

Film School Case Studies

The Social Network (2010). Drama; PG-13

Based on the book, this biographical movie explores the creation of Facebook, one of the most impactful social media creations to this day. Analyze listening patterns as Jesse Eisenberg, playing the role of Mark Zuckerberg, faces friends, rivals, and lawyers on his way to success.

TED Talks and YouTube Videos

These TED Talks and YouTube videos can be accessed by going to the Oxford Learning Link for It's All of Our Business or by typing the title of the video into a Google search window.

"It's not about the nail"

"Listen, learn, then lead" by Stanley McChrystal

"Want to help someone? Shut up and listen!" by Ernesto Sirolli

Office Space: Meeting with the Bobs

"The power of listening" by William Ury

"How to get people to listen to you" by Chad Littlefield

Bréné Brown on Empathy/RSA

After successful completion of this chapter, you will be able to

1. Create a professional social media presence.

2. Effectively research a company's mission, vision, and values.

3. Assess your knowledge of in-demand professional skills.

CHAPTER 7

Social Media and Interviewing: On Your Way to Work

WHAT DO YOU WANT to be when you grow up? That's a question we have been asked since we were children and before we know it, we reach adulthood. Some of us nail it early on: Activist Greta Thunberg started advocating for the environment when she was 8 years old. Others' paths zig and zag. Amazon founder Jeff Bezos wanted to be an archaeologist (Clifford, 2017), and Michael Jordan's father tried to steer him into playing professional baseball. (Coauthor of this text, Dan, wanted to be a Hall of Fame professional baseball pitcher, and the other coauthor Michelle was certain she would become an artist or a zookeeper. Instead, we became college professors and textbook authors.) We all end up being something, usually many somethings. According to the U.S. Bureau of Labor Statistics, on average, adults in the United States change jobs at least a dozen times before retiring, with nearly half of these jobs held before the age of 25 (Kolmar, 2022. Job interviewing is a recurring process, especially early in your life. Whatever profession we choose, communication plays a central role.

CHAPTER OUTLINE

- Online Networking
- Interview Preparation
- Know Your Value: A Subjective Inventory
- Interview Questions: Two Types
- Pep Talk: Check Your Mindset
- The Interview: Several Formats
- Interview Follow-up

4. Use a simple strategy for answering interview questions.

5. Navigate three types of interviews with ease.

The primary purpose of this chapter is to help job seekers navigate their career path, one which is inherently influenced by competent communication, from managing social media to post-interview correspondence. The chapter objectives are as follows: (1) introduce how to create compelling social media content for a business setting, (2) examine ways to assess one's value and confidence, and (3) traverse the stages of an interview: before, during, and after.

Online Networking

Have you Googled yourself lately? Even if you haven't, chances are the companies that are considering you for work have. Javier Quintero, recruiter for Embark Trucks, said, "Nine times out of ten, I barely glance at an applicant's resume, and go straight to social media to learn about them" (Quintero, 2019). The internet is full of social media horror stories about the blurred lines that exist between one's personal and professional life. Not safe for work (NSFW) pictures posted on what people thought were their private accounts, angry tweets that tag a business that happens to be a client or potential employer, and other blunders abound. Such mistakes can cost people their current jobs, employment opportunities, or reputation. What happens on the Internet stays on the Internet. With information available to many in a few quick keystrokes, savvy *use of social media is imperative in today's workplace*.

LinkedIn: The Professional Social Network

Specifically designed for business, LinkedIn is the foremost professional social networking website for job seekers, job posters, recruiters, and students looking for internships and contacts to build their resume for a future career in their chosen major or professional interest. LinkedIn boasts nearly 722 million members in 200 countries (Balch,

2022). Slightly more than 60% of LinkedIn users are between 25 and 34 years old, most with a college education (Tankovska, 2021). More important to the job seeker, there are more than 55 million companies listed on the site, and at any given time there are 14 million open job postings. A strong LinkedIn profile makes it easy to spot you in Internet search results, assess your skills, and connect with you for interviews.

"Every student should be on LinkedIn" (Patenall, 2021). Sree Sreeivasan, founder of Digimentors, a social media consultancy, says pointblank, "Every ninth grader should set up and maintain a LinkedIn profile" (quoted by Yavorski, 2021). Networking starts early.

As a college student, why should you care about establishing a LinkedIn presence? First, LinkedIn is not just a social networking site for immediate job seekers. LinkedIn is a great source of professional articles and a site to access expert-led video tutorials on everything from *The Art of Clowning* to *Ethical Hacking* and nearly everything in between (Marvin, 2019; Newberry, 2021; Petrone, 2019). It is a business education site. Second, LinkedIn can help you choose a college or graduate program. "Universities from around the globe have created LinkedIn pages that provide a trove of inspiration and information about their programs and their graduates" (Arruda, 2018). This is useful as a high school student, but it also is helpful for students who begin their higher education at a community college and plan to apply to a 4-year institution. Third, LinkedIn can provide a "one-stop shop" for building your resume as you proceed throughout your college education. Waiting until you are about to graduate from college and seek your first real career job to build a LinkedIn profile and resume will likely result in abundant lost information about your accomplishments in your years of education unless you accumulate details along the way. You can accumulate recommendations from a wide variety of mentors, teachers, and workplace supervisors. Awards and notable accomplishments can be added. Fourth, relevant mentors can be developed into a useful network of contacts. These contacts may provide internships

BOX 7.1   Student Spotlight

I have been on LinkedIn for about 2 years now, and I have created a community of 5.1k. LinkedIn helped me consolidate my post-secondary choices and find a career path I'm interested in. I was also able to share my thoughts and my passions with a community of like-minded individuals while learning from some of the most brilliant people. Being on LinkedIn enhanced my communication skills, and I have grown tremendously as a person. LinkedIn can be an intimidating platform for a student who is just starting out, but don't be afraid to reach for help. All the experts were once beginners once, and the people on LinkedIn are extremely welcoming.

Ella (Yi Xiu) Wang (She/Her) · 1st   **Wealthsimple Foundation**
High School Student | Summer Intern @ Wealthsimple Foundation
Talks about #music, #advice, #success, #leadership, and #studentvoices
Toronto, Ontario, Canada · **Contact info**

5,593 followers · 500+ connections

in which beneficial experience in your major and career path develop. Finally, you can build your professional presence, follow industries that interest you, and engage with professionals you might not otherwise have access to. Thus, LinkedIn is not just a site for those who have already begun their careers and are looking for advancement, but it is a platform that is highly relevant for college students who have yet to begin their careers.

When speaking about his involvement on LinkedIn, graduate student Shafeen Mahmood, said, "If it was up to me, I would incorporate LinkedIn essentials as a compulsory credit-bearing module at all colleges and universities." He continued to say that his LinkedIn activity helped him redefine his perception of college success, assess his business competition, build his personal brand, and it secured him an internship and multiple speaking opportunities.

Admittedly, there are some negatives associated with LinkedIn. First, it can be time consuming to constantly update your profile and interact with your network of contacts and mentors. Next, while some social sharing is permitted, it is not to be used like Facebook or Instagram, and remains primarily a professional platform. Also, there can be some privacy concerns, but LinkedIn does provide subscriber security. Unfortunately, as with all social media platforms, LinkedIn is not free of occasional internet trolls, sexual harassment, and scams. Overall, the pros outweigh the potential cons (Koirala, 2021).

Creating a Powerful LinkedIn Profile

Creating a powerful profile is highly important. Follow these recommendations to get your profile up and noticed.

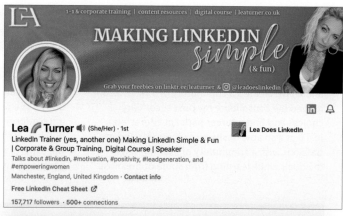

Compose a Compelling Headline

Your headline is the first sentence or words of your profile. *Since your headline is what appears in search results, it is the key to being found.* Make sure it grabs the right kind of attention by announcing your value, role, or both. Without your personal attention, LinkedIn will default to a headline based on your current job title and company. This hardly drums up any excitement or specificity about who you are or what you can do. If you haven't plugged in a title or company, it will default to "Unemployed at Unemployed." Yikes. You have 220 characters to get the right kind of attention. Use key words that showcase your special talents, title, or interests.

Graduate student Shafeen Mahood (https://www.linkedin.com/in/shafeen-mahmood/) touts his special awards and interests in his headline.

LinkedIn Coach Lea Turner (https://www.linkedin.com/in/lea-turner/) shows a bit of her personality by laughing at the fact that there are many people claiming the title of "coach" on the platform, and she highlights her specialties as well.

She also takes advantage of the opportunity to tell viewers what she talks about through the use of hashtags and has recorded a personal greeting/name pronunciation for others to hear.

You can also list your pronouns (as Lea did above) in your profile. LinkedIn's research concludes that "70% of job seekers believe it's important that recruiters and hiring managers know their gender pronouns, while 72% of hiring managers agree and believe this shows respect" (Hutchinson, 2021).

Try several headlines and watch the number of profile views each garners. No views? Consider tweaking it. *For those just starting your careers, strive for relevance instead of mystery.*

Provide a Profile Picture: Don't Be Camera-Shy

We all know that a picture speaks a thousand words (and so does the absence of one). *Profiles with headshots are up to 21 times more likely to be viewed than those without* (Callahan, 2018a). A picture completes your profile, instead of leaving it looking unfinished. Upload a recent head-and-shoulders shot of yourself that reflects approachability and competence. Though you are striving for professionalism, you do not necessarily need a professional photo shoot—just a genuine smile, the right lighting, and friends who can give you honest feedback about the picture you choose. Steer clear of sunglasses. Visually reinforce who you are with a background picture as well. When possible, showcase your personality or use an image that reflects what you do (industry), and/or where you are (city). LinkedIn offers a video feature as well where you can add a short clip to your profile so viewers can get a better idea of who you are and what you do. If you use this feature, make sure your video captures a mix of professionalism and your personality.

Which profile picture is the best? It depends on which jobs you seek. Photo 1 shows creativity and personality; it might be perfect for a job seeker in the media or creative arts. Photo 2 ignores the "no sunglasses" suggestion and seems to shout "model" wannabe. Photo 3, a blank picture, indicates that the job seeker might be lazy, shy, or hiding something.

Personalize Your URL: It's the Little Things

LinkedIn makes it easy to change your web address. Marine Corps Community Services says this is important because it makes you easier to find amongst the sea of LinkedIn users; enhances your credibility as a detail-oriented, tech savvy person; and looks clean on your resume, email signature, and business cards. When creating your profile, click "Edit public profile and URL" on the upper right side of the page, then click "Edit your custom URL." For example, there are more Michelle Waters in the world than she originally suspected, so Michelle's LinkedIn address is https://www.linkedin.com/in/i-am-michelle-waters/.

Craft a Strong Summary: Tell Your Story

Your summary continues the story that started with your picture and headline, and it highlights key elements of your qualifications. Make it good. *Think of your summary paragraph as your brand.* Define yourself in your own words. You can describe your character, explain what makes you tick, or showcase your successes. Jolie Miller (2018) of LinkedIn Learning says, "Don't tell me what you do, tell me why I should care. What's special about you?" She adds that on LinkedIn, it is acceptable to write your summary in first person or third, the former being the more approachable of the two.

Instead of only listing the jobs you have held in the experience section of your profile, *describe the value you have added to the company or position.* Mine your experience and expertise for instances where your efforts have saved employers time or money or have increased sales or customer satisfaction. List your responsibilities but be sure to pair them with a positive impact. Instead of simply saying you "increased revenue" show the numbers. If you are a creator who has been selling your original products on Etsy, specify how many units you have sold, how many return customers you have, and distribution range. You can highlight key words of customer feedback if applicable.

Get Recommendations on the Spot

Forget the outdated "references per request." Why wait until a potential employer checks your references when you can spotlight them right away on your profile? Aim to get two or three recommendations per job held. Consider asking previous leaders, coworkers, employees, mentors, and clients for words of praise. Draft a simple message to the appropriate LinkedIn connections and say something like, "Hello! I'm working on my LinkedIn profile and I would greatly appreciate it if you could write a couple of lines vouching for me and my work." Optionally, specify what you hope they spotlight, for example, teamwork or specific job skill, and leave a recommendation for them too in return when applicable.

Think of your LinkedIn profile as your professional online billboard: You want others to notice it for all the right reasons. It's where you introduce yourself to recruiters, potential employers, network connections, and peers in your field.

LinkedIn isn't the only social media platform that will help you find employment. Dancer, choreographer, and member of TikTok's Creator Fund, Zack Jot (https://www. tiktok.com/@zockjat), whose hip-hop dance posts went viral in 2020, says that the majority of his clients find him on Instagram or TikTok, making business offers based on what they see. He thinks of social media as an "unorthodox portfolio and resume" and recommends that creators and artists stay consistent with their online presence, posting quality content nearly every day. Keep in mind that 84% of recruiters and potential bosses will likely "Google" you and go beyond LinkedIn to check your Instagram, Facebook, Twitter, TikTok, Pinterest, and any other social media sites they can access (Gaynor, n.d.). *The best practice is to draw a line between your professional and personal life by keeping all accounts private except LinkedIn*. If you would like to have more of a digital presence for the public to view, consider setting up more than one account. For instance, have a personal Twitter account for friends, and another public account where you tweet more professional content.

Interview Preparation

Adequately preparing for an interview requires one to research, practice, and get in the right mindset. Preparation improves communication competence. Researching a company's history, mission, vision, and values does not only help you decide if the company is a good fit for you, but it also helps you present yourself as an informed candidate. You are also better prepared to ask good questions in the interview.

Researching the Company: Vision, Mission, and Values

Familiarizing oneself with a company involves much more than simply looking up their current stock market value or learning how to pronounce the name of the current CEO (the latter is important, however). In fact, thorough vetting of a company you would like a position with requires both time and commitment. Your research helps you in two ways: First, you can determine if this is even a desirable company. Do its values align with yours? Would you fit in with the company culture?

Second, if it is a company you are interested in, you enter the interview well-versed about the company, thus increasing your own confidence while impressing the interviewer with your diligence. *Start with an overview of the company*. What industry are they in and how do they make money? Who do they serve? Do they produce a service or product for another business (B2B), or do they work directly with customers (B2C), or both? What do their customers think of them? Study the organization's website, blog, and social media presence. Also look at their competitors and customer reviews. How long have they been around? How has leadership grown or stayed the same through time? Research the company's financials and look for relevant news items.

When viewing their website, look at the *About* tab. Familiarize yourself with any acronyms or verbiage special to the business or their field. *Study the company's mission, vision, and values*. These set the direction of an organization and can be used as measurements for alignment.

A **vision statement** represents a company's brand and overall strategic intent. It offers inspiration and direction for tomorrow. Ikea's (purveyor of many students' furniture) simple vision is *"to create a better everyday life for the many people" (Ikea.com)*. Everything they do should align with that vision. The American Society for Prevention of Cruelty to Animals (ASPCA) states that their vision is "that the United States is a humane community in which all animals are treated with respect and kindness" (ASPCA Mission, 2022).

A **mission statement** defines why an organization exists by announcing their primary objectives. It isolates what a company does *today* to get to tomorrow (the vision). According to their website, the ASPCA's mission has stayed the same since 1866. It is "to provide effective means for the prevention of cruelty to animals throughout the United States" (ASPCA Mission, 2022).

Google's mission is "to organize the world's information and make it universally accessible and useful" (about.Google, 2022). Twitter's mission is "to give everyone the power to create and share ideas and information instantly without barriers."

Both vision and mission statements are goal oriented. According to Bain and Company, mission and vision are sometimes interchangeable and very often blended into one statement. When preparing for an interview, more important than distinguishing between the mission and vision is to be well-versed in what a company does, why they do it, and where they are going, regardless how they spell that out. As of the writing of this chapter, many major companies researched such as Tesla, TED, Netflix, and Whole Foods state their mission on their web pages, but their vision is implied or combined in the mission statement. *If the company vision, mission, and values are not clearly defined or stated, be prepared to ask questions about them in the interview.*

Explore the company's culture and **values**. Are the values just words on the screen that sound good or are they threaded into how the company operates? Can you find examples of the company putting these values in action? Look at websites such as Glassdoor to see what current and former employees have to say.

Using the PREP Method: Matching Background to Company Values

Dropping stated company values into your interview vernacular does not demonstrate that you understand or can demonstrate them. Instead, *present specific examples of when you have demonstrated the values the company holds dear.* Be ready to speak about which value resonates with you the most, coupled with examples, if asked. Used as a model for organizing thoughts into responses, the **PREP method** works well for these kinds of discussions.

*P*oint: State your main idea/bottom line

*R*eason: Provide the reasoning as to why your point is valid

*E*xample: Give support in the form of a story, testimony or research

*P*oint: Restate your initial point for clarity

For example, if declaring how you embody the value of passion you might say

*P*oint: Of the three company values, I particularly resonate with passion. On your website, passion is defined as the desire "to excel and accomplish great things."

*R*eason: Through my college experience I've had many occasions to demonstrate my desire to be my best and go beyond what's expected of me.

*E*xample: I joined the local Save The Waves Coalition because of my love of the ocean. I held the title of membership coordinator. In the 2 years that I volunteered, I recruited 112 new members—a 60% increase from previous years.

*P*oint: Part of what made it easy to get others on board was my passion for the cause and commitment to the group.

Know Your Value: A Subjective Inventory

In a leadership workshop Michelle teaches on adding value to one's team, trainees begin the class by fighting for their jobs. Pretending they are at risk of being terminated, they are asked what they would say to their manager if they had 30 seconds to convince them to keep their job. It is an exercise in impromptu thinking and speaking, but more importantly, it is an opportunity for participants to pinpoint their worth. To prepare, they answer three questions:

1. What do you do better than others?
2. What value do you bring to the team?
3. Why are you the one for the job?

Most of the trainees balk at the initial idea. It is an awkward task and seems to contradict the humility required of a strong team player. But with the right encouragement, they are soon on their way to crowing their value. Regardless, where we are in our career, from first job search to nearing retirement, we should always be able to communicate effectively our strengths through detailed examples while simultaneously being aware of where we need to improve. Beyond getting a job, a reflective inventory of our strengths helps us develop, mentor, build confidence, and get results.

The "2020 Future of Jobs Report" (2020) compiled by the World Economic Forum (WEF) concludes that the increase in automation and the economic impact of the COVID-19 pandemic will greatly impact the transformation of jobs and skills by 2025. The WEF interviewed 200 experts across nine industries including aerospace, oil, and entertainment. The number one barrier to the adoption of new technology in the workforce is revealed as skill gaps in the labor market. Comparing research from the 2018 report, the expectation for employees to pick up new skills in the form of upskilling or reskilling rose from 65% to 94%. *Upskilling* is to teach or learn additional skills in order to improve and advance, whereas *reskilling* involves closing the skill gaps for performing one's current position or maintaining lateral movement within a company. In other words, if you are learning in hope of a promotion, you are upskilling. If you are enhancing your skillset accordingly with the changing technology in order to maintain expertise in your current role, you are reskilling. Both forms of learning are important to keep on your interviewing radar.

As of December 2020, the free job seeker site Indeed.com highlighted the qualities that employers want most: Along with communication, leadership, and teamwork skills that interviewers investigate, the Future of Jobs Report indicates that critical thinking skills, problem solving, and self-management (i.e., active learning, resilience, flexibility, and stress

TABLE 7.1 When Interviewing, Showcase Your Knowledge of In-Demand Skills

Skill	Examples	Possible interview question	Discussion points
Communication skills	Speaking, writing, listening, negotiating	*Tell me about a time when you found it challenging to communicate with someone. What was the situation? How did you navigate it? What was the result? What would you have done differently?* *What is one of your communication strengths? What are areas you could improve?*	Highlight specific examples of communicating successfully with not only managers and peers but also with people whose culture, language, and viewpoints differ from yours. Define your communication strength clearly and give examples. Be prepared to discuss which areas you are trying to improve. For example, you might say that you consider yourself to be a great active listener, and you are working on your presentation skills.
Leadership skills	Managing, mentoring; influencing people and ideas; giving and receiving feedback; strategic thinking	*Tell me about a time when you have taken the initiative to mentor someone or lead others. What is a change you led or influenced? How did you get others on board? What is a piece of constructive feedback you received that you acted upon? How do you influence change, especially if change is unwelcome?*	Discuss experiences with extracurricular groups or teams you have belonged to or tell about a time when you saw someone's potential and helped them grow. Demonstrate your humility and ability to accept feedback. Regardless of title, focus on examples of when you led change in a system, process, or person.
Teamwork skills	Collaboration, trust, communication, conflict management	*How has collaboration contributed to success in your life? What has been the most difficult part of collaborating with others?*	Note any projects or jobs where you have achieved results *with* others. What was the situation?
Learning/ Adaptability skills	Growth mindset, humility, resilience, ability to change	*What classes have you taken or skills you have learned recently? What was a change you resisted? How did you adapt? What is something you didn't know on a job but quickly learned? If you took the job, in what areas would you hope to grow?*	Isolate stories that highlight your ability and eagerness to grow and improve. Focus on examples of your willingness to adapt. Reference examples of times you took initiative to learn new skills. Tie back to the research you did on the company. Is there an emerging opportunity? Is there a specific corporate value you would like to strengthen in the professional realm?
Self-Management	Time management, productivity, prioritization, self-motivation, stress management	*How do you prioritize what to do on any given day while staying motivated to do it? What do you use to manage stress?*	Include experiences that demonstrate your ability to provide yourself structure and to produce results independently. Consider tools you use (One Note, Google Sheets, etc.) or projects you have managed. Don't say that you never get stressed. If applicable, emphasize your ability to remind yourself of the big picture. Discuss your stress relievers such as yoga, breathing techniques, sports, laughter, playing with your dog, or whatever you do for balance.
Problem-Solving skills	Managing challenges, decision making, productivity, strategic thinking, creativity	*Looking at our company, what challenges do you see on the horizon and what solutions would you propose? What trends do you see that will warrant changes?*	Give an example of improving processes or fixing issues. Research the company/industry to know their strengths as well as challenges or potential blind spots.

management) will be the top-growing skills in demand by 2025. Tout your prowess of these skills on your resume and cover letter, as well as in interviews.

Interview Questions: Two Types

You have researched the company, practiced your responses, and translated your experience into in-demand skills. Now it is time for the interview. Before you pick up that phone, log into that web meeting, or walk into that building, there is still more preparation to be done. An interview is a conversational exchange of information. Hardly linear, it is a two-way process of discovery. The interviewer seeks information about you, and you seek information about the company and the position. Come prepared to answer and ask good questions. In today's market, a company's interview questions are easy to find on sites such as Glassdoor.com. Gone are the brainteasing questions that companies like Google were once known for. Google's own extensive research on their interview processes found that asking a potential employee how many golf balls fit in a school bus, for example, did not actually predict anything of the candidate's success and were ultimately a waste of time (A. Bryant, 2013). *The two general types of questions asked in interviews are behavioral and situational.* **Behavioral interview questions** focus on the past, while **situational interview questions** explore the future.

Behavioral Interview Questions

A commonly asked behavioral interview question is, "Tell me about a time you experienced conflict with a coworker. What was the conflict and how was it resolved?" This question prompts the interviewee to use real-life examples in their past, the logic being that past experience is a strong predictor of future behavior—that is, if you did it that way then, you will likely do it that way again. The concrete nature of behavioral interviewing can uncover details

about a candidate's experience and their character. Answers take the form of a story, and often allow the interviewee to relax as they think of examples from their past. Interviewees are often coached by recruiters to use the STAR format for answering such questions.

> *Situation:* The background/setting of the example to be shared
>
> *Task:* The problem or challenge
>
> *Action:* The actions that were taken to solve the problem
>
> *Result:* The conclusion spurred by the action

If answering the question about conflict in STAR format, it might sound something like this:

> S: I was part of a small team of contracted window installers who did most of the installations for city-based projects.
>
> T: One of the top installers prioritized surfing over work, so whenever the swell was up, she would rearrange her lunch break and schedule for that day so she could surf. Though our group welcomed a somewhat flexible schedule, this began to inconvenience the clients and the team.
>
> A: Instead of judging her, I asked her more about her passion for surfing—why she loved it, what it gave her, and how she determines the best surf times.
>
> R: We decided that since low-tide mornings were consistently the best wave breaks, she would book customer appointments in the afternoon, and use the morning for in-office tasks that were moveable, if need be. It worked out well for all of us. I think my ability to ask questions instead of jumping to conclusions helped us solve the problem to everyone's satisfaction.

The downside of behavioral interviewing questions is that not all job candidates will have a good answer, particularly if they are new to the job market; the answers can take a lot of time; and stories may be embellished (Mayall, n.d.). Making hiring decisions solely based on behavioral interviews are about 12% more effective than flipping a coin (Schmidt, 2016).

This dated conclusion holds true in today's fast-changing world, as it is the adaptability, not simply the repetition, of our experiences that matters.

Situational Interview Questions

In contrast to behavioral interviews, situational interviews focus on the future and pose hypothetical scenarios. For instance, "What would you do if a recommendation you strongly supported was rejected by your team?" Answers to future-oriented questions can reveal the innovation and strategic mindset of job candidates. Still, candidates might create an answer that they think the interviewer wants to hear, and their aptitude and attitude may not be evident. The best interviews are a combination of the types of questions. Expect questions about what you did and how you'll do things. Go beyond simply researching the questions. Practice answering questions with a trusted peer or professional who can coach you on your presence and responses. Pre-interview role playing not only helps you polish your answers and organize your thoughts, but it also quells speaking anxiety. There's a saying that we are only perfect twice: at birth and in a job interview. Scrap perfection and instead aim for connection. As with any public speaking situation, authenticity is essential to a successful interview. Do not rehearse your answers to the point they become scripted and robotic. Interviewers want to know who you are, just as much as they want to know what you do.

Pep Talk: Check Your Mindset

Before starting an interview for a position you would like to attain, check your mindset. Do you think you can do the job? **Self-efficacy**, a term coined by psychologist Albert Bandura, is one's personal assessment as to whether you "can execute courses of action required to deal with prospective situations." (Lopez-Garrido, 2020).Essentially, if you do not have the confidence that you can succeed in an interview and be viewed as a potential job candidate, you are already starting off the interview process poorly. It is much more than an "I can do anything" mantra, however. Bandura recommends the following four steps to build self-efficacy:

1. *Mastery Experience*. An inventory of your past success can strengthen confidence. Mine your past for wins both big and small that support your bid for the position.

2. *Vicarious Learning*. Think of times when you have learned through others, merely by observation: for example, all the times that you have been on the receiving end of great customer service are learning opportunities. Perhaps you have not held a service position before, but you can identify good service when you see it, and in turn, aim to replicate it.

3. *Social Persuasion*. Assuredness is nurtured through others believing in your ability to succeed. Seek an advocate or coach who can remind you of your skills and value.

4. *Physiology*. Walk the walk; talk the talk. Act as if you are a success. Whether virtually or in person, maintain good posture, along with strong, natural eye contact, and speak up.

The Interview: Several Formats

After all that preparation, the time is here. Company research? Check. Question role playing? Check. Positive mindset? Check. You are ready for the interview. Having only one interview with a company is rare. Plan for several. While you'll take your knowledge and confidence to each, be aware of the nuances of different types of interviews along your job search journey.

One-on-One Interview

The one-on-one interview is most often face-to-face or through a videoconference. It generally lasts around 60 minutes. It might be with the hiring manager but can also take place with potential peers or other stakeholders.

Get there early. Whether onsite or online, promptness matters. If the interview is face to face, aim to arrive early so that you can navigate traffic, find the location, and review your notes before the interview. When interviewing through video, log in early to test the connection and the link. Receiving the pop-up screen that alerts you the meeting link is not valid will only increase your anxiety. Put yourself at ease by giving yourself the gift of time.

Greet your interviewer with purposeful energy. First impressions in on-site interviews used to begin with a handshake. The interviewer would silently assess the strength of your grip and make conclusions about you before the questions even began. A death-grip handshake might have sent messages of domination or confidence, whereas a limp handshake led to conclusions of lack of confidence or lack of

interest. COVID-19 essentially eradicated contact greetings such as the handshake, fist bump, and a hug. In April of 2020, as the pandemic escalated in the United States, Dr. Fauci said, "I don't think we should ever shake hands ever again, to be honest with you" (Knutson & Linebaugh, 2020). So, should you refuse the extended hand of an interviewer? That is up to you. As the saying goes, old habits are hard to break. Expect some awkwardness to ensue during this time of transition. If you are the one to extend your hand first, do not be surprised or offended if the kind bid is rejected. Go with the flow. If we do ever resume the archaic, germy habit of the handshake, use a firm, yet not overpowering grip, and pump your forearm slightly two to three times.

Of course, none of this is of concern when interviewing virtually. Still, follow the guidelines of in-person posture: Sit up straight, about an arm's length away from your screen and

As in-person greetings change, expect and accept the awkwardness of navigating new norms. If comfortable, you can follow the interviewer's lead; or politely say that you are not shaking hands anymore thanks to Covid concerns, but you are happy to be there.

keep your shoulders back; don't hunch. Also, look into your webcam and convey warmth and confidence by saying something along the lines of "Hello" or "It's great to meet you. Thank you for taking the time to talk."

Be interested and interesting. Tout your skills and experience and connect examples back to why you are intrigued by this specific opportunity and how you can add to the team. Now is not the time to give details about how you won the hula-hoop contest in fourth grade, *unless that story specifically relates to a quality your interviewer is looking for such as drive or risk-taker, but even that might be a stretch*. Storytelling is your friend in the interview. Tailor the STAR model and the PREP method to your needs.

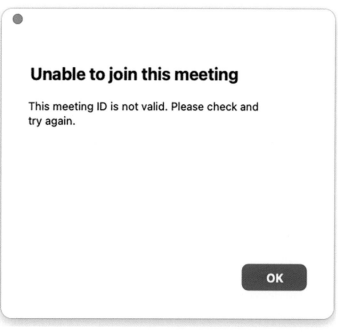

Unable to join this meeting

This meeting ID is not valid. Please check and try again.

OK

Being denied access to a virtual meeting only adds to an interviewer's stress! Log in early to test the link before the videoconference.

Take notes. To remember names and important details from the interview, come to the interview with a discrete notepad and pen or charged device. If using your laptop, be mindful of any stickers or branding you have used to personalize your computer. Everything speaks!

Keep your cool. Even with the best preparation, there are times when your mind might go blank or you'll be asked a question you did not anticipate. Famed former Green Bay Packers football coach Vince Lombardi said, "Perfection is not attainable, but if we chase perfection, we can catch excellence." When caught off guard, catch excellence by taking a breath and pausing. Do not ramble or make something up in order to fill the silence. Instead try asking a clarifying question ("Could you give me an example of what you mean?") or admitting you do not know ("I am not certain of that but would love to learn about it"). It is okay to pass on a question.

Monitor your nonverbals. Sit up straight; look the interviewer in the eye (if it is a virtual meeting, balance time looking at the person's image on the screen so that you can gauge their nonverbal signals and looking at the webcam

in order to convey the appearance of direct eye contact); and project confidence through the volume, cadence, and tone of your voice.

Finally, at the end of the interview, *thank the interviewer* for their time. Inquire as to when the hiring decision will be made and when you might hear from them about next steps.

Screening Interview

The **screening interview** is usually organized by a recruiter or company gatekeeper. They are most often conducted virtually or by phone. Do not expect a job offer after this type of conversation, since the objective of a screening interview is to identify candidates who are qualified to make it to the next level of interviews. The interviewer wants to weed out the poor prospects and propel the good ones to the next round. The interviewer will go beyond your resume, aiming to learn more about your experience, your personality, and your intentions. Questions commonly focus on what you are looking for in a job, work culture, and management style. They may also ask logistical questions about compensation expectations and availability. Be prepared to ask good questions as well about the details of the position, the company culture, and who you would be reporting to. Even though the interviewer might not be empowered to hire you, this interview counts as much as any other. There are several ways to demonstrate your competent communication skills in a phone interview:

1. *Come prepared*. Keep materials on hand such as your resume and company notes. Use a landline or be sure to be in an area with a strong cell signal.

2. *Eliminate distractions* such as text alerts, incoming calls, and background noises. Keep your energy up by standing through the call. (Fun fact: Standing puts less pressure on your diaphragm so you are apt to sound clearer.)

3. *Be your best*. Act as if it is a face-to-face interview.

Finally, at the end of the interview, *thank the interviewer* for their time. Inquire as to when the hiring decision will be made and when you can expect to hear from them about next steps.

Panel Interview

The **panel interview** brings all the fun of a firing squad, as three or more hiring managers interview you at once. Expect to spend between 45 minutes to an hour fielding questions from multiple stakeholders, in person or virtually. As with any type of interview, bring your A game: solid preparation and confidence. Follow the guidelines for the one-on-one interview and also do your best to *Learn the names and roles of all interviewers in advance*. This way you can better know which questions to ask which interviewer, and you can address them by name.

Monitor your nonverbal communication. Sit up, make eye contact with all interviewers equally, and speak loudly, clearly and at a reasonable rate. When in doubt, slow down.

As with each interview type, at the end *thank the interviewers* for their time. Inquire as to when the hiring decision will be made and when you can expect to hear from them about next steps.

Interview Follow-up

The interview is over! Exhale! Now you can sit back, slouch, and lace your fingers together as you wait for the job offer to come in. Hardly. In the space between interview and offer, there is more work to be done.

Express Gratitude: Pen a Worthy Thank-you Note

You worked so hard to make a great first impression, now follow that with a solid thank-you note to make a strong lasting impression. Email a note to each person you interviewed with as quickly as right after the interview and no later than 24 hours after the meeting. Keep it short but personalize it for each company. Thank them for their time, reinforce your interest in the company and position, and express your desire to hear from them.

Subject: Thank you for today's interview

Dear (interviewer's name, stated as they introduced themselves to you), Thank you for taking the time out of your busy schedule to talk with me about the (job title) position at (company's name).

I particularly appreciate the information you provided about the three branches of talent development, your company's commitment to the four core values, and the general scope of the open position. Your thoughtful questions gave me a chance to clarify my strengths and interest.

I look forward to hearing about the next steps.

Send a Follow-up Note: Remain Patient

As tempting as it may be to check up on the status of the position, Art Markman, professor of Psychology and Marketing at the University of Texas, counsels applicants to wait until *1 week after* the date the interviewer said they would get back to you. He explains that even though they might make an offer to someone else, that person might not accept the position and the job could open up for you. He suggests sending a note on par with the thank-you email, and no more than three paragraphs. Confirm your continued interest in the position, stay positive, and ask if they need anything else from you.

> *Subject: Follow up from 1/15 interview*
>
> *Dear (interviewer's name, stated as they introduced themselves to you),*
>
> *Hello!*
>
> *I am following up about my interview on (date) for the (position). I noted that we were to connect last week and I wondered if you had made your decision. I am still very interested in joining your team. I am impressed with (company's) innovative culture and think I could contribute positively to the projects we discussed.*
>
> *Is there any additional information I can provide? I look forward to hearing from you either way.*
>
> *Thank you, again, for your time.*

Get Better: Seek feedback

If you aren't offered the position but think the interview went well, it's acceptable to send an email requesting feedback. Keep it simple and upbeat.

> *Subject: Interview feedback request*
>
> *Dear (interviewer's name, stated as they introduced themselves to you),*
>
> *Hello!*
>
> *While I was disappointed that I didn't get the position of (job title) I interviewed for, I welcome feedback as to how I can improve my interviewing skills for future opportunities. Would you please tell me one thing I did well in the interview and one thing I could strengthen? I am always seeking to better myself and appreciate your perspective.*
>
> *Again, thank you for taking the time to interview me.*

SUMMARY

Finding a job can be an arduous process. Sharpening your business communication skills will help you increase your knowledge; it will increase your confidence and help you stand out to prospective employers. Whether entering the workforce, aiming for a promotion, or changing careers, the adage "Pay now or pay later"

applies. The implied meaning of that commercial phrase, originally from an oil filter commercial that aired in the 70s and 80s, is that you can be proactive and pay a price now (change your oil filter), or you can ignore the preparation and pay a much bigger price later (buy a new engine). By following the information in this chapter, your currency is your investment of time. You "pay now" by researching the company, refining your social media presence, and preparing for all parts of the interview. Conversely, if you don't do the pre-work, you could pay much more later, perhaps by missing out on a dream job. We champion the former: Pay now. Your due diligence will *pay off* later.

Film School Case Studies

The Intern (2015). Comedy/Drama. PG-13

Robert DeNiro plays Ben Whittaker, a 70-year-old widower who takes an internship at a web start-up. Analyze his performance during his job interview conducted by his boss played by Anne Hathaway. What type of interview is it?

TED Talks and YouTube Videos

These TED Talks and YouTube videos can be accessed by going to the Oxford Learning Link for It's All of Our Business *or by typing the title of the video into a Google search window.*

"The Internship"

"How do you spend a typical day?"

"The Pursuit of Happyness"

"How to Stay Calm When You Know You'll Be Stressed."

"Grit: The Power of Passion and Perseverance" by Angela Duckworth

After successful completion of this chapter,
you should be able to

1. Define conflict in both its constructive and destructive forms.

2. Understand the strengths and appropriate application of the five principal communication styles of conflict management.

3. Explore task, relationship, and value conflicts as they pertain to business communication.

Conflict Management: A Common Experience

(BASED ON REAL EVENTS—*names have been changed to permit slight alterations in some factual details.*) Open warfare raged for almost a year at public radio station K-I-L-L (slogan: "Live radio that'll knock you dead"). The station operated from facilities on the campus of Bayview Community College in Tsunami, California. KILL radio had 1,000 watts of power, enough to reach into the local Tsunami community (population 42,000).

The program director quit after a feud with the general manager (GM). The GM resigned soon after. His reasons included the volunteer staff (community members who were not students) inappropriately editorialized while reading news on the air and presented only one side on controversial issues, both violations of Federal Communications Commission (FCC) regulations for public radio stations. The FCC notes that "rigging or slanting the news is a most heinous act against the public interest," and "the FCC will investigate a station for news distortion if it receives documented

CHAPTER OUTLINE

- Nature of Conflict
- Communication Styles of Conflict Management
- Situational Factors
- Anger Management
- Virtual Communication and Conflict
- Culture and Conflict

4. Choose from several strategies for dealing with difficult coworkers.

5. Know how to manage anger at work, both yours and your coworker's.

6. Explore cultural responses to conflict and adapt communication accordingly.

evidence of rigging or slanting" ("The Public and Broadcasting," 2019). In addition, the volunteers were "insubordinate" when they refused to obey his directives concerning substitution of other programs for previously scheduled regular shows; and the volunteers threatened him with bodily injury when he ordered them either to implement his directives or terminate their association with the station.

The volunteer staff countered these allegations with the following: The GM showed them little respect and treated them abusively; they were overworked and underappreciated; and the GM never sought their input on programming and scheduling concerns. The volunteers issued the following demands: Programming should be determined by a consensus of the staff; program substitution should be made only when prior notice (at least 2 weeks in advance) has been given so staff members will not prepare material destined to be preempted at the last minute; and volunteers should run the station since they do the lion's share of the work and are the only ones with the necessary technical expertise. The volunteer staff threatened to quit en masse unless their demands were met.

The college supported the station with $85,000 annually but seriously considered a drastic cut in the station's budget due to the persistent conflict and because students were not actively involved in the station. The administration wanted the station to be a learning laboratory for students

interested in pursuing careers in broadcasting. The school's board of trustees got twitchy because of all the commotion. The local community highly valued the station and was upset. The college administration, in desperation, named the chair of the mass communication department as the new general manager and temporary program director of the station, a position he relished as much as poking a wasp's nest with a stick. What should have been done to manage this complicated conflict, and in most instances did occur, is discussed throughout this chapter.

The principal purpose of this chapter is to discuss communication strategies for managing workplace conflicts, such as the KILL radio fracas. Conflict in the workplace is a common experience. The most extensive and often cited study of conflict in the workplace was conducted by CPP, Inc. The study surveyed 5,000 full-time employees in nine countries from the United States and Europe and found that 85% of respondents address workplace conflict at various times, and 29% (36% in the United States) do so "always" or "frequently." Only 11% have never experienced a disagreement that escalated into personal attacks and project failures. An estimated 385 million aggregate working days are spent each year addressing conflicts (J. Hayes, 2008). The prevalence of conflict in the workplace finds further support from a more recent study of nurses, teachers, and social workers. This study found that 93% of the 1,299 subjects experienced conflict in their work settings (Tafvelin et al., 2019). Although conflict is common in the workplace, managing conflict competently is not so commonplace (Hastings, 2012).

In previous chapters, sources of conflict were discussed at length, such as rule violations, establishing a negative workplace communication climate, poor listening, and especially imbalances of power—"a fundamental element of every conflict interaction" (Canary & Lakey, 2013). Building on this foundation, *this chapter has the following objectives*: (1) defining conflict, distinguishing its constructive and destructive form; (2) discussing how to transact conflict effectively in the workplace; (3) learning how to deal with difficult coworkers; (4) exploring ways to manage your anger and the anger of others; and (5) recognizing cultural influences on conflict management in the workplace.

Nature of Conflict

The KILL Radio case study provides a means of explaining the general definition of conflict. In this section, destructive and constructive conflict are also differentiated.

Definition: Incompatible, Interconnected Struggle

In general, **conflict** is the expressed struggle of interconnected parties who perceive incompatible goals and interference from each other in attaining those goals (Wilmot & Hocker, 2021). You can see all elements of this definition in the KILL radio battle.

First, *conflict is an expressed struggle between parties*. If the participants in the radio station conflict had merely sat and stewed over perceived outrages, then no conflict would have existed because parties involved wouldn't have known there was a problem. Often the expression of a struggle is verbally manifested as in threatening bodily injury, such as occurred between the parties at the radio station. Occasionally, the expression is nonverbal, as in ignoring specific directions from the GM.

Second, *conflict occurs between interconnected parties*. For a conflict to exist, the behavior of one or more parties must produce consequences for the other party or parties. Clearly, consequences to opposing parties in the radio station conflict were evident. Both the GM and the program director quit, leaving the station in chaos.

Third, *conflict involves perceived incompatible goals* (Canary & Lakey, 2013). The staff demand that it run the station was incompatible with the role of the GM. The program director and the staff were engaged in a power struggle regarding programming decisions.

Finally, *conflict involves interference from each other in attaining desired goals*. Unless one party attempts to block the attainment of another party's goal, there is no conflict. Clearly, both sides in the KILL radio dispute interfered with attainment of respective goals.

Benefits of Conflict: Dissent Can Be Productive

Conflict for most people is as welcome as an IRS audit. Most conflict probably seems destructive given how poorly conflict is typically managed (Kerwin et al., 2011), and frequent conflict can be counterproductive because it can interfere with task accomplishment. *Moderate amounts of conflict can be a constructive force in the workplace if the conflict is managed competently.* Conflict can instigate positive changes, promote creative problem solving and innovative thinking, and encourage power balancing (Dovidio et al., 2009; Omisore & Abiodun, 2014). "The key to effective team negotiation and group decision making is constructive dissent—disagreements that respectfully and productively challenge others' viewpoints" ("Fostering Constructive Conflict," 2020). Constructive conflict in which teams are not only permitted to dissent but encouraged to express disagreement can prevent groupthink, a defective decision-making process that can produce disasters, as addressed more directly in Chapter 9. Although conflict can be constructive, it can also be destructive. So, what distinguishes the two?

Destructive or Constructive Conflict: Communication Differences

Destructive conflict is characterized by communication that is dominating, escalating, retaliating, competing, and exhibits defensiveness and inflexibility (Wilmot & Hocker, 2021). When conflicts spiral out of control, participants lose sight of their initial goals and focus on hurting their adversary. The KILL radio conflict was essentially a destructive conflict. Escalation, threats, inflexibility on both sides, and expressions of contempt and ridicule occurred. Neither side seemed able to work together to negotiate a mutually satisfactory solution to the conflict before the college Board stepped in and appointed a new GM.

Recognizing destructive conflict while it is occurring may not always be easy. *When it becomes obvious to you that "Gee, I'm getting stupid," you are engaged in destructive conflict* (Donohue & Kolt, 1992), but this requires a certain amount of self-awareness and mindfulness ("Conflict Is Destructive," 2018). When you take honest stock of yourself and realize that you are engaging in petty, even infantile tactics to win an argument, you are roaming in destructive conflict territory. Gossiping, backstabbing, and spreading malicious rumors are additional, obvious examples of stoking destructive conflict at work. Becoming physically and verbally aggressive can also be destructive. This does not mean that you can never raise your voice, express frustration, or disagree with others. *Conflict can remain constructive even when discussion becomes somewhat contentious*. When conflict becomes more emotional and impulsive than reasonable, and when you cannot think straight because you are too consumed by anger, then conflict has become destructive.

Constructive conflict is characterized by We-oriented, de-escalating, cooperative, supportive, and flexible communication patterns (Wilmot & Hocker, 2021). *The principal focus is on striving to achieve a solution between struggling parties that is mutually satisfactory to*

When coworkers escalate a conflict to the point of "getting stupid," they exhibit destructive conflict.

everyone. Even if no mutually satisfactory solution is achieved or even possible (e.g., you disagree with the company dress code, but it is set by "corporate" and cannot be changed locally), the communication process that characterizes constructive conflict allows conflicting parties to maintain cordial relationships while agreeing to disagree.

Communication Styles of Conflict Management

Communication is central to conflict management in the workplace. Our communication can signal that conflict exists, it can create conflict, and it can be the means for managing conflict constructively or destructively. Consequently, communication styles have been the center of much research and discussion. A **communication style of conflict management** is a tendency to manage conflict in a certain way. Individuals may exhibit a specific style, or an entire group may adopt a normative preference for a certain style of conflict management. There are five communication styles of conflict management: collaborating, accommodating, compromising, avoiding, and competing (S. E. Howell, 2014; "Thomas-Kilmann Conflict Mode," 2021).

Before delving into a discussion of these styles, let's clarify why we have chosen the term conflict "management," not "resolution." "Resolution" suggests settling conflict by ending it (Elgoibar et al., 2017), as if that is always desirable. *Since conflict can be an essential catalyst for growth, increasing conflict may be required to evoke change* (D. W. Johnson & Johnson, 2000). Women who file sexual harassment lawsuits provoke conflict to end an evil. "Managing conflict" implies no end to the struggle. Although some conflict episodes end, and are therefore resolved, conflict overall in the workplace is a continuous phenomenon that waxes and wanes.

Collaborating: Problem Solving

The most complex and potentially productive communication style of conflict management is collaborating, or what some refer to as problem solving. The **collaborating style** is a win–win, cooperative approach to conflict that attempts to satisfy all parties. The emphasis is on what Daniel Shapiro (2017), founder and director of the Harvard International Negotiation Program, calls the "relentless We." Conflict is viewed as "a shared challenge," not an us-against-them degeneration into tribal clashes. *Someone employing this style balances a high concern for both task and social relationships*. A collaborating style has three key components: confrontation, integration, and smoothing.

Confrontation: Directly Addressing the Problem The overt recognition that conflict exists in the workplace and the direct effort to manage it effectively is called **confrontation**. Although the news media are fond of using the term confrontation in a negative sense, as in "There was a violent confrontation between protesters and police," this is not the meaning relevant to this discussion. Confrontation as a conflict-management technique incorporates all the elements already discussed at length regarding assertiveness and supportive communication patterns. *The purpose of confrontation is to manage conflict in a productive way for all parties* (Dubrin, 2019).

The KILL radio case cried out for collaboration. The new GM should, and did, immediately meet with the volunteers individually and actively listened to their perspective. He let them tell their story without offering correction or rebuttal. Staff members felt unappreciated and undervalued. Supportive, confirming statements concerning the essential role volunteers played in the functioning of the station were made to all involved.

Not all issues are worth confronting. Members who confront even trivial differences of opinion or can't let a momentary flash of pique go unaddressed can be like annoying online pop-up ads. Groups must decide which issues and concerns are priorities and which are tangential.

Integration: Seeking Joint Gains Decision making often involves conflicts of interest.

Integration is a creative approach to conflicts of interest; it searches for solutions that benefit everyone. There are two key tactics: expanding the pie and bridging.

Expanding the pie refers to increasing resources as a solution to a problem ("Integrative Negotiation Examples," 2017). When faced with scarce resources, groups often become competitive and experience serious strife, warring over who gets the biggest or best piece of the limited resource pie (e.g., money, staffing, etc.). Parties in conflict, however, sometimes accept the inevitability of scarce resources—called the *"bias of the fixed pie"*—without fully exploring options that might expand the resources and empower the group ("Creating Value," 2020). For example, projects can sometimes be crowdfunded to raise money outside of traditional budgetary sources ("Crowdfunding," 2021).

Integrating the KILL radio station into the college curriculum was actually a fairly simple process. Involving students in the actual operation of the station as supervised interns earning class credit satisfied a primary concern of the administration and board. This also expanded the resources of the station by training additional individuals to help staff members who already felt overworked.

Bridging is the second type of integrative solution to conflicts. **Bridging** looks for overarching (sometimes referred to as superordinate) goals that find common ground to move beyond conflicts of interest toward mutual interest ("Four Conflict Negotiating Strategies," 2020). In the KILL radio station conflict, the overarching goal of all parties was to keep the station running. Violating FCC regulations could have resulted in the loss of the station's license, resulting in the shutdown of the station ("The Public and Broadcasting," 2019). No one wanted that to occur. Impetus to resolve the dispute was galvanized once the new GM made it clear that all parties must pull together in mutual interest (maintaining the viability of the station).

Smoothing: *Calming Troubled Waters* The act of calming the agitated feelings of group members during a conflict episode is called **smoothing**. When tempers ignite and anger morphs into screaming and shedding of tears, no collaboration is possible. A simple "I'm sorry" is a useful smoothing response. "Let's all calm down. Attacking each other won't help us find a solution" is another example of smoothing. Calming the emotional storm opens the way to confronting conflict and brainstorming integrative solutions. In the KILL radio case, smoothing hurt feelings was essential for the new GM to address. Smoothing statements (e.g., "We're starting fresh. I want us to work together") was delivered to the staff to calm troubled waters.

Since collaborating is such an effective communication style for solving conflicts of interest, why isn't it always used in these situations? There are several reasons. First, *collaborating usually requires a significant investment of time and effort along with greater-than-ordinary communication skills.* Even if you want to collaborate, it requires mutually agreeable parties. Second, *collaboration is built on trust.* If parties are suspicious of each other and worry that one will betray the other by not honoring agreements, then even an integrative solution may be rejected. Third, *parties in a conflict sometimes do not share the same emotional investment in finding a mutually agreeable solution.* Hypercompetitive group members want a clear "victory," not a solution that benefits all parties.

Accommodating: Yielding

The **accommodating style** yields to the concerns and desires of others. *Someone using this style shows a high concern for social relationships but low concern for task accomplishment.* This style may camouflage deep divisions among group members to maintain the appearance of harmony. If the task can be accomplished without social disruption, fine. If accomplishing the task threatens to jeopardize the harmonious relationships within the group, however, a person using this style will opt for giving members what they want, even though this may sacrifice productivity. *Generally, group members with less power are expected to accommodate more often and to a greater degree than more powerful members.*

Although we tend to view accommodating in a negative light, as appeasement, this style can be positive. A group that has experienced protracted strife may rejoice when one side accommodates, even on an issue of minor importance (Shonk, 2022).

Compromising: Halving the Loaf

With the **compromising style**, we give up something to get something. Some have referred to this as a lose–lose style of conflict management because neither party is ever fully satisfied with the solution. Compromising is choosing a middle ground. *Someone using this style shows a moderate concern for both task and social relationships in groups* (Zarankin, 2008). The emphasis is on workable but not necessarily optimal solutions.

In the KILL radio case, one or two experimental programs were tried as a compromise when community preferences did not match staff preferences in programming. Some compromise on program substitution (a 1-week prior notice, not 2 weeks as demanded) was also instituted with agreeable success.

Compromise evokes ambivalence—both negative and positive reactions (Jaffe, 2012). We speak disparagingly of those who would "compromise their integrity." On some issues, usually moral or ethical conflicts, compromise is thought to be intolerable. Yet despite this negative view, members of task forces, ad hoc groups, and committees of many shapes and sizes often seek a compromise as an admirable goal. Half a loaf is better than starvation—not in all circumstances, but certainly in some. *When an integrative solution cannot be achieved, when a temporary settlement is the only feasible alternative, or when the issues involved are not considered critical to the group, compromise can be useful*.

Avoiding: Withdrawing

Avoiding is a communicating style of withdrawing from potentially contentious and unpleasant struggles. Flights from fights may seem constructive at the time because they circumvent unpleasantness. Facing problems, however, proves to be more effective than running from them. *Someone using the avoiding conflict style shows little concern for both task and social relationships in groups*. Avoiders shrink from conflict, even fear it. By avoiding conflict, they hope it will disappear. It may instead increase relationship conflict (Cohen, 2020).

Avoiding, nevertheless, is sometimes appropriate (Elgoibar et al., 2017). If you are a

As Keith Ferrazzi and his colleagues (2021) suggest, "When it feels like there's an elephant in the room, [a metaphorical reference to an important controversial issue being avoided by participants], leaders of high-performing teams create what we call 'candor breaks' to encourage team members to share their thoughts and feelings." Avoiding the obvious difficult controversies even when they are small can lead to much greater and more troublesome conflict later.

low-power person in a group, and the consequences of confrontation are potentially hazardous to you, avoiding might be a reasonable strategy until other alternatives present themselves. Standing up to a bully may work out well in movies, but confronting antisocial types who look like they eat raw meat for breakfast and might eat you for lunch may not be a very bright choice. Staying out of a bully's way, although perhaps ego-deflating, may be the best *temporary option* in a bad situation.

If the advantages of confrontation do not outweigh the disadvantages, avoiding the conflict might be a desirable course of action. In some cases, tempers need to cool. Avoiding contentious issues for a time may prove to be constructive. ("Let's deal with this later when we've had a chance to simmer down a bit, okay?") We often make foolish, irrational choices when we are highly stressed. In addition, if differences among group members are intractable (e.g., personality clashes), avoiding the differences and focusing on task accomplishment may be a desirable approach. Again, in the KILL radio case, the demand that the volunteers run the station was pointless. There was no way that the college board would have approved considerable funds to support a public radio station run by unsupervised volunteers. More than likely, however, this demand was made without any expectation that it would be accepted. The GM wisely avoided the issue, no staff member raised it again, and it disappeared into the ether.

In most cases, however, avoiding rather than confronting is highly counterproductive (Elgoibar et al., 2017). Failure to address conflict promptly can lead to destructive conflict later, while addressing conflict without delay usually prevents escalation into destructive conflict.

Power-forcing is a hard bargaining style of conflict management that typically builds rigid verbal and nonverbal metaphorical walls in win–lose contests. The results are usually unproductive and often produce an impasse or destructive conflict.

Competing: Power-Forcing

When we approach conflict as a win–lose contest, we are using the **competing style**. This style, sometimes referred to as *hard bargaining*, is communicated in a variety of ways that are likely to produce destructive conflict: threats, criticism, contempt, hostile remarks and jokes, sarcasm, ridicule, intimidation, fault-finding and blaming, and denials of responsibility (Wilmot & Hocker, 2021). The competing style is aggressive, not assertive. It is not confrontation as previously defined; it is an attack. It flows from the dominance perspective on power. *Someone using a competing or forcing style shows high concern for task but low concern for relationships.* If accomplishing the group task requires a few wounded egos, that is thought to be the unavoidable price of productivity.

In the KILL radio case, power-forcing would have been required if staff violations of FCC regulations continued. Staff desire to editorialize on the air at will was irrelevant. The law could not be violated. Handling other issues effectively, however, reduced this issue to virtual irrelevance.

Communication Styles of Conflict Management

Style	Task—Social Dimension
Collaborating (problem solving)	High task, high social
Accommodating (yielding)	Low task, high social
Compromising (halving the loaf)	Moderate task, moderate social
Avoiding (withdrawing)	Low task, low social
Competing (power-forcing)	High task, low social

All five styles of conflict management show different emphases on task and social dimensions of groups. Nevertheless, someone using the competing style, for example, may in some circumstances manifest genuine concern for social climate. Low concern does not mean no concern. *All styles represent tendencies, not unalterably fixed ways of managing conflict in every situation.*

Comparing Styles: Likelihood of Effectiveness

Research clearly favors some conflict styles over others, even though more than one style may need to be used over the course of a conflict (S. E. Howell, 2014). Overall, the collaborating style produces the best decisions and greatest satisfaction from parties in conflict (Dubrin, 2019; Shonk, 2021c), avoiding typically produces poor results, and the competing/forcing style is least effective (Prieto-Remon et al., 2015). This is true for interpersonal and face-to-face or virtual groups (Paul et al., 2005). Collaborating encourages constructive conflict; competing tends to promote destructive conflict (Elgoibar et al., 2017; Somech et al., 2008). You have a choice. As author Max Lucado observes, "Conflict is inevitable, but combat is optional" ("103 Best Max Lucado Quotes," 2022).

Despite the clear benefits of collaborating, poor results of avoiding, the disadvantages of competing, and mixed results for accommodating and compromising, *we seem to use the least effective styles most often to manage conflict in the workplace* (K. W. Thomas & Thomas, 2008). Studies of doctor–nurse abuse, for example, found that avoidance was a chief style used by nurses (C. Johnson, 2009). One study showed that fewer than 7% of nurses confronted abusive doctors (Maxfield et al., 2005). Another study found that nursing students viewed their nursing educators as favoring the use of avoiding, with integration (collaborating) as the least likely conflict style used (Hashish et al., 2015). In the nursing profession overall, conflict styles are typically used in this order of frequency: compromising, competing, avoiding, accommodating, and finally collaborating (Iglesias & Vallejo, 2012). In a review of more than two dozen workplace studies, the power-forcing style was the most common approach used by managers, both male and female, with employee groups (Dildar & Amjad, 2017). Among employees engaged in conflict with their peers at work, "male employees consistently use more competing strategy (dominating) than female employees" (Rahim & Katz, 2019).

Even if the style with the greatest likelihood of success is chosen, when and how it is used must also be figured into the equation. *Confrontation used as a collaborative tactic can be highly effective, but it won't be if used in a hit-and-run fashion.* Confronting contentious issues 5 minutes before a group is due to adjourn a business meeting provides no time for anyone to respond constructively. Hit-and-run confrontations look like guerrilla tactics, not attempts to communicate competently and work out disputes. Likewise, when to use power-forcing is an important concern. *Competing/power-forcing should be a style of last resort, except in times of emergencies in which quick, decisive action must be taken and discussion has no place* (Elgoibar et al., 2017). Power-forcing typically produces psychological reactance (see Chapter 5). If you try to force before using other styles and are met with defiance, then you attempt to collaborate or accommodate, you may find that

Conditions for Communication Styles

	Appropriate	Inappropriate
Collaborating	Complex issues First approach Ample time	Trivial issues Last resort Time constraints
Accommodating	Trivial issues Issues significant only to one side Maintaining relationships Large power imbalance	Complex issues Issues significant to all parties Social relationships temporary Relatively equal power
Compromising	No integrative solution Temporary solution better than no agreement	Giving up too soon on critical issues
Avoiding	Issues are trivial Hazardous to confront Need temporary break	Issues are significant Ignoring disagreements may damage relationships May increase anger by ignoring issues
Competing	Timely decision required Last resort Disruptive member unresponsive to other approaches	Time is not a constraint First option Concern for positive social relations critical (especially collectivist cultures)

this sequence of styles will fail. Trying to collaborate after unsuccessfully power-forcing will be seen as the disingenuous act of a person whose bluff and bluster were challenged. On the other hand, temporarily withdrawing after a protracted feud has stalemated might allow heads to clear and passions to cool. Sometimes we just need a "time out," a chance to think calmly.

Situational Factors

Although some communication styles of conflict management have a higher probability of effectiveness than others, the choice of styles always operates within a context. To understand how to transact conflict effectively in the workplace, certain situational factors should be considered.

Task Conflict: Routine or Nonroutine

Whether conflicts regarding group tasks are beneficial or detrimental depends largely on the type of task, routine or nonroutine, performed by the group (Jehn, 1995; Yousaf et al.,

2020). A **routine task** is one in which the group performs processes and procedures that have little variability and little likelihood of change. General accounting and technical support are examples. Such routine business is also known as general operations. A **nonroutine task** is one that requires problem solving, has only a few set procedures, and has a high level of uncertainty, even risk (e.g., cleaning a hazardous waste spill at a business site). *Conflicts regarding routine tasks easily deteriorate into gripe sessions with little opportunity for resolution.* Buildings have to be maintained, bills have to be paid, equipment needs to be serviced, reports have to be completed. Dan serves on the local Metro Transit Board. All board members must complete a required financial disclosure form every year. Complaining about this tedious, time-consuming routine task is unproductive. You just do it because it is the law. These routine tasks may be boring and repetitive, even irritating, but they must occur or you are just asking for needless trouble. Conversely, *task conflict on nonroutine tasks can be beneficial by triggering group productivity and creativity* (Tafvelin et al., 2019).

Relationship Conflict: It's Personal

Conflicts are not always about task accomplishment. Some are about interpersonal or group relationships arising from differences in personality, style, even outright dislike between coworkers (Shonk, 2021a; see the next section on dealing with difficult coworkers).

We make style choices depending on our relationships with group members. Communication is transactional. Confronting coworkers about their narcissistic personality, for example, is usually a fool's errand. People do not change their personality easily even after concentrated effort and training (Vitelli, 2015). You may choose avoidance when personality clashes occur. You may even redesign your space to avoid volatile conflicts until a more favorable working arrangement emerges. The reality of power imbalances sometimes makes choosing accommodation a matter of self-preservation. Lower-power group members may want to collaborate. Dominating, high-power group members may see little need to collaborate since they can impose their will on subordinates ("Do it because I say so"). Accommodation may be necessary to avoid negative consequences of defiance.

A conflict initially about task accomplishment can easily become a relationship conflict that can have a toxic impact on teams, especially startup entrepreneurial groups (Kozusznik et al., 2020). When working on a group project, some group members may exhibit social loafing. Such lackluster effort from some members can trigger relationship conflict. Those members who wish to achieve a productive outcome may lash out at loafers. Anger can erupt, and relationship conflict can escalate into destructive conflict and poor overall group performance. As previously discussed, conflict is sometimes constructive, but not when it deteriorates into nasty relationship conflict (Tafvelin et al., 2019).

Establishing trust among team members is a key component necessary to prevent task conflict from mutating into nasty relationship conflict (Curseu & Schruijer 2010). How to build trust was discussed in Chapter 5. In relationships poisoned by mistrust, a collaborative attempt by one party may be seen as a ploy to gain some unforeseen advantage. Accommodating by one party, even as a gesture to change the negative dynamics of the parties in conflict, may be viewed as weakness and a sign that capitulation is likely to occur after a period of waiting. Also, research shows that perceived team performance impacts the rise or fall of relationship conflict in groups. *Low-performing teams experience increased relationship conflict; high performing teams experience the opposite* (Guenter et al., 2016). Finally, *developing relational closeness* with members of your group can act as a buffer against relationship conflict sprouting into harmful results. "Relationship conflicts are only harmful in relationally distant work groups in which members do not know each other well personally and do not feel close to each other" (Rispens et al., 2011). Sometimes just getting to know your coworkers or group members and finding common interests, pursuits, and life experiences may help build greater closeness (Shonk, 2021c).

Values Conflict: Deeply Felt Struggles

The most difficult disputes to manage are often values conflicts ("Four Conflict Negotiation Strategies," 2018). As noted previously, values are the most deeply felt views of what is deemed good, worthwhile, or ethically right. Beliefs are what we think is true or probable. "Smartphones are an indispensable means of communicating" or "Texting is more efficient than using email" are beliefs that do not ordinarily degenerate into fistfights or verbal assaults. How odd would that be if they did? We may clash over beliefs and still walk away as friends, especially if the ideas do not touch much on values. When disputes about beliefs spill over into value clashes, however, especially when the values are held passionately, then you have a conflict of a different ilk. Battles over sexual harassment, bullying, hate speech, and the like are fundamentally about values such as morality, respect, freedom, fairness, and equality. Such conflicts do not lend themselves easily to compromise (would you compromise your values?). Nevertheless, moving beyond demonization of those who fundamentally disagree on values and seeking a "values-neutral" attempt to understand without judgment may help to defuse what could degenerate into explosive, destructive conflict (Shonk, 2021c).

Unfortunately, when intransigent, dichotomous battle lines are drawn—friends versus enemies—power-forcing is often the style required for conflict management. The courts have had to settle polarizing issues by declaring what is permissible and what is prohibited. As noted in Chapter 3, company values and strict adherence to policies regarding sexual harassment, bullying, and gender bias, a systemic approach, can prevent power-forcing legal nightmares from occurring.

Dealing with Difficult Coworkers: Bad Apple Spoilage

Research by Will Felps and his colleagues (2006) on "**bad apples**"—disruptive members who poison the group ("One bad apple spoils the barrel")—demonstrates just how disturbing difficult coworkers can be ("Ruining It for the Rest of Us," 2008). They foment destructive conflict. A skilled student actor portrayed three versions of disruptive, or "bad apple" behavior in several small groups. He played a *jerk* who made insulting remarks to other group members, such as "Do you know anything?" and "That's a stupid idea." He played a *slacker* who wouldn't contribute during a 45-minute challenging group task, text messaged a friend, and responded with "whatever" or "I really don't care" to other group members' ideas. Finally, he played a *depressive pessimist* who put his head on the table, complained about the task being boring, and predicted group failure. (For additional bad apple behavior see "disruptive roles" discussed in Chapter 9.)

The results were startling. *No matter how talented team members were, those groups that had to deal with the one bad apple scored 30% to 40% lower on a challenging task than teams with no bad apple.* Disruptive behavior was also contagious. When playing the jerk,

Values conflicts are often the most volatile and challenging to address constructively. When left with perceived "no choice," power-forcing strategies (e.g., strikes) are often the result.

group members would respond to insults from the bad apple with insults of their own; when playing the slacker, group members would assume slacker behavior and say, "Let's just get this over with. Put down anything"; and when playing the depressive pessimist, other group members became cynical and disengaged.

There are several fundamental steps that should be taken by a group when dealing with a difficult coworker.

1. *Make certain the team climate is positive* (see Chapter 5). If your team creates a ruthlessly competitive, politicized climate where decision making is influenced by rumor mongering, backstabbing, deal making, and sabotaging the efforts of other members, then difficult team members will appear like flies at a summer picnic (Lafasto & Larson, 2001). As previously explained, although you may not be in a power position that mandates positive behavior, modelling such behavior can influence the group climate.

2. *The team should establish a clear code of conduct for all members*. This code should spell out specific unacceptable behaviors (e.g., insults, rudeness, threats, bigoted statements). The Joint Commission on Accreditation of Healthcare Organizations required just such a code of conduct for its 15,000 healthcare organizations because of disruptive behavior between doctors and nurses. The code is viewed as "an essential element" in addressing such disruptive behavior (Grenny, 2009).

3. *Change your communication in relation to a difficult person's behavior*. Disrupters thrive on provoking retaliation. Do not counter abusive remarks with abusive remarks of your own. Fighting fire with fire ignites a firestorm.

4. *Confront the difficult person*. If your boss is the difficult person, this likely will not be your appropriate choice. If the difficult coworker is a peer, however, and the entire team is upset by the behavior, then the group should confront the disrupter. Even truly abrasive individuals will find it tough to ignore pressure from an entire group. State what behavior is offensive and encourage more constructive behavior as detailed in Chapter 5.

5. *Separate yourself from the difficult person if all else fails*. Some individuals leave no other option except removal from the group, but this could be positive. One clothing retailer, for example, fired his top-selling employee who was a bad apple. The sales at the store skyrocketed nearly 30% once the bad apple was jettisoned from the small sales group (Sutton, 2011). If the difficult person is powerful, expulsion may not be an option. In this case, try putting physical distance between you and the problem person. Keep interactions to a minimum.

We have presented you with a rational model for handling troublemakers. Nevertheless, we are not strictly rational beings. Difficult people can provoke intense anger and deep frustration. In our own experience, even if we lost our temper and let our emotions get the better of us, this response seemed less problematic than ignoring or enduring the disruptive behavior. At the very least you have served notice on the troublesome group member that his or her pattern of behavior is unacceptable and will not be suffered in silence.

Anger Management

Conflict often produces anger and vice versa (Fisher & Shapiro, 2005). *Workplace anger is widespread*. One survey found that more than half (52%) of workers admit to losing their temper on the job (De Rose, 2018). Although it is not always harmful to dispute resolution in groups, anger can easily trigger a tit-for-tat response of retaliatory anger from others that disrupts constructive negotiations (Friedman et al., 2004). *The most commonly reported verbal and nonverbal communication behaviors associated with workplace anger include a potpourri of personal assaults*: yelling, swearing, hurling insults, using sarcasm, criticizing, crying, giving dirty looks, making angry gestures, throwing things, and physical assault (Glomb, 2002; C. Johnson, 2009). Thus, managing anger is an important aspect of constructive conflict management in groups.

Constructive and Destructive Anger: Intensity and Duration

Anger is sometimes justified. Your boss criticizes you, igniting justifiable anger because he did it in front of your coworkers and the criticism was unwarranted. Anger, however, can be counterproductive in the workplace. *Constructive and destructive anger can be distinguished depending on two communication conditions: the intensity and the duration of the anger expression* (Cash et al., 2018). The **intensity** of anger can vary from mild irritation to outright rage. The more intense the anger, the more likely it is that outcomes will be negative. Mild to moderate expressions of anger can signal problems that must be addressed in groups. In such circumstances, the anger can be constructive. One study found that moderate expressions of anger produced greater concessions during negotiations than either no anger or high-intensity anger (Adam & Brett, 2018). *Rage, however, is destructive*. It is the antithesis of competent communication. In the workplace, temper tantrums, ranting, and screaming fits make you look like a lunatic because you are "getting stupid." When used as a power-forcing strategy during conflict, it will likely provoke counter-rage, perhaps even leading to violence.

The **duration**, or how long the anger lasts, also determines whether anger is constructive or destructive. The length of an anger episode can vary from momentary to prolonged. Quick flashes of anger may hardly cause coworkers to notice. Even intense anger, if brief, can underline that you are very upset without causing irreparable damage. Prolonged expressions of anger, even if mild, however, can cause coworkers and team members to tune out and ignore you. Highly intense anger that is long-lasting is a combustible combination. *Venting our anger, despite popular notions to the contrary, merely rehearses our anger and can increase it* (Salters-Pedneault, 2019). "Blowing off steam" awakens our anger. It does not put it to bed.

Managing Your Anger at Work: Taking Control

There are several steps you can take to diffuse your own anger when you sense that it is approaching the "getting stupid" destructive stage of intensity and duration.

1. *Reframe self-talk*. There are numerous triggers for anger: you're treated with indifference by your boss or coworkers, you're impatient because of stress, your expectations are unrealized, you perceive unjustified criticism, past traumatic events, being a victim of abuse, among other experiences (McKay et al., 2018). Thoughts also trigger anger. If you think a coworker intentionally sabotaged your work, you feel righteously

Yes, expressing rage can make you appear deranged. Imagine attempting to communicate reasonably with someone who appears so out of control. Rage is anger intensity that is unproductive and ill-advised in just about any workplace circumstance. If faced with someone who is enraged, be asymmetrical—exhibit calm and resist matching rage with your own rage. "Two heads are better than one, but one is better than none" (Fisher & Brown, 1988).

angry, perhaps even vengeful. If you believe that no sabotage was intended and that there was merely a misunderstanding, then anger usually does not ignite or it subsides quickly when the misunderstanding becomes apparent. As a first step in managing your own anger, try assuming coworkers did not intend to harm you. View harm as accidental or simply the result of clumsiness unless there is clear evidence to the contrary. Reframing the way we think about events that trigger our anger can deflate the anger before it escalates (Leanza, 2015).

2. *Listen nondefensively*. When group members criticize, blame, or ridicule you, refuse to be defensive. Reframe the criticism or blame as a challenge or problem, not an opportunity for retaliation. Counter defensive communication from others with supportive communication (see Chapter 5).

3. *Deliberately calm yourself*. Exercise discipline and refuse to vent your anger (Shinn, 2018). When you sense anger boiling to the surface, deliberately slow your breathing. Count to 10 before responding to collect yourself. A cooling-off period often works well to calm your anger (Gottman & Gottman, 2006). Typically, it takes about 20 minutes to recover from a surge of adrenaline that accompanies anger (Goleman, 1995).

4. *Find distractions*. Ruminating, focusing your thoughts on what makes you angry, can bring them to a boiling point. Do not rehearse your anger by constantly revisiting past injustices or slights instigated by fellow group members. Distract yourself when old wounds resurface (Tartakovsky, 2018a). Play a video game, scan social media, play with the dog, or take a walk with someone and discuss subjects unrelated to the anger-inducing subject.

Do not attempt to employ all four of these steps at once. Pick one and work on making it an automatic response when your anger wells up, then try a second step, and so on.

Managing the Anger of Coworkers: Communication Jujitsu

Managing conflict constructively means defusing and de-escalating the anger of other group members so you can confront issues without eruptions of verbal or physical aggression as so often occurred in workplaces that required face masks to prevent the spread of Covid. *It is usually best to address the anger of a coworker, team member, or customer first before dealing with the substance of the dispute that triggers the anger*. Try these suggestions for defusing the anger of others (Lickerman, 2013):

1. *Be asymmetrical*. When a group member is expressing anger, especially if it turns to rage, it is critical that you not strike back in kind. Be **asymmetrical**, which means do the opposite. Counter anger with absolute calm (Martin, 2015). Stay composed. "What is needed in the presence of a hot-headed person? A cool-headed person" (Persun, 2018). Hostage negotiators are trained to defuse highly volatile individuals by remaining absolutely calm throughout the interaction. Imagine the outcome if hostage negotiators flew into a rage while talking to hostage takers. Imagine the outcome if you responded to the rage of a customer with your own

Actively listening when others are upset is an important asymmetrical communication approach to defuse potential destructive conflict.

rage. Use smoothing techniques to quiet the enraged group member: "I can see that you're angry, and I want to help, but I can't understand your concern if you yell at me. So let's talk about it."

2. *Validate the other person*. Validation is a form of the smoothing technique of collaborating and showing empathy. Be an active listener. Let the person know that his or her point of view and anger have some validity, even though you may not agree (Fisher & Shapiro, 2005). You can validate another person in several ways (Wignall, 2020). First, you can take responsibility for the other person's anger. "I made you angry, didn't I?" acknowledges your role in provoking anger. Second, you can apologize. "I'm sorry. You have a right to be angry" can be a very powerful validation of the other person. Apologies, of course, should be offered only when truly warranted. Third, actively listening and acknowledging what the other person has said can also be very validating. "I know it upsets you when I don't come to meetings on time" makes the other person feel heard, even if conflict remains.

3. *Probe.* Seek information from an angry group member so you can understand his or her anger (Seppälä, 2017). When you ask a question of an angry group member, it forces the person to shift from emotional outburst to rational response. Simply asking, "Can we sit down and discuss this calmly so I can understand your point of view?" can momentarily defuse a group member's anger. If your coworker or team member is expecting a kerfuffle and you do not take the bait, probing throws them a curve that can short-circuit their anger.

4. *Assume a problem orientation*. This is supportive communication. This step should occur once you have calmed the angry group member by using previous steps. Approach the anger display as a problem to be solved, not a reason to retaliate. The question "What would you like to see occur?" invites problem solving.

5. *Refuse to be abused*. Even if you are wrong, feel guilty, or deserve another person's anger, do not permit yourself to be verbally battered (Persun, 2018). Verbal aggression is unproductive no matter who is at fault in a conflict. "I cannot discuss this with you if you insist on being abusive. I can see you're upset, but verbally assaulting me won't lead to a solution" sets a ground rule on how anger can be expressed.

6. *Disengage*. This is the final step when all else fails to defuse a team member's anger. This step is especially important if the person continues to be enraged and abusive despite your best, most constructive efforts to calm the emotional storm (Martin, 2015). Firmly state, "This meeting is over. I'm leaving. We'll discuss this another time." Reporting such incidences to a boss or HR may be necessary.

Pointing a finger that exhibits anger and accusation does not have the same impact in a Zoom exchange as it does during an in-person exchange. First, if the Zoom meeting involves a group of coworkers, who exactly is the target of the pointed finger? You have a screen full of faces. Second, even if the finger is directed specifically at an individual so identified verbally, it does not have the same impact as someone pointing the finger a few inches from your face as opposed to a few inches from a computer screen with the target possibly miles, even time zones away.

Keeping track of all six steps to quell the anger of others, particularly when faced with an enraged person, is too much to expect. *Concentrate on one or two steps until they become almost a reflex reaction, a habit.* Being asymmetrical is the crucial first step, with validation a close second. The remaining steps can gradually become additions to your anger-defusing skill package.

The constructive management of conflict can occur only when anger is kept under control. This does not mean squelching anger. A group member can feel angry for good reasons. Anger acts as a signal that changes need to occur. Anger should not be used as a weapon, however, to abuse others. We want to learn ways to cope with and express anger constructively, not be devoured by it.

Virtual Communication and Conflict

Conflict is prevalent in virtual work environments. One survey of more than 1,000 U.S. workers found that "80% of remote professionals have experienced workplace conflict and many of them received text messages on a par with the trash talk you hear at actual boxing matches." A significant 42% of remote employees had a conflict with their boss, and 69% of these employees said that their boss cursed at them in virtual messages (Pieniazek, 2021).

As already discussed, not all conflict is counterproductive. Conflict that is competently managed can promote important, positive changes. There are differences, however, between virtual and face-to-face communication when conflicts arise. This is partly because developing trust and interpersonal bonds are easier to build when communicating in person than through social media (Tamir, 2020). *Destructive conflict is also more likely to be triggered when communicating virtually than when communicating face to face.* This is because of the **disinhibition effect**—the tendency to say online what you wouldn't normally say in person (Voggeser et al., 2018). "Blowing off steam," especially online (Martin et al., 2013), awakens our anger. It doesn't put it to bed.

A prodigious 84% of respondents in one survey "admitted they become more easily exasperated and enraged at others online than they ever would in person" (Macrae, 2015). Young people were particularly prone to social media rage, with 26% of 18- to 24-year-olds admitting they "are always worked up when using social media" followed by 18% of 35- and 44-year-olds with the same proclivity (Macrae, 2015).

Communication filters that operate in face-to-face communication to short-circuit emotional incontinence are less apparent when communicating electronically ("The Hidden Pitfalls of Video Negotiation," 2021). Nonverbal indicators of disapproval, such as a glance, a frown, or an eye-roll, are missing from text-only and audio-only interactions. What you wouldn't say to a coworker's face you might say in an email or text message. Misunderstandings can be a big problem because perceived slights, insults, or a negative tone in emails may not be quickly cleared up. Coworkers may have to stew over a perceived insult for a day, even a week, if an email response is not accessed right away.

Although this disinhibition effect is more likely in text-only or audio-only virtual communication, even in videoconferences with greater access to nonverbal cues, this disinhibition effect can play out negatively to provoke destructive conflict. Zoom or Skype meetings do not create the same feeling of presence that in-person discussions produce. *Social cues that support appropriate etiquette online are not as apparent* (Voggeser et al., 2018). Gestures can be more restrained, eye-rolling, even muttering under one's breath can be muted or indiscernible. Intemperate comments can be added to chat options during videoconferences.

Text-only communication, however, may be appropriate when face-to-face communication has a history of being awkward or intimidating. Sometimes we can be more honest and assertive in an email than in person. Words can also be more carefully chosen, and messages can be edited for tone more judiciously than you may be able to do when feeling angry and communicating face to face. How often have you replayed a hostile conversation in your mind and wished you hadn't made certain statements or had cushioned negative comments? In some instances, setting aside an angry email response

Virtual communication cannot always produce the same sense of closeness and warmth sometimes required to resolve highly emotional conflicts that ignite strong feelings among colleagues. Communicating an apology, for example, or smoothing hurt feelings just doesn't translate on Zoom the way it does in person. A hugging emoji of forgiveness is a poor substitute for a real in-person hug.

to a perceived insult or slight by a coworker and deciding, upon reflection, to delete it entirely is a wise choice. Email allows you to edit intemperate messages, but only by *adopting a standard practice of never responding heatedly to an email until you have had time to reflect, simmer down, and edit offensive remarks.*

Essentially, *virtual conflict management requires a higher dose of what has already been explained comprehensively throughout this text and will be discussed in ensuing chapters.* In-person initial meetings are critical to establishing cohesiveness and trust (Kahlow et al., 2020). Emphasis must be placed on developing and maintaining a positive, supportive workplace climate as detailed in Chapter 5. Procedural and behavioral ground rules play an important part in preventing discussions from devolving into destructive conflict (see Chapter 12). Additional approaches discussed in Chapter 9 (groups) and Chapter 10 (leadership) are also important.

Culture and Conflict

Cultures can vary widely in their preferences for communication styles of conflict management (Gunkel et al., 2016). Individualist and collectivist values significantly affect the communication styles of conflict management chosen when conflict occurs (Samovar et al., 2021. Individualist, low-context cultures tend to favor direct competitive/forcing or compromising styles of conflict management. Communication during conflict is explicit and direct. Americans as individualists "can become frustrated if conflicts are not managed openly and directly" (Canary & Lakey, 2013). Collectivist, high-context cultures favor avoiding or accommodating styles of conflict management. Assertive confrontation is considered rude and offensive. It is too direct, explicit, and unsettling (Sadri, 2018). It can be perceived as face-threatening (Merkin, 2015).

For example, avoidance of confrontation is "a core element of Thai culture. Expressions of emotion and excitement are seen as impolite, improper, and threatening" (Knutson & Posirisuk, 2006). A Thai avoids conflict and exhibits respect, tactfulness, politeness, modesty, and emotional control (Knutson et al., 2003).

Consider a comparison between typical Chinese and American approaches to conflict. Harmony is the essential foundation of Chinese communication (Chen, 2011). This philosophy translates into avoiding conflicts that might stir up trouble and disharmony. Conflicts handled ineptly might bring shame on the individual and the entire group. Thus, while Americans tend to focus immediately on task conflicts, Chinese tend to focus on relationship conflicts (i.e., saving or losing face) and avoid task conflicts until the relationships among all disputing parties have had time to build (Merkin, 2015). To Americans this may look like stalling to gain advantage.

Managing intercultural conflicts is challenging where expectations differ on the appropriateness of different communication styles. *Remaining flexible by employing a style that is well suited to cultural expectations is a key to effective conflict management in such situations* (Knutson et al., 2003). One study found that the more sensitive and accepting individuals are of cultural differences, the more likely they are to choose integration and compromising conflict styles and the less likely they are to choose avoiding and power/forcing styles (R. Yu & Chen, 2008). Competing/power-forcing is ineffective and inappropriate in most intercultural conflicts (Sadri, 2018). Always remember, however, that cultural generalizations are just that—generalizations. *Remaining flexible when managing cross-cultural conflicts means more than adapting conflict styles to typical cultural expectations of appropriateness. It also means adapting to individuals who may not embrace predominant cultural values* (Shonk, 2021c). Be careful not to stereotype an entire culture. Remain open to individual differences.

SUMMARY

Conflict is a reality of life at work. Although most people would prefer that conflict did not exist, it has both positive and negative aspects. Constructive management of conflict can turn a dispute into a positive experience. The five primary communication styles of conflict management—collaborating, accommodating, compromising, avoiding, and competing—all have pros and cons, depending on the situation. Nevertheless, collaborating has a higher probability of producing constructive outcomes than does competing. Situational factors, culture, and social media communication must be considered when managing conflict.

Film School Case Studies

The Social Network (2010). Biography/Drama; PG-13

Controversial Facebook CEO Mark Zuckerberg's meteoric rise to social networking superstar is presented in this well-made movie. Analyze the communication styles of conflict management used by Zuckerberg and others. What negotiating strategies are used, especially in response to a lawsuit filed against Zuckerberg contesting who came up with the initial idea for Facebook?

TED Talks and YouTube Videos

These TED Talks and YouTube videos can be accessed by going to the Oxford Learning Link for It's All of Our Business or by typing the title of the video into a Google search window.

"Anger at Work: How Negative Emotions Cloud Judgment"

Daniel Shapiro: "Negotiating the Nonnegotiable"

Lindred Greer: "Managing Conflict in Teams"

After successful completion of this chapter,
you should be able to

1. Recognize the essential function of group work in a business environment.

2. Identify the structure, rules, and roles associated with groups.

3. Explore complex ways to improve group decision making and problem solving.

The Nature of Groups: Working with Others

Winston Churchill, always armed with his sardonic wit, fired this salvo about working in groups such as on a committee: "A committee is the organized result of a group of the incompetent who have been appointed by the uninformed to accomplish the unnecessary." Some of our students have offered these caustic gems: "I've had the flu and I've had to work in groups. I prefer the flu"; "Working in groups is like eating tofu. I'm told it is good for me, but it makes me gag." Then there is this tongue-in-cheek suggestion: "Group work can be improved only if we threaten actual duels-to-the-death between slackers and perfectionists." This hyperbolic and negative view of working in groups is a common student reaction (Isaac, 2012; Muir, 2019). Surveys of full-time workers in the United States find similar results. One survey found that 95% of more than a thousand respondents agreed that working in groups serves an important function in the workplace, but only 24% preferred to do so ("University of Phoenix Survey," 2013). Another survey found that fewer than 10% of employees prefer to work

CHAPTER OUTLINE
- The Structure of Groups
- Creative Problem Solving

4. Practice methods that improve creative problem solving in groups.

exclusively in teams, while 43% prefer to work alone ("Organizational Dynamics Survey," 2016).

Often groups seem to be an impediment, not an aid, to decision making and problem solving. A survey of almost 19,000 workers found that the top "pet peeves" that spark actual hatred for working in groups include unfair workload, having to depend on others, and lack of full control over a project (Jerabek & Muoio, 2017). Having to depend on others who may not have the same motivation or commitment to produce excellent results can be annoying, even nightmarish. Groups can be time consuming, sometimes indecisive, conflict provoking, and slow to react to urgent needs. Personality clashes, irritating communication behaviors, and having to deal with difficult group members all encourage reticence to work in groups. Sorensen (1981) coined the term **grouphate** to describe how troublesome the group experience is for many people.

Despite these negative views, groups often outperform individuals working alone. For example, the Behavioural Insights Team in the United Kingdom conducted a series of experiments regarding ways to improve job hiring outcomes. Groups of five members were found to make far superior decisions compared to an individual (Michel, 2017). This group genius, or "wisdom of the crowd," is called synergy. **Synergy** occurs when group performance from joint action of members exceeds expectations based on perceived abilities and skills of individual members (Salazar, 1995). Thus, the whole is not necessarily equal to the sum of its parts. It may be greater than the sum of its individual parts. NASA did not reach the moon through the accumulated efforts of individuals working alone, and the Apollo 13 near-disaster "stands today as an example of . . . NASA's innovative minds working together to save lives on the fly" (Howell & Hickok, 2020).

Synergy is produced in several ways. First, *when group members are highly motivated to achieve a valued, common goal*—such as when grades, jobs, or lives are at stake, or members are highly motivated to help others—synergy likely occurs (Forsyth, 2014; "Teams Work Better," 2020). "If you want your teams to be engaged in their work, you have to make their work engaging" (L. McGregor & Doshi, 2020).

Second, *synergy is produced from relatively equal participation*, not individual, independent effort (Carey & Laughlin, 2012). For example, if employees work independently by completing individual assignments on their own, and their project group merely compiles the results, no synergy will occur. Google's Project Aristotle found that "if only one person or a small group [within a larger team] spoke all the time, the collective intelligence declined" (quoted in Duhigg, 2016). Assert yourself if the group tends to ignore you (see Chapter 4). *Relatively equal time speaking and active listening* among team members were found to be key to effectiveness.

Third, *groups whose members have deep diversity have greater potential to produce synergy* than groups with little such diversity (Pentland, 2016). For example, "When a group is composed of similar experts, they share biases. By comparison, people from diverse areas of expertise bring a variety of perspectives" (Moore & Bazerman, 2021). **Deep diversity** is substantial variation among members in task-relevant skills, knowledge, abilities, beliefs, values, experiences, perspectives, and problem-solving strategies (D. A. Harrison et al., 2002). Research shows that groups with deep diversity perform much better than those without such diversity (Reynolds & Lewis, 2017). Deep diversity and its attendant benefits are more likely to emerge from gender, ethnic, and cultural group diversity (Dixon-Fyle et al., 2020).

Finally, *groups are much more likely to be synergistic, rewarding experiences when group members are competent communicators* (Rogelberg et al., 2012). There is simply no substitute for competent communication, the exercise of knowledge, skills, sensitivity, commitment, and ethics that serves as a critical component of any successful group experience.

Most businesses and organizations have embraced the synergistic potential of working in groups. Four-fifths of both Fortune 1000 companies and manufacturing organizations employ **self-managing work teams**—teams that regulate their own performance

When groups lack deep diversity, are burdened by unmotivated social loafers, and members lack communication competence, **negative synergy**, or group decisions that are beyond bad, often result. Group synergy can be fostered when members exhibit knowledge, skills, sensitivity, commitment, and ethics while working in concert with each other.

free from outside interference while completing an entire task (L. MacDonald, 2019). In a survey of 6,000 employees conducted by Gensler Research Institute, *teamwork and collaboration were identified as the most important attributes of great workplaces* ("U.S. Workplace Survey," 2019). **Virtual groups**—groups whose members are connected by electronic communication technologies—have become a worldwide phenomenon. A major study of multinational corporations reported that 85% of employees work at least some of the time in virtual groups, and that "we cannot overstate the importance of virtual team work inasmuch as it is the basis of how global business is conducted today" (C. Solomon, 2016). When COVID-19 hit, virtual group work became a virtual necessity.

Because group work is unavoidable in the world of business, it is important to learn how to make that experience a positive one, and communication competence holds the key to that success. Thus, *the primary purpose of this chapter is to understand the nature of groups in the world of work, and to learn how to improve your communication in groups given this understanding.* Toward this end, this chapter has the following objectives: (1) to identify the structure of groups, (2) to explain the complex ways to improve group decision making and problem solving, and (3) to explore methods that improve creative group problem solving. *Special focus on virtual group effectiveness is addressed in Chapter 10 on leadership, Chapter 11 on teams, and Chapter 12 on meetings.*

The Structure of Groups

A **group** is composed of three or more individuals, interacting for the achievement of some common purpose(s), who influence and are influenced by one another. Two people qualify as a couple, or **dyad**, not a group. They engage in *interpersonal* communication. Typically, and for good reason, we do not refer to a couple by saying "Aren't they a cute group?" *There are qualitative, structural differences that distinguish a dyad from a group.* One study revealed that two individuals working together to solve a problem performed no better than two individuals working alone. Three individuals working together, however, proved to be the "tipping point" for significant improvement in problem solving compared to individuals working alone (Laughlin et al., 2006). Also, coalition formation and majority–minority communication processes can only occur in units of three or more members. Two individuals in agreement cannot logically form a coalition or argue against a "minority" of no one else. *A group dynamic, therefore, begins with no fewer than three individuals.*

Also, a group is not merely any **aggregation** or collection of unrelated individuals, such as 10 unrelated businesspeople waiting in line to buy plane tickets, or individuals standing in line at the unemployment office to apply for benefits. *To qualify as a group, three or more people must succeed or fail as a unit in a quest to achieve a common purpose.* That common purpose may simply be to make a decision, not necessarily to arrive at a common agreement (consensus) on an issue in dispute.

Every group has a discernible **structure**—a form or shape characterized by an interrelationship among its parts. In this section, group structure and its implications for the workplace are explored.

A mere collection of people is not a group. They can be in proximity to each other, but unless they are interacting to achieve a common goal, they are called an aggregation.

Group Size: Influencing Structure

Group size largely determines group structure and, consequently, how we communicate in the business environment. Adding even one member to a group is not an inconsequential event. As former newscaster Jane Pauley once observed, "Somehow three children are many more than two." The possible number of interpersonal relationships between group members grows exponentially

Group Size	Possible Relationships
3	9
4	28
5	75
6	186
7	441
8	1,056

as group size increases. Bostrom (1970) provides these calculations:

A triad, or three-member group, for example, has nine possible interpersonal relationships as shown in Figure 9. 1. Member A (executive) might perceive a different relationship (friendship) with member B (executive) than member B might perceive their relationship (collegues only). Same with member C (salesperson) who may have distinct perceptions of members A and B and vice versa.

Several challenges emerge as groups increase in size (Lowry et al., 2006). First, *the number of nonparticipants in group discussions increases when groups grow much beyond seven members*. Reticent members may be intimidated by the prospect of speaking to a group, especially a large one. Second, *larger groups easily become* **factionalized**—members of like mind may splinter into smaller, competing subgroups—to withstand pressure from other members to conform to the majority opinion on an issue. Discussion and decision making

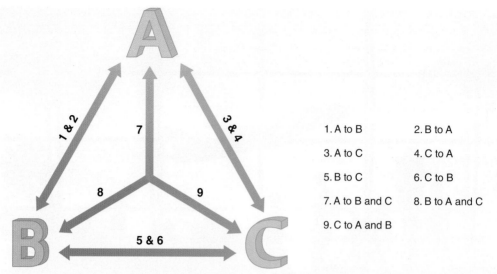

1. A to B	2. B to A
3. A to C	4. C to A
5. B to C	6. C to B
7. A to B and C	8. B to A and C
9. C to A and B	

FIGURE 9.1 There are nine possible interpersonal relationships with three group members.

can become fragmented. Third, *larger groups may take much more time to make decisions than smaller groups*. With more members, there are potentially more voices to be heard on the issues under discussion. Some of these voices may be difficult to silence, holding the group hostage to talkaholics' time-consuming monologues. Fourth, *even scheduling a meeting when all members are available can be a daunting task when groups grow large*. Schedule conflicts are almost inevitable with groups of more than seven. Finally, *group productivity typically decreases as groups grow larger*. Too many group members can create decision paralysis. Research shows that each member added to a decision-making group that starts with seven members reduces decision effectiveness by 10% (Blenko et al., 2010). If this **rule of seven** is taken to its logical conclusion, a group of 17 or more members "rarely makes any decisions." Another study of 2,623 members in 329 work groups found that groups composed of three to eight members are significantly more productive than groups composed of nine or more members (Wheelan, 2009).

So what is the ideal group size? Amazon CEO Jeff Bezos uses the "two-pizza rule"—a group is too large if it cannot be fed by two pizzas (Connely, 2018). That is obviously not a very precise rule (small, medium, or large pizzas? deep dish or thin crust? big eaters or nibblers?). *There is no single ideal-sized group for all situations*. Each group experience is unique. For example, complex, politically charged and economically complex business issues may require much larger groups (10 or more) just to give a voice to all interested factions. Groups may be faced with a trade-off between *speed* and *quality* of decision making. Smaller groups of three or four members are faster, but somewhat larger groups often produce higher-quality decisions because their knowledge base is greater. Offering a precise number, however, is arbitrary and debatable. Instead, *the smallest size capable of fulfilling the purposes of the group should be considered optimum*. The key point is to keep groups relatively small to reap the greatest advantages. As groups grow in size, complexity increases, and formal structure becomes necessary. Some small groups even evolve into large organizations.

Groups Versus Organizations: Structural Differences

What began as a very small business in 1940 with a half-dozen employees grew into more than 40,000 establishments in 120 countries employing almost 2 million workers (C. Smith, 2022). One of every eight workers in America has at some time been employed by this organization (Ashe, 2018). Can you guess what it is? If you guessed McDonald's, you are correct.

Small businesses sometimes grow into large organizations. Since you may work in both during the course of your career or job experience, knowing in what ways this transition from small businesses to large organizations produces changes in structure and attendant communication processes is important. *Small groups typically operate with an informal structure.* Communication is usually conducted as conversation rather than as formal public presentations. Procedures for managing conflict also remain informal. There is little need for formal grievance procedures; differences among three group members can usually be handled through discussion and a meeting. A meeting of a three-person group doesn't require formal communication rules of parliamentary procedure, such as **Robert's Rules of Order**, although larger groups may require such procedures. Smaller groups would appear silly using such formal rules. "Point of order," "Call the question," "I move to table the motion," and "I rise to a point of privilege" sound goofy when communicating with three or four friends or colleagues. ("Hey, relax! This isn't Congress.")

As groups increase in size, complexity increases. Thus, when small groups become large groups and, eventually, organizations, structure typically becomes more formal to cope with the increased complexity. Individuals receive formal titles with written job descriptions. Power is distributed unevenly. Those with the most prestigious titles typically are accorded the most status and decision-making power (and salary). The larger the organization, the more likely the structure will become a **hierarchy,** meaning that members of the organization will be rank ordered (see Figure 9. 2). This pyramid of power has those at the top—the CEOs, presidents, and vice presidents—wielding the most power, with middle managers coming next, and then low-level employees at the bottom.

Organizational structure alters communication. In most organizations, low-level

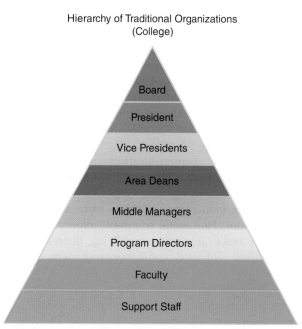

FIGURE 9.2   Hierarchy of traditional organizations (College).

employees' communication with those at the top of the power pyramid is restricted. If all two million workers in the McDonald's organization felt free to email or text message those at the top, information overload would overwhelm decision makers. Formal lines of communication, or networks, are established to control information flow. These chains of command can make **upward communication**—messages that flow from subordinates to superordinates in an organization—very difficult. Typically, *there are risks for low-level employees who communicate with bosses, especially if the information is negative.* Criticism and complaints can get you ostracized, perceived as a troublemaker, or even fired. The responsibility for establishing competent upward communication rests primarily with upper management and leadership. Developing a supportive climate (see Chapter 5) is vital. *Remember, however, that it is everyone's business to establish a positive communication work environment.*

Downward communication—messages that flow from superordinates to subordinates in an organization—also can be problematic. Communicating policy changes, giving rationales for assignments, explaining proper procedures and practices for the smooth running of the organization, motivating workers, and offering sufficient feedback to subordinates so that they know when they have performed well and when improvement is needed are vital messages. What you don't want in an organization is what former United Airlines president Ed Carlson once called NETMA—Nobody Ever Tells Me Anything.

Horizontal communication—messages between individuals with equal power, such as office workers in the same department—is another common communication pattern in organizations. Horizontal communication coordinates tasks, aids problem solving, shares information, enhances conflict management, and builds rapport. It is predominately informal, even casual. Do not underestimate the value of establishing these important lines of communication that provide important information not easily garnered through formal channels.

Task and Social Dimensions: Productivity and Cohesiveness

Every group and organization has two primary interconnected structural dimensions: task and social. As previously referenced when discussing conflict management styles, the **task dimension** is the work performed by the group and its impact on the group. The **social dimension** consists of relationships between group members and the impact of these relationships on the group. **Productivity** is the output of the task dimension. The extent of a group's productivity is determined by the degree to which it accomplishes its work efficiently and effectively. Five workers performing the same amount of work with the same proficiency as 10 doubles the group productivity. **Cohesiveness** is the output of the social dimension. The extent of a group's cohesiveness depends on the degree to which members identify with the group and wish to remain in it. Cohesiveness is developed primarily by encouraging compatible membership when possible, developing shared goals that members find challenging and exciting to achieve, accomplishing important tasks that meet these shared goals,

creating a positive group history of cooperation, establishing a positive group communication climate, and promoting acceptance of all group members by making each feel valued and welcome.

TASK DIMENSION—————→Productivity

SOCIAL DIMENSION—————→Cohesiveness

Cohesiveness and productivity are interconnected; one affects the other (Anwar, 2016). High cohesiveness alone does not guarantee group success, but it seems to be a necessary condition for successful task accomplishment. When groups lack cohesiveness, their productivity typically suffers (Wise, 2014). Small groups of exceedingly talented individuals will not accomplish tasks well if interpersonal relations among members are immersed in disharmony, anger, resentment, hostility, and rivalries. Low cohesiveness almost always dooms a group to poor performance and low productivity. Members who do not like each other and wish they were not a part of the group typically exhibit feeble effort and poor performance.

An especially challenging productivity-cohesiveness problem is that some individuals are social loafers in groups. **Social loafing** is the tendency of an individual to exert less effort on a task when working in a group than when working alone (Dean, 2021). Social loafing is exhibited by members missing or showing up late to group meetings, participating in a lethargic manner, or failing to start or complete individual tasks requested by the group. Social loafing often dramatically diminishes group productivity and cohesiveness and can engender grouphate. (See Box 9.1 for ways to address social loafing.)

Another difficult challenge besides social loafing is **groupthink**, defined by Irving Janis (1982) as "a mode of thinking that people engage in when they are deeply involved in a cohesive in-group, when the members' strivings for unanimity override their motivation to realistically appraise alternative courses of action." When disagreement is avoided because members fear disrupting group cohesiveness, error correction may be sacrificed. Groupthink is the opposite of critical thinking. Group members "go along to get along" even when decisions are

BOX 9.1   Addressing Social Loafing

The **collective effort model (CEM)** suggests that social loafing can be mostly prevented if group members are convinced that their individual effort will likely help in attaining valued results. If members view the task or their contribution as unimportant, then social loafing will likely occur, and synergy will be difficult to achieve. Instead of taking on more than your share, called **social compensation**, and letting the loafer slide, there are *several communication steps* that you and other group members can take to address social loafing (Dean, 2021; Synnott, 2016). The first few steps may be all that are necessary in some instances, but a complete list is offered just in case loafers are intransigent.

1. *Choose meaningful tasks.* Groups cannot always choose their tasks, and sometimes higher authorities give them tasks that are as dull as a gray day in January. If required to choose a project from a list of several options, choose the option most interesting to the entire group, not the option interesting to only one or two relatively dominant members.
2. *Establish a group responsibility norm.* Emphasize individual responsibility to the team and the importance of every member contributing a fair share to the successful completion of a task. Fairness and responsibility are important ethical concerns.
3. *Note the critical importance of each member's effort.* When members believe that their contribution is indispensable to group success, they often exert greater effort.
4. *Hold members accountable.* Provide each member with specific and easily identifiable

tasks. Face-to-face peer appraisal that focuses on development of each group member's strengths, not on criticizing weak effort, diminishes social loafing.
5. *Enhance group cohesiveness.* Members of weakly cohesive groups are more prone to social loafing than members of highly cohesive groups (Lam, 2015). Cohesiveness is enhanced by creating a positive group climate (see Chapter 5).
6. *Confront the loafer.* If the steps above are insufficient, either the leader of the group, a designated member, or the group should approach the loafer and encourage stronger participation, reaffirm the importance of the loafer's contribution to the team effort, and solicit suggestions regarding how the group might help the person become a contributor. Use supportive, not defensive communication (see Chapter 5).
7. *Consult a higher power* (not to be confused with divine intervention, although that would be impressive). If the above steps fail, consult a supervisor or someone with greater authority than the group members, and ask for advice. The authority may need to intervene.
8. *Boot out the loafer.* This is a last resort. Do not begin with this step, as many groups prefer to do. You may not have this option available, however.
9. *Sidestep the loafer.* If expulsion is not an option, reconfigure individual responsibilities and tasks so even if the loafer contributes nothing to the group effort, the group can still maneuver around the loafer and produce a high-quality result.

thought to be potentially disastrous. Dissent is discouraged, even punished. *Building a positive communication climate (see Chapter 5), constructing a deeply diverse group membership with a strong group identity, establishing collaborative leadership (see Chapters 10 and 11), and developing a group norm that both encourages constructive dissent and provides* *a psychologically safe environment for doing so all combat groupthink* (Heneghan & Mahtani, 2020; Packer & Van Bavel, 2021).

Finding the proper relationship between productivity and cohesiveness is a persistent dialectical struggle in all groups. Too much focus on productivity can strain interpersonal relationships within a group ("Work, work, work—that's all we ever do"). Too much focus on cohesiveness can lead to anemic effort on the task ("It's party time"). Both task and social dimensions should be addressed, not one at the expense of the other.

Norms: Rules Governing Group Behavior

Every group, large or small, has *norms* that guide behavior. **Norms** are rules, but they are *rules applied specifically to groups*. Norms provide structure that indicate what group members have to do (obligation), should do (preference), or may not do (prohibition) if they want to accomplish specific goals effectively and appropriately.

Types of Norms: Explicit and Implicit   There are two types of norms, as there are two types of communication rules discussed in Chapter 2: *explicit* and *implicit*. **Explicit norms** specifically and overtly identify acceptable and unacceptable behavior in groups. "No Smoking" signs posted around the corporate campus and laws prohibiting sexual harassment in the workplace are explicit norms. The Motley Fool, a stock advising company, has a corporate dress code that is certainly on the casual side, but the stated norm is to "not wear anything that would embarrass your parents" (O'Malley, 2019).

In groups, however, most norms are implicit. **Implicit norms** are observable patterns of behavior exhibited by group members that identify acceptable and unacceptable conduct. Examples might include the following: all members dress neatly, humor is never sarcastic or offensive, and no one says anything derogatory about any other coworker or boss. These norms are learned by how others react. Violate an implicit norm and

reactions from group members will undoubtedly set you straight ("Oops, the group is looking at me like I just suggested euthanizing all family pets. Big mistake."). Make fun of your boss in a business meeting expecting good-natured laughter, but seeing terrified facial expressions from participants instead, sends a message that you do not tease your boss.

Implicit norms may become explicit on occasion, especially when there is a norm violation. It should be apparent that checking or sending text messages, answering cellphones, perusing websites from a laptop, or blogging during business meetings violates implicit norms of appropriate employee behavior. These are common norm violations that may require explicit reminders during meetings to put away the electronic toys.

Conforming to Norms: Being Liked and Being Right   Group members tend to *conform* to group norms. **Conformity** is the inclination of group members to think and behave in ways that are consistent with group norms. *Conformity creates a sense of belonging, helps groups accomplish important goals, and can be a positive force.* Groups could not exist without some conformity. Group discussion would be tumultuous if there were no rules governing such interactions (e.g., taking turns speaking).

Conformity can also be negative. Unethical corporate behavior can be protected by employees who witness egregious transgressions but stay silent along with everyone else who realizes what is transpiring. Conformity to the norm not to be a "snitch" can be powerful. So, the often-dangerous consequences continue.

Members conform to group norms for two principal reasons: to be right and to be liked

Conformity to norms, in this case dress and meeting casualness or formality, is common in groups. We usually prefer to blend, not stand out alone in nonconformity.

(Aronson et al., 2016). We typically do not want to suffer the embarrassment of being wrong in front of our coworkers or supervisors, so we look to the group for information on correct behavior. We also are inclined to strive for acceptance from our group. We "go along to get along." Social acceptance, support, and friendship are often the rewards for conformity. Nonconformity typically triggers a negative response from the group, such as social ostracism at work, personal attack, or expulsion.

Roles: Expected Patterns of Behavior

Roles are patterns of expected behavior associated with parts that you play in groups. Roles and norms are interconnected structural elements of business groups. *Norms are broad rules that indicate expected behavior for every group member, whereas roles indicate specific behaviors expected of individual group members, not the entire group.*

There are two general types of roles: *formal* and *informal*. **Formal roles** assign a position. They are a standard part of the structure of organizations. Titles such as "president," "chair," or "assistant" usually accompany formal roles. Formal roles do not emerge naturally from group transactions; they are assigned. Normally, an explicit description of expected behaviors corresponds to each formal role.

In small groups and teams, roles are mostly informal. **Informal roles** identify functions, not positions. They usually emerge naturally from group transactions. The informal roles a group member plays are identified by observing patterns of communication. If a member often initiates group discussions, the member is playing the role of initiator-contributor. The group does not explicitly tell a member to play an informal role. Groups do, however, indicate degrees of approval or disapproval when a member assumes an informal role.

Informal roles are generally divided into three types: task, maintenance, and disruptive roles. **Task roles** advance the attainment of group goals. Their central communicative function is to extract the optimum productivity from the group. **Maintenance roles** address the social dimension of small groups. Their central

communicative function is to gain and maintain group cohesiveness. **Disruptive roles** are Me-oriented. Their central communicative function is to focus attention on the individual at the expense of group needs and goals. Group members who play these roles often deserve the label "difficult group member," addressed at length in Chapter 8.

Because competent communicators recognize the interconnectedness of the task and social dimensions of groups, they look for the optimum balance between task and maintenance roles to achieve group success. They also avoid disruptive roles. Box 9.2 identifies some common task, maintenance, and disruptive small group roles (Benne & Sheats, 1948; Mudrack & Farrell, 1995).

The list in Box 9.2 is not exhaustive. It is also a static list and description. *Informal roles in actual practice unfold transactionally, during discussion, debate, and disagreement. Consider the following transaction:*

> **Darise:** For our software presentation to the executive team, I don't think we should use slides at all for our Zoom presentation. Let's do something different, even surprising. (*initiator-contributor*)
>
> **Chanelle:** Does everyone agree? (*information seeker*)
>
> **Daniel:** I might have a better idea. (*information giver*)
>
> **Patrick:** This whole presentation just sounds boring. It's just a dumb Zoom presentation. (*blocker*)
>
> **Darise:** I don't see you offering anything more interesting, so why don't you stifle yourself? (*fighter-controller*)
>
> **Patrick:** Really? Stifle your own self! And who uses words like *stifle* anyway? (*fighter-controller*)
>
> **Chanelle:** Come on, you guys; this won't get us anywhere. This isn't bare-knuckle cage fighting. (*harmonizer-tension reliever*) We're a great team, so let's start acting like it. (*supporter-encourager*) Let's get back to Darise's suggestion. (*coordinator-director*). What do the rest of you think? José and Brittany, we haven't heard from you (*isolates*). Any thoughts? (*information seeker*).

BOX 9.2   Sample of Informal Roles In Small Groups

Task Roles

1. *Information giver*—provides facts and opinions; offers relevant and significant information based on research, expertise, or personal experience. "I have this report I found on this very subject . . ."

2. *Information seeker*—asks for facts, opinions, suggestions, and ideas from group members. "So, does anyone know why our new software is so buggy?"

3. *Initiator-contributor*—provides ideas; suggests actions and solutions to problems; offers direction for the group. "Maybe we should consider our first idea again, but from a different angle."

4. *Clarifier*—explains ideas; defines the group position on issues; summarizes proceedings of group meetings; raises questions about the direction of group discussion. "I don't think we're as far apart as it might seem. Consider everything we already agree should occur . . ."

5. *Elaborator*—expands the ideas of other group members; helps the group visualize how an idea or solution would work if the group implemented it. "I think your suggestion would work in the following ways . . ."

6. *Coordinator-director*—pulls together the ideas of others; promotes teamwork and cooperation; guides group discussion; breaks the group into subgroups to work effectively on tasks; regulates group activity. "Let me get everyone's work schedule so that we can find a time to meet."

7. *Energizer*—tries to motivate the group to be productive; acts as a task cheerleader. "Let's keep going; we're making real progress."

8. *Procedural technician*—performs routine tasks, such as taking notes, photocopying, passing out relevant materials for discussion, finding a room to meet, and signaling when allotted time for discussion of an agenda item has expired. "Our time allotment for this issue has expired. Does the group want to add more time for discussion or end it here?"

9. *Devil's advocate*—gently challenges prevailing viewpoints in the group to test and evaluate the strength of ideas, solutions, and decisions. "So, what happens if our plan doesn't play out as we hope it will? Do we have a backup strategy or are we just hoping for a miracle?"

Maintenance Roles

1. *Supporter-encourager*—offers praise; bolsters the spirits and goodwill of the group; provides warmth and acceptance of others. "Great job everyone."

2. *Harmonizer, tension reliever*—maintains the peace; reduces tension with gentle humor; reconciles differences between group members. "Let's try not to make this personal, and perhaps we need to take a break. I think we are growing weary."

3. *Gatekeeper*—controls the channels of communication, keeping the flow of information open or closed depending on the social climate of the group; encourages participation from all group members and open discussion. "We haven't heard from many of you. Any suggestions that you'd like to make?"

Disruptive Roles

1. *Stagehog*—seeks recognition; monopolizes discussion and prevents others from expressing their points of view; wants the spotlight. "Listen to me! I'm not done yet."

2. *Isolate*—withdraws from group; acts indifferent, aloof, and uninvolved; resists inclusion in group discussion.

3. *Fighter-controller*—tries to dominate group; competes mindlessly with group members; abuses those who disagree; picks quarrels, interrupts, and generally attempts to control group proceedings. "You're kind of slow to catch on, aren't you? Try keeping up if you can."

4. *Blocker*—actively tries to prevent actions and decisions advocated by others without offering alternatives.

5. *Zealot*—attempts to convert group members to a pet cause or viewpoint; delivers sermons on the state of the world; exhibits fanaticism—"one who can't change his mind and won't change the subject" (Churchill). "I know I keep saying this and you don't like it, but if you would just listen to me . . ."

6. *Clown*—interjects inappropriate humor during discussions and meetings; engages in horseplay; diverts attention from the group task with comic routines.

7. *Cynic*. This role is a climate killer. A cynic displays a sour outlook, engages in faultfinding, focuses on negatives, and predicts group failure ("We're never going to agree on a decent topic"). H. L. Mencken described a cynic as someone who "smells flowers [and] looks around for a coffin." When the group may need a cheerleader, the cynic becomes a *jeerleader* by providing a disheartening message ("I told you we wouldn't succeed. This was a stupid idea").

In this brief transaction, group members assume roles in response to members' communication. Some members play more than one role in rapid-fire succession, while others play only a single role, depending on reactions from participants.

Assuming appropriate task and maintenance roles during group discussion is a matter of timing. For example, a *devil's advocate* (check Box 9.2) is not needed during initial discussion. You do not want to kill potentially creative ideas by immediately challenging them. A *harmonizer-tension reliever* is needed when conflict emerges and threatens to derail the group discussion. This role is irrelevant if there is no tension or disharmony. Which roles to play at which time is an important aspect of leadership, discussed at length in the next chapter.

Structured Problem Solving: Standard Agenda

John Dewey (1910) described a process of rational decision making and problem solving that he called **reflective thinking**—a set of logical steps that incorporate the scientific method of defining, analyzing, and solving problems. The Standard Agenda is a direct outgrowth of Dewey's reflective thinking process. The **Standard Agenda** provides a structured problem-solving process composed of six steps that focuses on the problem before considering solutions. It is very similar to the structured decision-making process offered by professors of business Don Moore and Max Bazerman (2022). We prefer the Standard Agenda as more complete, especially because of the inclusion of the implementation step.

Problem Identification: What Is the Question?

The problem should be formulated into an open-ended question. For example, one study of 21 organizations, such as outdoor gear designing company Patagonia and Edmonds Inc., a car finder and appraisal online service, explored the question, "What makes a company culture great?" (O'Malley, 2019).

Problem Analysis: Doing the Research

To answer the main question, Michael O'Malley and his colleague, Bill Baker, spent 3 years researching companies that had appeared on reputable business publications such as *Fortune* and *Inc.* (see O'Malley, 2019). They interviewed executives, met with human resources departments, conducted focus groups with employees, and toured facilities of the 21 organizations that perennially appeared on several "best companies to work for" lists. From their research, they were able to ascertain criteria that not only revealed why these organizations are deemed "best companies," but how these criteria can be applied to a broad range of additional organizations, each capable of making internal decisions to improve their overall performance. *Establishing criteria before brainstorming answers to a primary question is essential.*

Solution Criteria: Setting Standards

Criteria are standards used to evaluate decisions and solutions to problems. There were five criteria O'Malley and Baker delineated:

1. *Put people first*. As Duane Hixon, founder and CEO of N2 Publishing explains, "Profit is necessary, but it is not the goal . . . Our purpose is to help people live better lives."

2. *Help workers find and pursue their passions*. Worker productivity is enhanced when their "area of work provides them with the greatest fulfillment."

3. *Bring people together on a personal level*. "The companies we visited celebrate special occasions and recognize important life-cycle transitions."

4. *Empower people to own their work*. This encourages workers to own their mistakes, not as opportunities to be reprimanded or punished, but to "normalize the acceptance of periodic failures" from which to learn.

5. *Create a space where people can be themselves*. Employees welcome a work environment that does not squelch self-expression but encourages an openness.

Solution Suggestions: Generating Alternatives

The group brainstorms possible solutions, or in this case specific actions that can be taken to meet criteria. Proper brainstorming technique is discussed later in this chapter. Some suggestions for meeting the criteria for "best companies" could include treating birthdays as paid holidays; engaging in social events such as monthly outings to baseball games, comedy clubs, theater shows, summer barbecues, and holiday parties among other possibilities, not "funishments"—those "rare and artificial teambuilding exercises that people are forced to take part in and required to enjoy" (O'Malley, 2019). Establish programs to assist employees in finding their passion.

Solution Evaluation and Selection: Deciding by Criteria

Software company SAS runs a program for employees that trains how to give presentations in the vein of TED Talks. PURE Insurance has Passion Program that gives employees $1,500 per year to explore whatever interests them. These address criterion 2 above. Software company BambooHR treats birthdays as paid holidays. Short film makers BAF, Inc., sponsors monthly outings, and Regeneron has spring flings and summer barbecues. These options bring people together (addressing criterion 3). BambooHR created an Oops Email Box for employees to announce mistakes and steps taken to correct them (addressing criterion 4). At N2 Publishing, the head of the mailroom composed and performed the company rap theme song. The Full Bloods is a cover band composed of workers from the graphic design department that performs at the company's monthly all-hands meetings (addressing criterion 5).

Solution Implementation: Follow-Through

A common failing of decision-making groups is that

once they arrive at a decision, implementation faces two challenges. First, **Murphy's law**—which states that anything that can go wrong likely will go wrong, somehow, somewhere, sometime—is often not considered. Failing to make a backup copy of a final written report for a group project, for example, is flirting with Murphy's malevolence. NASA specializes in redundant systems in its spacecrafts because it expects the unexpected to occur, and in the past it has.

A second problem is that, once a decision has been made, groups do not plan its implementation. One study found that only 30% of strategic initiatives in businesses are successfully implemented (Davis et al., 2010). Change can be an ordeal. One survey found that the number one barrier is "resistance to change" ("Survey of CEOs," 2007).

There are five conditions that reduce resistance to change. They are

1. *Group members have a part in the planning and decision making*. This gives them part ownership of the change. Conversely, imposing change ignites psychological reactance (Chapter 5).

2. *Change does not threaten group members*. If change cuts jobs or reduces employee compensation, there will be blowback. On the other hand, change that enhances employee compensation and benefits will be embraced.

3. *The need for change affects individuals directly*. Unhealthy working conditions that affect most employees can be a driving force for change.

4. *Change is open to revision and modification*. Change comes more easily when it is presented as a trial run instead of a permanent, unalterable edict from "on high."

5. *Three factors—degree, rate, and desirability of change—are considered*. Large, undesirable, rapid change produces much more resistance, typically, than relatively small, desirable change instituted slowly so organizations as systems can adapt (Rothwell, 2022).

Decision-Making Rules

There are three primary group decision-making rules: majority, minority, and unanimity. There are pros and cons for each.

Majority Rule: Tyrannical or Practical Although majority rule is a popular method of group decision making, *the quality of the group's decision is a particularly troublesome problem*. Majorities can sometimes take ludicrous, even dangerous positions. Racism, sexism, and other bigotry in the United States have been the products of majority rule. There are several deficiencies in majority rule applicable to most small groups. First, *deliberations are significantly shorter and less conscientious*. Deliberations typically end once a requisite majority is reached (Hoe, 2017). Consequently, less error correction takes place, sometimes resulting in faulty decisions. Second, *minority factions participate less frequently and are less influential*, thereby underutilizing the group's

Groups should consider what might go wrong before making a final decision. Once a bad decision is implemented, it is too late.

resources. Third, *members' overall satisfaction with the group is lower.* Minorities feel the "tyranny of the majority" when their point of view is ignored, and deliberations become combative and bullying.

Despite the disadvantages of majority rule, there are some clear advantages (Hastie & Kameda, 2005; E. Taylor et al., 2013). *When issues are not very important, when decisions must be made relatively quickly, when groups become large, and when commitment of all members to the final decision is relatively unimportant, majority rule can be useful.* Majority rule is efficient and provides quick closure.

Minority Rule: Several Types   Minority rule as a group decision-making method occurs in several forms. First, the group designates one of its members as an expert to make the decision. This method relieves group members from devoting time and energy to solving problems. Decision by designated expert, however, is mostly ineffective because determining who is the expert in the group is often difficult and contentious. Lack of group input also fails to capitalize on synergy.

Second, *a designated authority (usually from outside the immediate group) makes the decision for the group*, either after hearing discussion from group members or without their consultation. Sometimes the group advises the designated authority, and sometimes not. If group advice is treated as a mere formality, or the designated authority is a poor listener, then none of the benefits of group deliberations will accrue. Group members are also likely to vie competitively for attention, seek to impress the authority, and offer what the authority wants to hear, not what should be said.

Third, in some instances, *executive committees must be delegated responsibility for making certain decisions* because the workload for the larger group is overwhelming or the time constraints are prohibitive. The challenge here is to persuade the group to get behind the decision.

Finally, *minority rule can take the form of a forceful faction* deciding for the group by dominating less forceful members. On rare

occasions, this may be advisable when the minority faction consists of the most informed, committed members. Too often, however, dominant group members focus on personal gain more than on what is good for the group (Maner, 2017).

Unanimity Rule: Consensus   Group consensus is based on the unanimity rule. *Consensus* is "a state of mutual agreement among members of a group where all legitimate concerns of individuals have been addressed to the satisfaction of the group" (Saint & Lawson, 1997). *Consensus usually requires some give and take.* If all members can agree on an acceptable choice, even if this alternative is not each member's preference, then you have come close to achieving a true consensus. A **true consensus**, however, requires not just agreement, but commitment and satisfaction (DeStephen & Hirokawa, 1988). Members show commitment by defending the unanimous decision to outsiders, not undermining it by agreeing in the group but disagreeing outside of the group. Group members feel satisfaction with the decision-making process when a cooperative group climate and reasonable opportunities for all members to participate meaningfully in decision making occur (Gastil et al., 2007).

Groups that use a consensus approach tend to produce better decisions than groups using other decision rules. This occurs because full discussion of issues is required, every group member must embrace the decision, and minority members are heard (Lee & Paradowski, 2007). Women, who often are reticent to participate during group discussions when badly outnumbered by men, are more vocal when the unanimity rule is used (Karpowitz et al., 2012).

Nevertheless, there are three principal limitations to consensus decision making. First, *achieving unanimous agreement from group members is very difficult.* Some groups seem unable to agree even that gravity exists. Members who resist siding with the majority lengthen the deliberations and increase secondary tension (E. Taylor et al., 2013). Second, *consensus is increasingly unlikely as groups grow larger.* Groups of 15 or more rarely achieve a consensus. (Try getting 15 family members and friends to agree on a movie.) Seeking a consensus, however, even if never quite achieved, can still be beneficial. Third, consensus, because it takes substantial time, is *usually inappropriate when quick action is required*.

Several guidelines can help a group achieve a consensus:

1. *Follow the Standard Agenda*. Structured group discussion, not aimless conversation, improves the chances of achieving consensus.

2. *Establish a cooperative group climate*. Supportive patterns of communication encourage consensus; defensive patterns discourage it.

3. *Identify the pluses and minuses of potential decisions*. This encourages openness.

4. *Discuss all concerns of group members and attempt to resolve them*. Try to find alternatives that will satisfy members' concerns. This avoids groupthink.

5. *Avoid adversarial, win–lose arguments*. Do not stubbornly argue for a position.

6. *Request a "stand aside."* A stand aside means a team member has reservations about the group decision but does not wish to block the group choice. This avoids the blocker role.

7. *Avoid conflict-suppressing techniques such as coin flipping and swapping* ("I'll support your position this time if you support mine next time"). Conflict-suppressing techniques will not usually produce commitment to the group decision.

8. *If consensus is impossible, seek a supermajority* (a minimum two-thirds vote). It captures the spirit of consensus by requiring substantial, if not total, agreement.

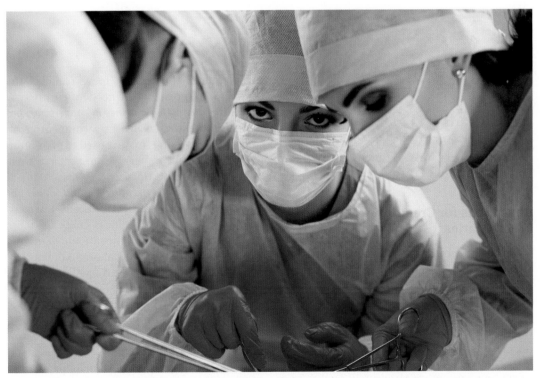

Both consensus and majority vote would be inappropriate for a surgical team performing an operation. "All those in favor of cutting here raise your hand"—does not work! Split-second decisions must be made, so minority rule, the chief surgeon making the decisions, applies.

TABLE 9.1   DECISION-MAKING RULES

Rules	Pros	Cons
Majority rule	Quick, efficient	Minorities vulnerable to tyranny of majority
	Expedient in large groups	Quality of decisions questionable
		Usually alienates minority
		Underutilization of resources
Minority rule		
Designated expert	Saves time	Expertise hard to determine
		No group input
Designated authority	Clear, Efficient	Members vie for attention
Executive committee	Divides labor	Weak commitment to decision
Forceful faction	Committed faction	Likely Me-, not We-oriented
Unanimity rule	Quality decisions	Time-consuming
	Commitment	Difficult
	Satisfaction	Tension-producing

Creative Problem Solving

Creativity does not just happen. There are conditions to be met. This section discusses these primary conditions.

Conditions for Creativity: Preliminaries

There are numerous conditions that trigger creativity. First, to borrow Thomas Edison's comment on genius, *creativity is more perspiration than inspiration.* This means devoting time and energy to the task, not hoping for imaginative ideas to fall from the sky and clunk us on the head.

Second, *creativity is spurred by challenges.* As the old adage says, "Necessity is the mother of invention." We are creative in response to some problem that requires a solution. The bigger the challenge, the more complex the problem, the greater is the need for creativity.

Third, *creativity flourishes in cooperative, not competitive environments.* In a competitive atmosphere, thinking "may be used to plan, strategize, and coerce rather than to problem solve and collaborate" (Carnevale & Probst, 1998).

Fourth, *creativity requires sound ideas, not just imaginative ones.* As Vincent Ruggiero (1988) puts it, creative ideas must be more than uncommon; they "must be uncommonly good." Creative solutions are original, but they also must work. I once heard a radio commentator read recipes submitted by children for preparing a Thanksgiving turkey. One child wrote, "Put 10 pounds of butter on the turkey and 5 pounds of salt. Cook it for 20 minutes." M-m-m-m-m good! Creative problem solving and decision making require both imagination and knowledge. Children create foolish things because they do not know any better. Competent communicators create effective solutions.

Fifth, *creativity requires many ideas*. Although sheer quantity does not guarantee great solutions, the fewer the ideas, the less probable is the discovery of at least one good idea. IDEO, the largest design firm in the world, generated more than 4,000 ideas for new toys. Of these, 230 were explored and only 12 were eventually produced by clients (Puccio et al., 2007).

Finally, *creativity requires breaking mindsets and thinking "outside the box."* Our **frame of reference** can lock us into a mindset, making solutions to problems difficult if not impossible to discover (Rathe, 2017). Worse yet, they can produce bad decision making (Moore & Bazerman, 2022). As the saying goes, "to the person with a hammer, every problem looks like a nail." Frames determine whether people notice problems, how they understand and remember problems, and how they evaluate and act on them (Bilandzic et al., 2017; Fairhurst, 2011).

Reframing is the creative process of breaking a mindset by describing the problem from a different frame of reference. For example, a service station proprietor put an out-of-order sign on a soda machine. Customers paid no attention to the sign, lost their money, then complained to the station owner. Frustrated and annoyed, the owner changed the sign to read "$5.00" for a soda. No one made the mistake of putting money in the faulty soda pop dispenser. The problem was reframed. Instead of wondering how to get customers to realize that the machine was on the fritz, the owner changed the frame of reference to one that would make customers not want to put money in the dispenser.

When groups become stumped by narrow or rigid frames of reference, interjecting certain open-ended questions can help reframe the problem and the search for solutions. In fact, Stanford professor Tina Seelig (2015) calls this **framestorming**—changing the framework for brainstorming before actually engaging in a brainstorming session by asking different questions. Our personal favorite is "What if . . .?" The group asks, "What if we don't accept this cutback in resources as inevitable?" "What if we tried working together instead of against each other?" Additional reframing questions include, "Why are these the only options?" "What happens if we reject the proposal?" "How could this be turned into a win–win situation for everyone?"

Meeting After Project Failure

Learning to reframe problems can significantly influence our perceptions (Tanner, 2020).

Creative Communication Techniques: Systematic Procedures

Creativity can be enhanced by utilizing systematic procedures. In this section, two are discussed: brainstorming and nominal group technique.

Brainstorming: Generating Lots of Ideas   Alex Osborn introduced the brainstorming technique in 1939. Brainstorming is a creative problem-solving technique that promotes plentiful, even zany, ideas in an atmosphere free from criticism.

There are several guidelines for using the brainstorming technique ("Brainstorming Rules," 2021):

1. *Encourage wild ideas*. Worry about the practical stuff after ideas have been generated.

2. *Do not evaluate ideas while brainstorming*. Idea slayers, such as "That will never work" and "It's completely impractical," should be squelched by members. Even a positive evaluation, such as "great idea," may be interpreted by those not praised as a negative assessment of their ideas.

3. *Do not clarify or seek clarification of an idea*. This will slow down the process. Clarification can come later after a list of ideas has been generated.

4. *Do not engage in task-irrelevant discussion*. Idea generation is significantly diminished when conversation is permitted. A brainstorming facilitator should invoke this rule.

5. *Stay focused on the topic*. You want all suggestions to be related to the topic. You are not looking for just any wild ideas, but relevant ones.

6. *Expand on the ideas of other group members*. Look for opportunities to piggyback on the ideas of others, generating additional creative ideas.

7. *Evaluate ideas generated once the brainstorming phase is completed* (Sawyer, 2017). The group needs to decide what ideas generated are best to implement.

Brainstorming normally is instituted during the solutions suggestion step of the Standard Agenda. Determining the quality of the ideas generated from brainstorming comes during the solution evaluation and selection step. Ideas are evaluated based on solution criteria established earlier in the Standard Agenda process.

Brainstorming, if done properly, can be highly effective (Goldenberg et al., 2013; Hansen, 2021). "The real genius to brainstorming isn't the number of ideas listed in a short period of time. . . . Instead, it's the many various combinations of ideas that can develop when individuals share their thoughts with each other. Those combinations could never occur apart from interaction" (Burkus, 2013). Brainstorming, however, is too often conducted improperly to produce the maximum results. Osborn suggested that *the proper brainstorming format should involve first an individual, then a group, followed by an individual brainstorming session* (Isaksen & Gaulin, 2005). Members should be provided with a well-defined problem a few days in advance so members can research it, think of ideas, and write down these ideas (*brain writing*). Then members meet as a group, initial ideas are posted on a large whiteboard or Post-it notes are affixed to a wall. These ideas are reviewed by participants, and then group brainstorming ensues. No, this isn't the final step. After this, individuals are given a few days to contemplate further ideas and a second group brainstorming session occurs. There is experimental support for the Osborn approach as the "most effective brainstorming process" (Korde & Paulus, 2017).

Members should belong to a longstanding group, not a zero-history group of strangers. Training and experience in how to use the brainstorming technique is vital because this improves idea generation (Baruah & Paulus, 2008). A trained facilitator improves brainstorming (Isaksen & Gaulin, 2005). Deep diversity also enhances brainstorming creativity: "Group genius can happen only if the brains in the team don't contain all the same stuff" (Sawyer, 2017). Brainstorming software, such as Ayoa, can be quite useful to aid brainstorming by offering a process for *mind mapping* as brainstorming progresses (Pewsey, 2020).

Electronic brainstorming for virtual groups can occur when group members sit at computer terminals and brainstorm ideas using a computer-based, file-sharing procedure. This offers an additional method for improving idea generation and creativity. Group members type their contributions, then send the file to a shared pool. Ideas are added and shared with group members. This can be done anonymously if group members fear a critique. This process somewhat parallels another creativity process called *brainswarming*, developed by cognitive psychologist Tom McCaffrey. Brainswarming is a complicated process best delineated by viewing videos that illustrate the technique (see video links at end of chapter for a detailed explanation).

Nominal Group Technique: Limited Interaction

Another common, creative problem-solving method is **nominal group technique** (Delbecq et al., 1975). Individuals work by themselves generating lists of ideas on a problem, then convene in a group where they merely post their ideas (on a chart, whiteboard, or computer screen). Interaction occurs only to clarify ideas, not to discuss their merits and demerits. Individuals then select their five favorite ideas, write them on a card, and rank them from most to least favorite. The rankings are averaged and the ideas with the highest averages are the ones selected by the group. Voting is anonymous, so reticent members participate more readily, and consensus occurs. Dominant members are neutralized. Cross-fertilization of ideas that comes from group discussion is constrained, however, by the highly structured procedures. As a result, *there is some evidence that brainstorming outperforms the nominal group technique in idea generation* (Baruah & Paulus, 2016).

SUMMARY

Working in groups can be a challenge. Groups can produce astoundingly positive synergy or stunningly awful negative synergy. A group is composed of three or more individuals, interacting for the achievement of some common purpose(s), who influence and are influenced by one another. Every group has a structure, a form or shape characterized by an interrelationship among its parts. The structure of groups is influenced by group size, task and social dimensions, norms, roles, the Standard Agenda, and decision-making and problem-solving rules such as majority and minority rules and consensus. Creative problem solving can be enhanced by brainstorming and nominal group techniques.

Film School Case Studies

The Martian (2015). Adventure/Drama; PG-13

Matt Damon plays the central character, an astronaut stranded on Mars and later rescued, to perfection. Identify the multitude of examples of creative problem solving depicted. What creative process does the technical group on the ground use to help solve the many problems?

Flight of the Phoenix (2004; 1966). Drama; PG-13

The original 1966 version of this taut drama about a plane crash and efforts of survivors to literally rebuild their damaged plane into a smaller flying machine to escape their plight in the desert is probably superior to the remake. In either case, examine the creative group problem solving required. What methods were used to create the final product? What decision-making rules (unanimity, majority, or minority rule) were used?

Apollo 13 (1995). Drama; PG

This dramatization of the nearly disastrous Apollo 13 space mission to the moon illustrates creative problem solving. What creative problem-solving techniques are exhibited?

TED Talks and YouTube Videos

These TED Talks and YouTube videos can be accessed by going to the Oxford Learning Link for It's All of Our Business or by typing the title of the video into a Google search window.

"U.S. Workplace Survey 2019"

"IDEO Brainstorming Video from IDEO U"

"Brainswarming"

After successful completion of this chapter, you should be able to

1. Recognize evolving theories of leadership, their strengths, and weaknesses.

2. Know how to gain leadership opportunities at work.

3. Differentiate between good and bad leadership practices.

CHAPTER 10

Competent Leadership: A Process More Than a Person

Scholars, philosophers, social scientists, even novelists have exhibited an inordinate interest in leadership. In politics, leadership is a buzzword and a subject of intense, although not always informed or fruitful debate. Conduct a Google search of articles, books, and viewpoints on leadership and you will get millions of hits. Enter "leadership" in the Amazon search window and more than 60,000 titles are referenced, and the list continues to grow. Business executives and management consultants regularly author books on leadership, mostly consisting of anecdotes that purport to prove allegedly sage advice garnered from years of corporate or executive experience or management training. Matthew Stewart (2009), a former management consultant turned disapproving critic, comments: "Upon putting the gurus' books down, however, I find that I get the same

CHAPTER OUTLINE

- Definition of Leadership
- Leader Emergence
- Competent Leadership Perspectives
- Virtual Group Leadership

4. Identify the strengths and limitations of five leadership perspectives.

5. Address cultural applications of leadership theory.

feeling I get after reaching the bottom of a supersized bag of tortilla chips. They taste great while they last, but in the end, what am I left with?"; he later answers, "platitudes," "bundles of non-falsifiable truisms," and "transparently unsubstantiated pseudotheories."

Clearly, *effective leadership is widely viewed as critical to business success* (Leimbach, 2018), but insightful academic research on leadership effectiveness is too often ignored, while the press and the popular culture lionize the flashy, quick-fix books by corporate celebrities. With few exceptions (some referenced in this chapter), they have mini-

mal merit. Fortunately, you do not have to depend on these self-promotional, personal testimonials on leadership. One highly acclaimed reference book takes more than 1,500 pages to review the vast research and theory on leadership (Bass & Bass, 2008), and much additional research has been conducted since this monumental work was released (see Moore & Bazerman, 2022; Dubrin, 2019).

This reservoir of research serves as the foundation for *this chapter's principal purpose, namely, to explore leadership effectiveness in the workplace and the essential role communication competence plays*. Just

Stanford business professor Jeffrey Pfeffer (2015) observes critically, "There are no 'barriers to entry' into the leadership industry; no credentials, rigorous research, knowledge of relevant scientific evidence, or anything else required to pass oneself off as a leadership expert." He notes that "anyone and everyone can write a book" on leadership, and "it seems that virtually everyone does.

imagine exercising effective leadership without communicating competently. *Competent leadership and communication are inextricably interconnected.* In far fewer than 1,500 pages, much to your relief we are sure, four objectives are addressed: (1) defining leadership, (2) discussing how to gain leadership in the workplace, (3) exploring the do's and don'ts of effective leadership in the world of business, and (4) addressing cultural applications of leadership theory.

Definition of Leadership

There is an evolving consensus among academics that leadership is a social influence process (Northouse, 2021). Influence is the essence of leadership (C. Johnson & Hackman, 2019). This influence can come from status, authority, personality, credibility, interpersonal and group relationships, and a host of other power resources; but it ultimately is exhibited through communication with others.

Leading and Managing: Different Influences

Have you ever worked for a manager, perhaps while employed at a juice bar, grocery store, sporting goods store, or some other service-oriented job, who seemed less capable to lead than a disoriented person lost in a maze? Ask employees how they respond to "being managed." On our campus, even referring to "managing" employees, whether they be faculty, staff, or student workers, is a surefire way to trigger a Krakatoa-like eruption of verbal rebellion. "Being managed" has negative connotations. As one report puts it, "Newsflash: No one WANTS to be managed. Even the term 'manage' evokes feelings of control and manipulation" ("People Hate Being Managed," 2021). *There are two primary differences between a leader and a manager* (Hackman & Johnson, 2019).

Difference 1: Positional Versus Interpersonal Influence In many of our leadership trainings, people think of leadership as a product of one's title: CEO, CFO, and even Project Managers are viewed as leaders. Sales reps, service providers, and receptionists are not. Leadership, however, can extend well beyond the power accorded a title. In fact, Driscoll's, a multibillion dollar international produce company for which Michelle has provided extensive training, expects all of their employees to be leaders, regardless of their title. In line with this viewpoint, we want you to *begin thinking of leadership as primarily a process not a person with a title*. Each of you, regardless of your level of experience, power position, and tenure on the job has leadership potential that can be actuated by communicating appropriately and effectively.

Managers are formally assigned the position of authority. Having positional authority, however, does not make a person a leader, especially an effective one. *A leader exercises interpersonal influence persuasively (leader–follower relationship), but a manager exercises positional influence, sometimes coercively (supervisor–subordinate relationship)* by issuing orders and edicts to garner compliance from others. One global report on leadership involving more than 7,000 business executives from 130 countries, concluded, "The whole notion of 'positional leadership'—that people become leaders by virtue of their power and position—is being challenged. Leaders are instead being asked to inspire team loyalty through their expertise, vision, and judgment" (Wakefield et al., 2016). *Using a power position makes a person a boss, maybe even a competent boss, but not automatically a competent leader*. This means that as a student working with peers, you will not exercise managerial authority; but you can become a competent leader on your project team, during discussion sessions, or in study groups by communicating competently with group members.

Difference 2: Maintaining Versus Changing Leaders work to change the status quo; managers typically maintain it. Managing involves, among other things, working with budgets, organizing tasks, solving problems as they arise, enforcing rules when they are broken, and keeping things running smoothly by carrying out policies and plans devised by those with greater authority (Bryant & Higgins, 2010; Gavin, 2019). The primary goal is efficiency, not transformation. If you were, say, a manager of a local fast-food restaurant, part of a national chain, you do not have the authority to decide, for example, whether the menu will offer more organic selections. That is a decision made by "corporate." You do not change the status quo. You implement it. As Muriel Wilkins, C-suite advisor and cofounder of leadership development firm Paravis Partners explains, a manager is "the individual who aims to keep things within the lines and the leader is the one who creates new lines" (quoted by M. Hoch, 2021).

Leadership implies change, not merely implementing or enforcing policies and rules. "Leadership deals with change, inspiration, motivation, and influence" (Dubrin, 2019). Some have called this **transformational leadership** (Bass & Bass, 2008). We agree with Rost (1991) when he claims, "Leadership, properly defined, is about transformation, all kinds of transformations." The social influence process (persuasion) that is the essence of leadership inherently implies transformations, small and large—changes in attitudes, beliefs, or behavior (Haslam et al., 2011). *All leadership, therefore, is transformational to a greater or lesser degree.*

Differences Not Categorically Exclusive: Matter of Emphasis   So, the terms *leader* and *manager* are not synonymous. Distinguishing the two, however, does not exclude one person from being both (Blom & Alvesson, 2015; Dubrin, 2019). Leaders are most effective when they can inspire followers and also manage a budget, problem solve, and organize a plan of action. Conversely, a manager may be interested in more than merely maintaining the status quo, thus exercising leadership by lobbying

Unlike leaders, if you act as a designated manager of a fast food restaurant, for example, you do not set the rules of operation. You may even believe that some of the rules and regulations are silly, but nonetheless you enforce them because that is your job as the manager. The goal is efficiency, not transformation. Does this preclude managers exercising real leadership in some circumstances?

for meaningful changes. *These distinctions between leaders and managers are matters of emphasis.* They are overlapping not completely separate categories. Thus, if you have the capacity to inspire and motivate your coworkers to make changes in your workplace, then you have the capacity to lead regardless of your place in the organizational hierarchy.

Leadership and Followership: Let's Dance

If you think that you are leading a parade but no one is following you, are you really a leader? Acclaimed business professor Warren Bennis (2007) notes, "The only person who practices leadership alone in a room is the psychotic." Leaders influence followers, but followers also influence leaders by making demands on them, requiring them to meet members' expectations, and evaluating their performance based on expectations (Avolio, 2007; Blom & Alvesson, 2014). A Deloitte survey of 1,531 Gen Z respondents (born after 1995) draws this conclusion: "Gen Z has the opportunity to shift the 'balance of power' between the employer and the employee to a model where instead of workers trying to fit into a box called a 'job,' organizations will need to tailor work around the curated skillset of a worker." The report continues: "We think Gen Z will have the ability to demand greater personalization in how they move along their career journey" (Gomez et al., 2019). Followers can also influence leaders dramatically by mounting responses to leaders' decisions on social media platforms (Gilani et al., 2019). Thus, *a definition of leadership must reflect the interconnected relationship between leaders and followers* (Dubrin, 2019).

Negative connotations have been associated with the term *follower,* however, such as powerless, passive, pliable, sheep-like, even unintelligent. Henry Ford, who pioneered the mass-production assembly line, articulated an apparent contempt for his workers who he expected to follow directions from their supervisors like robots: "The average worker," Ford asserted, "wants a job . . . in which he does not have to think." Ford further claimed that, of

the 7,882 operations necessary to construct a Model T automobile, 2,637 could be completed by "one-legged men," 670 by "legless men," 715 by "one-armed men," 2 by "armless men," and 10 by "blind men." Continuing in this vein of supposedly amusing contempt for the worker/ follower, he asked, "Why is it that when I ask for a pair of hands, a brain comes attached?" (Ford, 2003). This vision of followers parking their brains at the door and mindlessly obeying whatever orders are issued by those in powerful positions has been relegated to the trash can of archaic thinking (Henricks, 2018).

Modern researchers and scholars see leadership as a shared-power partnership (Dubrin, 2019). Leaders and followers act like ballroom dancers. One leads and the other follows, but they influence each other by communicating in tandem. If not, they will look like stumbling drunks on a binge. Thus, *leadership is primarily a process not a person* (Platow et al., 2015). When you look at leadership from this angle, there can be no doubt that focusing only on those in leadership positions without analyzing the complex communication transactions that take place between leaders and followers wildly misses the mark. Thus, a definition of leadership emerges. **Leadership** is a leader–follower social influence process, directed toward positive change that reflects mutual purposes of group members and is largely accomplished through competent communication.

It should become apparent as this chapter unfolds that opportunities for you to exercise leadership regardless of your age, experience, job resume, or a host of additional factors are plentiful. *You do not have to be accorded an official title or position within a group to exhibit competent leadership.* Learning early how to become a competent leader can boost your career choice and hasten your progress toward achieving personal life goals.

Leader Emergence

Individuals in the workplace are regularly appointed through formal processes to positions of authority, often called **designated leaders.** Designating someone to be a leader assumes that this person has the requisite abilities to inspire, motivate, effect change, and transform beliefs, attitudes, and behavior. Too often, however, designated "leaders" may have managerial skills that make them capable of implementing organizational policies and efficiently running day-to-day tasks, but they are incapable of providing true leadership. As previously explained, true leadership comes from interpersonal influence, not positional influence. **Emergent leaders**, the focus of this section, "are group members who significantly influence other group members even though they have not been assigned formal authority" (Dubrin, 2019). They rise through informal communication transactions, earning the admiration of employees and influencing them by exhibiting competent communication.

Emergent leaders can rise quite unexpectedly during challenges small and large. When COVID-19 struck, requiring everyone to bunker in a Zoom room, those more technologically savvy but lacking formal authority could exercise greater influence on their teams than a person with the formal title of chair, facilitator, or the like with limited technological skills to keep team transactions up and running smoothly. Some such individuals we have encountered who were responsible for chairing meetings had repetitive difficulty even remaining connected during Zoom meetings, requiring others to step into the breach and conduct the proceedings. In one case, the chair of a board of trustees kept appearing on screen during a Zoom meeting, then quickly disappearing into a blank screen only to soon reappear with hair askew and clothes disheveled, having obviously crawled under his desk trying desperately to find the cause of connection problems, which clearly were beyond his technical knowledge. The meeting continued without him, interrupted occasionally as the chairman came up for air to display his rather comical exasperation, as other group members swooped in to assume task roles (e.g., information giver; coordinator-director) despite lack of designated authority.

You do not have to be at the top of the organizational food chain to emerge as a leader. Even as a relatively new, low-level employee, you can influence your team in positive, productive ways. Also, leader emergence is not necessarily a one-time, permanent affair. *In long-standing groups, several leaders may emerge at different times*, rotating through the life cycle of the team, especially when circumstances change and team tasks differ markedly, requiring alternative sets of knowledge and skills. Again, leadership is more a process than a person. Thus, the leader emergence process in the workplace is a significant topic for exploration.

How Not to Become a Leader: Communication Blunders

A survey of Millennials reported that 91% aspire to be leaders (Haynie, 2016). *Another survey found that 81% of Gen Z respondents aspire to be leaders* (J. Miller, 2018). Why do people want to become leaders? There are numerous reasons, but the most obvious ones are *status* that comes from running the show, *respect* for doing a good job of guiding the group, *power* accorded leaders that allows them to influence others and produce change, and a *desire to help* others.

It is often easier to determine what you should not do more than what you should do if you are motivated to emerge as a leader. There are communication behaviors to avoid. Heed the following dictums:

1. *Thou shalt not exhibit Me-orientation.* Groups do not endorse would-be leaders who seem more interested in advancing self-oriented goals than group goals (Grace & Platow, 2015). Relationship building is strongly associated with perceived leadership (Horila & Siitonenm, 2020). (See Chapter 2 on We-orientation and communication competence.)

2. *Thou shalt not be uninformed.* Ignorance is not bliss; it's an abyss, a chasm of emptyheadedness. Leaders are expected to be relevantly knowledgeable. A previously cited Career Builder survey that identified the "most unusual" mistakes made by job interviewees seeking professional employment included one candidate who proudly offered "Fake it until you make it" as his

personal philosophy (L. N. Hayes, 2018). You can imagine how his tacit know-nothing confession was received by the hiring panel.

3. ***Thou shalt not manifest sluggish participation in group discussions***. Group members are not impressed by "vigor mortis." Remaining quiet will get you ignored.

4. ***Thou shalt not attempt to dominate conversation during discussion***. Although those who talk the most are perceived initially as potential leader material (Jones & Kelly, 2007), quality of participation, not mere quantity and volume, is what groups typically desire (J. Jiang et al., 2015). An armor-piercing voice demanding unyielding attention is "loudership" not leadership (Kluger, 2009).

5. ***Thou shalt not listen poorly***. As the sign says sarcastically, "Oh, I'm sorry. Did the middle of my sentence interrupt the beginning of yours?" Groups prefer leaders who listen effectively (Daimler, 2016). As Microsoft CEO Satya Nadella advises, avoid being an annoying "know-it-all," and become more of a "learn-it-all" by listening to others (quoted by McCracken, 2017). (See Chapter 6 on effective listening.)

6. ***Thou shalt not be rigid and inflexible when expressing viewpoints***. Group members prefer open not closed minds. The attitude of certitude provokes defensiveness, not a willingness to be influenced. (See Chapter 5 on communication climate.)

7. ***Thou shalt not display*** *"emotional incontinence."* Emotional outbursts, or what Birgitta Wistrand, CEO of a Swedish company, called "emotional incontinence," will likely brand you as unstable and unfit to lead a group of any size (Goleman, 2013).

General Emergence Pattern: Process of Elimination

In general, informal leaders emerge by a process of elimination (Bormann, 1990). Potential candidates are systematically removed from consideration. Employees in the workplace may be quite clear on what they do not want in a leader, but they may not be as sure about what they do want.

Two Phases of Emergence There are two phases to the process-of-elimination explanation of leader emergence. During the first phase, roughly half of the members are eliminated from consideration. The criteria for elimination are crude and impressionistic. ***Negative communication patterns—the "thou shalt nots"—weigh heavily.***

In the second phase, groups look for task-competent individuals who are committed to

If crying at work is perceived to be the ultimate workplace taboo (Selvin, 2017), it is nevertheless *a common occurrence*. One survey found that of 3,078 respondents, 5.2% admitted to crying at work daily, 8.3% did it weekly, and an additional 50% reported doing it occasionally (Bolden-Barrett, 2019). "Rightly or wrongly, workplace tears do not communicate leadership potential—especially if you're a man. While 59% of executives say crying makes a woman look bad, 63% believe it's a top mistake for men" (Goudreau, 2012). Emotional incontinence can be a leadership deal breaker. Better to cry in private if the need arises.

the group's goals, not personal advancement, to emerge as leaders. Leaders are expected to be doers, persons ready to act to help the work group achieve its goals (Platow et al., 2015). If the group feels threatened by some external or internal crisis (e.g., members with expertise fall sick or leave the group), *the team often turns to the member who provides a solution to the crisis*. Also, those individuals who *exhibit high levels of* emotional intelligence—"the ability to perceive, glean information from, and manage one's own and others' emotions"—emerge as work group leaders more readily than those who do not (Cote et al., 2010; Kim et al., 2021). In fact, based on two studies, "the ability to understand emotions was the most consistently related to leadership emergence" (Dubrin, 2019). This affirms the importance of sensitivity and skills in the communication competence model discussed in Chapter 1.

Gender and ethnic bias, unfortunately, plays a part in the leader emergence process. Issues of gender and ethnic bias were documented extensively in Chapter 3. The bias occurs even before issues of advancement within a company. Initial hiring decisions can be heavily influenced by such bias (Boateng, 2021). Research shows, for example, that male candidates applying for positions were judged more on leadership potential than leadership performance. Female candidates, however, were preferred based on demonstrated leadership performance instead of leadership potential (Player et al., 2019).

Finally, *members who acquire an advocate* who promotes them—their ideas, positions, and abilities—boost their chances of becoming a group leader (e.g., "Rodney has the most knowledge and experience dealing with technological glitches. I think he should address our problem.") A person can acquire an advocate in a variety of ways: through friendship, charisma, common interests and goals, or self-interest and pursuit of power. If more than one member gains an advocate, then the process can become contentious, or it may end in shared leadership.

Virtual Group Leader Emergence *Research on leader emergence in virtual work groups*

parallels these findings of leader emergence in standard, face-to-face groups. Degree of participation is an important consideration, as it is in standard work groups. The type and quality of the participation, however, matters. Virtual group participants have a negative view of those positioning themselves to emerge as leaders when their communication is perceived to be "dominant, opinionated, outspoken, uncompromising, and in pursuant of their own agenda." Virtual group participants have a positive view of those whose communication is "inclusive, collaborative, concerned about others, good listeners, and in search of consensus" (Shollen, 2010). More importantly, as a very large study of 220 student groups found, *doers are even more likely to lead virtual groups than they are in-person groups* (Purvanova et al., 2020). As lead author of the study, Radostina Purvanova explains, "Virtually, we are less swayed by someone's personality. . . . But those chosen as remote leaders were doers, who tended towards planning, connecting teammates with help and resources, keeping an eye on upcoming tasks and, most importantly, getting things done" (quoted by Cohen, 2020). Displaying emotional intelligence is more challenging in virtual groups, and charisma seems to have less influence on virtual group members.

Additional Factors: Implicit Theories of Leadership

When group members first meet, **implicit theories of leadership**—individuals' expectations, beliefs, and assumptions about what constitutes an effective leader—influence the dynamics that favor emergence of certain individuals as group leaders. Try this: Picture a leader. What came to mind? When survey respondents are asked to picture a "leader," they typically visualize a "male" (Koenig et al., 2011; Murphy, 2018). This is especially ironic because several studies reveal that women score markedly higher on measures of leadership effectiveness than men, even when both men and women make the assessments (Young, 2016; see also Post et al., 2021). In fact, Tomas Chamorro-Premuzic (2019), previously cited, has written a best-selling book titled *Why Do So Many Incompetent Men Become Leaders?* He concludes from voluminous research that "most leaders are bad and that most leaders are male." Studies also show that when asked to "think leader," respondents usually "think White" (Gundemir et al., 2014). Too often, those in power (disproportionately white men) merely replicate themselves when making hiring and promotional decisions. Gaining advocates (e.g., men supporting women as group leaders) and being assertive are especially important in overcoming *gender and ethnic bias* in leadership emergence, as already discussed in Chapters 4 and 5.

We develop prototypes in our minds of what qualities a leader should possess—decisiveness (Myers, 2017), confidence (Lipman, 2017), inspiration (Garton, 2017), to name a few. This can produce some odd choices (Williams, 2015). One disturbing study (Babiak & Hare, 2006) found that nearly 4% of 200 business executives qualified as **psychopaths**—"someone who has no conscience and feels no remorse or empathy" (Perman, 2011). *More recent research by forensic psychologist Nathan Brooks, however, bumps the prevalence of psychopathic business executives to an astounding 21%, about the same percentage as found "in a prison population"* (cited by Agerholm, 2016). Whatever the actual prevalence, these are power-crazed, "horrible bosses" not cold-blooded killers.

So why do psychopaths ever emerge as leaders? Initially, they are typically charming, confident, decisive, fearless, and mentally tough. They project an image of a powerful leader that dovetails with common implicit theories of leadership (Dutton, 2016). Nevertheless, they are domineering, ruthless, and manipulative (i.e., ethically challenged). They make toxic leaders who create negative workplace climates (Williams, 2015). *The negative qualities, however, may not become apparent until after the psychopath has emerged and subsequently solidified his or her formal position of authority.*

Similarly, **narcissists**—those who exhibit "a grandiose sense of self-importance; arrogant behavior or attitudes; a lack of empathy for others; a preoccupation with fantasies of unlimited success or power; . . . [and] a desire for excessive admiration from others" (Pfeffer, 2015)—frequently emerge as leaders in the business arena (Brunell et al., 2008; Nevicka et al., 2018). "Narcissists fit our conventional stereotype of what a good leader should look like" (Williams, 2015). They are outgoing, confident, decisive, even charismatic. They are especially successful emerging as leaders of new groups that have not had enough opportunity to observe and experience the narcissist's dark side (Watts et al., 2013). *Narcissistic leaders, however, can diminish worker performance* (Nevicka et al., 2011). This occurs because they lack concern for others, create negative work environments for subordinates, and hinder collaboration in teams (Braun, 2017).

The troubling emergence of psychopathic and narcissistic leaders in the world of business underlines an essential point: *those who emerge as leaders do not necessarily prove to be effective leaders.* Both psychopathic and narcissistic leaders are power-hungry, in-it-for-themselves individuals, not We-oriented team players. *Be careful not to let your implicit theories of leadership cloud your vision and allow yourself to be unduly influenced by those who initially may exhibit flash but lack substance, even ethics.*

Competent Leadership Perspectives

Voluminous research on leadership effectiveness permits several important conclusions. In this section, we explore what has been learned so far.

Traits: Marginal Enlightenment

In the early days of leadership research, the "leaders are born not made" was the popular belief. The search focused on determining what constellation of traits makes an effective leader. *This perspective views leadership as a person, not a process.* Thus, the hunt for the powerfully "heroic" and exceptionally talented individuals to idolize as model specimens of leadership became the focus (Henricks, 2018).

This journey has taken us to strange, dramatically bipolar, even absurd places. You can buy books on the leadership secrets of Meg Whitman, Barack Obama, Colin Powell, Eleanor Roosevelt, Margaret Thatcher, Nelson Mandela, Donald Trump, John Lewis, Alexandria Ocasio-Cortez, Steve Jobs, Attila the Hun, Genghis Khan, Osama bin Laden, and Santa Claus (not kidding).

There remains the common belief that a universal set of traits conflates with leadership effectiveness, sometimes with little consideration for ethical behavior. **Traits** are relatively enduring characteristics of an individual that highlight differences between people and that are displayed in most situations. There are physical traits such as height, weight, physique, beauty, and attractiveness.

There are personality traits such as being outgoing, sociable, or introverted and shy. There are traits associated with inherent capacities of an individual such as intelligence and quick-wittedness. There are also traits associated with consistent behaviors such as confidence, trustworthiness, and integrity.

A huge number of traits have been studied to discover the prototypical effective leader. A Pew Research survey of 1,835 adults found that when asked which traits are "absolutely essential" for a leader to possess, honesty was at the top of the list (84%), followed by intelligence (80%), and decisiveness (80%) ("What Makes a Good Leader," 2015). Stogdill (1948, 1974); however, twice reviewed hundreds of studies and concluded that *no universal set of traits assures effective leadership.* How could it be otherwise? For example, *a trait such as intelligence or confidence could be neutralized by unfriendliness, ethical indifference, laziness, arrogance, or insensitivity.* One study of 3,700 business executives used 60 traits to assess leadership (Stamoulis & Mannion, 2014). Who could possibly possess all or even most of these 60 traits without also possessing at least some neutralizing negative traits (recall the negativity bias)? A 25-year study by the Gallup Organization of 80,000 leaders found that the greatest leaders in the world do not share a common set of traits (Buckingham & Coffman, 1999).

The principal problem with the trait approach is the assumption that effective leadership resides in the person, not in communication transactions between leaders and followers (Northouse, 2021). There may be some essential traits necessary but not sufficient to be an effective leader. There is much more to leadership effectiveness than traits alone can explain. Yet common implicit theories of leadership tend to focus on traits (especially decisiveness, charisma) instead of more complex views of leadership effectiveness.

Styles: The Autocrat and the Democrat

Kurt Lewin and his associates moved away from the purely traits perspective and developed an approach to leadership effectiveness based on three leadership styles: autocratic, democratic, and laissez-faire (Lewin et al., 1939). **Autocratic style** is highly directive and does not encourage member participation. *It typifies the dominance form of power.* The **democratic style** encourages participation

What traits do these top business executives have in common? Age? Gender? Ethnicity? Attractiveness? Extroversion?

and responsibility from group members. Followers have a say in what the group decides. *It typifies empowerment and is well-suited to teamwork and team building* (Dubrin, 2019). The **laissez-faire style** is a sit-on-your-derriere style. It is "the avoidance or absence of leadership" in which individuals "avoid making decisions, hesitate in taking action, and are absent when needed" (Judge & Piccolo, 2004). Thus, it is non-leadership and has been dropped from serious consideration in most leadership research.

The extensive research comparing autocratic-directive and democratic-participative leadership styles shows both can be effective (Northouse, 2021). Democratic-participative leadership seems to work best when it springs naturally from the group itself. Not all groups and organizations, however, want or expect their leaders to adopt the participative leadership style (Glynn & DeJordy, 2010).

Nevertheless, one survey of business leaders reported that 76% of 1,400 respondents viewed use of an inappropriate leadership style to be among the biggest failures of leaders ("Critical Leadership Skills," 2014). Typically, it is the autocratic/directive style that is overused and can backfire (Green, 2018; Shonk, 2021a). It tends to tap into psychological reactance and resistance.

Situational Leadership: Be Agile

One weakness of the autocratic-directive/democratic-participative leadership style duality is that these styles are sometimes viewed as inflexible choices, as though one style is always better than the other. Individuals operate as either participative or directive leaders, but not both. *Realistically, though, a combination of both styles is required.* In organized sports, for example, the autocratic leadership style is

---

SELF-ASSESSMENT:
What Is Your Leadership Style Preference?

Fill out the self-assessment on leadership styles. *Note: The rating scale changes.*

1. I like it when my supervisor at work admits openly that they made a mistake.

STRONGLY DISAGREE			STRONGLY AGREE	
1	2	3	4	5

2. I want to be told what to do on the job, not have to figure it out for myself

STRONGLY DISAGREE			STRONGLY AGREE	
5	4	3	2	1

3. If my team were hiring a new applicant, I prefer that the entire team interview the candidate and make the final decision, not the team leader only.

STRONGLY DISAGREE			STRONGLY AGREE	
1	2	3	4	5

4. I don't want my boss to be my friend; I prefer that my boss remain aloof from the group so they can be objective when decisions need to be made.

STRONGLY DISAGREE			STRONGLY AGREE	
5	4	3	2	1

5. I do not think that my boss should reverse the decision of the team except in extraordinary circumstances (dangerous mistake).

STRONGLY DISAGREE			STRONGLY AGREE	
1	2	3	4	5

6. I prefer to be told what decisions have been made then informed what I should do to implement these decisions, not engage in time-consuming debate.

STRONGLY DISAGREE			STRONGLY AGREE	
5	4	3	2	1

7. I prefer having many opportunities to provide input before my team leader makes a final decision.

STRONGLY DISAGREE			STRONGLY AGREE	
1	2	3	4	5

8. I want my boss to make the important decisions, not get me and others on our team involved.

STRONGLY DISAGREE			STRONGLY AGREE	
5	4	3	2	1

9. I want my boss to encourage robust debate and differences of opinion before any decisions are made.

STRONGLY DISAGREE			STRONGLY AGREE	
1	2	3	4	5

10. I want my boss to be decisive, to make decisions confidently, and model a person who is totally in charge.

STRONGLY DISAGREE	STRONGLY AGREE			
5	4	3	2	1

Tally your total score and divide by 10. The higher your average score, the more you prefer participative leadership from supervisors/bosses/team leaders. The lower the average score, the more you prefer the directive leadership style.

---

preferred by some athletes but not by others (Turman, 2003). Also, consider a "temp worker" who is new on a job. Should this person participate on how the job should be accomplished when he or she has only recently located the restroom and may have an imperfect idea regarding what the job entails? No one style of leadership will be suitable for all situations (Glynn & DeJordy, 2010).

One popular situational leadership model offers four leadership styles: *telling* (high task focus, low relationship emphasis), *selling* (high task, high relationship), *participating* (low task, high relationship), and *delegating* (low task, low relationship). The primary situational variable

to consider when matching which leadership style is appropriate is the readiness level of an employee. **Readiness** is the ability (competence) and willingness (commitment) to accomplish a specific task. As readiness levels increase, leadership styles change. For example, an employee who is relatively unprepared to accomplish a task (low readiness) requires a telling style of leadership that is directive. An employee who is well-prepared and committed (high readiness) requires a delegating style that avoids micromanaging and trusts the employee to perform optimally.

Despite its popularity and permutations of this and other situational models (e.g.,

Leadership Grid; Situational Leadership II), as Dubrin (2019) notes, these theories "have not been researched for decades"; and what skimpy research has been done long ago on the validity of their prescriptions is inconclusive, even contradictory (Northouse,2021; Vecchio et al., 2006). Nevertheless, *the underlying premise of all situational models is sound, which is that one leadership style does not fit every situation, and leaders must adapt to changing circumstances* (Dubrin, 2019).

One way of analyzing changing circumstances in a less detailed, prescriptive manner is to simply consider *both the speed and quality of decision making*. For example, in a crisis situation in which swift action is imperative, the autocratic/directive style is most appropriate. Crisis teams (e.g., first responders) are trained to take swift action and to follow the directions of those in command. There is not time to deliberate options while a building is on fire and people need to be rescued. Nevertheless, when an actual emergency is not occurring, a democratic/participative leadership style could encourage fruitful, creative problem solving among team members to improve response times and decision making. *The situational leadership perspective rightly emphasizes the significance of context to leadership effectiveness and the importance of flexible use of styles to fit differing situations.*

Functional Leadership: Shared Leadership

The **functional, or shared leadership** perspective recognizes that "it's all of our business." Leadership is largely a process of empowering others to make better decisions (Moore & Bazerman, 2021). *This perspective truly embraces the view that leadership is more a process than a person* (G. Thomas et al., 2013). There are certain functions, or responsibilities, that must be performed for the group to be successful. Typically, these functions fall into two categories: task requirements and social needs. Finding the right blend of emphasis on task and social dimensions of groups is viewed as essential. Disney accentuates this blend in its employee training programs. When handling customer complaints, they tell employees that it does not matter who is to blame—it is now the

Some situations, such as emergencies, require prompt action and an autocratic/directive leadership style.

employee's problem to solve. Similarly, when adhering to their theme parks' reputation for cleanliness, every employee—no matter what their position—is held responsible for tidying up if they see something in disarray.

Leadership as a shared responsibility is demonstrated when any member steps in and assumes whatever role in the group (e.g., information giver, harmonizer, facilitator, etc.) is required that has not been filled by any other member (see Chapter 9 for a list of informal group roles and their attendant functions). No one, for example, has to be formally assigned the role of devil's advocate to function in this role when the need arises. If you see that your team has made a decision too quickly without adequate consideration of potential disadvantages, ask a relevant devil's advocate question, such as, "Before we finalize this decision, have we fully considered how much this will actually cost?" Similarly, when a group member dominates discussion, any other member can step in and play the gatekeeper role to quell the gabster (e. g., "I'd like to hear from some other members"). It does not have to be the sole responsibility of the designated leader (e.g., committee chair). *When you see the need, fill the void by assuming the appropriate role function.* This, of course, is unlikely to occur if autocratic leaders discourage group member participation.

Servant Leadership: Ethical Necessity

Ethical leadership is largely missing from previous perspectives. In Chapter 1, ethical communication criteria—honesty, respect, fairness, choice, and responsibility—were identified. One study of 195 global leaders ranked "high ethical and moral standards" as most important among 74 "leadership competencies" (Giles, 2016). Unfortunately, too often pragmatic concerns push the ethics of leader behavior into the background, or make them virtually invisible (Knights, 2017).

A key principle of ethical leadership recently gaining popularity is the dictum to "serve others." Ethical leaders are **servant leaders** who "place the good of followers over their own self-interests and emphasize follower development [empowerment] . . . They demonstrate strong moral behavior toward followers" (Northouse, 2021). Initially offered by Robert Greenleaf (1977), the concept of servant leadership has been studied and developed more recently (Spears, 2010; Walumbwa et al., 2010). Heavy emphasis is placed on caring for others, not advancing one's own self-interest. A leader must "operate beyond the ego, to put others first" (Knights, 2017).

Servant leadership embraces the five elements of communication ethics. A servant leader is scrupulously honest, respectful, and fair toward followers, provides choices for followers when possible, and is responsible for helping the group achieve goals in ethically acceptable ways. "A servant leader is therefore a moral leader" (Dubrin, 2019).

Servant leadership is also manifested by mentoring followers and empowering them to become leaders in groups. When asked, "how would you like to learn to lead," more than 60% of millennials responded, "I'd like a mentor." A remarkable 95% of those receiving mentoring from leaders received promotions at work within 18 months (Wartham, 2016).

As former Facebook Chief Operating Officer Sheryl Sandberg explains, "Leadership is not bullying, and leadership is not aggression. Leadership is the expectation that you can use your voice for good. That you can make the world a better place" (quoted by McFadden & Whitman, 2014). You are a servant not a master.

The servant leadership perspective is not just a "nice idea." Criticisms that servant leaders are subservient, weak leaders takes the incorrect view that leadership requires dominance and an autocratic style (Schwantes, 2016). Jim Olson, chief communications officer at Steward Health Care, counters this view: "There is a seismic shift occurring in leadership from command-and-control leaders to servant leaders." He continues: "The days of transmitting a single message or directive from the C-Suite and expecting tens of thousands of employees to read it, believe it, and embrace it are over. Today's leaders must pivot from talking, directing and controlling siloed divisions to supporting, enabling and inspiring teams of teams" (quoted by Henricks, 2018).

Servant leadership is about building relationships with employees and creating an atmosphere of empowerment. "Servant leaders develop cultures in which followers become servant leaders" (S. Brown & Bryant, 2015). Research shows that ethically congruent servant leadership benefits group members by reducing stress and producing team effectiveness (Sajjadi et al., 2014). The Cleveland Clinic, one of the world's premier healthcare providers, implemented a program of servant leadership in 2008. The results were impressive. Patient satisfaction was greatly improved following extensive training of staff in servant leadership (Patrnchak, 2015). Note that it was entire staffs that were trained in servant leadership, not just those with authority and titles, underlining again that effective leadership is a shared, collaborative communication process permeating all levels of groups and organizations.

Leadership Across Cultures: Few Universals

"Almost all of the prevailing theories of leadership, and about 98% of the empirical evidence at hand, are rather distinctly American in character" (House & Aditya, 1997). This has not changed appreciably in recent years. Can we apply the leadership effectiveness theories discussed in this chapter universally across cultures?

Research does suggest that some differences across cultures regarding leadership do exist (Sertel et al. 2022). Even though in the United States the importance of leadership is widely taken for granted, other cultures do not necessarily share this view (Plaister-Ten, 2017). A huge research project called GLOBE, conducted by a collaborative group of 170 scholars worldwide, studied 62 cultures and 17,300 individuals in 951 organizations. It revealed that status and influence accorded leaders vary widely among cultures (House, 2004). Americans, Arabs, Asians, the British, Eastern Europeans, the French, Germans, Latin Americans, and Russians tend to idealize strong leaders, erecting statues and naming streets and buildings after those thought to be extraordinary. German-speaking parts of Switzerland, the Netherlands, and Scandinavia, however, are generally skeptical of strong leaders and fear their abuse of power. In these countries, public commemoration of leaders is sparse. Leadership characterized as elitist, self-centered, and egotistical is perceived to be slightly effective in Albania, Taiwan, Egypt, Iran, and Kuwait. All other countries in the GLOBE study, however, especially Northern European countries, had a very negative opinion of such leadership. The participative leadership style, typically accepted or even preferred in Western cultures, is questionably effective in Eastern cultures (Dorfman, 2004). Directive leadership is strongly favored more in Middle Eastern cultures (Scandura et al., 1999).

There do seem to be a few universals in the cross-cultural research on leadership. The GLOBE study revealed strong endorsement by all cultures examined of such leadership attributes as having foresight and planning ahead; being positive, encouraging, dynamic, motivating, communicative, and informed; and being a team builder. Conversely, "the portrait of an ineffective leader is someone who is asocial, malevolent, and self-focused. Clearly, people from all cultures find these characteristics to hinder effective leadership" (Northouse, 2021). Less clearly, being individualistic, status conscious, and a risk taker was viewed as enhancing outstanding leadership in some cultures but impeding outstanding leadership in other cultures (Dorfman, 2004). Also, an in-depth study of 1,500 corporate executives and public-sector leaders in 60 countries and 33 industries found that among the North American

CEOs, 65% viewed integrity as a top trait for tomorrow's leaders, but only 29% to 48% of CEOs from other countries shared this view (A. Carr, 2010).

Again, even if agreement on a certain set of leadership traits existed across cultures, this would be very different from demonstrating effective leadership in actual practice. In any case, we still have much to learn about effective leadership across cultures.

Communication Competence: The Overarching View

"Extraordinary leadership is the product of extraordinary communication" (Hackman & Johnson, 2018) The leadership perspectives discussed in this chapter offer useful insights about leadership effectiveness, but ultimately all of these perspectives depend on competent communication. Those leaders rated as the most skillful communicators are deemed the most effective leaders (Riggio et al., 2003). A survey of 1,400 leaders, managers, and executives found that the "most critical leadership skill" by far was the ability to communicate effectively and "the biggest mistake leaders make" is "inappropriate use of communication" ("Critical Leadership Skills," 2014). A Harris poll asked 1,000 workers to identify the "communication issues that prevent effective leadership." Respondents listed the following: not recognizing employee achievements (63%), not giving clear directions (57%), not having time to meet with employees (52%), refusing to talk to subordinates (51%), taking credit for others' ideas (47%), and not offering constructive feedback (39%) (cited by L. Solomon, 2015). A similar list added poor listening, micromanaging, and refusing to consider different opinions and ideas from one's own (Haden, 2013).

Communication competence is at the heart of leadership effectiveness. Effective leaders create a supportive, positive climate, encourage open communication, stimulate cooperation and a collaborative spirit, empower others, show empathy, listen actively, and address conflicts in a timely manner. *Showing respect for followers is also a critical communication imperative for leaders* (van Quaquebeke & Eckloff, 2010) and a key element of ethical communication. A survey of 20,000 employees worldwide by Georgetown University Professor Christine Porath found that feeling respected by their superiors at work topped the list as the most important leadership behavior (cited by K. Rogers, 2018). Leaders exhibit respect by recognizing and appreciating the importance and worth of others. You compliment good work; and when mistakes occur, you engage in constructive dialogue to correct the error instead of criticizing and deflating the individual. You act politely toward group members. You show a genuine interest in others' opinions, and you don't blame others for your own mistakes. In short, *you exercise supportive communication not defensive communication patterns* (see Chapter 5). Because of the interconnectedness of leaders and followers, the more followers "feel respected by their leaders, the more they will 'return the favor' by being open to their leader's influence" (van Quaquebeke & Eckloff, 2010). Unfortunately, respect from leaders is highly desired by followers but too rarely experienced (van Quaquebeke & Eckloff, 2010).

Virtual Group Leadership

Virtual groups pose many unique leadership challenges (Bakken, 2019). "Long gone are the days when most teams not only worked side-by-side but also lived in the same cities, ate at the same restaurants, and even had kids who attended the same schools" (Grenny & Maxfield, 2017b). Establishing close, critical, interpersonal connections between a leader and group members is difficult in a virtual environment. One study found that 82% of virtual groups did not achieve their goals (Lepsinger, 2020). Poor leadership is a primary reason for such prevalent failure. A study of 15,000

Virtual groups present unique leadership challenges not experienced in standard in-person teams.

executives ranked leading virtual teams as by far their weakest skill ("The Ultimate Guide," 2021), and yet *"Leadership is the factor most important to the success of virtual teams"* (Lepsinger, 2020).

Distributed (shared) leadership is especially relevant (Eseryel et al., 2021). Exercising leadership with a dispersed group connected primarily or exclusively by electronic technology almost guarantees that "leadership focus shifts from individuals to networks of relationships because the Internet facilitates connecting so many people" (Dubrin, 2019). As also noted, there are cultural differences in attitudes toward hierarchy and authority. Multicultural groups may experience confusion and tension when there is no consensus regarding how leadership should be displayed.

Much of what has already been suggested in this and previous chapters need only be mentioned, but requires underlining the need for added emphasis above and beyond what should occur for in-person groups. Research shows that distributive, shared leadership "provides many benefits to virtual teams such as emotional stability, agreeableness, mediating effects on the relationship between personality composition and team performance" and building trust and strong personal relationships among members (Morrison-Smith & Ruiz, 2020).

Recognizing leadership of virtual groups as a shared responsibility, here are suggestions for enhancing effectiveness (Dubrin, 2019):

1. *Relationship building is essential* (Bakken, 2019). There are "degrees of virtuality" (Hacker et al., 2019). Occasional face-to-face meetings of virtual group members can help build social relationships, enhance cohesiveness, and strengthen group collaboration to solve problems (Trees, 2017). As principal facilitator, scheduling an in-person meeting is especially important as an initial meet and greet. Provide praise and recognition as warranted. Admittedly, this can feel more awkward in a virtual environment that can seem impersonal, but it is important. Staying connected electronically with all group members is vital. Send congratulatory emails when a task is completed well, especially if it is a team effort. Holding

virtual reward ceremonies, virtual parties, even mini lectures on shared interests all help create member connections. Again, *any of these options can be a shared effort, not strictly the role of the designated group leader*. Such shared leadership efforts create "commitment, trust, and cohesion among team members" (Morrison-Smith & Ruiz, 2020).

If some initial face-to-face contact is impossible, videoconferencing (Zoom meetings) must suffice as an alternative. When the virtual group first gathers, sharing information about yourself with team members helps to build bonds. Engage in video conversations as time together expands. Send pictures to the group. Share books and movies that you prefer. Engage in informal conversation to break down primary tension as you get to know each other. Connect with each other by texting, emailing, and using other social media options.

2. *Set up chat rooms* that solicit a variety of opinions before the group makes decisions ("Create Your Own Chat Room," 2020). You want to create a safe space for an exchange of differing points of view. Do not permit incivility during these exchanges. These chat rooms should never mimic blogging sites in which contributors engage in trashing anyone who disagrees. Chat rooms are not troll farms, spreading misinformation, inflaming emotions, and stoking conflict. Make sure that group members are active listeners not active antagonists.

3. *Follow the detailed blueprint for conducting virtual meetings and motivating member participation* offered in Chapter 12. Do not cut corners by ignoring some of the advice. Spending a couple of minutes before each virtual meeting interacting by sharing weather reports if members are geographically dispersed, recent activities, family outings, and the like as a warmup can also be fruitful.

4. Finally, *"exemplary communication skills"* are essential to virtual team effectiveness because the challenges posed by virtual teams are so complex (Grenny & Maxfield, 2017b). Setting clear goals, establishing clear roles, developing a positive communication climate by emphasizing supportive communication patterns, and promoting collaboration as a decision-making process are all critical to effective virtual team leadership (Lepsinger, 2020). *Confront any conflicts immediately* so they do not fester and grow (Ebrahim et al., 2009).

SUMMARY

Considering all perspectives and viewpoints presented, what do we really know about leadership in the workplace? Leadership is a leader–follower social influence process, directed toward positive change that reflects mutual purposes of group members and is largely accomplished through competent communication. It is primarily a process and not a person. When not designated, leaders emerge by a process of elimination. Our implicit theories of leadership initially and disproportionally lionize narcissists and psychopaths until this egregious mistake is realized, oftentimes too late. The key to effective leadership is the ability to adapt to changing situations and to exhibit communication competence in the process. This includes responding adroitly to changing circumstances resulting from the movement to virtual groups. The "one leadership style fits all" approach is doomed to fail much of the time. Leadership and communication competence are inextricably bound. No specific set of traits, particular style, set of functions or services will produce effective leadership without the knowledge, skills, sensitivity, commitment, and ethics of all team members participating in the leadership process together.

Film School Case Studies

42: The True Story of an American Legend (2013); Drama; PG-13

Chadwick Boseman plays legendary baseball player Jackie Robinson. What style of leadership does the Robinson character exhibit? Harrison Ford plays Branch Rickey. What leadership style does he exhibit and to what effect?

Gandhi (1982); Drama

Ben Kingsley's masterful, and Oscar winning, characterization of Mohandas Gandhi in his struggle against British rule in India depicts servant leadership. Explain in what ways this is true.

RBG (2018); Documentary/Biography; PG

This well-crafted documentary of Supreme court justice Ruth Bader Ginsberg shows a quiet leadership. What leadership style did Ginsberg typically exhibit? How did she become such a hero to so many young people? How did she exercise such influence on the Supreme Court?

The Devil Wears Prada (2006); Comedy/Drama; PG-13

Meryl Streep plays a boss from hell. Analyze her leadership style. Does it create a positive workplace climate?

TED Talks and YouTube Videos

These TED Talks and YouTube videos can be accessed by going to the Oxford Learning Link for It's All of Our Business or by typing the title of the video into a Google search window.

"Empathy—Best Speech of All Time" by Simon Sinek (Leadership)

"What It Takes to Be a Great Leader" Roselinde Torres

"The Crisis of Leadership and a New Way Forward"

After successful completion of this chapter, you should be able to

1. Distinguish teams from groups.

2. Identify qualities that make good and bad team members.

3. Scrutinize key communication elements that build and sustain effective teams.

Work Teams: A Special Type of Group

It began as a ragtag group of street performers led by Guy Laliberte. It grew into something wild and wonderful. In 1984, Laliberte contacted the government in Quebec, Canada, to sponsor a show he called Cirque du Soleil (Circus of the Sun). With a small grant from the government to perform as part of Quebec's 450th anniversary celebration of Jacques Cartier's discovery of Canada, Laliberte's vision came to fruition. He wanted to create a circus of a much different sort, one that would mix street entertainment with traditional circus acts. The success of Cirque du Soleil is unparalleled. From its modest beginning, it has grown into a billion-dollar business as the largest theatrical production in the world (Kingsford-Smith, 2017). Almost 200 million people in 450 cities on every continent except Antarctica have attended its "mix of circus acts, street performance, unparalleled acrobatic feats and the avant-garde" (Rinne, 2019). It is also a grand exercise in teamwork. Lyn Heward, the creative director at Cirque du Soleil, explains that what's necessary for success is "in having a passionate strong team

CHAPTER OUTLINE

- Definition of a Team
- Team Member Composition
- Building Teamwork
- Virtual Teams

4. Highlight characteristics of effective team leadership.

5. Address the unique challenges of virtual teams.

of people" (quoted by "Cirque du Soleil," 2011). The business became so successful that it offered team building and training modules for companies such as Google, Adobe, and Life Time Fitness, among many others (Xue, 2016). *Their modules parallel much of what is discussed in this and previous chapters, especially those that address power balancing, communication climate, listening, conflict management, and competent leadership.* Unfortunately, the massive success of Cirque du Soleil was seriously disrupted by the COVID-19 forced shutdown of arena performances in 2020, but the entertainment group announced in a June 23, 2021, press release that this "intermission is over" and announced "the long-awaited return" of its touring and residential shows.

In a starkly different direction, a disturbing study revealed the alarming statistic that more than 200,000 patients die each year from medical errors in hospitals (K. T. Kavanagh et al., 2017). Although the reasons for this stunning situation are complex, poor teamwork in our medical workplaces is emerging as a major cause (Mayo & Woolley, 2016). One study found that "more than 70% of medical errors are attributable to dysfunctional team dynamics" (Mitchell et al., 2014). The American Heart Association was so alarmed that it issued a "scientific statement" on the connection between teamwork and patient safety in the cardiac operating room. In part it said, "Nontechnical skills such as communication, cooperation, coor-

dination, and leadership are critical components of teamwork, but limited interpersonal skills underlie adverse events and errors" (Wahr et al., 2013). A comprehensive study conducted by Rice University in concert with four other organizations found that team training of health care employees can reduce patient mortality by 15% and medical errors by 19% (Hughes et al., 2016; see also Morley & Cashell, 2017). "When all clinical and nonclinical staff collaborate effectively, health care can improve patient outcomes, prevent medical errors, improve efficiency and increase patient satisfaction" (Bhatt & Swick, 2017; see also Hambley, 2020). One review of studies of teamwork in the medical field concludes that "communication and collaboration are crucial to the team function of nearly all frontline providers in and across the health care spectrum" (Dinh et al., 2020). With the appearance of COVID-19, "teamwork has become both more important and more challenging" (Tannenbaum et al., 2020).

Although the chances that you will ever join Cirque du Soleil are unlikely at best, and you may never enter a career in the medical field, the lessons these opening examples teach and *what makes teams work or fail across myriad environments will sooner or later become critically important to you.* The wisdom of teams is sometimes a tough sell in an individualistic culture such as the United States, where individual performance is extolled, and personal ego is celebrated. Nevertheless, the wisdom of teams has become increasingly embraced in the workplace for practical reasons (Middleton, 2019). As Dom Price, head of Research and Development at Atlassian explains, "90 percent of organizations claim to be tackling issues so complex they need teams to solve them" (quoted by Welker, 2017). One survey found that 37% of employees say that "working with a great team" is a primary reason for remaining at a company ("21 Collaboration Statistics," 2019). "One of the central pursuits of any organization . . . is how to assemble a high-performing team and set them up for success" (Wright & McCullough, 2018).

Consequently, *the principal purpose of this chapter is to explore how to build and sustain effective workplace teams*. Toward this end, there are five chapter objectives: (1) distinguishing teams from standard groups, (2) identifying qualities that make good and bad team members, (3) discussing key communication elements that build and sustain effective teams, (4) identifying what constitutes effective team leadership, and (5) addressing the unique challenges of virtual teams.

Definition of a Team

All teams are groups, but not all groups are teams. Teams are a special type of group. There are three principal characteristics that identify differences between standard groups and teams. First, *collaborative interdependence is the essence of all teams* (Kelley & Littman, 2005). Team members generally must work together to achieve their goals. When members work mostly for themselves, attempting to advance individual agendas (e.g., gaining promotions), that collaborative interdependence is missing. One workplace survey reported that 86% of respondents blamed lack of collaboration and poor communication for team failures ("How to Improve Collaboration," 2015).

Second, *a team requires complementary, not identical, skills* (Keller & Meaney, 2017). A kitchen staff in a fancy restaurant would perform badly if every chef were a master of desserts but none were able to cook more than the most basic entrees ("You want a burger—great! You want duck a l'orange—tough luck!"). In standard small groups, membership is usually a potluck. You may have lots of desserts but few main dishes. Also, new members of a student senate are not typically chosen for how well they might blend with and complement other

Collaborative interdependence is an essential ingredient in all successful teams. Each member of the team depends on working closely with other team members to coordinate its performance. Just imagine the calamity that would ensue if this Cirque du Soleil acrobatic group did not closely collaborate.

senate members. A study of 366 companies by consulting firm McKinsey & Company found that teams composed of diverse members exhibit greater creativity and perform better by as much as 35% when compared to more homogeneous groups (members with similar characteristics and backgrounds; Hunt et al., 2015).

Third, *team members have a sense of cohesiveness and oneness that exceeds the typical, standard small group*. Members feel an emotional attachment and an identity with teams not usually exhibited in standard groups. Sports teams are prime examples. A budget analysis group, however, is not likely to spark members' emotional connection to each other, a mutual bond that unites them in a common cause. Such groups probably desire to finish the task at hand and quickly move on to more pleasant undertakings.

With the three characteristics that distinguish teams from standard groups in mind, a **team** is defined as a constellation of members with complementary skills who act as an interdependent unit, are equally committed to a common mission, subscribe to a cooperative approach to accomplish that mission, and hold themselves accountable for team performance. Given this definition, obviously *not all small groups can become teams*. For example, a board of directors is a standard business group. Choosing a new CEO may be its specific goal. Board members, however, often do not have complementary skills, may become aggressive and hypercompetitive when advocating for a particular candidate, and debate may ultimately produce a split-vote decision with resulting anger. The goal is achieved (a CEO is chosen), but the process was not collaborative; it was adversarial.

Team Member Composition

Group members are the raw materials of any successful team. Assembling the optimum combination of individuals is the starting point for team building (Mayo & Woolley, 2016). "The best way to build a great team is not to select individuals for their smarts or accomplishments, but to learn how they communicate and to shape and guide the team so that it follows successful communication patterns" (Pentland, 2015).

Team Builders: Diverse, Complementary Skill Sets

Unlike standard groups, teams are not usually stuck with potluck when member composition is the focus. There are usually choices to be made. Who should become a team member depends on what each potential member has to offer the team. You want a diverse, complementary skill set.

Diversity: An Amalgamation   As already noted, diversity is a key element that separates a team from a standard group. Deep diversity—the substantial variation among members in task-relevant knowledge, skills, abilities, beliefs, values, perspectives, and problem-solving strategies addressed in Chapter 9—is critically important when assembling a team. At the IDEO design firm, diverse teams are essential to success (Chion, 2013). Sometimes *unicorns*—"people who don't necessarily fit in a prescribed role, but have a unique perspective and combination of quirky skills"—are hired to avoid creating homogeneous teams that can stifle growth and creativity because of members' sameness (Pham, 2019). When ABC's *Nightline* challenged IDEO to redesign the common grocery store shopping cart, a diverse team of individuals was assembled for the 5-day challenge captured on camera. Engineers and industrial designers collaborated and brainstormed with team members whose backgrounds included psychology, architecture, business administration, linguistics, and biology. Diversity expands the knowledge and skills pool for teams.

Communication Training: Developing Members' Competence   Competent communication is critical to team effectiveness, and high-performing team members typically exhibit superior communication skills. According to Professor Cathy Davidson, Google conducted two studies using "every bit and byte of hiring, firing, and promotion data accumulated since

Boards of directors and boards of trustees do not operate as teams. Members often represent opposing constituencies. Diverse membership is typically not required, as illustrated in this image. Collaboration is also not required, and members can become adversarial when representing constituent groups.

the company's incorporation in 1998" to determine what promotes team success (quoted by Strauss, 2017). The first study, *Project Oxygen*, found that among the eight most important qualities of Google's top performing employees, STEM (Science, Technology, Engineering, and Math) expertise was dead last. "Soft skills" such as communicating and listening, empathy, supportiveness of team members, critical thinking, and problem solving were more important. The second study, *Project Aristotle* showed that "the best teams at Google exhibit a range of soft skills: equality, generosity, curiosity toward the ideas of your teammates [listening], empathy, and emotional intelligence" (quoted by Strauss, 2017).

Communication training must be an integral part of the team equation for success (McEwan et al., 2017; Salas et al., 2012). These "soft skills" must be learned. Completing a college business communication class provides such critical training. Workplace training, however, is often

of dubious quality and efficacy. Dr. Eduardo Salas of Rice University notes, "If you send a group of executives into the wilderness for two days, they might have fun and learn something about one another—but it doesn't mean they'll magically develop teamwork skills" (quoted by Weir, 2018). Frequently, team training programs consist of little more than a weekend "dog and pony show" by an outside consultant, followed by "happy sheets" that indicate participants' degree of liking for the training. Liking, however, does not equal learning; and popularity ratings favor slick, cleverly packaged training programs that provide fun and entertainment but are as worthwhile long-term as a sugar donut to a diabetic. You get pumped before reality hits. Instead of these slick, superficial training sessions, you want ongoing, evidence based, systemic training programs, not a one-time event followed months later by a booster shot from another consultant with a different slick show. *Training should teach team members specific communication knowledge and skills relevant to the team's task* (e.g., design teams solving problems). Context-specific team training is effective in enhancing teamwork and team effectiveness (Salas et al., 2012). This is especially critical for high-risk, high-stress teams such as firefighters or emergency service workers.

One study of operating room staff found that those groups trained in effective teamwork had significantly reduced deaths from surgical errors than those groups that did not receive such training (Neily et al., 2010). A training program at Maine General Hospital essentially taught the difference between defensive and supportive communication skills to its medical teams. The results were nothing short of astounding: Team members were 167% more likely to address directly anyone demonstrating poor teamwork behavior, and the same percentage were more likely to speak up when a doctor or nurse exhibited disrespectful behavior (Grenny, 2009). Communication training builds teams! If you set your sights on a high-risk, high-stress career such as firefighting or emergency service work, context-specific

training is critical, and there is a plethora of college programs that provide such relevant training.

Team Slayers: Bad Attitudes and Communication Behaviors

For teams to be effective, *attitude is at least as important as aptitude*. "Good attitudes . . . do not guarantee a team's success, but bad attitudes guarantee its failure" (Maxwell, 2001). *Corresponding bad communication that easily flows from bad attitudes diminishes team performance*.

Egocentrism: Me-Deep in Omnipotence Those who communicate egocentrically reveal the "Me-first," arrogant attitude that promotes team friction and weakens team cohesiveness. Egocentrism can be a significant problem. One study of data from 750,000 employees about 69,000 managers found that egocentric managers with superiority complexes typically have "fatal flaws" and weaknesses that negatively impact teams. On the other hand, managers

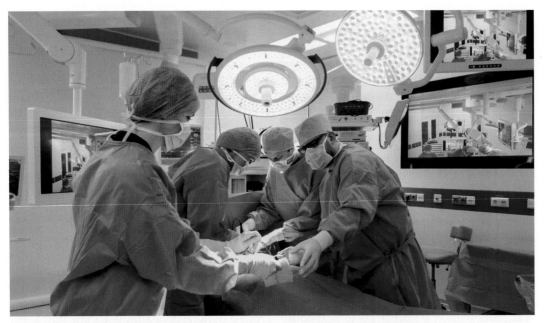

Team training is a vital part of team success. There is no magic to assembling individuals into a group, waving a wand, and declaring them a team. Surgical teams must undergo intense training, and communicating collaboratively is an important aspect of that training. The less they perform as a well-coordinated team that communicates competently, the greater the likelihood of medical errors and lethal consequences.

who exhibit humility and a motivation to improve (mindfulness) are more likely to have "profound strength" and virtually no fatal flaws (Zenger, 2015b). Chairman of software development company Virtugroup Neil Petch (2016) explains the main reasons egocentrics damage teams: "Ego-driven individuals are often led by an unhealthy overconfidence, convinced they are right regardless of the facts. But perhaps the bigger issue is that the businessperson with the inflated ego is far too often seeking glory for him or herself. 'Me' before the company. 'Me' before anyone else."

We-oriented members have a very different effect on a team than egocentric members. We-oriented members communicate with everyone equally, exhibit an infectious interest in others, listen at least as much as they talk, and socialize with all teammates (Pentland, 2012).

Cynicism: Communicating a Can't-Do Attitude

The attitude that most destroys teamwork and team effectiveness is cynicism (McKee, 2015). **Cynicism** is nay-saying, fault-finding, and ridiculing. *When you may need a cheerleader, you get a jeerleader instead.* Cynics are quick to mock human frailties and imperfections and to deride the beliefs of others. They predict failure and look for someone or something to criticize, sapping the energy from the team while spreading their negativity to coworkers (Makela et al., 2020).

Experience and talent are not contagious, but attitude is (Weir, 2018). *What you want in a team member is the communication of an optimistic, can-do attitude, not a cynical can't-do attitude*. An optimistic attitude nourishes a team's spirit, braces it for coming challenges, and encourages aspirations to rise and motivation to increase. For example, on April 29, 2007, an overturned gas tanker-truck burst into a fireball and literally melted 165 feet of elevated freeway on the Interstate 80/I-580 connector ramp in the San Francisco Bay area. Initially predicted to take many months and create a gridlock traffic nightmare, the repair of this collapsed section of roadway was completed in only *18 days*. Clinton C. Meyers, the contractor on the job, explained how his crew managed to complete the monumental repair in so short a time: "I've got a tremendous organization behind me of dedicated can-do people. . . . This shows what you can accomplish when everyone works together as a team" (quoted in May, 2007).

Abuse: Incompetent Communication That Kills Teams

In Chapter 3, we documented widespread abuse in the workplace. Abuse consisted of bullying, sexual harassment, and gender bias. When team members are abused in these ways, collaboration is not possible. Members cannot perform successfully under such a negative communication climate of abuse. Research shows that supervisor abusive communication is a significant problem, and abuse that is perceived to be intentional is particularly destructive (Schyns et al., 2018).

Building Teamwork

Building teamwork is a complicated process that unfolds over time. In this section, key aspects of building teamwork are discussed.

Developing Team Goals: The Four Cs

Setting specific goals is an important step in the team-building process (Klein et al., 2009). Wharton management professor Andrew Carton (2017b) explains it this way: "Articulating a common goal or a common purpose has powerful implications, especially for groups . . . because it galvanizes collective energy. It gives people a common cause that they can all rally around." Research at IDEO found that effective goal setting improved the success of project launches by 12% (DeVries, 2019). There are *four criteria for setting effective team goals that we call the 4 Cs*.

Clear Goals: Everyone on the Same Page

For teams to become effective, clearly stated and understood goals are essential (Van der Hoek et al., 2016). Ambiguous goals, such as "do our best" or "make improvements," offer no clear direction for teams. "Complete the study of traffic congestion by April 15," or "raise $350,000 in donations within 2 years for a scholarship fund for business majors," are clear, specific goals.

A clearly articulated goal is apparent when all members can identify how they will know when the **charge**—the team task—has been accomplished. For example, is an oral or written report required? Does the team report its results to a higher authority? Are there statistical measures that indicate completion (e.g., $350,000 is raised for the scholarship fund)?

In some cases, the goals will be specified by the organization within which teams operate. In other instances, the team will decide through discussion what goals they wish to pursue. In either case, the number of goals should be limited to what can reasonably be accomplished within the specified time period. *A few clear goals that each team member can recite from memory are preferable to goals that are too numerous for members to recall.*

Cooperative Goals: Interdependent Effort   Cooperative goals require interdependent effort from all team members. Members share information freely, offer advice, share rewards, and apply their abilities to make every team member optimally effective (Mayo & Woolley, 2016). *Research clearly shows that cooperative goals enhance team performance*, while pursuing individual goals within a team structure diminishes team performance (Tjosvold & Yu, 2004; Van Mierlo & Kleingeld, 2010).

A **superordinate goal**, a specific kind of cooperative goal that overrides differences that members may have because it supersedes less important competitive goals, is particularly effective for developing teamwork (Sherif et al., 1988). When a group faces a common predicament that jeopardizes its very existence, for example, survival becomes the superordinate goal that can galvanize members to pull together in common cause.

Challenging Goals: Denting the Universe   Accomplishing the mundane motivates no one. Teams need challenging goals to spark members' best efforts. *Members need to feel that they are embarking on a shared mission, with a common vision of how to translate the dream into a team achievement.* The team that built the first

A challenging goal cements team cohesiveness and builds teamwork.

successful Macintosh computer had this elevated sense of purpose. Randy Wigginton, a team member, remembers: "We believed we were on a mission from God" (Bennis & Biederman, 1997). Steve Jobs, the team leader, promised team members that they were going to develop a computer that would "put a dent in the universe". Amanda Steinberg, founder of DailyWorth, made her mission "to cultivate the self-worth and net-worth of women around the world" (quoted by Vozza, 2014).

Changing the world, of course, does not have to be the team's dream. More down-to-earth visions can easily motivate team members, such as, "double office space for computer programmers," "provide free lunches in the company's cafeteria for all employees," or "make the corporate campus safer by replacing old lighting systems with brighter, energy-efficient systems." Your team may not put a dent in the universe, but it may just dent the status quo.

Commitment to Goals: A Passion to Succeed   In a massive study for the Gallup Organization of 1.4 million workers in 66 countries, one key finding was that coworkers who share a commitment to quality is a key to great team performance (Buckingham & Coffman, 2002a). Commitment is a key element of communication competence. It is also essential to team success.

One principal way to create commitment is to have team members share in setting goals for the team (Pentland, 2016). Although not always possible, whenever participatory goal setting can be instituted, it is advisable to do so. Team members typically respond better to goals that they have had a hand in creating than to those that are foisted upon them by others. Please note that even if you are a novice employee, this does not prevent you from being assertive and suggesting participatory goal setting if your team leader is skipping this important step.

Developing a Team Identity: Unifying Members

A group becomes a team when it establishes its own identity, both to team members and to outsiders. **Team identity** is the sense members feel that they are a part of a group, that they belong. There are many benefits that derive from team identity. Research supports that team identity "is associated with higher levels of altruism, collective behaviors, cohesion and ultimately team performance while at the same time it is associated with lower levels of conflict, social loafing, and tardiness" (Robert & You, 2018). *Consider some key strategies for developing team identity.*

Symbolic Convergence: Communicating Fantasy Themes   Ernest Bormann (1986) developed what he termed **symbolic convergence theory**. Moving beyond an analysis of the individual, Bormann focused on how people communicating with each other develop and share stories that create a "convergence," a group identity that is larger and more coherent than the isolated experiences of individual group members. These stories, or fantasies, create a shared meaning for team members. As Daniel Coyle (2018) explains, "Stories are not just stories; they are the best invention ever created for delivering mental models that drive behavior."

Bormann defines fantasies without the negative connotation of "delusions" or "flights from reality." **Fantasies**, he says, are the dramatic stories that provide a shared interpretation of events that bind group members and offer them a shared identity. These fantasies will have heroes and villains, a plot, conflict—anything a well-told story would have (Kafle, 2014).

The fantasy theme serves as a motivation to team members to strive for goals and a vision that are extraordinary, not merely ordinary. Most start-up companies begin with a fantasy theme. Team members share a common vision and experience, and fantasies provide a shared interpretation of events. Each member can relate additional stories that play on the fantasy theme, creating **fantasy chains**—a string of connected stories that dramatize and amplify the theme. In this way, a team creates its own identity.

In our own college department, composed of between 9 and 12 members over the years, a common **fantasy theme**—a consistent thread that runs through the stories told by departmental members—is the challenge to survive and thrive among many much larger departments with far greater clout. We periodically tell the story of our early days at Cabrillo College when our department was under attack from some members of the administration. We relate the drama over the battle for full-time replacements of two retiring instructors; how part-time faculty had their hopes for full-time positions dashed; how this battle pitted us against the college president at the time; and how we went before the college board, the faculty senate, and the faculty union to make our case. Each new member of the department gets to hear a retelling of this story, embellished somewhat over the years. The story serves to create a team identity as a small but determined team.

After the department exhibited substantial growth in student demand, the fantasy theme became "empire building." Initially seen as a dubious undertaking, the theme eventually gained adherents. It permitted departmental members to imagine a time when the department would be regarded as a major player on campus, a result finally accomplished after years of coordinated rhetorical effort by all members of the departmental team. *The fantasy theme serves as a motivation to team members to strive for goals and a vision that are extraordinary, not merely ordinary.* Department members shared a common experience, and fantasies provided a shared interpretation of events. Each member of the department could relate additional stories that played on the fantasy theme, creating fantasy chains.

Solidarity Symbols: Unifying Creatively   Another way to develop team identity is by creating "solidarity symbols" (Kelley & Littman, 2001). A team name, logo, uniform, or style of dress can all serve as solidarity symbols. The jeans and T-shirt attire often found at companies such as the highly successful design firm

Solidarity symbols, such as standard business attire, serve to create a team identity. Of course, the attire needs to fit the context. This might make a nice poster to reinforce the message, "In Business, We All Need to Pull Together in Common Cause" (with a woman calling the shots).

IDEO is an example (Chion, 2013). In fact, T-shirts with individualized inscriptions or sayings—humorous, profound, or just plain whimsical (e.g., "I Might Look Like I'm Doing Nothing—But in My Head I'm Quite Busy")—help establish the loose climate characteristic of design teams. During the Covid-19 pandemic, some businesses allowed, even encouraged, employees to wear masks with amusing messages to create a sense of camaraderie ("I Got a Mask; I Need a Cape"; "My Cussing Muffler"). In other instances, an entire team may wear T-shirts with the same inscription, such as a computer-programming team that wore T-shirts with the inscription "No Coffee, No Code" or "Thank God It's Pi Day." Some businesses require more formal attire, but the effect is the same—to create a team identity.

Team Talk: The Language of We   Team talk is another strategy for creating a team identity and cohesiveness. "A shared language bonds a team together and serves as a visible sign of membership" (Bolman & Deal, 1992). Cirque du Soleil refers to auditions as "treasure hunting," intense training sessions as "boot camp," and describes teams as "family" (Baghai & Quigley, 2011).

Teams establish an identity, a oneness, when they speak in terms of "we" and "our" and "us," not "he/her/they" (Carr, 2017). This language of shared identity is especially important for team leaders to use. For example, it is better for a team leader to say "*We* have to get this done by Friday" than "*You* have to." Team talk emphasizes interdependence and avoids terminology that emphasizes individuality. Use terms such as *teammates* and *team members* instead of coworkers or employees (DuBrin, 2019). IDEO has "design community leaders" not "project managers." Groups at Pixar animation studio provide "notes" on initial versions of films and they "plus" them with suggestions for changes. As Coyle (2018) explains, "These might seem like small semantic differences, but they matter because they continually highlight the cooperative, interconnected nature of the work and reinforce the group's shared identity." The language of *individual* blame and criticism is avoided. Effective teams speak of *collective* blame for failure and give collective praise for success. This is the language of team accountability. Team failure is "our" failure. Team success is also a matter of collective responsibility, and team talk should reflect this.

Designating Roles: Beware of Duplication

Unlike most informal small groups in which roles emerge from the transactions of members, *teams often require a formal designation of roles.* You do not want **role ambiguity** that produces confusion when team members are unsure of the parts they are expected to play (Klein et al., 2009). *A team must have every group function covered by a qualified member playing a specific role so there is little or no duplication of effort.* In a Gallup study of 80,000 managers and 1 million employees (Buckingham & Coffman, 1999), one manager, named Michael, who ran a highly successful restaurant in the Pacific Northwest was asked to tell about his best restaurant team ever. He told of his waitstaff of four individuals: Brad, Gary, Emma, and Susan. According to Michael's description, Brad was a professional waiter who aspired to be the best waiter in town. He could anticipate what customers wanted. Gary always smiled and was cheerful. Everyone liked him, especially the customers. He had an optimistic attitude. Emma was the unspoken team builder. She regularly assembled the team and alerted the crew members to potential problems. Finally, there was Susan, the greeter. She was lively, energetic, and pleasant. She kept track of customers at lunch who typically needed quick service to return to work. She was attentive.

Michael noted that each team member had his or her clearly defined role. "Brad is a great waiter, but he would be a terrible manager.... He respects the customers. He is less respectful of some of the new employees" (Buckingham & Coffman, 1999). Qualities that made Susan a great greeter would not necessarily translate into being an efficient waitperson. Emma worked well with her team members, but she had a quiet personality not particularly suitable for a greeter. Gary would have been a weak team builder. His joking around went too far. Finding the appropriate team member for each vital role permits full utilization of the team's resources.

The original reason that a person is asked to join a team may make role designation automatic. It is not unusual, however, to find that the roles originally contemplated for team members do not work well and must be changed to make the team more effective. *One of the responsibilities of a team leader is to make determinations regarding role designations.*

Team Empowerment: Enhancing Members' Capabilities

"Highly empowered teams are more effective than less empowered teams" (Jordan et al., 2002). This is true for both face-to-face and virtual teams (Kirkman et al., 2004). A key element of team building is structuring team empowerment. This section is an enhancement of our earlier discussion of empowerment in Chapter 4.

Definition of Empowerment: Four Dimensions The concept of **empowerment**, previously discussed generally, is the process of enhancing the capabilities and influence of individuals and groups. Research by IDEO of more than 500 organizations found that "teams that are empowered enough to challenge the status quo, have autonomy and clear processes have 69 percent higher success rates" (Aycan et al., 2020).

Regarding teams specifically, there are four dimensions of empowerment: potency, meaningfulness, autonomy, and impact (Kirkman & Rosen, 1999). **Group potency** is "a team's generalized confidence in its ability to perform across a variety of situations" (Woodley et al., 2019). It is a can-do group attitude. There is a strong relationship between group potency and team performance. Those teams whose members are confident that their team can perform effectively, not just on a single task but across many different tasks, typically perform effectively, whereas teams with low group potency do not perform as well. Feeling empowered to perform effectively as a team can contribute significantly to team success (Kennedy et al., 2009; Woodley et al., 2019).

Meaningfulness is a team's perception that its tasks are important, valuable, and worthwhile. Meaningfulness is enormously important to team success (Carton, 2017a). When

A kitchen crew in a restaurant either has clearly defined roles or teamwork falls apart and a real mess can ensue.

team members view a task as very meaningful, social loafing disappears, and they work harder collectively than they would individually (Karau & Elsaid, 2009). "It coalesces their energy and effort and can build what are called *social contagion effects*, where one person's excitement spreads to another person" (Carton, 2017b).

Autonomy is "the degree to which team members experience substantial freedom, independence, and discretion in their work" (Kirkman & Rosen, 1999). A survey of more than 5,000 knowledge workers globally found that a substantial majority desire greater autonomy, especially regarding flexibility to work anywhere, not just in an office. In fact, 59% of these respondents reported that "they would not work for a company that required them to come into a physical office five days per week." The same percentage also reported that such autonomy is more important than salary and benefits (Reisinger & Fetterer, 2021).

Choice empowers team members. Steve Jobs once said, "It doesn't make sense to hire smart people and tell them what to do; we hire smart people so they can tell us what to do." Team autonomy means that important decision making is a flexible, shared undertaking, not a mandate from a team leader. Because of interconnectedness, no single team member entirely runs the show. Nevertheless, *autonomy does not mean that teams have no supervision or guidance*. "Leaders can foster autonomy by assuming the role of mentor or coach instead of micro-managing teams" (Aycan et al., 2020). Teams with a great deal of member autonomy and with limited supervision (primarily facilitation and coordination) are far more effective than teams with virtually unlimited autonomy (Ancona & Isaacs, 2019).

Impact is the degree of significance given by those outside of the team, typically the team's organization, to the work produced by the team (Kirkman & Rosen, 1999). Impact is often manifested by change outside of the team. If a team makes proposals for change in an organization, but those proposals are mostly ignored and little

Working in teams on desirable tasks can be extremely meaningful and can produce the social contagion effect that spreads excitement throughout the team and nourishes empowerment.

change occurs, the message communicated is that the organization is indifferent to the team's suggestions. The team then feels disempowered, and a "Why bother" attitude likely ensues.

Hierarchical Organizations: The Enemy of Team Empowerment   Traditionally, organizations have been hierarchical, meaning that members of the organization are rank ordered in a kind of pyramid of power: CEOs, presidents, and vice presidents are at the top of the pyramid, upper management is next, followed by middle and lower management, and finally the common workers are spread out at the base. Top-down decision making is the rule, with those at the top of the power pyramid issuing edicts to managers, who in turn tell the worker bees what to do. Employees at the bottom of the pyramid mostly check their brains at the door because they will not be asked to participate in decision making and problem solving. Their role is merely the "heavy lifting."

Hierarchy in traditional organizations is the enemy of empowerment and negatively impacts team effectiveness (Greer et al., 2018). Although some degree of hierarchy provides necessary structure for organizations, flattening traditional, rigid hierarchy somewhat is desirable. *Empowerment flattens the organizational hierarchy by sharing power.* The organizational system becomes more open with information and communication flowing in all directions, with few gatekeepers overly restricting the flow, and with decision making across the organizational spectrum encouraged. Groups can flatten hierarchies and encourage more egalitarian communication by monitoring the speaking times of participants. Reducing the speaking times of more dominant, loquacious participants can make room for those members who are less inclined to fight for the floor to be heard by the group (Khademi et al., 2020). This flattening of the hierarchy is often manifested by self-managing work teams.

Self-Managing Work Teams: The IDEO Model   Self-regulating teams that complete an entire task are called **self-managing work teams**. Most Fortune 1000 companies use self-managing teams within their organizational system (L. MacDonald, 2019). *Self-managing work*

teams embrace empowerment. After sufficient training and education, team members share responsibility for planning, organizing, setting goals, making decisions, and solving problems. They have a great deal of autonomy, and since they control much of their own decision making and problem solving, team results seem meaningful to members and have impact on organizations. As self-managing teams manifest success, group potency increases, further reinforcing members' desire to continue with the team.

Design firm IDEO, a model for self-managing work teams, has a flattened hierarchy characterized by few titles and no time clocks or specified vacation schedules. Employees are free to transfer to overseas offices in London or Tokyo or to transcontinental offices in Chicago or New York, as long as someone from those offices agrees to swap jobs. A team of designers, not "the boss," chooses new team members. At IDEO, employees are treated as equals who set their own schedules (typically 50- to 60-hour workweeks) while meeting demanding standards and strict deadlines. Designers can pick project teams and even occasionally specific projects to tackle.

Leadership and Empowerment: Some Supervision Required   *Teams require leadership even if they are self-managing.* In fact, a survey by the Association of MBAs consisting of current MBA students and graduates found that 58% listed "poor leadership" as a top-three reason why their teams failed (N. Allen, 2018). IDEO has substantial member autonomy but some supervision by team leaders. Remember that leadership is primarily a process not a person. A team may have a designated leader (coach, manager, project director), but *leadership in teams is a shared responsibility.* Linda Hill, professor of business administration at Harvard Business School, puts it succinctly when she notes that effective team leaders "understand that their job is to set the stage, not to perform on it" (quoted by Cook, 2015). Team leaders do not act like bosses if they hope to be effective. The days of "command and control" team leadership are quickly ending, increasingly being replaced with "inspire and empower" distributive leadership (Safian, 2017).

From designing the first manufacturable mouse for Apple to advancing the practice of human-centered design, IDEO has long been at the forefront of creating change through design. (David Kelley, founder of IDEO, in the center of the photo.)

The most effective team leaders are teachers and facilitators—skill builders (Handrick, 2017). They are open to input from team members. One person cannot be expected to know everything, so effective team leadership encourages the sharing of knowledge and wisdom. Autocratic/directive leadership typically operates from fear—fear of making a mistake, of looking foolish, and of being criticized. A team leader wants to drive away fear. Those who fear failure can be paralyzed into a play-it-safe stasis. Project Aristotle, previously referenced, found that the number one thing separating high performing teams from others is **psychological safety**—where team members were free to make mistakes, ask questions, and take risks. As discussed in Chapter 5, trust in the workplace cannot exist in the absence of psychological safety. It "has been well established as a critical driver of high-quality decision making, healthy group dynamics and interpersonal relationships, greater innovation, and more effective execution in organizations" (Edmondson & Mortensen, 2021). *Effective team leaders create a climate in which making a mistake is an expected part of learning.* At IDEO, there is a saying, "Fail often to succeed sooner." When mistakes are made, members are encouraged to learn from the errors. They are not ridiculed or made to feel stupid.

Establishing Individual Accountability: Providing Feedback

Team accountability diffuses the blame for failure and spreads the praise for success. Team building, however, also requires **individual accountability**, which establishes a minimum standard of effort and performance for each team member to share the fruits of team success. Team effort is not truly cooperative if some members are slackers who let others do all the

---

BOX 11.1 Typical Characteristics of Empowered Teams

1. Teams set their own goals and rules.
2. Team members often set their own work schedules.
3. Teams usually design their own workspace.
4. Workspace is divided relatively equally among members.
5. Members devise and embrace rules for appropriate member behavior.
6. Teams, not outsiders, are accountable for team performance

7. Teams determine their membership and remove members who are deemed ineffective or disruptive.
8. Team members are trained to communicate collaboratively and supportively.
9. Decision making is typically democratic, and leadership is primarily distributive.
10. Team members do not ask for permission from the team leader to take risks or make changes, but they negotiate with the team and strive for consensus.

---

work. You must have a mechanism for individual accountability to discourage social loafing (Kozlowski & Ilgen, 2006). A team needs to catch errors, lapses in judgment, and slip-ups.

Individual accountability standards should not be set so high that they assure failure. Opportunities for social loafers to redeem themselves should be available. *The focus should be on raising all team members above the minimum standards—way above if possible— not on looking for ways to designate failures* (Druskat & Wolff, 1999). Minimum standards agreed to in advance by the group might include the following: no more than two missed meetings, no more than two incidents of tardiness or early exits from meetings, work turned in to the team on time, and work of satisfactory quality as determined by peer appraisal.

Individual accountability is different from ranking group members' performances or distributing rewards based on merit. *Individual accountability merely provides feedback that establishes a floor below which no one should drop, not a ceiling that only a very few can reach.*

VIRTUAL TEAMS

Although distinctions between virtual groups and virtual teams are rarely offered by researchers and theorists, there are differences.

They have electronic technologies and remote communication in common, but they differ in the same ways that conventional face-to-face groups and standard teams differ: degree of cooperation, diversity of skills, level of group identity, and commitment of members. For example, online class discussion groups are virtual groups but not virtual teams. Class members join online discussions to fulfill class requirements and share opinions. Little cooperation is required, class members are not chosen because of skill diversity, no real group identity is necessary or developed, and commitment to the online discussion may be lackluster and sporadic.

Everything discussed so far that builds group and more specifically team success has to be magnified for virtual team effectiveness. Choosing team members with diverse knowledge and skills is important to any team, but it is especially critical to virtual teams. As Keith Ferrazzi (2014), a consultant on virtual team development, explains, "We've found that successful virtual team players all have a few things in common: good communication skills, high emotional intelligence, an ability to work independently, and the resilience to recover from snafus that inevitably arise." You don't just plug in random individuals and expect them to flourish magically in a virtual environment. Individuals who can provide supportive communication, avoid defensive communication, exhibit shared leadership by playing key informal roles when certain functions need attending to, and can stringently avoid egocentrism, cynicism, and, of course, abuse of other team members are all essential to virtual team success. Exhibiting empathy that recognizes the inevitability of technological glitches, "challenges that people of historically underrepresented genders, races, ethnicities, language abilities, and other marginalized groups face in their organizations," and a host of problems that can arise in a virtual environment is especially critical (Meluso et al., 2020). *Be understanding and kind.*

Keeping virtual teams small, fewer than 10 members and preferably even smaller at 4–5 members, is also important for virtual team success. The larger the virtual team and the more spread out members' locations are (i.e., time zone differences), the more complicated and potentially frustrating and secondary tension producing this can be (Hadley & Mortensen, 2022). Advice offered on conducting and participating in virtual group meetings (Chapter 3) is particularly essential as teams grow in size. *When keeping virtual teams small is not possible because the task is especially complex, shared leadership becomes even more critical to success.* Trying to navigate in a large virtual team is too complicated for a single leader to exercise effective control, nor is it desirable (Meluso et al., 2020).

SUMMARY

Teams have a higher level of cooperation, team members have more diverse skills, there is a stronger group identity in teams, and teams usually require greater allocation of time and resources than what is found in most standard small groups. Developing effective teams begins with assembling effective team members. The best team members eschew egocentrism, cynicism, and abusive communication practices; and they are experienced and have strong problem-solving abilities, are optimistic, and have received communication training. You

build teamwork by developing team goals and team identity, designating clear and appropriate roles for each member, structuring empowerment into the fabric of the team, and having competent leadership. Competent team leadership is a shared process. Team leaders should foster participative leadership and insist on a cooperative team climate that they themselves also model.

Film School Case Studies

Apollo 13 (1995). Drama; PG

Identify and analyze what made the teams depicted so effective in this crisis situation.

TED Talks and YouTube Videos

These TED Talks and YouTube videos can be accessed by going to the Oxford Learning Link for It's All of Our Business or by typing the title of the video into a Google search window.

"How Google Builds the Perfect Team" Charles Duhigg

"Cirque du Soleil: An Artistic Example of Cooperation"

"Deep Diversity: Managing Diverse Teams at Work"

"IDEO Shopping Cart Project"

"How to Build Your Creative Confidence" David Kelley

"Atlassian"

"Simon Sinek: Why Good Leaders Make You Feel Safe"

After successful completion of this chapter,
you should be able to

1. Create a robust agenda
that clarifies the order of topics
for discussion, participation
methods, and timing.

2. Use communication
competence to participate fully
in any meeting, regardless of
your role as meeting leader or
participant.

3. Navigate virtual meetings
with ease.

CHAPTER 12

Meetings: A Perpetual Challenge

Do you ever remember anyone saying, "I sure wish we had more meetings?" Columnist George Will once remarked, "Football combines the two worst things about America: it is violence punctuated by committee meetings." You may disagree with Will's opinion about football, but most seem to agree with his assessment of meetings. A Harris poll found that almost half of the 2,066 respondents would suffer "any unpleasant activity" instead of attending a meeting, with 18% of this group preferring a trip to the DMV, 17% preferring to watch paint dry, and 8% opting for a root canal ("Meetings," 2015). In a more recent survey of *more than 19 million participants* from the United States, Germany, Switzerland, and the United Kingdom, *100% of respondents* said poorly organized meetings were a waste of time and money (Doodle, 2019). How much money? Gallup estimates the United States wastes 37 billion dollars a year on unproductive meetings (Gandhi, 2019). In a leadership class Michelle teaches to mid- and upper-level managers across the globe, participants create individual "job pie charts"

CHAPTER OUTLINE

- Meeting Preparation: A Leader's Job
- Conducting a Meeting
- Participating in a Meeting
- Virtual Meetings

with proportioned wedges that depict the average time devoted to their main activities at work. Most participants end the activity exasperated, exclaiming that they have too much to do and that ultimately, they need a bigger pie! Next, they are encouraged to create a job pie chart that represents their *ideal* proportions of work activities. Looking through a lens of engagement, productivity, and passion, they are asked what they would *ideally* be spending time on at work? What they add varies, depending on their job titles. What they want to decrease or eliminate does not. After conducting this activity with hundreds of managers on three different continents, the answer is always the same: *the number one area employees wish to decrease is their time spent in meetings.*

Despite this dismal perception and waste of resources, "Meetings-R-Us." Non-managers attend an average of eight 1-hour meetings a week, while managers attend 12. CEOs top the list with 60% of their time spent in meetings (Rogelberg et al., 2013). With all that time, one might conclude that meetings are a vital part of any thriving business, and they can be. Meetings are an essential vehicle for collaboration and communication. Great minds come together enabling the possibility of synergy, decision making, and camaraderie. Meetings provide a place to share information, create strategies, and make agreements. They permit face-to-face participation on issues of mutual concern where each member's ideas and arguments can be heard and evaluated simultaneously by all group members. Meetings are an unavoidable and potentially significant part of a successful business if conducted competently, but there's the rub.

So, why are meetings met with the same dread one might experience waiting for midterm test results? Consultant and author Patrick Lencioni (2004) specifies two reasons: (a) most meetings lack drama and therefore are boring, and (b) they lack context and purpose. Personified as Azkaban's dementors of the business world, poorly designed meetings can suck the happiness (i.e., engagement) out of even the most well-intentioned attendees.

Consequently, *the purpose of this chapter is to explain how to conduct effective meetings.* Toward this end, chapter objectives include (1) determine what to do before, during, and after a meeting when you are the leader; (2) explore how to use communication competence to participate fully in any meeting, regardless of your role; and (3) learn how to navigate virtual meetings with ease.

Meeting Preparation: A Leader's Job

So, you have decided to call a meeting. Meeting preparation is critical. Having a clear purpose and a clear agenda are the top two indicators of successful meetings.

Clarify the Purpose: Avoid Aimlessness

Spend a moment to consider *why* you are meeting. **Don't call a meeting if—**

- The purpose of your meeting can be achieved as (or perhaps more) effectively through an email or phone call.
- It is a routine occurrence that has little value.
- You have a message for one person but want to make it appear like it's for everyone.

Once you have decided that a meeting is required, *determining a meeting's purpose cascades into every decision you make about the meeting* including whom to invite, what to discuss, and how to discuss it. The purpose is the *rational outcome, that is, the tangible, measurable result that needs to be achieved through meeting.* Much like the thesis of a research paper, the purpose of your meeting should be clear, specific, and meaningful, and all meeting content should align with that purpose. As important as it is for you to clarify the meeting's purpose, it is equally important to communicate it to those coming to the meeting so they can best prepare.

To determine the purpose, begin with broad strokes: what is the overarching objective of the meeting? *Most meetings are called to distribute information, generate ideas, solve a problem, or make decisions* (Goff-Dupont, 2019; Lauby, 2015). Which best suits your meeting? Once you have determined the general objective, it is time to refine it by creating your purpose/impact (P/I) statement. Follow this template:

> *The Purpose of this meeting is to* _____ *in order to* _____ *(Impact).*

For example, instead of routinely calling the team together for the Monday staff meeting, drill down to the importance of *why* you are calling a meeting and *what* the most desirable result will be after its conclusion. Steer clear of vague descriptions. Aim for P/I statements that

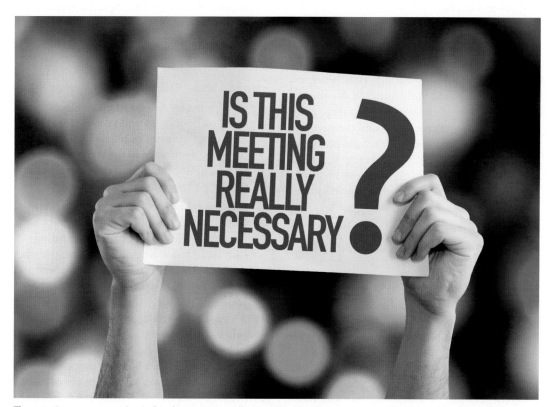

The question on everyone's mind, is this meeting really necessary? Be clear on your meeting purpose before calling the meeting and reiterate to all in the agenda and when the meeting begins.

capture the detail needed to gain clarity and momentum around the required gathering. If there is no clear purpose and/or no valuable impact, do not have a meeting. For example,

> *The purpose of Monday's meeting is to check in with everyone in order to be updated.*

This statement fails to signify the importance of the meeting, and the stated impact is weak, at best. Conversely, here is a better P/I statement:

> *The purpose of Monday's meeting is to review team member's weekly goals and discuss prioritization of clients in order to ensure the right people are working on the right priorities.*

Here is a compelling sample of a P/I statement for a brainstorming meeting:

> *The purpose of our brainstorming session is to gather a minimum of five strong, feasible accounts to pursue in order to meet our year-end quotas.*

Do not get lazy with your P/I statements or ignore the process altogether to save time. Doing this correctly will likely save you time, over time. Pointless meetings that serve no useful purpose and have little or no impact simply frustrate attendees and encourage cynical views of the organization *and* the meeting coordinator. One of work life's little pleasures is the surprise notification, "Meeting has been canceled." Eliminating meaningless meetings will amplify the value of truly purposeful and impactful ones.

Create an Effective Agenda: Simple Steps

Once you have determined your purpose for calling a meeting and its likely impact, consider *what* you need to do in the meeting to achieve your P/I, *how* you will do it, and with *whom*. Many who work at the *Harvard Business Review* have a "no agenda, no meeting" rule (Rousmaniere, 2015). The agenda serves to keep the meeting on track and on topic, communicates participation expectations, specifies the processes used throughout the meeting,

and highlights what pre-meeting preparation is needed. Creating an agenda takes time, but if done correctly, it saves time. Here is how to do it (see also Table 2.1):

1. *Revisit your P/I statement.* Print this at the top of your agenda. (Consider displaying it for all to see at the actual meeting.) Begin with the end in mind.

2. *From your P/I, draft your agenda items.* What must be done? In what order? By whom? What affects the entire team? What can be saved for an email, a one-on-one, or a different meeting? If you already know who is attending the meeting, seek input about agenda items from them as well (see 6).

3. *Check alignment.* Compare drafted agenda items to your P/I statement. Are you including items that will get you to your desired impact?

4. *List your agenda items as questions* in order to encourage participation and drive clarity. Instead of simply putting the words "employment engagement" next to a bullet, for example, write, "What should we do to encourage the engagement of seasonal employees?" (Schwarz, 2017).

5. *Identify the lead.* Next to every agenda item question, label who will take the lead on each topic. This not only saves you from being the only voice in the room, but it increases contributions and thwarts surprises during the meeting.

6. *Manage your guest list.* Now that you know your meeting's purpose, general agenda items, and who is responsible for leading each topic, it will be easier to determine who needs to attend and who does not. Steer clear of automated distribution lists. Ask yourself, "Whose attendance is absolutely necessary?" Consider key decision makers, subject matter experts, stakeholders, and influencers. For decision making meetings, don't shy away from inviting those with dissenting opinions. Still, do not needlessly invite peripheral individuals simply because you do not want to leave anyone out. Keep the meeting size as small as possible to

promote productive engagement. Former Apple CEO Steve Jobs, no stranger to arrogance, declined a meeting with Barack Obama because the president had invited too many people for his liking (Semarjian, 2018).

Once you have carefully curated your guest list, you will have more clarity around meeting logistics such as the timeline, required meeting space, and activities. You will also have a better idea if you should prepare participants by sending any materials for them to read before the meeting, such as reports, articles, or even the presentation slide deck.

7. *Seek input.* Email your list of agenda items (not the completed agenda—you are still working on that) to meeting attendees and get input as to what they'd like to include. Encourage clarity by having them define what and why: *What* would they like added to the agenda and *why* is it necessary to include in this team setting (Schwarz, 2017)? If their request fits the purpose of the meeting, add it to the agenda. If not, consider how it can be addressed in an email, a one-on-one, or a different group meeting.

8. *Choose the best process for each agenda item.* As your purpose/impact statement meets the rational outcome of a meeting, carefully considered processes impact the meeting's *experiential outcome. The experiential outcome targets the dynamics we want meeting attendees to have.* Less tangible than the rational outcome, the experiential outcome might focus on collaboration and trust. How do you want people to engage in the meeting? How will they feel after the meeting has concluded? Recently, when Michelle facilitated a meeting to establish a charter for a newly formed team, creativity and collaboration escalated as pairs created flip-chart pages that captured their interpretation of the group's purpose and then presented their ideas to the larger group. Perhaps an adequate result could have been achieved by going around the conference table and seeking input from each attendee; but that tired method does little, if anything, for engagement, and

surely spurs tedious predictability. Change the monotonous meeting script by trying different methods of involvement and inclusion. Other techniques we have used include creating small breakout groups that debate a question for 5 minutes and then come back and discuss with the larger group; or having each meeting participant "vote" for their favorite idea on a prepared flip-chart using a colored sticky dot (found in office supply stores). Many virtual meeting platforms offer similar capabilities such as breakout rooms, shared whiteboards, and poll voting. Carefully planned processes can dramatically affect the quality of participation.

The standard "I talk/You listen" *approach is tedium times tedium equals tedium squared*. Try breaking free from the traditional meeting equation. Do not waste an opportunity to nail a positive outcome because of unfortunate tradition, meeting malaise, and/or lack of courage to try a different approach.

9. *Estimate time needed.* Designate the anticipated time needed for each agenda item, considering the time needed to solicit information, have discussions, and make decisions if needed (See Table 1). While you are likely to win praise for early meeting dismissal, you will lose the attention (and often the respect) of many when meetings go over time because of your poor planning. Check your time allotment and estimates with the meeting contributors. If you have granted 5 minutes for them to present, check to make sure they can fill that time. Is it too much? Too little? Once timing is agreed upon, hold participants to it. Also, feel free to make estimates outside of the 5-minute increments we see on a clock's face. For example, some agenda items will only take 2 minutes, others might merit 17 minutes—schedule them accordingly.

One way to improve your time estimates is by monitoring the time it takes to get through processes and agenda items in the *meetings you attend or have attended*. Through *reflection-inspection, a study of what went well and what didn't,* curiously investigate the meeting's underpinnings. What topic or discussion took too long and could have been shortened? What was rushed through, needing more attention? Another time consideration is meeting length. Do not be trapped by the antiquated 1-hour meeting time frame. Some meetings will require more time, but many will need less. **Parkinson's Law** states that work expands to fill the time available for its completion. Translated to meetings, it means that if 1 hour is automatically assigned for every meeting, it will take (at least) 1 hour to get things done.

A final time saver is the *assignment of pre-reads*. Pre-reads are simply materials you assign for review before the meeting begins. Increase attention while decreasing monotony by nixing the typical background review/how we got here talk at the beginning of meetings. Distributing information that can be easily read by all before the meeting saves time on the agenda and prepares participants for conversation. *Pre-reads should be concise and essential to the discussion*. Avoid encyclopedic-sized pre-read attachments to the announcement of a meeting unless you like being ignored or teased.

Keep in mind that whatever the choice, the approximated meeting time should accommodate your meeting's purpose and plan.

10. *Create your final agenda.* After all that pre-work, you are finally ready to roll with your agenda. Use a simple three-column grid to capture the timeline, topic, and lead on each agenda item. Once you are pleased with the purpose and the plan, send out your completed agenda so participants know what to expect when they attend.

Attachments (pre-reads) can easily become unmanageable and stressful. No group member is likely to pre-read lengthy attachments, so they usually become useless appendages to emailed agendas. Brevity should be the watchword for attachments whenever possible.

TABLE 12.1 Sample Agenda with Time Estimates

Agenda for Group Project Team Meeting, Monday, 8:00 a.m.–9:00 a.m.
Purpose/Impact: *The purpose of our brainstorming session is to gather a minimum of three strong focus areas to consider for our final group project.*

Time	Topic/Question	Leader
8:00–8:02 (2 minutes)	Welcome: What is the purpose of this meeting?	Anne
8:02–8:06 (4 minutes)	Connect before Content Ice Breaker: What one word describes your current level of interest in our project?	Arun
8:06–8:11 (5 minutes)	Assignment Review: What are the criteria for the final group project?	Anne
8:11–8:18 (7 minutes)	Brainstorm in pairs: What topics could we present and why?	All
8:18–8:33 (15 minutes)	Group Brainstorm: What topics could we present and why?	All
8:43–8:47 (4 minutes)	Which ideas merit further exploration? Vote for top 3	Arun
8:47–8:55 (8 minutes)	Determine next steps: Who will do what by when (WWDWBW)? When will we meet again?	Anne and Arun
8:55–9:00 (5 minutes)	Revisit Parking Lot: Issue? Action item? Agenda? Rate the meeting plus 1	Anne

Get There First: Remember Murphy's Law

Whether you are the meeting facilitator or meeting attendant, arrive early to the meeting, whenever possible. There is no need to make a grand entrance. This is not a coronation. Anticipate problems: Arriving early will give you an opportunity to double-check the room and equipment for problems. Notice the room's layout—are there enough chairs, adequately spaced apart, and is a table required and available? Test the equipment and your Internet connection (if using) before the meeting starts. Check the temperature of the room: If it is too hot or too cold, adjust the room's temperature control. If not possible, consider sending a quick text or email to attendees suggesting they dress accordingly. While they might sound trivial, these little considerations such as seating, climate, and technology can greatly influence the conditions necessary for a participative group.

Before the meeting, write your P/I on the whiteboard, on a flip-chart, or someplace for all to see. This statement will be the backbone of your time spent with the group and will stave off tangential conversations meant for different meetings.

Conducting a Meeting

Benjamin Franklin said, "If you fail to plan, you are planning to fail." Though that typically holds true, simply having a plan (P/I statement and carefully conceived meeting agenda) and preparing the meeting room does not guarantee success. There are additional steps required when actually facilitating a meeting.

Begin on Time, End on Time: Punctuality Is a Virtue

Begin your meetings at their stated time and end them accordingly. Do not wait for the terminally tardy to arrive. By starting a meeting on time only to say the meeting will start when a few more people arrive, you are teaching those who are present that being on time does not really matter. If you will just wait around for people to join, why should anyone bother to be punctual for your next meeting? As for meetings that run late, consider that others may have back-to-back meetings scheduled; and while it is a big deal to you, yours may not be the most important one of the day to others.

Communicate Ground Rules: Avoid Chaos

While many might assume professionalism and competent communication are unspoken yet understood guidelines for how to behave in the workplace, it is not so often the case. There are two types of ground rules: **procedural ground rules** that help the meeting process and **behavioral ground rules** that assist in managing contributions and communication (Schwarz & Heinecke, 2016). Common procedural ground rules include,: "Turn off phones," "Start every meeting on time," and "No multitasking." They should be specific to the group's needs. One team Michelle consulted had a standing ground rule of "No corn nuts in the meeting." Evidently, a member of that group loathed the smell of the crunchy snack. Silly as it sounded, the ground rule was unique to the group and helped them bond. Impactful behavioral ground rules focus on the way people are expected to participate at the meeting. "Stay curious and ask tough questions" permits participants to challenge ideas and information and reinforces psychological safety previously discussed. "Stay on topic and monitor time" encourages people to be mindful when contributing. "Don't leave anything on the table: discuss the undiscussables" calls out the need to confront the tough topics.

Ground rules not only help the flow of the meeting, but they also make communication expectations known to all. Well-established ground rules can also eliminate the counterproductive but all too common "meeting after the meeting"—the informal conversations where employees discuss what they *really thought* about the meeting.

Stay on Track: Parking Lots, Jellyfish, and Perception Checks

Choosing the right participants, starting on time, and sharing the well-designed, detailed agenda will help keep your meeting on track, but good meetings require competent communication. If you are the leader of a meeting, you are responsible for not only monitoring the time and the energy; you are also responsible for encouraging participation and corralling those who see your meeting as their personal stage. Discourage stage hogs. This may require purposeful interruption. Prompt contributions from those who use the meeting time to zone out. Divert the talkaholics with a comment, such as "Let's hear from others," "George, what are your ideas about X?," or "Let's keep our comments targeted so everyone can join the conversation."

Establish a visual **parking lot** for questions and topics that are worthy of discussion but not on the agenda. Put the words "Parking Lot" on a white board or on a piece of flip-chart paper that is easily accessed by all. When an item comes up that is important though not necessarily relevant to this meeting, encourage participants to capture it on the parking lot. This ensures the importance of participant contributions and concerns, while keeping the meeting on track. At the conclusion of your meeting, take 2 to 3 minutes to revisit the parking lot. Determine whether or not each item has been *resolved, needs action, or requires further exploration*, perhaps in the form of a follow-up conversation or meeting. Take a picture of the parking lot with your phone so you can refer to it later if needed.

A light and humorous method that empowers all meeting attendees to monitor time, contributions, and communication is by saying "*jellyfish*" (or some other agreed upon, neutral term) when conversations veer off-track (Frisch & Greene, 2017). Gelatinous jellyfish are the drifters of the sea. Invoking their name reminds people not to drift. Saying "jellyfish" or "this sounds a little *jellyfish* to me" suggests getting back to the originally stated goals (remember the P/I statements?) of the meeting. For best results, we recommend a "jellyfish sandwich" of sorts. Introduce the term in the ground rules, use it respectfully throughout the meetings, and follow it with use of the parking lot, capturing interrupted ideas for future discussions.

Of course, you are not limited to jellyfish. Australian start-up Atlassian swears by squeezing a rubber chicken named Helmut to keep things on track (Castles, 2017). We both have used a snorting pig toy that sits in the middle of the conference table. Almost any word or object will work, *as long as all meeting attendees know what it is and how to use it*. Introduce the concept at the beginning of a meeting. Let participants know that anyone can use it, regardless of stature, for the purpose of maintaining meeting focus. This helps participants monitor their own contributions, and it is a safe way for all to interrupt constructively if conversations get hijacked or derailed.

Dan has used a Kermit the Frog puppet with everyone trying to impersonate his Muppet voice ("It's not easy to intervene") when meeting discussions veer off-track. Such light-hearted methods to keep conversations focused can transpose stuffy, tedious meetings into more enjoyable yet meaningful discussions.

The success of the jellyfish concept depends on your work culture, meeting participants, and even the meeting topic. In an informal business environment where employees generally get along, and the meeting topic will not make or break the company, it can be very effective. In other meetings, however, no matter how well it is set up, it can fall flat, sound offensive or be misused. To be most effective, it needs to be understood, agreed upon, and used correctly. Teams with strong psychological safety can use it with ease.

Not surprisingly, some reject the jellyfish idea, saying that it wrongly assumes the person who calls jellyfish is making an accurate assessment to stay on track (Schwarz & Heinecke, 2016). What was called out as a tangent might actually be a helpful addendum to the conversation that was interrupted. Conversely, they might be jockeying for some type of conversational control. Regardless, misusing the concept might result in stifling people's contributions at the expense of keeping the meeting on track (Schwarz & Heinecke, 2016).

Better for many groups is unanimous agreement around a ground rule that invites respectful, direct inquiry. For example, whenever anyone in the meeting senses another is off-track, they can do a quick perception check. As discussed in Chapter 6 on listening, **perception checking** has three parts: (a) neutral description of an observable fact, (b) two possible interpretations of the aforementioned fact, and (c) a request for clarification. For example, "You're talking about next quarter's budget (neutral description), and I am unclear how that relates to the research we're reviewing for next quarter's changes, or maybe I missed something in your explanation (two possible interpretations). Will you help me make the connection, or, if we have veered off-track, should we put this on the parking lot so it can be addressed at a different time (request for clarification)?" Even the most perfectly crafted perception check can come across as rude or dismissive if paired with contradicting nonverbals. Keep your voice tone, eye contact, and posture in alignment with the intention of your communication: respectful, direct inquiry intended to keep the topic, and thus, the meeting, on track.

Concluding Meetings: Do Not End with a Whimper

With so much planning around the facilitation of a meeting, it would be a shame to end it with a shoulder shrug while saying "That's it." Great meetings close with purpose. Every participant should leave knowing who does what by when (WDWBW). Allow a few minutes for these useful questions (Axtell, 2015):

- Is there anything left that needs to be said before we adjourn? (check for completion)
- How do you feel about where we ended up? (check alignment with decisions)
- Who is doing what by when to ensure progress before our next meeting? (ensure agreement on next steps)

After the Meeting: Clean-up Time

The meeting is over, but you are still not finished. Jot down any must-dos or reminders as soon as you can while they are fresh in your mind. This might include your list of *who does what by when*. Check to see if anyone outside of the meeting needs an update. Next, revisit the parking lot—what requires follow-up from you? Should you schedule a one-on-one or will an email or phone call suffice? Finally, start planning your next meeting. Based on your own perceptions or any feedback you collected, note what worked particularly well and what you'd like to change.

Participating in a Meeting

Chances are you will not always be the one running a meeting, and while the facilitator impacts the success of any meeting, so do the participants. This short list will have you standing out as a star performer.

Belong or Be Gone

Just because you are invited to a meeting does not mean you belong there. Carefully vet all meeting invites. In his short TED Talk, "How to Save the world (or at Least Yourself) from Bad Meetings," information security manager, David Grady, proposed the acronym MAS for Mindless Accept Syndrome: "an involuntary reflex in which a person accepts a meeting invitation without even thinking why. A common illness among office workers worldwide." Likening wasted time to stolen property, he recommends clicking "tentative" instead of immediately selecting "accept" when a meeting invitation pops up in your email or on your calendar. Buy yourself some time and start asking good questions of the meeting coordinator to ensure your time and attention are necessary.

Be Prepared: Don't Act Like a Potted Plant

Elevate your pre-meeting knowledge by requesting the meeting agenda and asking the person who coordinated the meeting how they would like you to contribute. Are you there to observe? Participate? Take notes? Critique? We have both been removed from several meetings by making such inquiries. Specific clarification of your role will help you prepare and show up the best way possible. Beyond educating you, this quick check-in drives the meeting coordinator to clarity around his or her own desired inputs (participant contributions) and outcomes (goals). If you are truly needed at the session, complete any necessary pre-reads or research. Write down any questions you hope to get answered. If you have a suggestion for an agenda item, send it to the coordinator in advance so they are not caught off guard and can work it into the agenda.

Preparation includes punctuality, regardless of your meeting role. Make the meeting a priority, not an afterthought. If you are on time, you are late. Aim to arrive 5 minutes early. Secure parking (if traveling for the meeting), find the room, set up your seat, say hello, and center yourself. Long ago a company Michelle worked for imposed a $25 penalty for arriving even 1 minute late for the weekly check-in meeting. It is amazing how quickly people prioritized getting there early.

Preparation also means coming prepared to listen, not half-listen while you discreetly text status updates on all of your social media accounts. Research shows that when it comes to cell phones, simply silencing them during the meeting isn't enough. In fact, people who leave their phones in a different room when they attend a meeting have significant increases in their ability to process relevant information, reason, and solve problems. It turns out it is the mere *presence* of a phone that is distracting, not the alerts (Ward et al, 2017).

WAIT: Avoid Stage Hogging

Overlay consultant Laura Schloff's acronym **WAIT**: "Why Am I Talking?" (Lublin, 2017) to your verbal contributions. Before talking, determine your intention (to contribute, to challenge, to add, to encourage, etc.), and ask yourself if your comment will add or subtract from the conversation. In effort to be clear and to the point, think before you speak. Do not ramble. Look for a balance of contributions. Do not always be the first one to comment on a presentation or proposal, particularly if you're not senior management or an expert. If nobody raises what you were going to say then continue, but be mindful of the impact of how you make your contribution. Model excellent participation—others might follow your lead. (Top tip: These suggestions are applicable for communication beyond the meeting, too.)

Be Attentive: Silence Can Be Golden

You are sending messages even when you're not speaking. Watch your posture, facial expressions, and tone of voice. Posture should be attentive (standing or sitting up straight, facing the leader or screen, arms uncrossed). Facial expressions should convey interest, not boredom or disbelief. Tone of voice should be congruent with the level of respect you are trying to convey. Stay curious, listen well, and ask relevant questions. Examples of inquiries that expand rather than close a conversation in meetings include

- *What do you think?*
- *What makes you think that?*
- *Tell me more*

- *I think/believe/assume/suppose*
- *From my point of view/viewpoint*
- *On the one hand/on the other hand*
- *I never thought of it like that–I see where you're coming from*
- *I don't know if I agree, but I understand*
- *I'm unclear how that connects with the objective. Can you please clarify?*
- *Ideally, how do you see this turning out?*
- *Will you please give me an example?*

When committing to any action item, make sure you understand all it entails, such as due date, check-ins, and scope. Then, build trust and display your competence by following through as soon as possible.

Virtual Meetings

Virtual meetings take the form of teleconferences (audio only) and videoconferences (video and audio); and while they were quickly becoming a workplace meeting norm before 2020, when the COVID quarantine emerged, it forced everyone to adapt quickly to the online meeting environment. In April of 2020, Zoom's daily user count skyrocketed 378% from the previous year's statistics as businesses and families alike sought connection through the virtual platform (Bary, 2020). Microsoft Teams reported a 1-week increase from 32 million to 44 million active users per day during the same time period (Bary, 2020). Virtual meetings follow several of the same guidelines established for successful face to face meetings. For the best participation and meeting outcome, however, some important challenges need to be addressed. First, let's look at the advantages and disadvantages of virtual meetings. Next, we will cover facilitator tips for driving engagement, followed by simple strategies that will help virtual meeting participants show up at their best.

Pros and Cons: A Mixed Bag

Virtual meetings save time and money. Meeting others online axes travel costs such as flights, food, gas, lodging, and eliminates venue charges, should the meeting be held out of the office. Virtual meetings also allow remote or global employees instant access and connection with the rest of the team. Pragmatically, virtual meetings can be recorded so people who missed the meeting can catch up. But limitations include distractions disguised as multitasking; a lack of nonverbals from the meeting facilitator and participants that can lead to misinterpreted communication; and finally, the absence of interpersonal interactions that build trust and connection with a team, including small talk, handshakes, and getting coffee together before or after the meeting (Speagle, 2017). A 2020 study of 20,000 employees from the United Kingdom and the United States noted that people have a love–loathe relationship with virtual meetings. Many (45%) chose videoconferences as their preferred way of connecting with colleagues, but over half (56%) said they would like to spend less time on video calls. In the same study, participants ranked technology issues, such as slow internet connections and trouble dialing into a meeting along with the communication frustration of people talking over one another, as their top videoconference frustrations (Mendoza, 2020). With these limitations in mind, it is no surprise that one of the biggest challenges that leaders of virtual meetings encounter is keeping participants engaged and connected.

Facilitating Virtual Meetings: New Challenges

To avoid surprising anyone, the meeting invitation should specify that cameras are expected to be on. When cameras are required, people are more engaged. They cannot hide or multitask (we have heard of people who work from home and do all of their house cleaning while muted on audio-only conference calls), and expressions are easier to read (Edinger, 2018). Conclusions from Forbes Insights, the strategic research practice of *Forbes* media, in a July 2017 global survey of executives, supports the **preference of videoconferences to teleconferences**. From the more than 300 executives surveyed, 62% agreed that when compared to teleconferences, videoconferences significantly improve the quality of communication, while 50% said that videoconferencing improves comprehension ("5 reasons why," 2017). Researching which virtual meeting medium (video vs. telephone) executives prefer is similar to asking children if they prefer broccoli over Brussels sprouts—and we cannot assume a fondness for the overarching category.

Unique virtual meeting challenges emerged in 2020 as people seamlessly moved from one meeting to another without ever leaving their homes or their screens. Virtual meeting attendees reported feelings of exhaustion and dread when boardrooms and classrooms took solely to the virtual platform during the pandemic (Gillespie, 2020, Supiano, 2020). Adding insult to injury, when meetings leaked past the workplace boundaries over into our social lives for virtual happy hours and birthday parties, it is easy to see how the lines blurred and novelty wore off. The overlap of our work lives and social lives is only one component of "Zoom fatigue," however. The fatigue is enhanced as our brains are required to process more information in lieu of the missing nonverbal elements present

Technological glitches can ruin virtual meetings. Anticipate problems and check all equipment and connections prior to the meeting commencement.

Zoom fatigue is real. Learning and development specialist Gianpiero Petriglieri summarized the virtual meeting run-over quandary best when he told the BBC, "Imagine if you go to a bar and in the same bar you talk with your professors, meet your parents, or date someone. Isn't it weird? That's what we're doing now."

in face-to-face meetings. We are working harder to decipher message cues such as tone, facial expression and pitch—elements essential to the processing of messages. Even pauses are cause for distress. "Silence creates a natural rhythm in a real-life conversation. However, when it happens in a video call, you become anxious about the technology" (quoted by Jiang, 2020). As anyone who has experienced the frustrating stop-start dance of interruption when trying to contribute at the same time as others on conference calls can attest, our latest way of communicating disrupts conversational cadence. The merest millisecond delay of accessing the mute/unmute button takes more than twice as long as what we experience in-person (Yorke, 2020). No wonder we are so tired.

To strengthen interpersonal connections, *open a virtual or a face-to-face meeting with a 5-minute icebreaker.* Invite participants to take turns sharing brief updates about what's going on in their lives, personally or professionally. This helps people connect before diving into the meeting's content. When most of the workforce was thrown into working from home during the COVID quarantine, many meeting facilitators took advantage of unusual ways of connecting with their teams. A favorite icebreaker we learned from Will Wise and Chad Littlefield, founders of We Connect, prompts those on the call to take 30 seconds to find an

object in their new workspace (which often doubled as their living room, bedroom, or even kitchen) that represents a part of who they are. On many of the calls we attended while quarantined, people chose to disclose more about themselves by choosing items not normally found in their traditional office spaces, sharing everything from pets to personal mementos.

As the facilitator, you are in charge of moving the meeting toward stated objectives. *Consider rotating helpful roles* such as timekeeper, whose sole job is to remind others of time constraints, and note taker, who captures meeting highlights and commitments, summarizing them quickly at the meeting's close (Tsao, 2017). Bestselling author and business consultant Keith Ferrazzi suggests recruiting several volunteers to act as "Yodas" in each meeting. Wise peacekeepers, the Yodas keep a pulse of what's not being said, call out difficult to discuss topics, and help others follow agreed-upon ground rules (Ferrazzi, 2017)

Finally, *call on people directly* to increase participant involvement. In the spirit of transparency and fair warning, let attendees know early on that you'll be calling on people directly to solicit their input and collaboration (Axtell, 2015).

Participating Virtually: Unusual Considerations

Several considerations will influence the impression that you make and the impact you have when attending virtual meetings. As with face-to-face meetings, if you're on time, you're late. *Log into the website or set up your call early*—at least 5 minutes before the meeting begins. Forget about sneaking in unnoticed—there's typically a chime that alerts others when someone has joined or left the online meeting site. Have your meeting's access code and/or pin at your fingertips. Once you've successfully logged into the meeting, test your camera, your Internet connection, and volume.

Zoom meetings can devolve into chaotic messes without careful organization and attention to details.

When preparing for a video-conference, *dress as you would dress in the office* to convey respect and professionalism—even if you are working from home and still wearing fluffy bunny slippers. Steer clear of stripes and bright, bold accessories that will be distracting (Zimmerman, 2010). Check out your background, too. Stacks of dirty dishes or piles of papers send messages you might not want to convey.

As you "enter" the online meeting room, *announce yourself*—first and last name, without interrupting anyone if a conversation is already in progress. A simple, "Hi all. Dan Rothwell, here" is typically sufficient, though in some meetings you will want to include your role, if need be. People will not only know you have arrived, but they will be more attuned to your voice and know who you are. Similarly, use people's names when asking questions or encouraging participation.

When the meeting begins, *pay attention.* "The key to a successful video conference or phone conference meeting is to remember that you are in a meeting. Give your full attention to the participants as you would if you were in the same room," says Susan Colaric, assistant vice president for Instructional Technology at Saint Leo University in Saint Leo, Florida (Zimmerman, 2010). As it sometimes happens with monotonous lectures in the classroom, it can be humiliating to be called on only to realize you have no idea what is being asked. It is awkward for all involved, and in business meetings, it diminishes your credibility and professionalism. Pay attention.

Review Table 12.2 for a comprehensive list of tips for getting the most out of virtual meetings.

Next, make sure you *know how to mute yourself.* Though the mute button slows the flow of communication, it is imperative for people in busy, noisy environments that would distract from the meeting. And while you might not even notice your barking dog or the blaring background music of the coffeeshop you are in, your fellow meeting attendees surely will. "Look around" the virtual room. Just as we familiarize ourselves with a physical meeting room, choosing the best seat and noting the exit, for example, we can do something similar in the virtual meeting room: Locate the mute, chat, and exit buttons so you can access them with ease.

TABLE 12.2: A Participant's Guide to Successful Video Conferences

Before the meeting	
Make some time: Check the meeting platform, the invite, and your Internet connection	**Try a test run.** If using the meeting platform for the first time, Microsoft Teams, Zoom, Google Hangouts, and WebEx all have test links you can try before your meeting. **Download** any required meeting software. If joining the meeting by cell phone, **check to be sure you have a strong signal**. If joining by computer, use a wired connection over Wi-Fi; and check your camera, speakers, and microphone. When working from home, **be aware of any Wi-Fi dead zones** before your meeting begins. Move your router to a central location. Make all HGTV hosts cringe by keeping it visible and in an unobstructed area. Wipe off those fingerprints: **Make sure your camera lens is clean.** **Sign into the meeting a few minutes early** to make sure the meeting invite is valid. Contact the meeting organizer if you cannot join through the provided link. Once in the virtual meeting room, look around. **Find your communication options and know how to use them:** Locate chat, mute, screen share, and video icons so you can participate without hesitation once the meeting begins. **Keep the meeting password handy,** especially if you need to log in again anytime during the meeting. Things happen. Pro tip: If you have back-to-back virtual meetings and a less than stable connection, **restart your computer** or, at the very least, log out of and back into the meeting application between meetings. **Close all unneeded applications,** as well. **Improve connection** even more by reducing movement: Keeping your computer in the same spot (not moving it around during the call) and turning off a ceiling fan, tv, or any other movement in your visual background improves video streaming.
Get ready for your close-up: Appearance, camera, and lighting	**Position your webcam at eye level or a bit higher,** but no higher than your hairline. Sit far enough away from your camera so that your shoulders are showing. Don't be a webcam zombie: washed out and weary. **Ensure that you are clearly visible and illuminated.** Appearance matters, as much as, if not even more than, in a face-to-face meeting. **Sit facing your light source.** Lighting from above and below casts unflattering shadows (Think telling scary stories around the campfire with a flashlight under your chin.) Natural lighting is great. Three-point lighting—creating dimension and eliminating shadows by using a key light, fill light, and backlight—is even better. Face your key light, the main light source. Place a fill light on either side, at about face level, and use a backlight to separate yourself from your background. **If you wear glasses, beware the glare.** Let others see your eyes by paying closer attention to the angle, height and distance of your light source. A large, soft light, above eye level and off to the left or right, can greatly decrease glare. **Avoid filters,** particularly of potatoes. One department head conducted an entire meeting as a *virtual spud.* **Dress appropriately**, as you would if you were meeting in an office. Avoid distractions such as stripes or logos on clothing or hats that impede eye contact.
Look behind you: Backgrounds	**Everything speaks:** Keep your background clean and free of anything that will take meeting participants' eyes reason to roam. Let the focus be on you, not the piles of paper (or dishes!) behind you. Even decorations such as family photos can be a visual distraction. **Clear the clutter,** but don't make your background so sterile that you're one screenshot away from a mugshot. If you must choose between sterility or clutter, pick the former. If using a virtual background, test it before the meeting to make sure your system supports it. *Choose a virtual background that contrasts with your hair, skin, and clothing.* Be sure your background doesn't compete for your attention (visual noise), particularly when uploading your own background image. Your colleagues may all know you love Disney, but announcing your loyalty to the House of Mouse by using a background of Mickey and Minnie in each videoconference might detract from your professionalism.
Get ready to roll!	**Keep a pen and paper nearby for notes.** **Grab a beverage** (but consider that the container will be seen on the call—not a good time for your "I hate meetings" mug). When working from home, put pets away, and put a "Do not disturb" Post-it on your door.

During the Meeting

Monitor your nonverbals	Your goal is to appear attentive, yet natural. Keep these in check: **Posture:** Sit up straight or stand up tall. Whether sitting or standing, limit unnecessary movement. **Eye contact:** When talking, look into your camera often, not just the images on the screen. This makes it appear as if you are looking your audience members in the eye. When listening, look at the people on the screen so you can capture their nonverbal messages. **Vocal qualities:** Use your indoor voice. Keep volume loud enough for all to hear but avoid shouting. **Facial expressions:** *Show* others you are listening. Follow along with the conversation and reflect your reactions accordingly. You can show you're paying attention by nodding in agreement, smiling for encouragement, or raising your brow in surprise. Whatever the case, be authentic. **Gestures:** Make them purposeful and relevant. As with a public presentation, know what your hands are doing.
Eliminate the desire to multitask	**Commit to the meeting**. Though tempting, this is not the time to get up and use the bathroom (as *celebrities* and *others* were caught doing), scroll your Amazon cart, or tidy up around you while others are watching. Remember: Your audience can see you!
Participate	**Mute and unmute with ease.** Since you logged in early, you already know where the mute button is—now is the time to use it! For meetings with many participants, commit to the sequence: Mute when you're not talking, unmute when you have something to say, mute yourself when finished speaking, repeat. To paraphrase an overheard tweet: "not muting is the new reply all." **Say your name.** Say it upon entering the meeting so people not only know you are there but they can better identify your online voice. To avoid confusion in meetings with multiple participants, say your name before speaking up. For example, say, "This is Michelle again, I have a question about the process" and then proceed. **Narrate yourself.** To avoid looking like you're not paying attention, let meeting participants know what you're doing when you are looking away for prolonged periods of time or silence. For example, say, "I am looking up the details of that right now . . ." or "Let me pull up the latest version of that report." You can also let the meeting host know why you need to go off camera or leave the meeting by sending them a private chat. **Get comfortable with silence.** Whether it be from lagging Internet or fumbling for the unmute button, expect delays from others who ask and answer questions. "Even a delay of five-tenths of a second is more than double what we're used to in in-person conversations" (Yorke, 2020). Make it less awkward by employing patience. **Know how to interrupt.** The rules of interrupting vary with meeting size. Smaller group meetings of say three to five familiar attendees can more easily mimic the cadence of a normal conversation, with people exchanging ideas quickly, though at times clumsily. As the participant list grows, however, so does the complexity and formality of interrupting. If prescribed, follow the leader's protocol on participation by using the hand-raise symbol or raising your real hand for all to see when you have something to say. (Likewise, understand that simply because you are raising your hand on camera doesn't mean it's being seen by all—it depends on how others are viewing the meeting.) You can also type questions in the chat (if this feature is used), or save comments to the end of a meeting. To ensure comprehension and etiquette, use transitions liberally. Say some iteration of, "Before we move to the next agenda item, I have something to add." And if your contribution isn't on the agenda or would derail the timing of the meeting, indicate such by saying something like, "I just thought of something that could support that. Can I say it now or should I wait until the end (or after) the meeting?" Again, be patient. Be polite.

After the meeting

Exit with ease	In most video calls, there are those few people who don't know how to exit the meeting and stare awkwardly at the screen, mumbling apologies, while trying to figure it out. Remember all that meeting orientation prework you did? It pays off when you can smoothly say goodbye and exit the meeting with the press of a button at a meeting's end.

SUMMARY

Although many people would like to eliminate the preponderance of meetings, they are still a prominent vehicle of communication in the business world. When leading a meeting, it's imperative to think the meeting process through, beginning to end. Before the meeting, identify the meeting purpose, carefully craft the guest list, and create a worthy agenda. During the meeting, keep participants engaged and keep the meeting on track. After the meeting, tend to unanswered questions and action items. As a meeting participant, aim to arrive at the meeting early and prepared, and monitor your contributions—find the delicate balance between too little or too much communication. Whether virtual or face to face, implementing these guidelines will help immunize yourself and others from the delirium of meeting madness.

Film School Case Studies

The Hobbit: An Unexpected Journey (2012). Adventure/Fantasy.

Examine the ability to shift the mood and participation of a chaotic meeting in the first portion of this film.

TED Talks and YouTube Videos

These TED Talks and YouTube videos can be accessed by going to the Oxford Learning Link for It's All of Our Business or by typing the title of the video into a Google search window.

"Authenticity in Meetings"

"How to save the world (or at least yourself) from bad meetings" by David Grady

"How to Have a Hybrid Meeting That Works for Everyone" by Heidi Grant

"9 Brilliant Virtual Meeting Tips in Under 9 Minutes" by Will Wise and Chad Littlefield

"This Meeting Should Have Been an Email" by Chad Littlefield

After successful completion of this chapter,
you should be able to

1. Explain the importance of strong business writing skills in the workplace.

2. Adapt each written messages to the recipient after answering five pre-writing questions.

3. Distinguish the pros and cons of six types of business writing.

CHAPTER 13

Business Writing: Representing Yourself with Words

A Google search of "how to choose an avatar" yielded 1,520,000,000 results (in .7 seconds, at that). Avatars are cartoon representations of oneself, typically used online in social media platforms and gaming. The *Personality and Social Psychology Bulletin* published research in 2015 that concluded one's online avatar "can communicate accurate and distinctive information regarding personality" (Fong & Mar, 2015). An avatar acts as a representative for the user.

Written business correspondences do the same. *In a business environment, written messages send distinct information about the writer.* The words fill in for the writer's physical presence. In turn, the reader forms an impression about who is behind the keyboard and the business they represent. The recipient also comes to conclusions about the writer's mind, specifically if it is cluttered or well-organized. In a survey on the importance of business writing, one anonymous respondent summed it up well by saying "if we can't

4. Analyze the anatomy of an email and improve your abilities in each area.

5. Improve your tone, spelling, and grammar in written business correspondences.

Bitmoji, the personalized emoji app, lets users customize their avatar's skin shade, hair color, hair style, jawbone, chin, nose, eyes, eyebrows, facial hair, and outfits to use on platforms such as Snapchat, Facebook, Gmail, iMessage, and even Slack. As online avatars such as Bitmoji stand in for us, so does our written communication.

write succinctly and clearly then we aren't clear in our thinking" (L. Brown, 2019). We might not need this chapter if we spent as much time planning and proofreading our written messages as we did choosing the perfect hairline for our online avatars.

Although a chapter on business writing may sound as exciting as a spore fair, our goal *is to help you create clear, purposeful messages that are easy to comprehend and actionable for recipients.* The chapter objectives are as follows: (1) to discern when to write and when to have an oral conversation, (2) to understand why strong written skills matter in the workplace, (3) to analyze your audience and tailor the messages accordingly, (4) to distinguish different types of business writing, and (5) to know how to avoid common business writing mistakes.

Writing Versus Conversing

Written communication carries many benefits in the workplace. It allows the communicator to

- Get many people's eyes on the same information at once
- Attach reference materials such as videos, images, or supporting documents
- Avoid speaking
- Think ideas through thoroughly
- Organize information clearly
- Maintain a record of correspondence

On the other hand, spoken conversation in the form of a phone call, video call, or face-to-face is preferred in order to

- Build relationships with new and seasoned employees
- Solve complex problems
- Discuss sensitive issues
- Give constructive feedback
- Manage workplace conflict

The Case for Writing Well

Ernest Hemingway once commented on the challenge of writing well: "Sometimes it comes easily and perfectly; sometimes it's like drilling rock and then blasting it out with charges." Ultimately, you must take it seriously as an important bedrock function in the world of work. It can be hard work, but it is significant. In this section, we explore several reasons why writing well in the work environment is essential.

The High Cost of Weak Writing Skills

Writing well is more than simply making a good impression. Poorly written messages decrease productivity and cost businesses money. Supported by his studies in 2016, business writing expert Josh Bernoff concludes that poor writing in the workplace not only wastes time and money but also erodes leadership effectiveness, decreases workplace productivity, and disintegrates trust (Bernoff, 2016). In her

Your writing gives readers a glimpse into your mind. Let's show them organization and clarity of ideas instead of crumpled rough drafts.

research on the "digital communication crisis," Erica Dhawan surveyed nearly 2,000 American business employees and found a preponderance of frustration around unclear messaging. *The time employees wasted trying to decipher unclear messages added up to an annual loss of $188 billion dollars of productivity nationwide* (Dwahan, 2021b).

The emotional tone of an online written message can also easily be misinterpreted as hostile, impersonal, or disagreeable because vocal tone, facial expressions, posture, gestures, and the normal array of nonverbal cues are missing (Myers, 2017). One study found that the *tone of our emails is misinterpreted 50% of the time* (Kruger et al., 2005). Internationally acclaimed business consultant Erica Dhawan (2021a) has coined the term **digital body language** to identify the myriad signals our digital world presents that heightens our awareness of how a message is presented online but can cause confusion, even calamity. It encompasses "such things as punctuation, video call first impressions, abbreviations, signatures, and the time it takes us to press *Send*." Its implications can be illustrated with a few examples. Simple punctuation can produce misunderstandings online, blending the verbal with the nonverbal. Dhawan notes, based on research, that in text messages, ending sentences with periods is "more likely to be considered insincere," but not in emails. She further notes that "exclamation points, arranged throughout texts and emails, convey friendliness" unless attached to all-caps words ("NOW!!!"), which can communicate hostility. Effective online written communication can be highly challenging.

Business Writing Is an Occupational Requirement

Business writing expert and author Laura Brown (2019) set out to determine if business writing matters anymore. Her research concluded that it does. She surveyed professionals from five diverse industries in 2016. A large majority, 69% of respondents, indicated that business writing is "very important." Nearly 20% said it was "important," and none said it was not important at all. The annual survey of employers from diverse occupations and professions conducted by the National Association of Colleges and Employers (see Gray, 2021) ranks written communication skills as a top five "attribute employers seek on a candidates resume," with 73% of respondents indicating its importance.

In sum, our writing stands in for ourselves when we cannot or need not meet face-to-face. Poor writing costs us billions in lost productivity, and most professions require some degree of writing skills.

Competent Business Writing

With many considerations, business writing has become more complicated and challenging than at any time in history. It is not a simple task, as explored in this section.

Types: So Many Options

Email, instant messages, texts, posts, letters, reports, and proposals are forms of business writing (see Table 13.1). Email is still the giant of the category. German consumer data company Statista recorded over 304 billion emails sent and received per day worldwide in 2020. The projected tally for 2025 is a whopping 376 billion. The popular workplace instant messaging service Slack has over 10 million daily users (Slack, 2019) and is ultimately expected to dethrone email in the next few years (L. Brown, 2019). Conversations through email, text, and messaging are *asynchronous*, meaning they are out of synch, and not in "real time." The pause between the initial message and the response is beneficial because it allows one to think through their response. It is also challenging because gaps in response time can cause anxiety and can lead to false assumptions. If you email your manager to request time off but hear nothing in response, it is easy to jump

TABLE 13.1 TYPES OF BUSINESS WRITING

Form of Written Communication	Definition/Example	Pro/Con
Email	Messages sent electronically through a computer network	Pro: Still the preference for most written business communication Con: Delayed response time or confusion around who should respond can decrease productivity
Social Media Posts	Using platforms such a Twitter and LinkedIn, individuals can promote information about their company	Pro: Promote yourself, the company's brand, and successes to a wide audience Con: Rude or careless posts and engagement can break your reputation
Instant Messages	Messages sent through the Internet Example: Slack and Microsoft Teams	Pro: Quick way to communicate with other team members. Can be longer than texts. Are more secure than texts Con: Can be used to exclude team members or departments
Texts	Messages sent through cellular phone service	Pro: Quick way to communicate with team members Con: Can be hacked
Reports	Summaries, analyses, or recommendations about particular situations at work	Pro: The standard for explaining a problem and offering a solution. Con: Can be very time consuming
Proposals	Written persuasive appeals to win a job or project	Pro: Follow a fairly standard flow of development Con: Require extensive knowledge of topic, audience, budget, and persuasive strategy

to the conclusion that she is disappointed or doesn't care. In reality, she may not have received the message, or perhaps she is moving the schedule around to accommodate you. To minimize confusion when engaging in asynchronous communication, assume positive intent. It is a great foundation for maintaining curiosity and positivity in relationships.

Regardless of the form of written communication, a clear understanding of how to use each form at work increases efficiency and decreases confusion. For example, teams should be clear on expectations around acceptable hours for messaging, expected response time, and digital communication norms.

- **Hours:** Are employees to be available after normal workday hours? What is the earliest one can send a message? If messaging after hours, is a reply expected?

- **Response time:** While each company might determine its own times, the suggested response rates are 24 hours or less for email, within 30 minutes for texts, and as soon as possible for instant messages (Dhawan, 2021a)

- **Norms:** Each business or team should determine norms around language (e.g., is swearing allowed?), tone, and what is considered *not safe for work* . It is equally important to know the guidelines for what can be and cannot be posted online.

If you are not in the position to influence these ground rules, ask about the expectations for digital communication. If no standards are in place, model the way by demonstrating impeccable written skills.

Audience Analysis: Good Writers Respect Their Readers

Grab a friend and ask them to partake in a quick listening experiment. You'll be the *tapper* and they will be the *listener*. Next, think of a common song, something that many people know like the "Jingle Bells" or "It's a Small World," for example. Don't reveal what song you are thinking of. Tap out the rhythm on a table or wall. Don't hum. Don't even gesture or make facial expressions that go along with the song. Just tap a few stanzas. Let your friend guess the song. Don't be surprised if they get it wrong. Finally, reveal what song you tapped. Thank them for playing along. For fun, reverse roles and have them tap out a different, well-known song for you.

When you were the tapper, did you think it was obvious as to what song you were tapping? Was it frustrating to you that they couldn't identify it? If so, then, congratulations! You just experienced the curse of knowledge. The **curse of knowledge** is an error in thinking, or a cognitive bias, when we know something so well and we erroneously assume others know it too. This bias can disrupt the effectiveness of our emails, texts, and reports.

The more familiar we are with something, the harder it is to believe that others aren't familiar with it. This phenomenon was demonstrated in 1990 when Stanford graduate student, Elizabeth Newton, ran the tapper/listener experiment you just tried. Out of over 100 songs, listeners were only able to correctly identify three, even though the tappers were confident that the songs would be obvious to the listeners. More than a fun party trick, this concept has widespread application in the world of communication. Innocently enough, because of the curse of knowledge, people—just like the tappers—tend to assume a shared base of knowledge with their audience. This inadvertently leads to exclusion, frustration, and misunderstanding when communicating.

The curse of knowledge creeps into all types of communication such as presentations, marketing pitches, instruction, conversations, and email. It is a possible occurrence any time someone with a specialized skill communicates to someone who doesn't have that same level of expertise. *Once we know something, it is hard to think that others don't know it too*.

Here are some examples of the curse of knowledge and its impact on others:

- The team tunes out when a presenter shows slides with overly detailed graphs that use abbreviations they do not know.

- A Gen Z employee uses abbreviations in text that are common to them but unfamiliar to older recipients.

- An email from top management announces the implementation of a new software system but fails to communicate that it will ultimately make the employees' task much easier. The management assumes the benefits are obvious, but the employees don't know that. They, in turn, resist because it just seems like a lot of extra work for nothing.

- A flier that promises to *start humaning by creating thumb-stopping content* ends up in the recycle bin because it doesn't make sense to the reader.

When addressing this cognitive bias, the challenge is to make messages clear and inclusive, without "dumbing it down" and insulting the audience's intelligence. The following tips help break the curse of knowledge and to improve the effectiveness of your written communication, especially when you are attempting to explain information you know well.

1. *Shrink your blind spots.* They say you don't know what you don't know. But now you know. Awareness that the curse of knowledge exists might reduce the number of assumptions we make.

2. *Think back to when you were a novice.* What explanations, metaphors, or examples helped you understand concepts you were trying to share? What were the challenging parts? Might the recipients of your message struggle with that, too?

3. *Determine your audience's base level of subject knowledge.* Is your audience comprised of experts, laypeople, somewhere in between, or a combination? Often, this can be assessed by asking, "Hey Jo, I'm going to send you an update about the XYZ program so we can make the final decisions together. Before I send out the specifics, what do you know about the program already? I respect your time and don't want to waste it on details you do not need." Meet the recipients where they are at and take them further. When your audience has varied levels of subject knowledge, respectfully acknowledge

the experts while simplifying for the novices. "Anisha and Saul know this project inside and out. So that the others on this thread have the same information, I will review the top three reasons our customers are asking for this change."

4. *Assess your shared vocabulary.* "**Jargon** refers to terms, expressions, or acronyms that are specific to a particular industry or professional group" (Z. C. Brown et al., 2021). Considered communication shortcuts, jargon bonds a group by its inclusivity. For example, a Disney cast member (employee) would easily understand what to do if there was a *Code V* (guest/customer vomit). Restaurant employees could share frustration over a *four-top of campers* (i.e., a party of four who stayed seated long after they completed their meals). A nurse who is told to grab a *banana bag* will know to fetch a specific IV fluid bag for a patient.

The email message in Box 13.1 seems laden with industry jargon. Coming straight from a Fortune 500 company, however, it made sense to all who received it because they knew the abbreviations and had context for the information provided.

Used within the group, jargon provides an ease of communication and a sense of community. Applying these industry shortcuts to those outside the specified field, however, can lead to exclusion and confusion. Saying something such as, "Let's circle back when we get our eyes on the metrics so we can leverage the momentum of the mission-focused targets" might make you feel smart, but your message isn't clear and will likely get lost in your jargon. Remember, your goal is to communicate your message to your audience as effectively as possible, not to show everyone you know the latest buzzwords. *When in doubt, leave jargon out.*

5. *Have someone with the same knowledge base as the recipient read your message before you send it.* While we recommend you read any of your written communication at least twice before you send it, you can break the curse of knowledge (and catch errors) by having another set of eyes on your message. Ask for feedback about what makes sense to them and what doesn't. Have them

BOX 13.1   Example of Audience-specific Email

To: (Sales Team)

From: QRST

Re: Numbers for domain expansion

Hi,

I double checked with engineering and as it turns out we can max-out the PPDD configuration with 18 disk packs, currently the four DDs have 15 disk packs each. This means we can add an additional 360TB per machine.

The math behind that is: each RAID6 disk pack has 15, 8TB disks (15 disks x 8TB = 120TB) 3 disk packs is 3x120TB or 360TB raw/288 usable. This will bring each Data domain to XXDD07 & 08 to 1.92PB raw/1.5PB usable.

I worked with Gauri today to pull the individual server stats and you are getting some great de-duplication (high) 65,020,993:1 down to 1.54:1 across 4,734 clients. If we use a conservative 30:1 we can look at 45PB of protection.

The only caveat I need to point out is that we ideally need 8U of rack space in a rack next to the current Data Domain, 5U for the DS60 DAE disk enclosure and ~3U for cable management.

I'll work up a quote for 360TB for each DD if that is OK with you.

Thanks

---

summarize what you wrote and check their interpretation for accuracy. Adapt your message as needed.

6. *Other things to consider when matching the content of your message to its reader include their level of interest and their attitude toward you and the topic.* For example, members of the accounting department might be thrilled to hear about the new software system that will be installed in the next quarter, and they might require little background about the choice. Another department, such as sales, for example, might be resistant to the system and the challenges it will bring. Written communication for this audience should include more of the rationale and benefits of the overhaul.

With any communication, your goal is to get the message to your audience as effectively as possible. Analyzing your audience and avoiding the curse of knowledge helps make this happen (see Table 13.2).

Write Well: Choose Your Words Wisely

When Yahoo CEO Marissa Mayer sold the company to Verizon for $4.4 billion in 2017, she sent this paragraph in an email to her employees:

> The strategic process has created a lot of uncertainty, but our incredibly loyal and dedicated employee base has stepped up to every challenge along the way. Through the first half of the year, we met our operational goals and overachieved on plan. But, further, there are things that you cannot measure, like the passion of the people behind the products. The teams here have not only built incredible products and technologies but have built Yahoo into one of the most iconic, well-liked companies in the world. One that continues to impact the lives of more than a billion people. I am incredibly proud of everything we've achieved, and I am incredibly proud of our team.

Simply *incredible*, or at least that is the word she favored four times to describe her employees, products, and technologies, and her pride for Yahoo's achievements and her team, in one brief paragraph. **Semantic satiation** is our brain's way of decreasing meaningfulness of oft-repeated words. When our brains are exposed to excessive repetition of a word or phrase, the rapid-fire of neurons in our brains dampen the potency of redundant

TABLE 13.2 WRITING STRATEGIES FOR SPECIFIC AUDIENCE TYPES

Audience	Strategy
General	Present information simply and clearly
Technical	State "how to" information; be direct
Experts	Provide specifics, consider decisions to be made, use their vernacular
Skimmers	Highlight main points first
Skeptics	Provide examples and sources
Indifferent	Show what's in it for them, why they should care
Hostile	Consider their viewpoints, look to move them one step closer to neutral by using sound reasoning

information. In a world in which the average employee spends *more than* 3 hours a day reading, writing, and replying to emails at work (Naragon, 2018), our messages should stand out, not disappear. Lazy repetition and use of certain terms have lost their impact because of saturation. In 2021, watered-down words and phrases used in print and conversation included "bandwidth," "granular," and "it is what it is" (Petras & Petras, 2021). Repetition of the words essentially make them cliché, meaningless, exclusive, or insincere. Similarly, excessive casual use of the words *amazing,* which means "causing great wonder or surprise" and *awesome,* which is "an emotion variously combining dread, veneration and wonder" (Merriam-Webster, 2021) has watered down the state of astonishment each implies. A good writer speaks plainly and pays more attention to their verbs than their adjectives and adverbs.

Writing Pre-work: Step Away from the Keyboard

Whether it be an email, proposal, or any form of business writing in between, many people plunge into crafting the greeting and first sentence of a message, with little forethought. As discussed earlier in the chapter, doing so only increases the risk of making a bad impression, increasing the recipient's frustration, and wasting time and money. Before putting a fingertip to the keyboard or pen to paper, answer these questions:

1. *What is my writing purpose?* Clarity on *why* you are writing will make *what* you are writing much simpler. **The purpose of most written business communication *is to inform, to request, to persuade, to connect, to update, to answer, to apologize, to thank, or to instruct.*** Ask yourself, *"What do I want the reader to do after viewing this message?"* Everything in your communication will tie back to that purpose. Clarifying it before you type helps you determine what to include and exclude from your message. You would not be as overt to announce, "I'd like to persuade you to move Wednesday's standing meeting to Thursday," but once you begin to construct the persuasive email, you might say something such as, "I would like to share three reasons why Wednesday's standing meeting would be more impactful if moved to Thursday." Determining your writing purpose helps tighten your message.

2. *Who will read this?* This is your *primary audience:* the intended recipient or recipients. Do not include too many people because of office politics or ignorance. Go back to the purpose of your message and determine the decision-makers, doers, and those who need to be in the know.

3. **Who else might read this?** This is your *secondary audience.* Messages are seldom private. At work your communication might be shared or forwarded. Consider anyone beyond your primary audience who might receive the message or document.

4. *What does my audience know and what do they think of message/topic?* Bring in that audience analysis work you did to break the curse of knowledge. To bolster credibility, you should know if they are familiar with you and your expertise. Knowing how much they know about the topic will not only help you avoid the curse of knowledge, but

5. *What must I say and what might I say?* Next, consider the most important information to include and secondary details that support it. These questions are a culmination of the information in the questions above. If the information does not have starring or supporting roles in your written communication, cut them out. Knowing what to include or exclude enhances message clarity and the likelihood that you will receive a response. Emails that didn't exceed 200 words or 10 sentences had a 50% response rate. However, the response rate dropped to 36% for messages with fewer than ten words (Fidler, 2022; A. Moore, 2016).

Anatomy of an Email

Mark Lugris (2021), CEO and Content Director of Lugris Communications, notes, "the importance of email in business communication cannot be underestimated. Not only does email enable immediate response, it also ensures we keep track of all outgoing and incoming communication. Email is also cost-effective and provides invaluable marketing opportunities." With email still reigning as the primary form of business communication, this section takes a closer look at emails, offering suggestions as they apply. We will identify each part of an email, coupled with strategies for optimizing the strength of your messages.

The Setup

Messages from an email start way before the greeting. This section shows the correct setup of an email message.

TO   This is where you populate the email address of your primary audience. To avoid sending any email before it is ready, *fill this in last.* Too many messages have been sent before they were ready! *Use rank order when needed.* For example, put your manager's email address ahead of your co-worker's address.

CC   This is your secondary audience. Include people whose response or action is not necessary but should be in the loop. Though it might be tempting to include many, *limit the number of recipients*. When many are included on an email, chances for the *diffusion of responsibility,* the psychological phenomenon where people are less likely to take action when others are present increases, and therefore the likelihood of a response decreases. According to leadership expert and author Pat Lencioni, *"When I send an email to one person, there's a 95% chance I'll get a reply. When I send to ten people, the response rate drops to 5 percent. When you add people you drastically decrease the exclusivity and make people feel they don't need to read the email or do what you ask"* (quoted by Shipley & Schwalbe, 2010). For each email address you type into the CC line, ask yourself why they should be included and what you expect them to do with the information in the message. Be kind. Aim not to flood people's inbox with email that doesn't concern them.

BCC   Including anyone in the *blind carbon copy* line essentially says, "I want you to know and I don't want others to know that I want you to know" (Shipley & Schwalbe, 2015). We liken it to a gossipy whisper behind the recipient's back. *Handle the BCC with extreme care;* best use: to keep a list of email addresses private.

SUBJECT LINE   *Always fill it in.* Write your subject lines with the same degree of intention and attention as you would write a research paper. The subject line of an email (or lack thereof) often determines if a message reaches your target audience (thank you, spam filters) or if it is opened at all. If your subject-free message is opened, you risk frustrating your reader even more when they try to decipher what it is all about. In 2021, the average American worker was on track to receive 121 email messages per day (Norquay, 2021). By 2022, 347 billion emails will be sent and received per day ("25 Mobile Email Statistics," 2021). With such back and forth, we owe it to each other to write worthy messages, starting with the first thing a person sees: the subject line. *Follow these tips for creating strong subject lines*:

1. *Write it first*. Instead of making it an afterthought, much like putting a stamp on a letter, craft the subject line first. This will help set the tone for the message (Ward et al., 2021). Also, you will be able to align everything in the email back to the umbrella of the subject line.

2. *Think mobile*. Between 85% and 90% of people check email on their mobile devices (99 firms). Because different email servers display a varied number of characters from one device to another, the recommended sweet spot is 40 characters.

3. *Be specific*. Add a date and/or detail for specificity and organization (e.g., "Notes from 10/11/22 sales meeting").

4. *Start the subject line with a key word or phrase* if your message is time-sensitive or requires a response, such as "Action requested" or "Input needed." Follow that with the related subject. For example, "Confirmation: Menu for Friday's HR training."

5. *Purge meaningless subject lines from your mind, fingertips, and keyboard*:

   - Meeting
   - Update
   - Checking in
   - Hi!
   - Status
   - FYI
   - Quick Question
   - Urgent

6. *Change the subject line if the subject of the email changes during a conversation*. Have

Watching the USA Volleyball team take gold in the 2021 Olympics was thrilling. Watching people volley an email message back and forth is not. Know when to change the subject line. Also know when to change the channel. If the back-and-forth of a text, instant message, or email conversation is not productive, it might be time to switch to phone, videoconference, or face-to-face communication.

you ever had an email exchange that paralleled a volleyball rally? The communication volleys back and forth and somewhere along the lines the subject of the message changes. When that happens, change the subject line. This helps frame the message as well as file it.

Attach Files Remember "attachment anxiety" mentioned in Chapter 12. Attach only the most critical files; and, if possible, keep the attachments short. Otherwise, they are likely to be ignored.

The Body

The body, of course, is the main substance of your email. There are several key components that make this substance effective.

Opening: Consider formality Politeness and respect matter. Use an opening such as Dear, Greetings, or Hello followed by the recipient's name (Ms., Mr., Bob Brown, etc.). Depending on the relationship of those involved, as an email message goes back and forth between recipient and sender, the formality of the greeting can be decreased or dropped.

Lead with the Most Important Information
With so many things vying for our attention, the bottom line of your message should become the top line of the email. For example, if you wanted information on the new-hire orientation, indicate that immediately.

Not this:

> Hello Jamie,
>
> I am so excited to be a part of your team. I look forward to learning from you and I hope I will be able to provide value to the group. I already appreciate the way everyone has made me feel welcomed.
>
> I see that I am scheduled for the new hire orientation on Wednesday. Are there materials I can review in advance, or are they distributed when we meet?

But this:

> Hello Jamie,
>
> I am scheduled to attend Wednesday's new hire orientation. May I review any materials in advance or are they distributed in the meeting? I'd like to be as prepared as possible.
>
> I am grateful to be part of your team and look forward to learning from you.

Increase readability and clarity by using ample white space. This is best achieved by keeping paragraphs short and including bulleted lists when possible. When assigning roles or responsibilities, type names in boldface for ease of scanning. Email is not the vehicle for flowery prose and verbose meanderings. Earn your reader's respect by keeping it simple.

The Close

The close is the conclusion of your conversation. It is an opportunity to leave on a positive note, reaffirm your purpose, and make a call to action, when appropriate. It is also your final shot at making a good impression. Good closing statements are clear, kind, and concise.

Not this:

> Thanks!

But this:

> Thank you for reviewing my request. May we arrange a time to meet on Thursday to discuss it further? I look forward to hearing from you.

Signature Block Online writing assistant site, Grammarly, lists *regards, best,* and even *cheers* as acceptable sign-offs. They strongly caution against cheeky spellings (thx, rgrds), love, blessings, and *sent from my iPhone.*

Following your signoff, include

full name

title and company name (include hyperlink)

phone numbers (mobile and office)

Link to social media, if desired, such as LinkedIn

Cultural Variations Despite the above advice, digital closings are not universally standard and perceived similarly across all cultures.

"Power scanning" has become an increasing problem with emails, especially long ones. Queries are missed or emails are just ignored as too lengthy.

Dhawan (2021a) notes just a few of many differences:

> English email closings are likely to sound cold to Arabic speakers, who sometimes end their emails with more gracious expressions, including . . . "Accept an abundance of respect and appreciation." Nigerians typically close emails with a variant of "Stay blessed." A recent comparative study by Korean and Australian academics suggests that how we close out an email has a significant effect on whether or not the recipient feels respected. In the study, 40% of Korean respondents found Australian emails to be impolite, compared to 28% the other way around.

In high power-distance cultures (see Chapter 3), a sign-off with an accompanying formal title (if any) is desirable. "In more egalitarian cultures, there's no need to trumpet the fact that you're the 'Visionary Founder' of blah-blah-blah" (Dhawan, 2021a), but including a formal title in a formal business email is appropriate.

Careful Composition

Although this may seem like an English composition class, there are at least three remaining issues regarding business writing. They are tone, spelling, and grammar. We can only

---

BOX 13.2   How Many Errors Can You Find?

Subject:

Today's meeting was a disaster. Did you edit or practice this presentation? We looked like amateurs. And the slides went by so quickly that I don't think anyone is better informed because of it. What a waist. We look like a bunch of idiots. Do you expect to get sales out of this or do you you want to cruz by like you always do?!?! ☻ ☺

We can't boil the ocean, but we can make a dent.

Also, I looked around and saw many people not paying any attention. We are back in office. I expect more. No more zooming. The gals in the back were scrolling TikTok and taking selfies, I am sure of it. ☻

Since most of you forgot how to submit an expense report, I'm attaching the guidelines. BTW: Get your expenses to me by Tuesday.

Let's get it together. We are all in this together.

Answers are at end of chapter.

provide basic suggestions in our remaining space, but we encourage you to dig deeper by consulting myriad websites that address these challenges.

Tone: Difficult Writing Challenge

In chapter 8, we introduced the online *disinhibition effect*. It happens when "we drop our guard, forego formalities, and express ourselves online in frank, uncensored ways we would never dream of doing in person" (Dhawan, 2021a). Essentially, the screen of a computer or phone detaches us from the human interaction, and we forget our manners. Online disinhibition effect, coupled with the lack of physical gestures, eye contact, and vocal inflections, can lead to poor assumptions and interpretations on either side of the message.

Tone can be described as mood, voice, style, and cadence. It reflects how you feel about your subject and your co-communicator. Common tones in writing include formal, informal, worried, encouraging, friendly, aggressive, assertive, and passive. With so many choices and the chance of so many interpretations, it benefits us to check our tone. When rushed, we might send a text to a coworker that says, "You need to do XYZ now." We have both been on the receiving end of these types of texts and emails, and they don't do anything to increase our fondness of the sender or our drive to fill the request. Instead, the tone is aggressive, and the sender sounds disappointed. It is hard to tell. Eliminate online disinhibition effect by checking the tone of your message. Read it out loud. If you wouldn't say it the exact same way to their face, rewrite it. Also, ***don't compose messages when angry***. Step back, catch your breath, and remember that you are in a professional setting.

Tone and Texting   When initiating a new text/instant message thread, say hello before conveying the idea that popped into your mind; the idea that you felt an impulsive urge to type up and then had to immediately press send. Before you text an out-of-the-blue command or query to a coworker, telling them what you need from them, warm up the conversation with a greeting. It can make a sizable difference in how

they interpret the rest of your text. Check the tone of these texts/IMs:

"I need XYZ from you."

"Hi. I need XYZ from you."

"Hi! I'm checking in about XYZ. Can I get that by day's end?"

The extra time devoted to checking your tone will ultimately save you and your message's recipient time. You won't need to deal with the ramifications of someone thinking you were rude or demanding, and the recipient won't waste time wondering why you were curt. Exceptions include seemingly abrupt texts permissible in emergencies, or when that is the standard, acceptable way of communicating.

Tone and Email   If initiating a new email thread, warm up by setting the tone and intention, and think about adding some context. Imagine how Sam might react to either of these versions of the same message.

"Sam: We need to meet about project XYZ. Contact me ASAP."

or

"Hello Sam. Let's set up a meeting to discuss the XYZ project." Specifically

- *status update re: milestones and deadlines*
- *extra resources needed (if any)*

What is your availability on Tuesday?
Thanks!

The first example is curt, authoritative, and emotionless. It might put Sam on the defense. The second shows respect while giving a clear picture of why they need to meet. A few seconds and a few words can make a big difference.

Punctuation and emoji can be added to enhance tone. Use exclamation points, but use them sparingly and with purpose (Dhawan, 2021a). A single exclamation point can emphasize joy and excitement. Review your message. If everything is exciting and noted with an exclamation point, then nothing is exciting. One suffices. Do not use an exclamation point to convey anger, as it can come across as harsh, or even that you are screaming. Similarly, a message typed in ALL CAPS indicates anger. Finally, emoji are acceptable in the workplace and can stand in for the emotion and nonverbals that are missing in synchronous communication. As with exclamation points, use emoji sparingly so they carry the intended impact.

Spelling/Grammar 101

Even in the day of acronyms, abbreviations and textspeak, spelling counts! Business etiquette expert Jacqueline Whitmore (2017) says that in the business world, eliminating spelling and grammatical errors is essential for three reasons:

1. It reduces the chance your message will be misunderstood or misinterpreted.

2. It reflects the writer's credibility, intelligence, and reliability.

3. It indicates that you care about how you do business.

Even with spellcheck in place, some words are easily confused, and thus, misspelled.

1. *It's* is *only* a contraction of *it + is*, as in "It is" or *it + has*, as in "The report is late; it's got to be done today." *It's* is never possessive, as in "The business raised *its* rates." Never, ever. You would never say, "The business raised *it is* rates," which is exactly how you would have to decode "it's" in this sentence.

2. *Fewer* applies only to things you can count such as cars, whereas less applies to things you cannot count and are measured, like sugar. "There are *fewer* cars on the road." (If you said "less cars" it would mean there were partial cars driving around.) "I'd like *less* sugar in my coffee." (You could say fewer only if you are referring to fewer grains of sugar, and that would just be weird.)

3. *Lose* or *loose*: When you lose something, you lose an O. You don't "loose face" (unless your facial flesh is sagging). You "*lose* face."

4. Which is which, *i.e.* or *e.g.*? And where does the punctuation go? *I.e.* comes from the Latin phrase: *id est*. It means "it is." Use *i.e.* interchangeably with the phrases "in other words" or "in essence." It typically provides

more specificity. "Today I'm going for a challenging run, *i.e.*, the forest trail, during my lunch break." We can interpret this as the person above is running the forest trail, which they find challenging, on their lunch break. *E.g.* stems from the Latin phrase *exempli gratia* and means "for example." Lists often follow e.g., and rarely follow i.e. Both *i.e.* and *e.g.* are lowercase, except at the beginning of a sentence. Place a period after each letter. Even though they are Latin, there is no need to put either in italics. In general, place a comma after *i.e.* and *e.g.* For emphasis, both can be placed in parentheses with the rest of the listed items.

5. *There* is a place. "*There* is a chair over *there*." *Their* is the possessive form of *they*. "It's *their* chair. *They're* is a contraction of *they + are*. "*They're* tired of these silly examples."

6. *Your* is the possessive form of *you*. "It's *your* choice. *You're* is a contraction of *you + are*. "*You're* expected to know the difference."

7. *Affect* or *effect*? *Affect* is a verb; it indicates action and change. (A is for action.) This post might *affect* your spelling. *Effect* is a noun; think of cause and effect. Appearing smarter might be an *effect* of this post. Except every so often, *effect* is a verb meaning to make something happen ("We *effected* a major change in policy"), and honestly, that just underlines the complexity of the English language.

There are many more such common errors (e.g., *like* vs. *such as*). Therefore, you might want to consult the many grammar websites available that provide dozens of common mistakes.

SUMMARY

Writing well still matters in today's workplace. Not only do your written words represent you, but poorly written messages waste time and money. Long gone is the simplicity of an in-house business memo. It has been replaced with a flurry of email, texts, and instant messages. Write well by considering your audience, planning your message and avoiding common writing errors.

Answers for BOX 13.2

No subject line
No greeting
Misspellings
Wordy
Jargon
Sexist
Two subjects thrown into one email
Lacks professionalism

TED Talks and YouTube Videos

These TED Talks and YouTube videos can be accessed by going to the Oxford Learning Link for It's All of Our Business or by typing the title of the video into a Google search window.

8 Email Etiquette Tips- How to Write Better Emails at Work

How to Write an Email (No, Really) Victoria Turk TEDxAthens

After successful completion of this chapter,
you will be able to

1. Address speech anxiety and make a plan to decrease it.

2. Analyze the five types of audiences and tailor your presentation to their needs and expectations.

3. Determine the best way to organize speech content.

Developing and Organizing Business Presentations

When Adlai Stevenson introduced John F. Kennedy in 1960, he compared the skills of ancient orators, saying that when Cicero was done speaking, people always gave him a standing ovation and said, "what a great speech"; but when Demosthenes finished speaking, people said, "Let us march!" and they did (Robbins, 1986). Stevenson used the example to illustrate the difference between information and persuasion, and ultimately the power of public presentations. While you might not be moving masses to march for a worthy cause, a command of the spoken word is required in today's modern workplace.

One survey reported an impressive 92% of respondents viewed presentation skills as "critical to success at work" (Noar, 2018). As communication consultant Carmen Gallo (2021) explains, "Public speaking is no longer a 'soft skill.' It's your key to success in any field." Public speaking is an essential business skill, made more relevant by the explosion of video conferencing in which you present from your office, and by the rise and popularity of TED Talks (Smedley, 2017).

4. Adequately prepare for virtual business presentations.

As business author Steve Bustin explains, "You can now watch great speakers on YouTube, and when people go to conferences or work events, they expect the speakers to be that good . . . the bar has been raised" (quoted by Smedley, 2017). Employers, however, do not believe most job applicants possess such skills, mainly because applicants have received little or no training in public speaking (Grant, 2016).

Oral presentational knowledge and skills translate into knowing how to present complex ideas clearly and fluently, keeping an audience's attention, critically analyzing important issues, conducting effective research, making reasonable arguments, and supporting claims with valid proof. Skilled presenters entertain, inspire, lead, and educate their audience. They get people to listen, to contemplate, and to change their minds. This is an impressive array of practical knowledge and skills to bring to the business arena. Whether speaking to an audience of 200 customers, inspiring your project team, or pitching an idea to your boss, being a skilled presenter will ensure that you elicit credibility and respect wherever you go.

But what really is a business presentation? Presentations at work include informing people about updates, policies, and processes or persuading people to agree, change, follow, buy, or act. Business presentations more specifically can include a *sales pitch* to a potential customer about your cloud storage plan; a *request* to your company's Chief Financial Officer for an increased budget to spend on new software; a *field report* that alerts others to this week's sales strategy; an *update* about the status quo of the three initiatives assigned to your team; and an *overview* in the new-hire orientation about the company's values and what they look like in action.

Given the importance of competent public speaking in the workplace, *the principal purpose of this chapter is to explain how to develop your business presentations always with your audience as a central focus.* The main objectives of this chapter are (1) address the causes of speech anxiety and provide strategies for decreasing it, (2) discuss ways to analyze your speech audience and tailor your presentation to their needs and expectations, and (3) provide ways to organize your presentations effectively to meet those needs and expectations

Addressing Speech Anxiety

Mark Twain once remarked, "There are two types of speakers: those who are nervous and those who are liars." Overstated, but *speech anxiety is a significant problem for many people.* A survey by Chapman University of 1,500 respondents puts the fear factor at 62% ("The Chapman University Survey," 2015). Another study of college students found the fear factor to be 64% (Marinho et al., 2017). Others have claimed an even more pervasive problem (Black, 2019). With the advent of COVID-19, what consultant Eleni Kelakos (2020) has dubbed **Zoom performance anxiety**—the added fear of presenting speeches in the somewhat uncomfortable and awkward online platforms--has amplified this problem. "Public speaking and presentations took on new meaning with Zoom sessions and webcams and our speech anxiety, undoubtedly, grew, as well" (Prentiss, 2021).

Speech anxiety is often the very first concern individuals experience when asked or told to make a presentation to coworkers and supervisors. So, let's address this issue first. If you belong to the vast majority of individuals who endure significant speech anxiety or even mild jittery "butterflies" in the pit of your stomach, then this next section usefully addresses the causes of such anxiety and offers strategies to address it effectively.

Causes: Dysfunctional Anxiety

Let's begin with some positive news. *Individuals who experience low to moderate anxiety that is under control typically give better presentations than those individuals who experience little or no anxiety* (Motley, 1995). If you care very little about the outcome, you'll experience little anxiety, but your presentation will likely be lackluster or worse. Understanding the causes of **dysfunctional anxiety**—the fear of public speaking that reaches an intensity that interferes with giving an effective presentation—is the first step in learning to address speech anxiety constructively.

How you think about speaking to an audience will largely determine your level of speech anxiety (Bodie, 2010; Tsaousides, 2017a). Self-defeating thoughts that can sabotage your speech are grounded in the excessive concern that your audience will judge and reject you. Though you might not be able to turn it off completely, it is essential to turn down the volume of your dysfunctional self-talk by examining what triggers it.

Catastrophic Thinking: Fear of Failure
Wildly exaggerating the magnitude of potential failure is a common source of stress and anxiety (Ackrill, 2012). Catastrophic thinking, or **catastrophizing** as it is often called (Legg, 2019), sees only failure, not the opportunity for exhilarating success that comes from embracing challenges. Don't paralyze yourself with catastrophic, unrealistic thinking. Instead of focusing on all that could go wrong, list at least three possible positive outcomes of your presentation.

Perfectionist Thinking: No Mistakes Permitted
Perfectionists anguish over every perceived flaw, and they magnify the significance of even minor defects, often before, during, and after their presentation. Examples include, "I feel so stupid. I keep mispronouncing the name of a consultant that I quoted"; and "I completely forgot to explain that slide—I bet nothing made sense." Flawless public speaking is a desirable goal but an unrealistic expectation. A few mistakes might make you appear more relatable than someone who speaks flawlessly but is disconnected from the audience because they read the entire presentation.

The Illusion of Transparency: Being Nervous about Looking Nervous
Substantial research shows that those who fear public speaking are often overly worried about appearing nervous to their audience. This **illusion of transparency**—the overestimation of the extent to which audience members detect a speaker's nervousness—is usually just that, an illusion (MacInnis et al., 2010). Telling a person not to be nervous, of course, is about as realistic as telling a person not to sweat in a sauna. Research shows, however, that identifying the illusion of transparency can improve overall performance (Savitsky & Gilovich, 2003). Your nervousness is far more apparent to you than it is to your audience.

Novelty of the Speaking Situation: Fear of the Unknown
We often fear what is unpredictable or unfamiliar (Carleton, 2016). For inexperienced speakers, the mere novelty of the speaking situation may trigger speech anxiety, especially if you have little experience presenting. What if you trip over your words? How will you know if your listeners are interested? What if everyone just stares? *Sometimes the cause is the cure: Alleviate speech anxiety by giving speeches.* Speak often to a variety of audiences and watch your fear decrease. Similarly, you can start small by speaking up in meetings and asking questions at public events.

We may think that our speech anxiety is obvious to an audience, but it is rarely evident unless our illusion of transparency, our excessive worry that our anxiety shows, makes it obvious. Never tell your audience, "Gosh, I'm really nervous." Don't call attention to your nervousness. Simply take a deep breath and proceed with your presentation.

Strategies: Managing Anxiety

Your goal is to manage your anxiety, not eliminate it completely. Seasoned presenters, Mark Bonchek and Mandy Gonzalez, say that the fear of public speaking "never goes away entirely. Instead, it's about having *less* fear—think of it as being fear-*less*" (Bonchek & Gonzalez, 2018). As the international presentation club Toastmasters says, you might not eliminate the butterflies in your stomach, but you can get them to fly in formation. In this section, several ways to manage your speech anxiety that are supported by research are presented.

Prepare and Practice: Novelty to Familiarity
When you are adequately prepared to make an effective presentation, novelty and unfamiliarity associated with the speaking situation is diminished. *Begin necessary research well in advance, organize and outline your presentation carefully, and practice your speech.* Giving speeches to a variety of audiences, even just for practice, will gradually build your confidence and reduce your anxiety. Zoom with friends and practice giving virtual speeches.

Gain Perspective: Rational Thinking   *Learn to recognize the difference between rational and irrational speech anxiety* (Tsaousides, 2017b). A colleague of Dan's and a longtime business consultant, Darrell Beck, concocted a simple formula decades ago for determining the difference: *the severity of the feared occurrence times the probability of the feared occurrence*.

Severity is approximated by imagining what would happen if catastrophic failure did occur: your knees and hands shake violently, and you go blank, perspire profusely, babble incoherently, and you feel nauseated, and you eventually faint. Imagine all of this occurring, the entire mess. Would you quit your job? Would you renew your passport and make plans to leave the country? Would you hide from colleagues, afraid to show your face? None of these effects seems likely. Even a disastrous speech does not often warrant significant life changes. A few moments of disappointment, mild embarrassment, or discouragement is about as severe as it gets.

Next, consider the *probability* of this nightmare scenario actually happening. It is highly improbable that all or even most of these feared occurrences would transpire. Stop catastrophizing and predicting utter failure. Chances are excellent that it is not going to happen if you prepare adequately. If you try to "wing it,"

Giving a speech is not an Olympic event. The communication orientation concentrates on clarity of your message and the focus on your audience not yourself to address speech anxiety.

however, eschewing adequate preparation, you may fly into the metaphorical mountain.

Communication Orientation: Reframing One of the best ways to turn the dial down on speech anxiety is to switch your focus. Stop ruminating about how you might embarrass yourself and what your audience thinks about you. ***Start thinking less about yourself and more about your audience.*** The more you think about meeting their needs, the less likely you will worry about yourself. The **communication orientation** focuses on making your message clear and interesting to your listeners (Tsaousides, 2017b). Think of your presentation, whether in person or online, as more of a conversation than a performance. When talking with a friend or even a stranger, for example, you rarely notice your tone, gestures, and posture. Instead, your focus is on being clear and interesting, even having some fun. Approach your presentation in a similar way. Based on research, ***the communication orientation is the most successful method for anxiety reduction and control*** (Motley, 2011).

Audience Analysis

Any business presentation begins with an analysis of your audience. This next section explores different audience composition and expectations, along with strategies for meeting their needs.

Types of Audiences

There are five general types of audiences: captive, committed, contrary, concerned, and casual. Each poses specific challenges for you, the speaker. In Chapter 6, we discussed at length the listening process, but remember that communication is a transactional process between speaker and listener. If you are fortunate, your audience may be comprised of effective listeners; but chances are that as a speaker, you will need to engage your listeners in different ways depending on the type of audience you are addressing, members' expectations, and their needs.

Captive Audience: Disengaged Listeners

Captive audience members are required to be there and likely had no say in the command to attend. *Power, especially in its dominance form, can be an issue with captive audiences.* Listeners may attend a presentation only because those with greater power (e.g., supervisors) insist.

As a presenter, gaining and keeping a captive audience's attention is top priority. Make your message meaningful to your listeners. If you are discussing elements of a budget, tie the data to your listeners' concerns and explain the importance of any changes. Anecdotes and relevant stories that highlight your main points can prevent listeners from nodding off. Light humor, used judiciously, can also gain and maintain the attention of a captive audience. An animated delivery (see Chapter 16) also can gain and maintain an audience's attention.

Committed Audience: Agreeable Listeners

A **committed audience** voluntarily assembles because members want to invest their time and energy listening to and being inspired by a speaker. A committed audience usually agrees with the presenter's position already. An example of a committed audience is a **mastermind pod**—a group that assembles to mentor, learn, and hold each other accountable and meets to brainstorm approaches or share strategies on a compelling project. Seek to maintain or enhance the audience's level of commitment, lead them toward decisive action, and encourage them to spread the message and inspire others to act. When an audience is already on your side, use emotional appeals accordingly by matching the audience's feelings of hope, excitement, angst, or interest.

Contrary Audience: Hostile Listeners

A **contrary audience** is initially resistant to your position on your speaking topic. They enter the room already on defense. For example, if you are presenting arguments as to why your team needs a bigger budget, people in other departments who either haven't had their budgets increased or perhaps whose resources will be negatively affected if your budget is changed, might come to the situation armed with resistance and counterarguments. While presenters should be knowledgeable about their topic no matter what type of audience they have, it is vital that you come to the presentation well-informed and equally aware of any possible objections. Bring worthy evidence to back up all of your claims (see Chapter 15). Seek common ground. If necessary, when animated objections emerge, ask audience members to disagree without becoming disagreeable.

Concerned Audience: Eager Listeners

A **concerned audience** is one that gathers voluntarily to hear a speaker because listeners care about issues being discussed. They are a motivated audience that wants to learn more. An example might be the people who come to hear about proven employee engagement strategies for employees who work from home.

The best approach to use with a concerned audience is to offer new ideas and information in a stimulating and attention-getting fashion. Given the right information, concerned listeners may shift to becoming a committed audience. If you do a sloppy job, however, they can become a contrary audience, and you might lose credibility with them.

Casual Audience: Unexpected Listeners

A **casual audience** is composed of individuals who become listeners because they stumble upon a presentation, stop out of curiosity or casual interest, and remain until bored or sated. Individuals who attend business conferences may sample different presentations out of curiosity or schedule availability. They are often inclined to leave if the presenter does not immediately grab attention (or provide chocolate—a common conference handout).

When addressing a casual audience, aim to connect with listeners immediately and create curiosity and interest. Be excited about your topic. Help casual listeners see how it relates to them. Unlike a captive audience, members of a casual audience are free to leave at a moment's whim and will, if you haven't considered them and in turn, given them a good reason to stay.

Each type of audience—captive, committed, contrary, concerned, or casual—presents its own challenge to a speaker. Often an audience is comprised of representatives from each category, meaning there are several strategies to keep in mind. If you have a group that is mostly made up of committed audience members, but you know that a few people attending are contrary, you'll need to combine strategies for both. In this case you might engage the energy of the committed members by carefully laying out the next action steps, while also respectfully providing sound evidence that will reduce some of the objections for those not yet onboard. *One of the biggest mistakes a presenter can make, however, is to deliver a canned presentation that has not been adapted to your specific audience.*

Audience Type and Persuasion

Rarely do we give a presentation in the workplace just for fun. Sad but true. *Most presentations in the workplace are either informative (i.e., describe, explain, demonstrate, educate, update, clarify) or persuasive (i.e., sell, convince, pitch).* When persuading any group, pay close attention to these three areas: Credibility, emotional appeals, and logic bolstered by evidence.

1. **Credibility**, what Aristotle called *ethos* as noted previously, meaning trust or moral character, can be a two-stage process. *Antecedent credibility* is your reputation preceding the speech. Do your listeners already perceive you to be a believable and trustworthy source of high moral character and worthy of respect? **Acquired credibility** is the care you show for you audience and their concerns, the competence you display in your delivery, and the authenticity of your evidence that likely bolsters your believability and trustworthiness. You might not need to bolster your credibility with favorable audience members, but keep a sharp eye on ways to convey your good reputation,

good will, and good research when speaking with those not yet convinced. Your audience doesn't care how much you know until they know how much you care. Will they see you as trustworthy and supportive? Be sure they do.

2. **Emotional Appeals** is what Aristotle called *pathos*. To think that emotion is not a part of the workplace is a gross misjudgment. Emotions such as happiness, hope, excitement, anger, and determination can be very motivating when trying to persuade, when expressed appropriately and to the right degree. Are you excited about the ease the new software system will provide? Are you dismayed by the lack of inclusivity in the rules you are trying to change? There may be a place in your speech for that emotion. Aim to elevate the emotion of the audience members who are in favor of your persuasive proposition. Rally their support. For the contrary or even casual audiences though, too much emotional appeal might backfire. If you are trying to convince a group to purchase a gym membership but they are already reluctant to do so, layering the emotional appeal of how much they will love it, or the fear appeal of how much they risk by not getting in shape, may make them walk away. Find the sweet spot by tailoring your use of emotion to the audience type at hand.

3. **Logic/Evidence**, is what Aristotle called *logos*: Most persuasion requires laying out logical arguments supported by strong evidence. Do you want a raise? Building a case on credibility and emotion alone won't cut it. Make a case as to why you deserve a raise by noting your hard work supported by citing examples of your work and salary history. Would you like to expand the boundaries of the project your department is leading? Develop arguments that such expansion has several important benefits and offer solid support through fact-based evidence that supports your request. The contrary audience will need the most evidence from the most respected sources (see Chapter 15).

Audience Composition

Whether informing or persuading, as workplaces and global virtual groups become more diverse and commonplace, **demographics**—characteristics such as age, gender, culture, and ethnicity, and group affiliations—require more attention. Audiences often are composed of diverse members, so there are competing attitudes, beliefs, and values among listeners, making audience adaptation especially challenging. Recognize that few audiences are entirely of one mind.

Age: Generation Gap   Generalizations based on age define what we consider to be a generation gap in cultural beliefs and practices. *Diversity in age can be challenging* (Henry & Yeung, 2020). A study by Pew Research Center reported the largest generational differences in the United States in decades ("Generation Gap," 2018). Those 65 years and older differ significantly from those 18 to 29 on issues of politics, religion, social relationships, use of technology, and other topics. Generalizations based on generation gaps should be embraced cautiously, but generational differences do pose significant challenges for those making presentations (Dhawan, 2021a).

As a speaker, develop the content of your speech so that it relates to the experience of your listeners. References to insider trading, mutual funds, problems of leadership in corporations, and retirement accounts don't necessarily speak directly to the experience of young employees. Older employees, however, may relate to detailed explanations of such topics. Also, don't assume older audiences embrace rapidly changing technology, its advantages, and its necessity as readily as younger generations. Many do, but often not quite as readily as digital natives might.

Gender: The Importance of Inclusivity   Gender differences in perception and behavior do exist, as discussed at length in Chapter 3. Thus, develop your speech from different perspectives to include all listeners. A presentation on sexual harassment in the workplace, for instance, should concern everyone, regardless of gender identification—male, female, transgender, genderfluid, bigender, or nonbinary—as abuse in any form pollutes the workplace environment. If using hypothetical examples in your presentation, do not use gender stereotypes. All men are not bosses, and all women are not office assistants. That's a yesteryear notion.

Ethnicity and Culture: Sensitivity to Diversity
Large cultural and ethnic differences in beliefs and values exist and are also reviewed in Chapter 3. Embrace the potential diversity of your audience by being inclusive in your use of language and show sensitivity to the main point that difference is not deficient (Dhawan, 2021a). For example, as the 17th edition of the *Chicago Manual of Style* notes, "some people identify not with a gender-specific pronoun [he or she] but instead with the pronoun *they* and its form or some other gender-neutral singular pronoun; any such preference should generally be respected" (quoted by M. Grant, 2021).

Group Size: It Makes a Difference   Chapter 9 discussed the many effects of group size on decision making and problem solving in groups. Tailoring your presentation to the anticipated size of your audience is also important. Presenting your speech behind a podium when your audience is composed of only three or four members is overly formal and awkward. If you plan to offer a handout, knowing in advance how many listeners are likely to attend can prevent embarrassing apologies for failing to provide enough copies, or piling a stack of a hundred handouts and realizing that fewer than a dozen individuals have attended your presentation. It signals a failure of expectations. The size of your audience might also influence which visual aids you will use, as explored more in Chapter 16. For these reasons, try to get an accurate head count before you present.

Top presenters are sensitive to additional and often less-obvious audience composition factors such as sexual orientation, income, and education level. Prioritize respect and inclusivity in every speaking situation.

How to Analyze Your Audience

At this point you might agree that there is a lot to know about your audience, but you might be wondering how a presenter would know all of this. When possible, the best way to gather information about your audience is through *direct observation*. If you are presenting to peers in your company, you know their demographics. If your audience is made up of your team members, you have the advantage of gathering information about them firsthand, through observation. You know what they know about your topic, how they get along with you and each other, and you likely share a common vocabulary (e.g., jargon, acronyms, and abbreviations).

If you are not a member of the group that comprises your audience, *query your contact person*. Ask questions about the group's shared history, age, and diversity. Ask what the audience expects from you. Michelle (the coauthor of this textbook) learned this one the hard way. She delivered a lunch-and-learn presentation about team dynamics to an insurance group and had been in brief contact with a new liaison. It was only after her workshop that participants revealed the internal email invitation specified that the topic would be about dealing with difficult customers (another topic she had discussed briefly with the liaison, but understood it was to be presented the following month). She was lucky that the audience played along, but she didn't feel good about missing their expectations. While some people reported that they derived something useful from the presentation, it wasn't what they expected, and perhaps was not how they would have chosen to spend their lunch hour. As a presenter, ask good questions and be crystal clear about what has been communicated to your audience about your presentation. If possible, ask to be copied on email correspondences about your presentation.

When applicable, *survey your audience*. Distributing a short query through a service such as Survey Monkey will help you find out more about their topic knowledge and expectations. When teaching new groups about giving better

Know your audience. Consider age, gender, size, diversity, and the reasons audience members are attending your presentation. A speech that is a massive success for one audience can be a dismal failure with an audience markedly different in composition. Always adapt your speech to the audience at hand.

business presentations, Michelle sends all enrolled participants a short survey about their level of speech anxiety and speaking experience. By gathering this important information, she can adjust how much time she allocates to those topics.

Other Considerations

With any audience, be sure to consider the time of day that you are presenting. Research concludes that 10:00 a.m. is the best time for audiences to absorb and remember information. Logical reasoning piques between 11 a.m. and 2 p.m. After 2:00 p.m. is the time block in which we are most busy, distracted, or both (Matyszczyk, 2016). Though you might not have control of the presentation time slot, based on this information you can still strategize ways to connect with them and tailor your presentation. Sometimes merely acknowledging the time ("It's 2:00, which means that afternoon fatigue is probably kicking in. Stay with me—I have some wonderful information to share with you!") shows that you have not switched into autopilot mode and are reading from a script. Instead, you are present and connected.

What do they think of you? We recently overheard someone say, "We would care less about what people think of us if we knew how seldom they think of us." This is not the time to ascribe to such words. It is essential to gather information about what your audience thinks of you. What is your reputation with the audience? Do they know you? Do they have good will for you? Are they aware of your expertise? Knowing this will help you define how much credibility you'll need to establish in your introduction.

What do they think about the topic? Is the topic something that benefits them? What is in it for them? Clear answers to those questions are essential for connecting your audience to the topic. Knowing the audience's position toward your presentation topic can help you add or subtract supporting materials that will aid in their comprehension.

Respect your audience's time. Every time you hold an audience for longer than they expected, you lose a little bit of their trust. Also, if you are one of many speakers or part of a full agenda, going over your allotted time takes away from someone else's.

Though it might seem like a lot of work, a thorough analysis of your presentation audience can help alleviate speech anxiety, craft a more meaningful message, and ultimately, it will help you communicate your ideas as effectively as possible.

Organization

Now that you know how to quell your fears and analyze your audience, it is time to organize your information so you can present it in a coherent, memorable way that makes sense to your listeners. We'll start by identifying the speech's general purpose. From there we will create a purpose/impact statement that guides the development of your presentation. Finally, we will do a deep dive on presentation flow and organization of ideas.

The Introduction: How to Begin

A presentation is comprised of three main parts: the introduction, body, and conclusion. Regarding your introduction, before you start speaking, the audience is subconsciously asking two questions: *Why should I listen?* and *Why should I listen to this person?* Your job as a presenter is to answer these questions and get them acclimated to you, your speaking style, and your agenda. A complete introduction should be no more than roughly 10% of your total speaking time. It should accomplish five goals: get the audience's attention, make a clear purpose statement, establish your topic significance, build your credibility, and preview your main points.

Get the Audience's Attention: Break the "Ho-hum" Barrier   The ho-hum barrier is the invisible wall that exists between you and your audience. They think, "Ho-hum, another pitch." "Ho-hum, another update." "Ho-hum, another training." Starting your presentation with a monotone *"hellomynameisDanandtoday-Iamgoingtotalktoyouaboutleadership"* does not do anything to pique your audience's interest, nor does it stoke the fire that you need to build your own confidence. An attention getter can be a thoughtful quote, a compelling or amusing story, a powerful question, or a startling statistic. Whatever you choose, make sure it is connected to your topic and your audience. Walking over to the wall, sliding the dimmer switch all the way up and saying "Let's shine some light on the topic of blockchain" is corny and irrelevant. For years, Michelle has taught sales teams in global companies how to hone their speaking skills. In a sales update to 50 employees from all areas of California, a sales manager reported that she shifted the energy in the room from bored to interested by taking a chance with a fresh opener. She worked in the agriculture industry and needed to provide valuable information about the forecast in what was one of the rainiest seasons the business had encountered. Instead of launching into the numbers, she paused, made eye contact with her audience, and then thoughtfully glanced at the rain pouring outside the conference room. She then said, "By a show of hands, how many of you came here today by boat?"

The audience laughed and the ho-hum barrier was broken. She acknowledged the challenge of the weather presented for not only travel but also for their company's product. When retelling her presentation experience, she said that she was less anxious when she connected with her audience. She took a risk and tried something new—and it paid off.

Make a Clear Purpose Statement: Provide Intent Identifying a general purpose and creating a purpose/impact statement are essential elements of your speech introduction. A **general purpose** identifies the overall goal of your presentation, and it tells the audience why you are giving the presentation (to inform, persuade, or entertain/eulogize). *As already mentioned, most presentations in the workplace are either informative or persuasive.* Some informative presentations can be persuasive. You might be demonstrating the impressive features in the new conference room, and an unexpected

Immobility when speaking is dull. Be animated. Show some enthusiasm to grab and keep your listeners' attention. Lively facial expressions and moderate body movement creates attention. Rigid posture and facial immobility can act like a sedative.

consequence of your informative presentation could be that your audience members are persuaded to get these features in more conference rooms throughout the corporate campus. Also, there is an informative element to any persuasive presentation. Your job is to know your general purpose and stick with that. *Ask yourself if your goal is to inform or to persuade.*

Much like the Purpose/Impact statements created for a meeting agenda in Chapter 12, carefully narrow your general purpose to a **purpose/impact statement** that cascades into all parts of the speech's organization. Your purpose/impact (P/I) statement serves to guide the development of your presentation, enabling you to focus on what to include and exclude. It also signals to your audience what you hope to accomplish from your presentation.

> *(Purpose)* The purpose of this presentation is to _____ in order to/so *(Impact)* _____.

Not this:

General purpose: To inform

Purpose/Impact: To talk about the software update so people know it

But this:

P/I: To educate my team about the new software update so they can easily access the premium features.

Not this:

General purpose: To persuade

P/I: To increase our software budget so we can buy what we need

But this:

P/I: To specify the limitations of our current software in order to get funding for a new system.

Establish Topic Significance   After you have their attention, focus on those two key questions: *Why should your audience listen? What's in it for your listeners?* Tell your audience how they will benefit from tuning in to your talk. This part really gets back to why you are speaking. Surely, it is not just because you think it is fun, had time to fill on your calendar, or just

wanted to hear yourself talk. You are speaking for a reason—to inform or persuade, and you are speaking to this particular audience for a reason. This can be as transparent as saying, "Today's update about the weather's effect on product shipment will help you answer reseller and customer queries with ease; you'll have the most current information and answers that are in alignment with our brand." This is also a great place to speak a conversational form of your P/I statement that guided your presentation development.

Establish Your Credibility   Your antecedent credibility can be reinforced in your title, your reputation, and your apparent experience. If you are not a part of the group or your reputation doesn't precede you, you can acquire credibility by stating your title ("As the leader of product development") or assuring your listeners of your topic knowledge ("I have spoken with other industry leaders and extensively researched the competition"). You might also reveal the sources of research you consulted ("The most current issue of *Harvard Business Review* features automation and its impact on our field"). You can also tout your sources in the body of the presentation as well (see Chapter 15 on supporting materials).

Preview Your Main Points   Previewing the main points or organizational pattern of your presentation gives listeners a chance to find their way if they drift off, and of equal importance, it helps them anticipate what questions to ask at the speech's conclusion. Such a roadmap can segue into the main event: *"I am going to discuss three reasons to reject the latest proposal: cost, safety, and loss of benefits."* Now everyone knows that these three points will constitute the body of your presentation.

The Body

Typically, the body of your presentation will focus on two to five well-developed main ideas, depending on your time limit. The body of your presentation should have a logical, well-designed flow. It typically consumes about 80% of your speaking time.

Organizational Patterns: Several Choices The standard outlining format is reviewed in Table 14.1. Within that format, strategically organize your main ideas so they are easy for your audience to follow and retain. Paying attention to the organization and development of your main ideas (vs. "winging it") also aids your own familiarity and retention of the material. There are six common ways to organize your ideas: *topically, chronologically, problem–solution, spatially, cause and effect, and Monroe's Motivated Sequence.* Use the chart in Table 14.2 to differentiate among common organizational patterns and to choose which one or combination of patterns might work best for your business presentation.

While these organizational patterns can be used independently to structure the body of your speech, they may also be nested together.

For example, you might be giving a demonstration of the new technology in the conference room using a topical pattern that can be paired with a spatial pattern when reviewing the room's layout. For example,

P/I: To educate all senior leaders about the new conference room technology so they can use it with confidence in upcoming meetings.

I. Layout of the room

    A. Wall controls in the back

    B. Cameras in each corner

    C. Supplies in cabinet

II. How to connect for virtual conferences

III. Capabilities of smart screens

While there are many ways to organize the body of your speech, the most important thing

TABLE 14.1 GUIDELINES FOR OUTLINING

While it might be tempting to organize the draft of your presentation using bullet points, much is gained through creating a thorough outline. Using the standard outline format, complete with appropriate symbols and indentation, helps develop your purpose/impact statement so that you can see the logical progression of your ideas and arguments.

I. Roman numerals denote the main points that support the P/I

  A. Capital letters mark primary subpoints that support the main points
  B. Another primary subpoint for thorough development
    1. Standard numbers show secondary subpoints that support the secondary subpoints
    2. Another secondary subpoint for thorough development
      a. Lowercase letters indicate tertiary subpoints
      b. Another tertiary subpoint

II. Roman numeral for the second main point, and so on.

Each successive set of subpoints is indented to separate the main points visually from the primary, secondary, and tertiary subpoints. Thus, you would not format an outline as follows:

  I. Main point
    A. Primary subpoint
    B. Primary subpoint
      1. Secondary subpoint
      2. Secondary subpoint
        a. Tertiary subpoint
        b. Tertiary subpoint
  II. Main point

You can see that lack of indentation merges all your points and can easily lead to confusion.

We encourage the development of ideas to the secondary subpoint, so your points are well supported.

TABLE 14.2

COMMON PRESENTATION ORGANIZATIONAL PATTERNS, USES, AND EXAMPLES

Organizational Pattern	Definition	Best Uses	Example
Topical	Information is chunked into categories (main points) that support your speaking purpose	Use when the main points are not necessarily related to each other, but each is related to the topic	Purpose/Impact: To announce the organization's new sexual harassment program in order to gain compliance, company-wide I. The new mandates II. How to access in the Learning Management System III. Next steps for rolling it out, company-wide
Chronological	Main ideas are sequenced by time, either forward or backward	Use when there is a logical progression of information, steps or a process	P/I: To educate the community about the history of your organization so their knowledge extends beyond what we sell I. 2015: Founders II. 2018: Acquisition III. 2021: Today's leadership and commitment to community
Spatial	Geographically organize information around location or space	Use to help listeners differentiate locations	P/I: To orient new hires to the company campus so they can navigate it with ease Sales and Human Resources are in building 200 I. Information Technology is in Building 250 II. Finance is in building 275
Cause and Effect	Illustrate causal relationships by explaining the cause and how it leads to the effect (or effects)	Use to inform or persuade	P/I: To present the results of our philanthropy partnership so we can continue the good work I. For the past year, our company has distributed our product to over 25 local, nonprofit businesses, free of charge II. 19 of those companies have left positive social media reviews, thus building our brand loyalty
Problem–Solution	Present a dilemma followed by a recommendation to solve it	Use to persuade	P/I: To influence the adoption of a new dress code, company-wide, in order to have a more inclusive work culture I. Today's dress code is outdated and reflects gender stereotypes II. We should adopt an inclusive, gender-neutral dress code, company-wide
Monroe's Motivated Sequence	An expansion of the problem/solution format that harness the psychology of persuasion; uses five steps: Attention Need Satisfaction Visualization Action	Use to persuade	P/I: To influence the adoption of a new dress code, company-wide, in order to have a more inclusive work culture I. Imagine not being able to bring your authentic self to work II. The current dress code limits self-expression and while encouraging exclusion III. A new, updated dress code will help employees express their individuality and will reflect the diversity of our clientele IV. Now imagine a place where employees are happier and customers more at ease V. Let's adopt the new dress code immediately

of all is that you do it! A well-organized speech increases perception of your competence and enhances the audience's cognizance of your topic. As seen in the example above, sorting the subpoints also helps you assess what needs to be developed, if all categories are included, and whether or not the presentation design is balanced (see also Table 14.1).

Transitions: *Making Connections* Transitions serve to connect one point to the next. They can be used to preview what is to come, summarize a complex point before moving on to another, or a combination of the two. There is a ***preview transition, such as*** "The next point I'll be reviewing is the new process that all front desk employees will use when dealing with customer complaints." There is a ***summary transition*** such as "To repeat, when dealing with difficult customers, aim to follow the L.A.S.T. conversation framework. *Listen* fully to their complaint so we understand the issues. *Apologize* for the inconvenience. *Solve* the problem to the best of our abilities. *Thank* the customer for working with us to make it right." There is also a ***review-preview transition***, such as "Now that we know the L.A.S.T. conversation model we will be using to solve customer problems, let's take a look at some techniques for keeping your cool in challenging situations."

While suitable for any type of business presentations, transitions are particularly helpful in technical presentations when your audience does not share the same level of knowledge as you. *Transitions increase the audience's comprehension of a complex topic. Use them liberally, particularly between your main points.*

The Conclusion

Your conclusion should end with a bang, not a whimper. A strong conclusion is approximately 5%–10% of your speaking time and has three parts: a summary, call to action, and a final thought.

The Speech Summary: *Pulling It Together* By this point, you may have noticed that your presentation is filled with purposeful redundancy. Strategic repetition not only reinforces your key takeaways but also provides guidance for your audience members whose minds will inevitably wander. Begin your conclusion by saying something such as, "In closing, I'd like to remind you that adopting a new dress code is in alignment with our company's inclusivity initiative. As mentioned, it is practical, affordable, and easy to adopt." The summary is succinct and wraps up your main points.

Call to Action: *The Persuasive Finish* If persuasion is your goal, a call to action is essential. Too many professionals skip this part, claiming it feels too sales-like. You have taken your audience this far, so you need to be intentional and specific about what you want them to do. Even if you already articulated that in a problem–solution organizational pattern, your audience needs to know exactly what you are asking of them. To be consistent with the dress code example, there are many actions you might like your audience to take. If they are a committed audience, you might ask them to come to the next meeting about this issue, show their support by emailing HR, or spread the word about the importance of the new dress code. If they are a contrary audience that is resistant your topic or call to action, moving them to immediate action might not be possible, but you can move them one step closer to neutral. That counts as persuasion.

If your goal is not persuasive, use this portion of your conclusion to remind the audience why the topic should matter to them. Remember how they were wondering why they should listen? Repeat that. For example, if you are giving an informative presentation to new hires about the company's history, remind them that a broader knowledge of the company helps give them context and brings the possibility of richer conversations with clients.

Final Thought It is so tempting to slap on a "thank you" and sit down. Instead, as you opened with an attention getter, close with a final thought. Use a relevant quote, short story (perhaps one that you started in the introduction and you are now concluding), or a rhetorical question. Keeping in line with the dress code presentation you might say, "I'd like to close with something Sheryl Sandburg said: "We cannot change what we are not aware of, and once we are aware we cannot help but change." Then take a nice pause.

Let your final thought sink in.

And then (and only then) can you say the words most presenters are dying to say: "Thank you" and "Any questions?"

Q&A: They Have Questions, You Have Answers

Resist the temptation to flee the room or sit down. There is one more step to your presentation's flow: The question–answer period. Use these strategies for maintaining your credibility and your connection with the audience all the way until the end.

1. *Anticipate questions*. You created the speech with the audience in mind. If you correctly anticipated audience's objections or concerns, you will be ready to address them if you haven't already done so in the presentation.

2. *Maintain professionalism*. Too often we have seen polished presenters morph into much less-confident versions of themselves in the Q&A. Channel confidence through your posture, eye contact, and vocal delivery (see Chapter 16 for more).

3. *Listen closely*. Even if you think you know what the audience member is asking before they get to the end of their question, listen closely to ensure you understand their query. Don't assume. If you don't understand the question, ask them to repeat it, or summarize what you think they are asking and check for accuracy. "I think you're concerned about the time this implementation will take away from other initiatives, is that correct?"

4. *Answer the question that was asked*. Be clear. Be concise. Do not use someone's question as a springboard for a tangential topic you wish to address. Ask the audience member if you answered their question after you have responded. Use the PREP method from Chapter 7.

5. *Address unasked questions*. You might feel relieved when no one speaks up to ask a question, but this usually isn't a good thing. A lack of questions might indicate that your audience is disinterested, tired, or confused. Keep a couple of questions in mind. When the audience stares in silence say, "A concern that people often have is _____ and I want to assure you that _____." You can also increase audience participation by asking them questions: "Is there any point that I need to clarify further?"

You're on Mute: Tips for Presenting Virtually

With the use of Zoom skyrocketing, videoconferencing is here to stay. By 2025, an estimated 70% of the world's workforce will be working

---

BOX 14.1 Presentation Prework

Don't wait until your next presentation to use these tips!

- Speak up often—get used to hearing your voice.
- Practice good posture and eye contact whenever you can.
- Monitor your "ums" in casual conversation.
- Listen for interesting metaphors or news items that relate to your topic and that you can use to keep your audience's attention throughout your presentation or to help them understand a complex topic.
- Practice upcoming presentations with a live person—someone who is representative of your audience—when possible.
- Remember, your job as a presenter is to get your ideas across as clearly and effectively as possible.
- And, most importantly: YOU GOT THIS!

at least 5 days per month remotely (Castrillon, 2020). Companies such as Twitter, VMWare (a subsidiary of Dell Technologies), and Reddit are offering employees the option of working from home (WFH) 100% of the time, indefinitely. Virtual presentations are obviously on the rise.

The same guidelines and advice for in-person presentations apply for virtual presentations: Lessen your anxiety, analyze your audience, and organize your ideas. *Use the chart in* Table 14.3 *as a guide* that also provides unique tips relevant to virtual presentations.

Hybrid Presentations: Upping the Ante

To this point we have covered the basics of in-person and virtual presentations. But what if they are both? By 2025, more than 40 million American professionals will be working entirely remotely (Guruprakash, 2022). This greatly increases the chance that you will present to an audience comprised of people who occupy the same physical space as you and to others who are tuning in virtually. The content of your presentation may stay the same, and prioritizing inclusion will help you meet the needs of both audiences.

Blending both audiences is best achieved by setting up the room correctly, making eye contact with all attendees regardless of location, and involving remote participants when possible. To best set up the room, see the presentation from the audience's perspective. The camera is the eye of the remote participants, no matter where their actual eyes/images are

TABLE 14.3   VIRTUAL PRESENTATIONS

Before the Presentation	
Prepare and practice	**Try a test run.** If using the meeting platform for the first time, Microsoft Teams, Zoom, Google Hangouts, and WebEx all have test links you can try before your meeting.**Download and update** any required meeting software. When joining by computer, use a wired connection over Wi-Fi, and check your camera, speakers, and microphone. If presenting from home, **be aware of any Wi-Fi dead zones** before your meeting begins. Move your router to a central location. Wipe off those fingerprints: **Make sure your camera lens is clean.** **Sign into the meeting a few minutes early** to ensure the meeting invite is valid. Contact the meeting organizer if you cannot join through the provided link. **Assign a cohost** to monitor the chat feature or assist with technology issues. This helps you keep your focus on the presentation. **Find your virtual communication options and know how to use them:** Locate chat, mute, screen share, and video icons so you can participate without hesitation once the meeting begins. **Keep the meeting password handy,** especially if you need to log in again anytime during the meeting. Things happen. **Do a dry run-through** of your virtual presentation. Record it if possible.
Get ready for your close-up: Appearance, camera, and lighting	**Position your webcam at eye level or a bit higher**, but no higher than your hairline. Sit or stand far enough away from your camera so that your shoulders are showing. Don't be a webcam zombie: washed out and weary. **Ensure that you are clearly visible and illuminated.** Appearance matters. **Sit or stand facing your light source.** Lighting from above and below casts unflattering shadows. Natural lighting is great. Three-point lighting—creating dimension and eliminating shadows by using a key light, fill light, and backlight—is even better. Face your key light, the main light source. Place a fill light on either side, at about face level, and use a backlight to separate yourself from your background. **If you wear glasses, beware the glare.** Let others see your eyes by paying closer attention to the angle, height, and distance of your light source. A large, soft light, above eye level and off to the left or right, can greatly decrease glare. **Forgo filters.** Do take advantage of Zoom's "Touch up my appearance" feature if using that platform. You might also turn on the "adjust for low light" setting if need be. **Dress appropriately**, as you would if you were meeting in an office. Avoid distractions such as stripes or logos on clothing or hats that impede eye contact.

(Continued)

TABLE 14.3 *(Continued)*

Before the Presentation	
Look behind you: Backgrounds	**Everything speaks:** Make your background add to your message, not detract. Keep your background clean and free of anything that will take meeting participants' eyes reason to roam. Choose a background that enhances your professional image and your message. Zoom offers virtual backgrounds, and other platforms like Microsoft Teams can blur your background. Know what tools are available before your audience arrives. **Clear the clutter,** but don't make your background so sterile that you're one screenshot away from a mugshot. If you must choose between sterility or clutter, pick the former. If using a virtual background, test it before the meeting to make sure your system supports it. *Choose a virtual background that contrasts with your hair, skin and clothing.* Be sure your background doesn't compete for your attention (visual noise), particularly when uploading your own background image.
Get ready to roll!	**Keep a pen and paper nearby for notes.**
During the presentation	
Monitor your nonverbals	Just as with a live presentation, be animated and energetic. Err on the side of over animated vs. monotonous. You need to fight a bit harder to keep a virtual audience's attention. **Posture:** Sit up straight or stand up tall. Whether sitting or standing, limit unnecessary movement. **Eye contact:** When talking, look into your camera often, not just the images on the screen. This makes it appear as if you are looking your audience members in the eye. When listening, look at the people on the screen so you can capture their nonverbal messages. **Vocal qualities:** Pace yourself. With the lack of nonverbal cues from your audience, you might be tempted to plow through your presentation. Don't! Instead, vary your volume, pitch, and rate, just as you would do in a meeting room. Use your indoor voice. Keep volume loud enough for all to hear but avoid shouting. **Facial expressions:** *Show* others how you feel about what you are saying by engaging your facial muscles and eyebrows. Emote. Be authentic.
Engage your audience	Sure, it's your speech, but you need to make sure the audience is following along. Engage them by asking questions that they can answer out loud or through the chat, launch polls that relate to your topic, or invite questions at points of the presentation by encouraging participants to use the "raise hand" symbol to speak. Invite people to unmute themselves and turn on their cameras when talking. Call on people directly if applicable. If it is a large audience, have your cohost monitor the chat or alert you when people have questions. It can be very distracting to do it all as a presenter.
After the presentation	
Stick around	When possible, be the last to leave. Stay for questions.
Evaluate your performance: How did you do?	First, take notes on what you think you did well and what you would like to have done differently. Next, solicit feedback from your cohost or audience. Say something like, "I am looking to improve my presentations. Can you tell me one thing I did well, and one thing that would have made my presentation more effective?" Finally, if the presentation was recorded, take the time to watch it and learn. Pay attention to your strengths as well as your areas for improvement. Speaking is a skill. Great speakers commit to continuous improvement.

being displayed in the room. In a recent hybrid presentation that this textbook's coauthor Michelle gave, the room was set up before she arrived. The in-person participant's desks were arranged in a half circle, and a large screen with images of the three remote attendees along with the webcam closed off the top of the circle. Michelle was asked to *present from inside the circle.* In order to include all, she needed to turn around and speak to the webcam to engage the remote folks, but also spin the other way to maintain connection with those seated in front of her. It wasn't her first choice of setups, but the group acknowledged the awkwardness and appreciated her inclusion of everyone. If given the opportunity, set the webcam and computer up in line with the in-person audience. If not, go with the flow, but not at the expense of keeping your back to virtual participants or forgetting they are there. Keep them engaged by checking in with them ("Those who are joining virtually, can you see the chart?"), and asking questions directly to them ("Let's hear from the remote crew—is there anything you would add?").

SUMMARY

Love it or hate it, presenting is often a part of the professional world. Unlike the grade you worked for while giving speeches in college, or the certificate you might have earned in presentation programs, strong presentation skills at work can help you close a business deal, get more resources for your team, spread important messages to your department, and build your positive reputation in the workplace. Speech anxiety is a normal part of the process. Appease it by acknowledging it and putting it into perspective. Get your audience on board as the coauthors of your presentation. A thorough audience analysis not only gives you information vital to your presentation development, it also takes your focus off of yourself. Identify the general purpose of speaking, and then identify the impact you intend to make. Finally, structure your presentation like a well-planned workout: Warm up (introduction) workout (body of the speech), and cool down (conclusion).

Film School Case Studies

Don't Look Up (2021) Netflix; Rated R

There are several instances in this film where researchers Dr. Randall Mindy (Leonardo DiCaprio) and Kate Dibiasky (Jennifer Lawrence) need to present essential information to the public on a televised news program called *The Daily Rip*. Look for ways they build or detract from their credibility, and how they adapt the information and their delivery to the audience at hand.

TED Talks and YouTube Videos

These TED Talks and YouTube videos can be accessed by going to the Oxford Learning Link for It's All of Our Business or by typing the title of the video into a Google search window.

"How to NOT Get Nervous Speaking in Front of People"

"No Freaking Speaking: Managing Public Speaking Anxiety"

"How Not to Be Awkward In Conversation"

"This Talk Isn't Very Good: Dancing With My Inner Critic by Steve Chapman"

Tutorial on Virtual Speeches: "Worst (and Best) Practices for Giving Online Speeches"

210.24

209.22

210.74

1,218.38

208.33

26.42

456.60

1.015

19.05

2510.41

51.41%

149.16

7,513.08

23.30

2,168.02

29,240.68

1. Effectively support speech ideas with impactful examples, statistics, and testimony

2. Critically evaluate supporting materials through tests of relevance, credibility, and sufficiency

Critical Thinking and Supporting Materials

Critical thinking has never been more important or challenging in the world of business given the eruption of fake news, fabricated studies, "alternative facts," and proliferating conspiracies disseminated on social media (Chan et al., 2017; Datz, 2020; Debies-Carl, 2017). A Rand Report cleverly dubs this deterioration of critical thinking practices as "truth decay" (Kavanagh & Rich, 2018). The COVID-19 virus unleashed what the World Health Organization dubbed a "massive infodemic" in which the desire to learn about this novel virus exploded, but so did the dissemination of misinformation. Holding your breath for 10 seconds is not a test for COVID-19, Vladimir Putin did not release 500 lions onto the streets of Moscow to keep residents indoors to fight the spread of the virus, and eating sea lettuce does not prevent anyone from getting infected with COVID-19. These are just a few examples of the misinformation spread on social media sites at the outset of the pandemic (Fleming, 2020).

Jonathan Swift long ago noted, "Falsehood flies, and the truth comes limping after it." Researchers at the Massachusetts

CHAPTER OUTLINE

- Examples
- Statistics
- Testimony
- Evaluating Supporting Materials

Institute of Technology confirmed this by conducting a study on lies and false information spread on Twitter. Their results are troubling: *Fake news is 70% more likely to be retweeted than real, substantiated news; and it takes the truth six times as long as misinformation to reach 1,500 people*. Truthful information rarely spreads to more than 1,000 people, but the top 1% of false news routinely spreads to between 1,000 and 100,000 people on Twitter. They found that "bots" were not the culprits in spreading nonsense, but instead it is people who are more drawn to the novel, surprising, and emotional nature of most false information, rumor, and conspiracy theories that spread like wildfires on social media (Vosoughi et al., 2018).

Michael D. Rich, president and CEO of the RAND Corporation and coauthor of the "truth decay" report, explains *the danger to businesses from misinformation and blatant disinformation* this way: "The reason that engineers focus on data and measurement and science and calculations and analysis is that, if [they] don't, the bridge they're designing could fall. Businesses can lose market share and go out of business. There are consequences" (quoted by Brian Bolduc, 2020). The coauthors of the RAND report continue: "Whether acquiring a company or making a capital investment, successful business leaders start with verifiable facts" (Rich & Kavanaugh, 2021). The *Global Fraud and Risk Report* of September 2019 "found that 84% of businesses felt threatened by market manipulation

through the spread of disinformation, most commonly fueled by 'adversarial' social media" (quoted by Hodge, 2020). Research from Internet analysis firm MOZ discovered that "companies risk losing 22% of their business if potential customers find just one negative article [negativity bias] on the first page of their internet search results. This figure balloons up to 70% if four or more negative stories are found on the same page" (Hodge, 2020). The negative stories don't have to be true.

Wild unsupported assertions and playing fast and loose with the truth pollutes any workplace environment and leads to egregiously bad decision making and problem solving. Clearly, knowing how to evaluate information and claims is critical in the business arena for everyone involved.

Consequently, the purpose of this chapter is to explain ways to build supporting materials that improve critical thinking and business presentations essential to competent decision making and problem solving. Typically, supporting materials are discussed only in relation to making speeches, but they are also critical in promoting thoughtful and competent workplace decision making and problem solving at all levels. Thus, the following chapter objectives include (1) explaining types of supporting materials, (2) ways to make supporting materials effective for presentations, and (3) exploring criteria for evaluating supporting materials for presentational effectiveness and enhancing decision making and problem solving in the workplace.

Examples

Supporting materials are the examples, statistics, and testimony used to bolster your theme or viewpoint. *Supporting materials accomplish four specific goals*: (a) to clarify points and avoid misunderstandings, (b) amplify ideas for impact, (c) credibly support claims (assertions) to counter truth decay, and (d) gain interest in positive ways. *This is an audience-centered process*. For example, some audiences require greater clarification of points than others: a group of lawyers won't require examples to clarify legal procedures nearly as often as a lay audience assuredly would. This section covers the types of supporting materials and ways to present them effectively to accomplish these four specific goals.

Types of Examples

A well-chosen example is often memorable for audiences and may have a great impact on listeners. There are four types of examples: hypothetical, real, brief, and extended.

Hypothetical Examples: It Could Happen   Hypothetical examples describe imaginary situations concocted to make a point, illustrate an idea, or identify a general principle. Hypothetical examples help listeners envision what a situation might be like, or they call up similar experiences listeners have had without citing a historically factual illustration that may not be readily available. As long as the hypothetical example is consistent with known facts, it will be believable.

What life changes might occur if hypothetically, because of unexpected circumstances, you can't finish your college degree? What would be the likely effects if you suddenly lost your job, were laid up in a hospital for 3 months, or became permanently disabled? What if your employer provided inadequate health insurance? Imagine the effects a job promotion might have on your career. How might you deal with the failure of your start-up business? Hypothetical examples like these help listeners picture what might happen and motivate them to take action that could prevent or prepare them for such occurrences.

Real Examples: It Did Happen   *Because real examples are factual, they are more difficult to discount than hypothetical examples*. A real example can personalize a problem. Hypothetical examples can be discounted as simply "made up." Unlike hypothetical examples, real examples can make an issue concrete for listeners that hypothetical examples cannot accomplish. For example

> If you're standing on a street corner in South Lake Union or Belltown [Seattle], chances are you're standing in front of an Amazon office building. You'll be surrounded by blue badges but, if asked, you might struggle to point out the exact building where the

This is the ostentatious Apple, Inc. corporate campus (on the left). Unlike some companies such as Amazon's corporate headquarters in Seattle pictured here, that purposely try to blend into their surroundings, Apple apparently desires to stand out dramatically.

people wearing them work. Even as it has transformed a once-sleepy neighborhood of warehouses and shipyards into a buzzing technology hub, Amazon prefers to blend into its surroundings wherever possible. (Dol, 2020)

"In contrast, Apple Inc. celebrates its ostentatious main corporate campus: Apple Park is Apple's new, 175-acre corporate campus. Its 2.8 million-square-foot main building, or 'spaceship,' is considered to be one of the most energy-efficient buildings on earth. The campus and nearby visitor center opened in 2017, and will house 12,000 employees" ("Apple Park," 2020). Juxtaposing these two real examples can help make the point that corporations present their brands and images in a variety of ways. One company prefers to blend in and another prefers to stand out. *You don't have to say "what if" when you can say "what is."*

Brief and Extended Examples: Timing and Impact

Often a brief example or examples can make a point well. The examples are clear, and no explanation or elaboration is required. If you are trying to illustrate how to attract attention for your business by choosing a clever name, you could offer a potpourri of business names, such as

Curl Up and Dye (hair salon)

Broken Egg (breakfast restaurant)

To Thrill a Mockingbird (pet store)

Waste Not, Want Not (septic disposal)

Nailed It (nail salon)

An extended example is a detailed story or illustration. Terry Hershey, a Protestant minister who for more than three decades has presented enormously popular presentations at the annual Religious Education Congress in Anaheim, California, tells this story to make the point that we learn very early in life to fear making mistakes:

There's a terrific story about a first-grade Sunday school class. The children were restless and fussy. The teacher, in an attempt to get their attention, said, "Okay kids, let's play a game. I'll describe something to you. And you tell me what it is."

The kids quieted down. "Listen. It's a furry little animal with a big bushy tail, that climbs up trees and stores nuts in the winter. Who can tell me what it is?" No one said anything. The teacher went on. "You are a good Sunday school class. You know the right answer to this question. It's a furry little animal with a big bushy tail, that climbs up trees and stores nuts in the winter." One little girl raised her hand. "Emily?" "Well, teacher," Emily declared, "it sounds like a squirrel to me, but I'll say Jesus." (Hershey, 2021)

Be careful not to overwhelm your audience with too many statistics in a cluttered manner.

Unfailingly, when Hershey tells this story, the audience roars with laughter. The story is brief, humorous, fits the audience perfectly because it has religious overtones and a moral, is delivered in an animated style (you had to be there), and is told fluently, as though Hershey has told this story many times. You can imagine, however, how this story could be used to make an important point about risk taking in the workplace and its relationship to creative problem solving. You don't want employees constantly worried about making mistakes and looking to provide only contributions that are safe and what one might think a boss wants. That can lead to groupthink (see Chapter 9).

Making Examples Effective

Using examples effectively requires skill. Well-chosen examples can make a presentation come alive. Here are some basic tips.

Use Relevant Examples: Stay on Point   Examples should be relevant to the point you make. If employees are deeply concerned about the possibility of losing their jobs during a recession or pandemic, presenting facts and figures on how well the stock market is doing to assuage such fear doesn't address the concern. Employees may not own any stock, and even if some do, their stock portfolio may be a weak substitute for months of unemployment or a looming necessity to change careers. Although sometimes it is tempting to offer a funny story or tell a quick joke when making a presentation at a business conference or during a workplace meeting to "loosen up the audience," if the story or joke is not directly relevant to an important point you need to make, skip it. Audiences usually find such irrelevant ploys irritating and counterproductive. They can feel tricked into laughing for no good reason.

Choose Vivid Examples: Create Strong Images
Examples that are vivid can be impactful. For example, descriptions offered in one study of workplace bullying reveal a bubbling cauldron of vitriol waiting to be spewed daily on long-suffering victims. As one victim described such an event, "[She] was intimidating—right in your face—less than an inch away from your face, where her spit would hit you in the face. She would scream at us, her face getting all red and her eyes watering." Another victim described it this way: "He'd scream and yell every day. Veins would pop out of his head; he'd spit, he'd point, he'd threaten daily, all day long to anyone in his way . . . He'd swear profusely" (quoted in Lutgen-Sandvik, 2006). Rage (and apparently flying spit) appear to be common manifestations of workplace bullying, and these vivid descriptions underline its seriousness with impactful depictions.

Stack Examples: When One Is Not Enough
Sometimes a single example does not suffice to make a point clear, memorable, interesting, or adequately supported. Note the value of using plentiful examples stacked one on top of another. Adam Grant (2016) makes the point that original ideas are often overlooked or rejected:

> Studio executives passed on hits ranging from *Star Wars* to *E.T.* to *Pulp Fiction*. In publishing, managers rejected *The Chronicles of Narnia*, *The Diary of Anne Frank*, *Gone with the Wind*, *Lord of the Flies*, and *Harry Potter* . . . [which] sold more copies than any book series, ever. The annals of corporate innovation are filled with tales of managers ordering employees to stop working on projects that turned out to be big hits, from Nichia's invention of LED lighting to Pontiac's Fiero car to HP's electrostatic displays. The Xbox was almost buried at Microsoft; the laser printer was nearly canceled at Xerox for being expensive and impractical.

A single example would have made the point, but stacking several relatable historical examples provides additional punch.

Statistics

Statistics are measures of what is true or factual expressed in numbers. ***They can provide magnitude and allow comparisons***. For example, the first Internet website was info.cern.ch, created by Tim Berners-Lee in December 1990 ("How We Got," 2008). The number of websites (not webpages) worldwide jumped to 24 million by 2000; and by 2010, it had exploded to more than 200 million sites ("March 2010 Web Server Survey," 2010). In 2014, the number of websites had reached an astounding 1 billion; and by 2018, it had reached almost 2 billion before receding somewhat a few years later (Huss, 2021). The magnitude of the Internet today and its astronomical growth (comparison) are exhibited by stacking statistics to show a trend.

Statistics, however, can be manipulated to distort truth. Later in this chapter, several fallacious uses of statistics are discussed. Nevertheless, when statistics are used validly, they can add real substance to your presentations and enhance decision making and problem solving. A well-chosen statistic can support claims, show trends, correct false assumptions, validate hypotheses, and contradict myths—perhaps not as dramatically and memorably as a vivid example, but often more validly and effectively.

Make Statistical Comparisons: Gain Perspective

An effective way to make statistics have meaning for listeners and provide perspective is to use statistical comparisons. For example, one study a few years ago asked more than 800 business people and employed adults to choose from a comparative list of three options. Which business venture would they prefer to start: (a) one that made $5 million profit with a 20% chance of success, (b) one that made $2 million profit with a 50% chance of success, or (c) one that made $1.25 million with an 80% chance of success? Which option would you choose? The entrepreneurs were significantly more likely to opt for the last choice with the least risk than employed adults (Xu & Ruef, 2004). This is a nice way of gaining perspective on aversion to risk in the world of business, especially among CEOs.

Use Statistics Sparingly: Don't Overwhelm

Stacking statistics should be used sparingly and only to create an impact on the central points in a speech. Audience members will tune out if they become weary hearing you stack a mountain of statistics. For example

> The Deloitte Global Millennial Survey 2020 of more than 27,000 Millennials and Generation Z respondents found that 48% of Gen Z and 44% of Millennials reported that they are stressed all or most of the time. Three-fourths said the pandemic has made them more sympathetic toward others'

needs. More than half of Millennials and nearly half of Gen Zs are saving money. Half of all respondents report that it is too late to repair the damage caused by climate change. More Millennials said they would prefer to stay with their employers for at least five years than would prefer to leave within two years. Also, 27% of Millennials and 23% of Gen Zs reported working fewer hours, while 8% of Millennials and 5% of GenZs said they were working longer hours without a corresponding bump in pay. Only about a third of both groups reported that their employment income status had not been affected by the COVID-19 pandemic.

Simply rattling off this abundance of statistics is likely to leave listeners swimming in a statistical swamp. If all of these results are truly important to relay to an audience, presenting these findings on PowerPoint slides and permitting digestion and exploration of each point made from the statistics is warranted.

Testimony

Testimony consists of conclusions offered publicly by experts on a topic or a firsthand account of events by witnesses. This section discusses both types and offers ways to use testimony competently.

Testimony of Experts: Relying on Those in the Know

We live in an often baffling world of mind-boggling complexity. None of us can be expected to know enough to make rational, informed decisions without the help of experts. When choosing a college major, seeking assistance from expert counselors is an advisable practice. What are the odds that a start-up small business will be successful? Consult experts before taking the plunge. Does raising the minimum wage bolster or hinder economic growth? Ask the experts. Does accepting "fringe benefits" as compensation in lieu of salary violate tax laws? You better consult experts if you hope to stay out of prison. Combined with statistical evidence (data), expert testimony can be powerfully informative and persuasive. As Tom Nichols (2017) explains

> Experts are the people who know considerably more on a subject than the rest of us, and are those to whom we turn when we need advice, education, or solutions in a particular area of human knowledge. Note that this does not mean that experts know all there is to know about something. Rather, it means that experts in any given subject are, by their very nature, a minority whose views are more likely to be "authoritative"—that is, correct or accurate—than anyone else's.

We need experts who in many cases spend their adult life studying subjects and receiving training that can prove critical for business teams in making high-quality decisions and solving complex problems. Businesses often hire consultants for such purposes. Management consulting is almost a $250 billion industry in the United States ("Management Consulting," 2021).

Relying on the uninformed or scarcely informed opinions of nonexperts is asking for disaster. David Dunning (2017), one-half of the pair that identified the Dunning-Kruger effect (see Chapter 1), notes that a study by the Financial Industry Regulatory Authority asked 25,000 individuals to rate their financial knowledge before taking a test that measured their actual financial literacy. The almost 800 of these respondents who had actually filed for bankruptcy scored, not surprisingly, in the 37th percentile on average on the test, but they rated their financial knowledge above those who had not filed for bankruptcy. Almost a quarter of the bankrupt group gave themselves the highest knowledge self-rating. *Confidence is a poor indicator of expertise. Credible credentials and experience in one's area of expertise are far more reliable.*

Testimony of Nonexperts: Ordinary Folks Adding Color to Events

You do not have to be an expert or an eyewitness to world events to add compelling testimony to your speech. Twitter is replete with examples of ordinary folks offering sometimes compelling, frequently clever and amusing responses about trends and experiences relevant to business and the workplace.

For example, let's say that you want to make the point that employees' dissatisfaction with their jobs is epidemic. You can cite credible survey results, of course, but a few well-chosen Twitter tweets can sometimes resonate more with an audience and bolster the impact of survey data, such as

> "My office has started random urine testing of employees to detect traces of hope or optimism";

> "I hate my job. The work sucks. The people suck. The pay sucks. (Looks up and sees motivational poster on wall.) Well this changes everything";

> "I just walked in on two coworkers crying in a conference room and I was like, 'Mind if I join?";

> "I was put in charge of morale at work, so I suggested leaving me alone. I didn't know they meant 'everyone's' morale.".

Follow the example of newspapers, television news media, and documentary films. They all use interviews with "common folks" to spice up a story and personalize coverage of events.

Using Testimony Effectively: Beyond Quoting

When you cite testimony to support your speech or make a point during a meeting, you have to decide whether to quote exactly or merely paraphrase. Typically, you use a direct quotation when the statement is short, well phrased, and communicates your point more eloquently or cleverly than you can. **Paraphrasing**, discussed in Chapter 6, is *communicating the concise essence of a source's message—it is advisable when a direct quotation is not worded in an interesting way, such as in most government documents, or when a quotation is very lengthy and needs to be shortened.* Whether directly quoting or merely paraphrasing, however, there are a couple of ways to present testimony appropriately and effectively during your speech.

Quote or Paraphrase Accurately: Be Ethical It is imperative that you not misquote or inaccurately paraphrase your source supporting your claims or an opponent in a debate or discussion. When quoting someone's testimony, ***do not crop the quotation*** so it takes on a different meaning than communicated in context. ***Do not delete important qualifiers*** from any statement. For example, a message such as: "The economic indicators show a slight, but steady increase in sales for the rest of this year but there are warnings in the data that portend a likely downturn to follow" should not be paraphrased inaccurately as: "The economic indicators show a steady increase in sales for the future." Editing quotations to change the meaning of the speaker's intended message is unethical. It is dishonest, and as explained in Chapter 1, honesty is an essential criterion for ethical communication.

Quote Experts Only in Their Field: No Generic Experts Quoting experts outside their field of expertise runs the substantial risk of promoting inaccurate claims supported by invalid and unreliable supporting materials. As Tom Nichols (2017) explains, "Experts can go wrong, for example, when they try to stretch their expertise from one area to another. This is not only a recipe for error, but is maddening to other experts as well." As Nichols further notes, a microbiologist is not by virtue of education an expert on art, and an economist cannot credibly pose as a pharmacologist. Remember our earlier explanations regarding the inapplicability of CEOs' advice on leadership effectiveness (Chapter 10). Being a CEO of a major corporation does not make one an expert on leadership theory and practice. What works for someone in such an enormous power position does not readily translate to a small business owner or a mid-level project team leader.

Evaluating Supporting Materials

The three main types of supporting materials have been explained, and basic ways to use them effectively in your speeches and

Consult *snopes.com* to correct urban myths, disinformation, and implausible statistics, such as the spiders and sex statistics that are silly manufactured stats. The Internet is a common source of implausible and often ridiculous statistics. Make sure that the sources of your statistics are credible.

discussions at work have been addressed. Competent use of supporting materials, however, goes deeper than the basic advice offered so far. You can stack statistics effectively for maximum impact on your listeners, but what if the statistics are made up or inaccurate? For example, way back in 2003, Microsoft asserted that 30 million PowerPoint presentations are given *every day*. Yet, "nothing and no one has substantiated this claim of 30 million" (Bajaj, 2020). How would you calculate accurately such a statistic? *Why has the figure remained unchanged on multiple websites two decades later* (see "PowerPoint Coaching," 2022; Sahni, 2021; Shpitula, 2022)? Has PowerPoint not expanded its use since 2003? This is not a credible statistic, and it never was.

You want to use high-quality supporting materials, and this requires a careful assessment based on specific criteria. *There are three primary criteria, or standards, to evaluate supporting materials: credibility, relevance, and sufficiency*. This section discusses these criteria and explores the errors that occur, called fallacies, when using supporting materials for presentations and decision making and problem solving in the workplace.

Credibility: Is It Reliable and Valid?

A key criterion for evaluating supporting materials that provide the underpinnings of claims made by speakers, **credibility** is determined by reliability and validity. **Reliability** means consistency, and **validity** means accuracy. This means that a source of information should be consistent when citing facts and interpreting data. The facts and the data should also be accurate. For example, quoting the *Harvard Business Review*, which we cite quite often, is credible. It is rated by Media Bias/Fact Check as "least biased based on balanced story selection and editorial positions. . . . We also rate them High for factual reporting due to proper sourcing and a clean fact check record" (Van Zandt, 2020). *Harvard Business Review* is both a reliable and valid source for business information and insight.

Evidence used to support claims is often not credible, however, and determining the difference between reliable and valid evidence and its opposite is essential. It can also be challenging. Stanford researchers gave 263 college students two tasks. One task had students evaluate the trustworthiness of a "news story" whose source was actually a satirical website. A second task asked students to evaluate a website claiming to sponsor "nonpartisan research" but was actually created by a Washington, DC, public relations firm headed by a corporate lobbyist. Students were permitted to "use any online resources" to help with their evaluation. More than two-thirds of these students did not recognize the bogus "news story" as satirical. A whopping 95% never identified the PR firm as actually partisan, not nonpartisan (Wineburg et al., 2020). Students rarely explored additional websites to investigate the veracity of the "news story" and the "nonpartisan research" site.

The Internet can be a phenomenal resource for finding high-quality information, but it also provides a monsoon of misinformation. For example, one of us received from a friend the following email attachment with the source vaguely cited as "the Internet" used to assert the claim that these teachers deserved to be fired:

These are actual comments made on student's report cards by teachers in the New York City public school system. Teachers were fired from their jobs as a result.

1. Since my last report, your child has reached rock bottom and has started to dig.
2. I would not allow this student to breed.
3. Your child has delusions of adequacy.
4. Your son is depriving a village somewhere of an idiot.
5. Your son sets low personal standards and then consistently fails to achieve them.
6. The student has a "full six-pack" but lacks the plastic thing to hold it all together.
7. This child has been working with too much glue.
8. When your daughter's IQ reaches 50, she should sell.
9. The gates are down, the lights are flashing, but the train isn't coming.

10. If this student were any more stupid, he'd have to be watered twice a week.

11. It is impossible to believe that the sperm that created this child beat out 1,000,000 others.

12. The wheel is turning but the hamster is definitely dead.

Confident that public school teachers would not have written these "actual comments," especially on a report card, we used the Internet, ironically, to check on the credibility of this supposed Internet report. We chose one of the comments, typed it verbatim into the Google search window, and located websites that printed the same list of comments but claimed that the list was garnered from British military officer fitness reports, employee performance evaluations, military performance appraisals, and appraisals of federal employees. There were 672 Google hits that printed this list of comments attributed to various sources. The list is almost certainly fabricated. How would anyone have gathered these comments? Who has unfettered access to student report cards, and what teacher would be foolish enough to make such objectionable comments on a report card sent home to parents, risking legal action or termination of employment? If supporting materials are implausible, then credibility should be questioned.

Even credible sources can provide misinformation, and that is doubly troubling. Research shows that corrections of misinformation are ineffective when the misinformation has been repeated multiple times and was originally provided by a credible source. When corrections, however, are provided by a credible source, corrective messages tend to be more successful in changing peoples' minds (Walter & Tukachinsky, 2020).

Several common fallacies significantly diminish the credibility of supporting materials. Recognizing each of them can help you determine the credibility of sources and information provided. We have chosen only the most common such fallacies, not an exhaustive list.

Biased Source: Something to Gain *Special-interest groups or individuals who stand to gain money, prestige, power, or influence if they advocate a certain position on an issue are biased sources of information.* You should consider their claims as dubious. Look for a source that has no personal stake in the outcome of a dispute or disagreement—a source that seeks the truth, not personal glory or benefit.

Check for bias (a source that gains something by taking certain positions). Research shows that ideologically leaning Internet news sources (e.g., Daily Kos; Drudge Report) have a strong biasing effect that produces "a distorted understanding of evidence, potentially promoting inaccurate beliefs" (Garrett et al., 2016). A Stanford University study showed that more than half of the college students participating thought the American College of Pediatricians (APC) was a reliable source after accessing the group's website and given the opportunity to do a wider search online to check on this group. The Southern Poverty Law Center identifies the APC as a hate group because of its "history of propagating damaging falsehoods about LGBT people, including linking homosexuality to pedophilia, and claiming that LGBT people are more promiscuous than heterosexuals, and . . . a danger to children" ("Meet the Anti-LGBT Hate Group," 2015). A quick Google search easily reveals these details. Also, almost two-thirds of the same college student participants failed to recognize the political bias of a tweet about the National Rifle Association by the liberal group MoveOn.org (Wineburg et al., 2016). Clearly, we are not doing a sufficient job of teaching students to recognize source bias.

One media bias chart provides a quick indicator of political leanings.

Websites are often biased. For example, any website providing nutritional information while pushing vitamins, minerals, and other "health" products (e.g., GNC, Vitacost, or Vitamin World) is biased. In contrast, WebMD and MayoClinic.com are more neutral sites that do not push products, and they provide useful medical and health-related information.

Incomplete Source Citation: Something to Hide? A complete citation of the source of

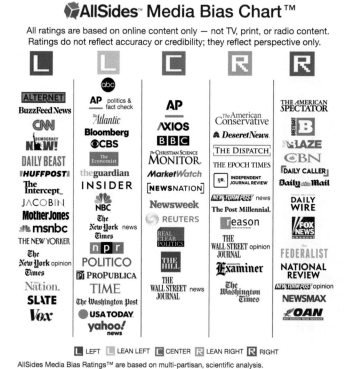

FIGURE 15.1 This is a helpful chart that identifies the media bias for a multitude of sources.

your information adds credibility to your claim, if your source is qualified. *A complete citation includes, as a minimum,* (a) the name of the source, (b) the specific title or expertise of the source (if not obvious) to build credibility, and (c) the specific publication in which the evidence can be found with the relevant date of the publication.

It is easy and common to cite sources incompletely. Citations with references only to a vague title, such as "Dr. Smith" or "Professor Jones," or worse yet "some people" are incomplete. What type of doctor or professor or person is being cited? What are his or her specific credentials to speak as an expert on a particular topic? Even references to qualified experts leave us wondering how current they are if the publication source and date are missing. *When you cite your sources completely, you signal to your audience that you have nothing to hide,*

and your transparency likely increases your credibility, assuming that your source is of high quality and the citation is recent and not out of date.

Relevance: Does It Follow?

Supporting materials must have relevance; they must relate directly to claims made. Consider two fallacies that fail the relevance test: ad hominem and ad populum.

Ad Hominem Fallacy: Diversionary Tactic The **ad hominem fallacy** is a personal attack on the messenger to avoid the message. It is a diversionary tactic. Ken Gosnell (2018), CEO and servant leader of CXP and leadership consultant, explains, "Often a leadership attack can cause the organization to lose focus or cause the leader to question their own ability to lead. Leaders should pursue truth without being distracted." As Dr. Nir Kossovsky (2017), CEO of Steel City Re, which analyzes the reputational strength and resilience of companies, notes, "Reputational threats are inevitable, which every company acknowledges, but social media and online 'news' sources make discerning the truth difficult. . . . Regardless of their validity, battles waged in the volatile court of public opinion measurably impact a company's brand, market cap, margins and income."

Note, however, that if a well-supported claim raises the issue of a person's credibility, character, or trustworthiness, the attack is not irrelevant to the claim made. Personal attacks, however, that are intended merely to inaccurately slander a person as a distraction from important facts, issues, and policies are fallacious and unethical.

Not all personal attacks are ad hominem fallacies. Bernie Maddoff, who died in prison in 2021 while serving a 150-year sentence for epic securities fraud, was justifiably reviled. As one investor and Madoff victim testified at court sentencing, "He stole from the rich. He stole from the poor. He stole from the in between. He had no values" (quoted by Balsamo & Hays, 2021).

Ad Populum Fallacy: Arguing from Popular Opinion

Claims should be weighed on the basis of valid reasoning and high-quality supporting materials that bolster that reasoning, not on the whim of the majority, which could change in a flash. The **ad populum fallacy**—basing a claim on popular opinion alone—lacks logical relevance. For example, a 2016 Chapman University survey found that almost a quarter of respondents do not believe astronauts landed on the moon, almost half believe in haunted houses, and more than half believe the U.S. government isn't telling the truth about the 9/11 terrorist attack (Poppy, 2017). More than 40% of Americans do not know that Earth orbits the Sun in a year-long cycle. A startling 52% of Americans do not know that dinosaurs and humans did not roam Earth at the same time—they were 65 million years apart (Sidky, 2018). Considering these results, basing a claim on mass opinion is logically irrelevant. It doesn't matter if, hypothetically, even 100% of the American people believe charisma is a necessary quality for effective leadership in business. What do the data show? (See Chapter 10 discussion.)

Sufficiency: Got Enough?

The person who makes a claim has the burden to prove that claim. This means that sufficient supporting materials must be used to support a claim you make. Sufficiency is a judgment. There is no precise formula for determining it. Generally, high-quality supporting materials and solid reasoning meet the sufficiency criterion. Several fallacies, however, clearly exhibit insufficiency.

Self-Selected Sample: Partisan Power   A **random sample** is a portion of the population chosen in such a manner that every member of the entire population has an equal chance of being selected. A **self-selected sample** attracts the most committed, aroused, or motivated individuals to fill out surveys on their own and answer polling questions. Printing a survey in a business magazine or blogging site and collecting those that have been returned is an example of a self-selected sample. Calling an 800-number to answer questions about the state of the economy or whether respondents lost their jobs during COVID-19 are additional examples. *Any statistics from a poll or survey that depend on respondents selecting themselves to participate provides results that are insufficient to generalize beyond the sample.* The common practice of soliciting internal organizational polls of employees to measure worker engagement and sentiment are criticized by Rajeev Peshawaria, author of the book *Open Source Leadership* (2017). He notes that some employees are too busy to fill out such surveys, some employees don't trust that their criticisms will be kept anonymous, and the samples are self-selected and therefore unrepresentative (see Korman, 2020).

Note that the problem is not an insufficient sample. Self-selected samples often involve huge numbers of respondents. Increasing the number of respondents does not improve the results (unless you survey everyone in the population) because the sample is unrepresentative.

Inadequate Sample: Large Margin of Error

So what is an adequate sample size? In general, the margin of error—a measure of the degree of sampling error accounted for by imperfections in sample selection—goes up as the number of people surveyed goes down. Margin of error applies only to random samples, not self-selected samples. An adequate sample size will have a margin of error no greater than *plus or minus 3%–4%*. A poll of 1,000 people randomly selected typically has a margin of error of about plus or minus 3%. This means that if the poll reports 51% of respondents believe that Amazon founder Jeff Bezos deserves to be worth almost $200 billion, then the actual result, if every adult American were surveyed, could be between 48% and 54%.

Years ago, a study conducted at 103 California companies created major news. Results showed that 17.8% of job applicants tested positive for drug use. The margin of error for the study, however, was a bloated 7.8%. Thus, the true results if every applicant had been tested instead of only a small sample actually could have been 25.6% (17.8% *plus* 7.8% margin of error) or a far less concerning 10% (17.8% *minus* 7.8% margin of error; "Pre-employment," 1990). No poll is without some margin of error because it is usually impractically expensive and time consuming to survey every person in a population; but increasing the sample size improves the chances that the poll is accurate if the sample is random, not self-selected.

Hasty Generalization: Arguing from Example

When individuals jump to a conclusion based on one or only a handful of examples, especially vivid ones, they have made a **hasty generalization** (Govier, 2010). The mass media tend to sensationalize each new scientific study that gets published, for example. This is especially true when pharmaceutical companies tout their latest and greatest drug (with corresponding lists of sometimes startling side effects, including potential death). A single study, however, is insufficient to draw any general conclusion. In science, studies are replicated before results are given credence because mistakes can be made.

Correlation as Causation: How Related?

We all are prone to draw causation (x causes y) from mere correlation. A **correlation** is a consistent relationship between two variables. A variable is anything that can change. Finding a strong correlation between two variables doesn't necessarily have significance.

Correlations suggest possible causation, but correlations alone are an insufficient reason to claim probable causation. Kids with big feet are better readers than those with small feet. Why? Do big feet cause reading proficiency? No! Children with big feet are usually older, and older children have had more experience reading. Increases in U.S. spending on science, space, and technology correlate almost perfectly with increases in the number of suicides by hanging, strangulation, and suffocation. Likewise, the divorce rate in Maine correlates with the per capita consumption of margarine in the United States (Vigen, 2015). Do these correlations prove causation? Hardly! The statistics or examples don't necessarily connect logically as a cause–effect relationship. Thus, arguing, for instance, that working virtually is responsible for a drop in a company's productivity and profit merely because the two things occurred together does not prove causation, merely correlation. Other facts such as inept leadership, economic forces beyond the control of an organization (e.g., a major recession or pandemic), or poor decisions made by boards of directors could be the real causes.

SUMMARY

The dangers posed by "truth decay" to businesses is real and significant. There are three types of supporting materials that are used to provide evidence bolstering claims made by a wide variety of individuals and groups: examples, statistics, and testimony from experts and nonexperts. Each has its strengths and weaknesses. In general, you evaluate the value of each supporting material based on three criteria: credibility, relevance, and sufficiency. Learning and applying these criteria competently makes you a critical thinker and can improve both decision making and problem solving in business.

Film School Case Studies

What Women Want (2000); Rom/Com; PG-13

A full-of-himself, chauvinistic advertising executive magically acquires the ability to hear what women are really thinking. Analyze the use of supporting materials. Are business decisions based on credible evidence? The Nike commercial, presented to actual Nike ad representatives by the Mel Gibson character late in the film, is exceptional, but is it based on any evidence?

TED Talks and YouTube Videos

These TED Talks and YouTube videos can be accessed by going to the Oxford Learning Link for It's All of Our Business or by typing the title of the video into a Google search window.

"Chimamanda Ngozi Adichie: The Danger of a Single Story"

"Emily Dressler: Don't Be Fooled by Bad Statistics"

"Fighting Truth Decay to Preserve the Value of Facts."

"Scientific Studies" John Oliver (Warning: Raw Language)

"The Four Most Dangerous Words? A New Study Shows" Laura Arnold

"Truth Decay and the Technology Threat" (Harris, Foroohar)/DLD Munich 20

After successful completion of this chapter,
you should be able to

1. Select the type of visual aid most appropriate for any given business presentation

2. Improve your use of PowerPoint and other slide software

3. Determine which of four types of delivery is most suitable for your presentation

CHAPTER 16

Visual Aids and Delivery

Think of a bear. How would you describe what you just thought of? You may have thought of a brown bear, or a polar bear, or a teddy bear. Maybe it was a big bear, a baby bear, a Chicago Bear, or Yogi Bear. What we can almost guarantee is that you didn't think about the letters B E A R. Why? Harvard researcher Elinor Amit explains: "This is the way our brains are wired, and there may be an evolutionary reason for this (because) we haven't always been verbalizers. For a long time, we understood our world visually, so maybe language is an add-on" (Reuell, 2017). MIT neuroscientists concluded that our brains identify images seen for as little as 13 milliseconds (Trafton, 2014). Clearly, *we cannot rely solely on text to drive communication*.

Steve Jobs knew this when he introduced the iPhone in 2007 and with it offered a brand new way to view content. He prioritized the presence of visual media and put it right in our pockets. Instagram further propelled the visual revolution in 2010, giving everyone the ability to add "amateur photographer" to their list of talents. Pinterest, TikTok, and

CHAPTER OUTLINE
- Becoming Visual
- Delivering the Goods

4. Increase the impact of your business presentation by employing effective vocal and physical delivery tips

similar companies gave us easy visual ways to communicate to broad audiences. Cisco projected in 2020 that by 2022, online videos would make up 82% of all consumer Internet traffic (McCue, 2020). This estimate is 15 times higher than it was in 2012. Visual communication has permeated all facets of life, including our business presentations.

The visual aids a presenter selects to reinforce their ideas, and the way they use their voice, facial expressions, and body movement to deliver that message, are essential additives to stellar business presentations.

The purpose of this chapter is to focus on visual aids and presentation delivery. We have two main objectives: (1) to examine the benefits and variety of visual aids available, and (2) to explore effective delivery of business presentations.

Becoming Visual

Harnessing the power of visuals aids in presentations has several benefits. First, effectively chosen visual aids *clarify intricate points and processes*. A complex sales cycle will be easier for an audience to comprehend if a clean, clear, process map accompanies the presenter's narration. Second, effective visual aids *gain and maintain audience attention*. Because of our hardwired attachment to visuals, a carefully curated image that reinforces the theme of our presentation is a strong way to begin. Third, visual aids *enhance speaker credibility*. Presenting accurate, well organized, information visually makes it appear knowledgeable. Fourth, using visual aids can *improve your delivery*. Referencing a visual aid allows a more natural, conversational delivery. It can ease speaker apprehension because it shifts the focus from you to your visual aid. Effective visual aids can also *make your presentation more memorable*

(Alexander, 2018). With all of these benefits, visual aids merit a closer look.

Types of Visual Aids: Making Appropriate Choices

Too often in the workplace presentation slides such as PowerPoint or Google Slides are the only visual aids considered. Depending on the presentation purpose, there are many other powerful aids to choose from. Whichever you choose, carefully consider how it contributes to or detracts from the purpose of your speech. This section discusses making appropriate visual aids choices and identifies both strengths and limitations of each type.

Objects and Models: Keeping It Real Although Elon Musk had no trouble bringing a Tesla truck onto the stage of his presentation in order to demonstrate his unbreakable glass (which broke), often the objects we seek as our visual aids are too large, too small, expensive, fragile, rare, or unavailable. ***Models can often act as effective substitutes***. If Emergency Medical Technician instructors need to train new hires how to give COVID-safe CPR, for example, a model is the perfect visual aid to accompany the demonstration. Few would volunteer to have their chests pounded. When possible, use objects and models to offer 3-D comprehension of your topic.

Charts, Graphs, and Diagrams: Delivering Data Visually Statistical bombardment causes numeric mind meltdowns. As already noted in Chapter 15, this happens when a presenter throws number after number after number at the audience, hoping to make a point that is only obvious to themselves. Instead, the audience is left frustrated and confused. Numbers are important, however. Data journalist, Alexandra Samuel said, "Knowing how to develop and deliver data-driven presentations is now a crucial skill for many professionals, since we often have to tell our colleagues stories that are much more compelling when they are backed by numbers" (Shwarztberg, 2020). A chart is a graph, table, picture, or diagram used to make information simple to understand. Graphs are the most used visual representation of information in business presentations. A **graph** is a diagram that plots the variance between variables. A **line graph** is useful for showing a trend or change over a period of time. A **pie graph** depicts a proportion or percentage for each part of a whole. A pie graph should depict from two to six "pie pieces." Much more than this will make the pie graph difficult for your audience to see, let alone decipher (see Figure 16.1). **Bar graphs** compare and contrast two or more items or show variation over a period of time. Used properly, they can make a dramatic visual statement (see Figures 16.2 and 16.3). By default, you might make charts and graphs in Excel; but many sites such as Tableau, Infogram, and Creately are simple to use and offer creative ways to organize presentation data.

Maps: Places and Processes When geography is central to your speech or a key point, there is no good substitute for a map. Imagine teaching a geography class without showing maps. "Picture the Arabian Peninsula" does not work for a geography-challenged audience. If you are giving a new-hire orientation, displaying a map of the building or corporate campus is helpful for audience comprehension. Process maps, on the other hand, map out the steps of a business operation. Arrows show the order of the steps and ovals show the beginning and end of the process. They are helpful as visual aids because they can be used to illuminate processes, identify roles, and spot inefficiencies.

Google the "world's worst PowerPoint slide ever" and sure to pop up is the slide depicting the U.S. military strategy in Afghanistan to Commander of U.S. and NATO forces at the time, General McChrystal in 2010 (see p. 277 Figure 16.4). At first glance we might all agree that it is the spaghetti soup of visual aids, and while most are quick to condemn it for its apparent information overload, it might not have been so awful if we knew the purpose it was meant to convey and how it was referenced. If the purpose was to visually communicate the complexity of the strategy in just a glance, then the goal was achieved. If the presenter made use of zoom-in features to highlight specific parts of the process as they spoke, then it might have been effective. Seldom can visual aids be judged without knowing the context for which they were used.

Tables: Factual and Statistical Comparisons Tables are effective for depicting blocks of information. A **table** is an orderly depiction of statistics, words, or symbols in columns or rows. A table can provide easy-to-understand comparisons of facts and statistics. *Tables, however, are not as visually interesting as graphics, and they can become easily cluttered with too much information.*

Tables will be a visual distraction if the headings are too small to read, the columns or rows are crooked, and the overall impression is that the table was hastily drawn. With readily available computer technology, there is little excuse for amateurish-looking tables. Tables have been used repeatedly throughout this text.

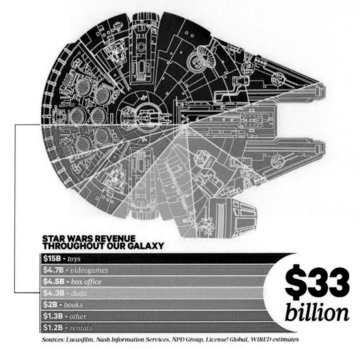

STAR WARS REVENUE THROUGHOUT OUR GALAXY

$15B - *toys*
$4.7B - *videogames*
$4.5B - *box office*
$4.3B - *dvds*
$2B - *books*
$1.3B - *other*
$1.2B - *rentals*

$33 *billion*

Sources: Lucasfilm, Nash Information Services, NPD Group, License! Global, WIRED estimates

FIGURE 16.1 This pie and bar graph combination is aesthetically appealing, but is it effective? What would make it better? What adaptations might you make?

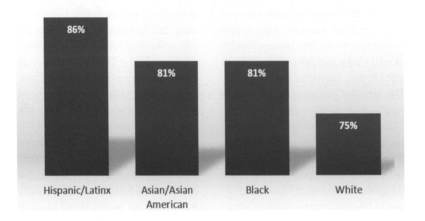

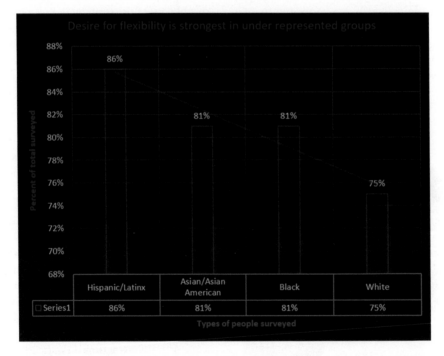

FIGURES 16.2 AND 16.3   These two graphs show the same information, yet the top graph is far more effective than the bottom one. Note the difference color, layout, labeling, and spelling make when presenting visual information.

No matter which option you choose to visually present data, follow these guidelines for success:

1. *Check visibility.* You might be next to the data, but your audience is further away. When practicing, stand as far away from the screen as your furthest audience member will be and check visibility. Too small? Enlarge and enhance.

2. *Talk through it, but not to it.* Highlight one conclusion from each slide. Announce it by

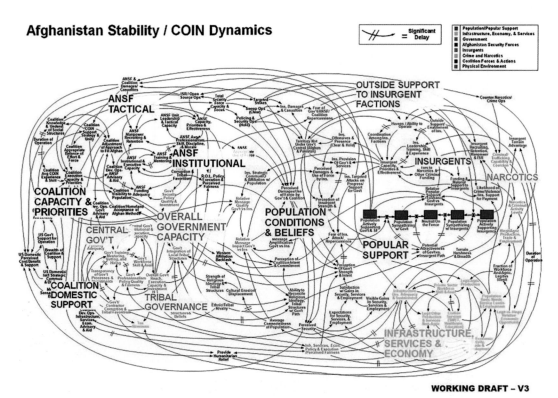

FIGURE 16.4   Often referenced as the world's worst PowerPoint slide, this may have been effective depending on how the presenter used it. What would you have done differently?

using phrases, such as "The data illustrates . . ." "These numbers prove . . ." While talking about the data, be sure to keep your focus on the audience, not the graph.

3. *Clearly label all parts of the chart.* Axes and pie pieces, for example, should be labeled with clear, easy-to-read, easy-to-comprehend words. Steer clear of abbreviations and acronyms that are not known by your audience.

4. *Practice crowd control.* For example, if you have 10 points of data on a bar graph but only two are critical to your discussion, enlarge those and eliminate the others instead of fitting everything on one slide. You can still speak to the other data if needed, but it doesn't necessarily require visual representation.

5. *Reinforce the message.* Consider placing a slide with one important word or one

critical number after data-heavy slides to visually reinforce the takeaway.

Photographs and Images: Very Visual Aids
The many photographs included in this text-book underline the effectiveness of this visual aid to make a point, clarify a concept, and draw attention. To be most effective, photos should be large enough for all to see (without distortion or pixilation). Ownership matters, too. Outside of photos you may have taken yourself, you can purchase quality images on sites such as Getty Images and iStock Photos. Free quality photos are available at sites such as Pixabay, Pexels, and Unsplash. *It is imperative that you never use an image that is watermarked.* Used to discourage copyright infringement, a watermark is a semitransparent logo or stamp that is superimposed onto images. It is a visual distraction and detracts from the purpose of the image.

The real failure in this image is the Shutterstock watermark that demonstrates it isn't available for free distribution. When you project an image that is watermarked, you tell your audience that you don't care about copyright laws, you don't care about the effectiveness of your visuals, and you don't really care about them enough to find a more appropriate image to share.

Choosing Media: Showcasing Your Visual Aids

There are many ways to showcase visual aids. A multimedia presentation may be too complicated to master in time for a recently assigned presentation, or the proper equipment may not be available to execute it effectively. On the other hand, showing very simple visual aids to an audience of experts may be viewed as condescending. *Ask yourself,* "*Do I need a visual aid and, if so, which medium works best to accomplish my purpose?*"

Whiteboards and Flip Charts: Visual Aids On the Go   Most meeting rooms come equipped with either a permanent or portable whiteboard. Many also have flip charts—the large pads of paper that rest on an easel. Both are great for capturing the audience's ideas (e.g., *brainstorming) or creating diagrams and processes in real time.* Tables, drawings, and graphs all can be drawn on them in advance,

accurately and neatly. Presentation material can be outlined before the meeting begins or as you proceed. With whiteboards, mistakes can be immediately, and easily, corrected or erased. With flip charts, the page can be turned, and you can start over or switch to a new topic. Flip charts have the added advantage of tearing off pages and posting them in other parts of the room, particularly easy to do if they have self-adhesive on the back. Whiteboards and flip charts offer the benefit of evolving an idea or process with a draw-as-you-go technique. This allows for interacting with your audience. If you have real artistic ability, this art-in-progress can be quite impressive.

Guidelines for either whiteboards or flip charts include

1. *Can my audience see it?* For best visibility, both mediums are suitable for audiences of 30 or fewer. Whiteboards and flip charts are best suited to smaller audiences.

2. ***Can my audience read it?*** If you are sure they can *see* the whiteboard or flip chart, ensure they can *read* it. Use the appropriate type of markers for each (we prefer low-odor, dry-erase markers for whiteboards and Mr. Sketch scented markers for flip charts), and make sure that your markers are not dried out. Also, use up to three dark colors: one as the base and others for subpoints or emphasis. Print don't write; and print clearly enough and large enough for the person in the very back of the room to read with ease. Before your presentation walk to the back of the room and test this out.

3. ***Can I use it effectively?*** Creating your visual aids as you go, as with whiteboards and flip charts, requires you to possess the content knowledge and confidence to convey messages credibly. You wouldn't want to run back and forth between your notes and the board or chart, scrambling for the next bullet point or step in a process.

The bigger, better relative of whiteboards and flip charts is the SMART Board. They are not always available due to their expensive nature, but they offer the ability to write, draw, add virtual pages, link to your computer desktop and access programs, take screenshots, and record your visual presentation. They are a fantastic tool for collaboration, too. A number of tutorials online can help you learn to use this option (*see link at end of chapter*).

Handouts: *Information To Go*   Tables, maps, drawings, PowerPoint slides, or even photographs can be made into a handout, that is, a visual aid that is given to the audience members before, during, or after a presentation. One significant advantage of a handout is that the listeners can keep it long after the speech has been presented; it can serve as a useful reminder of the spoken material. A handout can also include a great quantity of information to be studied carefully as a presentation unfolds (e.g., budget details). Giving audience members access to your handout prior to your presentation helps if the material on it will be an integral part of your presentation. In this case, the handout will not distract, but rather will assist audience members' message comprehension. Distributing a handout before your presentation and assigning it as a pre-read can save you a great amount of time. Audience members will come to the meeting prepared with any background information required (assuming they actually read the pre-read, which, in our experience, is not always the case) and they will be able to have questions at the ready. If possible, we discourage passing out information during your presentation. It can easily disrupt the flow of the presentation, waste valuable time, and distract the audience. Most audiences expect a copy of any slides used in a presentation to be emailed to them at the end of the discussion. If you intend to do this, save your slides as a PDF so recipients can neither see any notes that you put in the notes section, nor can they modify the slides. Also, be sure to have your contact information in the footer of the deck. For virtual presentations, you can add a PDF version of your presentation to the chat window, and participants can download it from there.

Video Excerpts: *Visual Power*   If a picture is worth a thousand words, a well-chosen video clip might be worth twice as much. Movie excerpts, YouTube clips, TED Talk highlights, and videos you have recorded yourself can powerfully tell stories that words alone cannot. Videos can be dramatic, informative, and emotionally charged. Not only are they great attention grabbers, but they are increasingly what people are used to experiencing.

It can be tricky, however, to incorporate video excerpts smoothly into your presentations. First, the sound on a video will compete with the speaker for attention. If you are playing it in a video meeting, it might be distorted. Too many Zoom presenters are well versed at saying, "Can you hear that? Is it loud enough? No? Let me check. Hold on." If you are using a video, mute and or pause it when you are trying to explain a point, unless the video excerpt is very short, such as 30 seconds or less, and sound is essential. Longer video excerpts with sound may be effective in lengthy presentations. Second, a video can easily upstage you, the presenter. We don't come with the lights, action, and special effects that many clips do. Video, with its dramatic action, can make your speech seem tame, even dull, by comparison. Also, be careful that any dramatic action depicted in a video excerpt is not overly graphic and offensive. For example, a video clip of on-the-job heavy equipment injuries should come with a warning before showing the scene, if the scene is deemed absolutely necessary to make the point. The warning allows audience members to choose whether to view the scene. Short video clips should support, not be, the main message. *This is a presentation not a movie.* Typically, use only a few brief video excerpts (30 seconds) when your presentation is short. Whenever possible, add subtitles.

If you use a video excerpt during your talk, cue it properly so you will not have to interrupt the flow of your presentation by looking for the right place to start the excerpt. Whenever possible, embed video directly into a slide presentation to avoid interrupting the flow of your presentation. Test, test, test your links again when you get to your meeting room, whether it be a physical space or virtual one.

Projection Options: Blowing It Up   There are several choices for projecting images onto a large screen. Document cameras, such as the ELMO series, offer similar advantages of the aged-out overhead projectors. Almost any image from a magazine, book, or pamphlet or a simple object can be projected onto a large screen. They also can magnify very small images a hundredfold, and they allow you to zoom in and out on images. Some versions of this technology have wireless remote control, split-screen, masking, and highlighting capabilities. Becoming familiar with this equipment is essential to using it effectively.

Light-emitting diode, or LED, projectors and laser projectors connect with computers and can display video, slide shows, and other content on a large screen. Through experience, the biggest challenge regarding this equipment is having the right AV cable to connect your computer with the projector. For example, if you are using a Mac, but the connections available are only for PCs, you will not be able to project your presentation. If presenting in an unfamiliar venue, check with your contact person to ensure seamless projection. Bring your own connector, or, better yet, bring your presentation on a USB drive to avoid any issues.

Computer-Assisted Presentations   PowerPoint is probably the most widely available and utilized example of a computer-assisted presentation, although other computer-assisted presentational software options such as Prezi, Keynote, and Google Slides are worthy competitors (Abbamonte, 2021). PowerPoint continues to dominate as a computer-assisted, visual aid tool. Space does not allow a comprehensive "how-to" explanation for preparing PowerPoint slides. There are several excellent sites on the Internet that provide step-by-step instructions (*see access to link at end of chapter*). We do have several suggestions for making slides magnificent.

Let's distinguish what presentation programs such as PowerPoint and Keynote are and what they are not. Slides are meant to complement your oral presentation, not replace it. If an audience can gather all they need to know by reading your slides independently of you, save them the time and simply send them your slide deck in an email. *Slides are not giant note cards for you to read from, either.* They augment, enhance, illustrate and/or explain your message. They don't stand in for you, the presenter.

A carefully created slide can enhance credibility, evoke emotion from your audience, and illuminate important information. The slide (on p. 281) does all three. The statistic (logos), $26.1 billion, is set apart from the other text. It is larger and bold. The congratulatory high-five evokes happiness (pathos). Finally, credibility of the statistic is enhanced by citing a prominent executive in the company. The speaker's credibility (ethos) is subtly enhanced by citing the source of the image, thus giving credit where credit is due (logos).

Slides do have many limitations. *The biggest drawbacks of PowerPoint presentations are the time it takes to prepare the slides, the potential for glitches to occur during the actual speech, and the tendency to become so enamored with the software capability that it detracts from the actual speech.* "PowerPoint presentations are often so poorly executed that they actually obstruct the brain's cognition of the material being presented" (Hoffeld, 2015). You might check out award-winning comedian Don McMillan's amusing YouTube presentation "Life After Death by PowerPoint" to see what not to do in this regard (*see access to link at end of chapter*). It

Simple PowerPoint slide that conveys credibility, emotional appeal, and evidence.

never gets old. To avoid getting swept up in all the bells and whistles that presentation software has to offer, visual aid expert Dave Paradi recommends doing these three things: determine, analyze, prepare or DAP. First, *determine* if the information you are covering needs a slide. Not everything you say needs an accompanying visual. Next *analyze your audience*. What types of visuals would best suit them? Might they resonate with a short YouTube clip, or would a short bullet-point list of information be better? Finally, *plan* your visual aid before you create your visual. If you already have an idea of what your slide will look like (colors, images, layout, and graphics), you won't be as tempted by the fun features that, as Don McMillan said, can "suck the life out of you" (McMillan, 2009).

Slide Design: The Basics   Human eyes can register and form meaning from 36,000 visual messages per hour. In contrast, adults can read 15,000 words per hour (Balliett, 2020). For the biggest bang *use fewer words and more images*. Remember that this is a *visual* aid not a mere text reproduction. Visual presentation expert Nancy Duarte says, "Each slide should pass the glance test: People should be able to comprehend your slide in three seconds. Think of your slides as billboards. When people drive, they

only briefly take their eyes off their main focus, which is the road, to process billboard information" (Duarte, 2012).

Slides should be prepared with highly contrasted colors. David Paradi of *Think Outside the Slide* advises avoiding the following color combinations because they clash, are hard to read, or will be difficult to decipher for people with a color deficiency: red/green, orange/blue, red/blue. Instead, he advocates for the high contrast pairings of a dark background with light text and images or a light background with dark text and images (Paradi, 2022a) Note that your company may already have a prescribed template or palette to work from.

Text needs to be readable. In 2002, Microsoft issued six new fonts to its Vista system, which would be known as part of the ClearType font collection. These six fonts translate flawlessly to any version of PowerPoint. They are Calibri, Cambria, Consolas, Candara, Corbel, and Constantia. This is helpful if you will be giving a PowerPoint presentation from someone else's computer. Today many other fonts are heralded for their viewing ease such as Verdana, Tahoma, Helvetica, and Gil Sans. Whichever you choose, select it for its primary purpose: readability. *The font chosen will determine which size to use, since font types vary in appearance*. Aim for titles from

36- to 44-point size, and text between 28- and 32-point size. Labels and source citations can be between 18- and 24-point size (Paradi, 2022b).

The presentation community is divided on how many words are allowed on each slide. For years, Seth Godin swears by limiting it to six (Godin, 2007). In order to keep the focus on what is important, others take a page from Twitter's original guideline of adhering to no more than 140 characters (not words) per slide. Our recommendation is to stop counting words and characters, and instead look at the slide objectively to see if it has *short phrases instead of sentences, plenty of white space, photos, images and graphs in place of words whenever possible, and is easy to quickly comprehend*.

Pairing Visual Aids: The Power of Partnership

In the summer of 2021, a senior executive greeted over 100 employees at the quarterly all-hands meeting. He used a photograph of the China's Zhangjiajie Grand Canyon Glass Bridge as his only visual aid. After giving his team some background information about the bridge (e.g., it's the longest glass bridge in the world and was designed to sway when walked upon), he asked for a show of hands as to who would welcome a walk across the bridge, and then who would prefer to pass on that opportunity. The room filled with smiles and chuckles. Next, he invited his audience to call out the one word that best described the bridge. Scary, exhilarating, challenging, innovative, daring, beautiful, and amazing were some of the descriptors he heard. He scrawled each word on the whiteboard. He then told the audience that the bridge was a metaphor for their company, and like it or not, they all walked across it together during the pandemic—and they survived. He said that the words they used to describe the bridge could also be applied to the company's recent challenges and successes. He continued by giving detailed examples of each.

Would you cross this bridge? Have you? Often there is no good substitute for a powerful photo.

TABLE 16.1 USING POWERPOINT AND OTHER SLIDE SOFTWARE EFFECTIVELY

Topic	Tips
What it is	A complement to your oral presentation More visual than verbal
What it isn't	*Not* a giant note card *Doesn't* take the place of you
Your job as a presenter	Get your message to your audience as clearly and effectively as possible. If slides help with that, use them.
Your goal	Make one point with each slide
Before you open any slide software	**Determine** your speaking purpose, **Analyze** your audience, **Plan** your content When possible, create a draft of your ideal slide on paper. This separates thinking about making a slide from the mechanics of making a slide
Fonts and Text	Use the 6 C fonts: Calibri, Cambria, Candara, Consolas, Constantia, Corbel. They transfer between PCs and Macs. Titles: 36- to 44-point text Body: minimum 18 point; max 32 point Don't over animate Check spelling and grammar
Images	Avoid Clip Art or overly used images Check usage rights: Google>Images>Tools>Usage rights>labeled for noncommercial reuse Don't use images with watermarks Don't stretch your images to fit the screen Free usable images: Creativecommons.com, Wikipedia, pixabay.com, pexels.com, powtoon.com, unsplash.com, etc.
Color	Use high contrast colors for impact and for those who have color deficiencies Consider the emotion or mood the color sends; align with the tenor of the message
Add video	Test the video/Check the volume
Graphs and charts	Less is more Remove excessive background clutter Reduce number of colors Be able to explain your information simply
Delivery	Practice with your slides Don't turn your back to the audience Gesture to the screen, not the computer Speak a transition when advancing slides (Next we will see . . .) Stay audience-centered Be prepared to speak even if your visual aids fail In PowerPoint, use the B key to turn your screen black and the W key to turn your screen white. This is useful when you don't want an image projecting on the screen.

In contrast, the leader could have bombarded his employees with overcrowded slides filled with messy graphs and meaningless statistics. He didn't. He did, however, verbally announce some of most important facts and numbers he wanted the team to know, and he sent them a follow-up fact sheet at the meeting's end.

Several attendees said it was the best all-hands meeting they had ever attended.

This example illustrates visual aid excellence. The executive paired a stunning photo with a tactile flip chart to drive home the message he intended to deliver. Similarly, you might choose to combine PowerPoint and video clips and whiteboards. Or you could start your virtual presentation with slides but stop sharing your screen to hold up an object that is pertinent to your talk or conduct a visual poll that all participants can see. Whichever combination you choose, be sure to practice with it ahead of time so that it doesn't detract from your content, nor diminish your confidence and credibility.

Anticipate Problems   The more complicated your technology, the greater the likelihood that problems will occur before or during your presentation. Projection bulbs burn out unexpectedly, computers crash, programs will not load. Have a backup plan. If the audience is small (30 or fewer), a hard copy of PowerPoint slides, for example, can be prepared just in case your computer fails. Show up early and do a quick test to verify that all systems are GO! Think about what might go wrong and anticipate ways to respond.

Delivering the Goods

Effectively presenting your message, research, and visual aids is the final key to giving an empowered presentation. Delivery that is unpolished, over the top, or insincere undermines your credibility and overall effectiveness. Appropriate delivery, on the other hand, reflects confidence, content knowledge, and concern for your audience's experience. In this portion of the chapter we review the four delivery methods, and then discuss the dos and don'ts for delivery. *Virtual presentations can benefit from reviewing especially technical advice offered in* Chapter 12 *for virtual meetings*.

Delivery Method: One Type Doesn't Fit All Occasions

When you approach speaking situations, you choose, consciously or not, one of four delivery methods. Each of these—manuscript, memorized, impromptu, and extemporaneous—is discussed in this section.

Manuscript Speaking: Prepared Text   A **manuscript speech** is one that is read from prepared text. Use it when exact wording

is necessary. Legal presentations, political speeches, and press releases most often default to the manuscript method of speech delivery. After creating the script, the presenter typically reads it from a teleprompter that scrolls the manuscript line by line. Teleprompters are easily purchased online, or there are many teleprompter apps that run on smart phones and computers.

A few basic guidelines should be uppermost in your mind when faced with delivering a manuscript speech. First, *do not use a manuscript as a crutch* because you experience speech anxiety. Use a manuscript because message precision is critical in a specific context. Match your tone to the occasion, and *speak conversationally*. You are presenting important information to your audience, not reading out loud from Tolstoy's War and Peace. *Practice repeatedly* so you can frequently look at your audience for longer than occasional glimpses. Reading becomes especially apparent and detracting when giving a presentation virtually. *Use vocal variety and some body movement* (see later discussion) so your presentation doesn't sound dull and appear stilted. Body movement, of course, is not an option in virtual presentations unless you are standing while delivering, as would be the case if your speech is given to a large, in-person audience but offered virtually as well. Finally, if possible, *be flexible*. When appropriate, break from your manuscript.

Memorized Speaking: When a Manuscript Won't Do   There are times when holding a script would be out of place, and teleprompters or cue cards are not options. Still, exact wording might be necessary. In these situations, memorizing shorter presentations is a good option. A brief acceptance speech at an awards ceremony, or a few key lines or quote in a lengthy speech, may benefit from memorization, especially if what you memorize is emotionally touching or humorous (no one wants the punch line of a joke to be read).

Global CEO Coach Sabina Nawaz says that if you must rely on exact wording, memorize your speech "cold."

> Knowing a script or presentation cold means taking the time to craft the words and sequence of what you plan to say, and

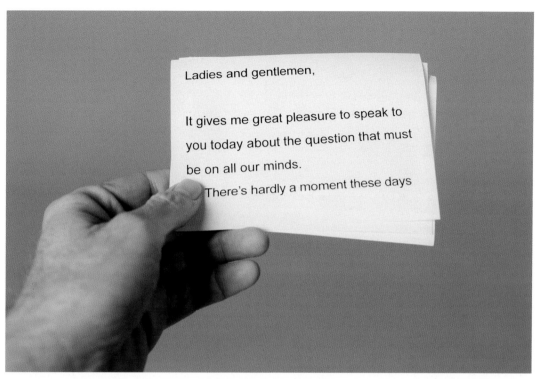

If a teleprompter isn't available, you might be tempted to write your presentation out word-for-word on note cards. We discourage this. The writing will be too small to read comfortably from a distance. Writing much on a small surface naturally leads to having a large stack of note cards. From experience, we have seen speakers crumble when those cards get out of order, are inadvertently turned upside down, or fall from their nervous hands.

then rehearsing them over and over until you could recite them backwards if asked. It's memorization on steroids, but modified according to your needs and speaking venue—whether you require mastery of key bullet points to land with your audience or need to learn a speech word for word until it's as familiar as your own name. (Nawaz, 2020)

Famed presenter and Apple founder, Steve Jobs, reportedly walked around the house for days reciting his 2005 Stanford Commencement address, which is still one of the most quoted commencement speeches in modern history (Schlender, et al, 2015). By the time he delivered it, he had strategically imprinted the speech's content, organization, and delivery in his mind.

To deliver a speech cold, Nawaz recommends doing three things. First, *batch your presentation into natural sections.* Aim to memorize small chunks in order, then add the transitions (which can often be less structured) into the memorization process. Next, *practice your presentation repeatedly*. Finally, *have a back-up plan,* should your memory fail you. Decrease your anxiety by pausing, taking a breath, and saying something like, "I seem to have lost my place." There is no need to apologize. Audiences typically connect with this display of humanness. Keep notes handy if you are having a difficult time remembering what comes next.

Impromptu Speaking: Off-the-Cuff Presentations

An **impromptu speech** is an address delivered without preparation, or so it seems. Without warning you are asked to speak in a public forum. This happens most often in meetings where you are not the main speaker but are suddenly called upon to give an update on a project that wasn't on the agenda. It can also happen when another presenter fails to show up, and you share the same knowledge base. One advantage of impromptu speeches is that audience expectations

Forget something? It happens to the best of us. Pause, catch your breath (in order to decrease your body's physiological response to stress), and let the audience know you are searching for your next thought. Glance at a key word note card if possible.

are likely to be lower than for speakers given adequate time to prepare. If you give a strong impromptu presentation or answer, audiences will be impressed. If you fumble for each word, you might lose your credibility.

First, *anticipate impromptu speaking*. As Mark Twain once remarked, "It usually takes me more than three weeks to prepare for a good impromptu speech." If you have any inkling that you might be called on to give a short presentation of any kind, think ahead about what you might say. Be prepared. Do not wait until you are put on the spot.

Next, *formulate a simple outline for an impromptu speech*. Begin with a short opening attention strategy—a relevant story, a humorous quip you have used successfully on other occasions, or a clever quotation you have memorized. State your point of view or the theme for your remarks. Then quickly identify two or three short points that you will address. Finally, *summarize what you said*. You are not expected to provide substantial supporting material for your points during an impromptu speech, but if you have

some facts and figures memorized, you will impress your audience with your ready knowledge. Impromptu speaking is usually more informal than a standard speech, so be conversational in tone and presentation. The PREP format introduced in Chapter 7 applies well here.

Point: State your main idea/bottom line

We are on target to meet our quota for this quarter.

Reason: Provide the reasoning as to why your point is valid

Raley's just signed a contract for 10,000 units and we have deals with Target and Walmart in the pipeline (expand on this).

Example: Give support in the form of a story, testimony, or research

We've done the research and if the demand for our product continues, we should double our profits by early next year (expand on this).

Point: So yes, we are well on our way to meeting our quota, and the future looks bright.

Extemporaneous Speaking: A Conversational Combination   An **extemporaneous speech** is delivered from a prepared outline or notes. There are several advantages to this method of delivering a speech. First, even though fully prepared in advance, *an extemporaneous speech sounds spontaneous* because you do not read from a manuscript. Instead, you *memorize structure*, glance at your outline or notes, and put the rest of your thoughts into words on the spot. In this sense, extemporaneous speaking is a combination of manuscript, memorized, and impromptu delivery methods. There are several benefits of this delivery method. The extemporaneous style is the most conversational, thus the most relatable of the four. Unlike the others, however, you are not glued to a script, searching for the next memorized word, or coming up with a speech on the fly. You are able to maintain adequate eye contact, and adapt your presentation as needed. For example, if you notice a few of your audience members convey expressions of confusion, you can back up and clarify complex information. (The curse of knowledge, explained in Chapter 13, might be at play!) The major drawback to this type of delivery is time. It can take a great deal of time to construct a thorough speech outline and even more to practice it conversationally. We recommend memorizing the first and last lines of your presentation, so you will clearly know how to start and how to conclude. Memorize the main points you aim to convey, then practice wording the rest several different ways.

Developing Competent Delivery

The method of delivery does not resolve many of the delivery challenges you face when presenting a speech and specific ways to address these challenges. This section discusses these challenges with numerous tips on how to improve your delivery.

Eye Contact: Connecting with Your Audience

Eye contact is the first step to building trust with your audience. Even across cultures, a fair amount of eye contact during speaking is important to enhance credibility and to connect with listeners. Research shows that the typical preferred duration of direct eye contact is 3 seconds (Binetti et al., 2016). This means that we can handle about 3 seconds of direct eye contact and then we become twitchy and want to avert our gaze to break connection. Aim to look at each audience member for about 3 seconds and avoid prolonged stares. Don't make the rookie mistake looking solely at the person you most want to impress, like your boss. Advice provided in Chapter 12 regarding eye contact in virtual settings includes look at your camera often, not just the images on your screen; and vary your eye contact from camera to your screen and back to your camera, taking in your entire visible audience.

Voice: *Developing Vocal Variety*   Strive for vocal variety called **inflection**. *Raise and lower the pitch of your voice.* Vary your voice enough to avoid a monotonous sameness to your pitch. "Pitch variance can convey enthusiasm, interest, and active deliberation, whereas a monotone voice sounds dull and mindless" (Schroeder & Epley, 2015). The same research also shows that pitch variance influences employers' view of job candidates' competence and intelligence. Monotony can also be avoided by *varying the volume of your voice* from loud to soft. A loud voice signals intense feelings. It will punctuate portions of your presentation much as an exclamation point punctuates a written sentence. Do not be excessive, however. Speak loudly only when you have an especially important point to make. All points in your speech do not deserve equal attention. Be careful not to shout when presenting virtually.

Speaking softly can also induce interest. When you lower the pitch and loudness of your voice, the audience must strain to hear. This can be a nice dramatic twist to use in a speech, if used infrequently. Vocal variety signals shifts in mood and does not permit an audience to drift into the hypnotic, trance-like state produced by the white noise of the monotone voice. Practice vocal variety on your friends during casual conversations. Experiment with different voice inflections and volume.

Fluency: *Avoiding Excessive Vocal Fillers*   A common delivery challenge is to exclude **vocal fillers**—the insertion of um, uh, like, you

BOX 16.1 Put It to the Test: Vocal Variety

Try it! Say each sentence twice. The first time, speak it with no inflection; the second time, vary your volume, pitch, and rate in order to make the trivia come to life. Top tip: slow down when you are speaking a number.

Did you know . . .

- *Dolphins have two stomachs—one for food storage and one for digestion?*

- *An elephant seal can hold its breath underwater for more than 100 minutes?*
- *Four million American's quit their jobs in June 2021?*
- *77% of remote workers report that they are more productive when working from home?*

know, know what I mean, whatever, and other variants that substitute for pauses and often draw attention to themselves. Such dysfluencies are common in normal conversations. Despite how common they are, vocal fillers when giving a speech are not always problematic and they often go unnoticed by listeners. Actually, error-free speaking may strike some audiences as too slick and insincere (Erard, 2008). *Research reveals that an optimum frequency of vocal fillers is about one per minute, but the average speaker uses about five per minute when they are not nervous, but even more often when they are anxious* (Zandan, 2019).

If you slip into a habit of using vocal fillers frequently in your conversations, you will very likely suffer the same problem when giving a speech. It can be a tough habit to break. First, develop your own awareness of this habit by paying attention to your conversations. Next, ask for feedback from a friend or coworker. Let them know you are trying to improve. They can tell you when they hear an overuse of any particular word.

Speaking Rate: Finding the Right Pace Sean Shannon, a Canadian residing in Oxford, England, recited the famous soliloquy "To be or not to be . . ." from Shakespeare's Hamlet at 650 words per minute (wpm; see access to link at end of chapter). Talking at 650 wpm is clearly possible, but how fast should you speak to an audience? Moderately fast and rapid speaking rates (180–210 wpm) increase the audience's perception of you as intelligent, confident, and effective compared to slower-paced speakers (between 92 and 145 wpm; Smith & Shaffer, 1995).

Some listeners, however, may not be able to keep pace with you if you are attempting to speak at the pace of someone who has downed three hyper-caffeinated energy drinks. Listeners' comprehension of speech declines rapidly once the speaking rate exceeds 250 wpm (Foulke, 2006). Normal conversational speaking pace ranges between 140 and 180 wpm (McCoy et al., 2005). Because people generally are accustomed to a fairly standard conversational pace, *speaking at a normal conversational rate is appropriate for most speaking situations*. One analysis of TED Talks determined that the average speaking rate was 173 wpm (Barnard, 2018). Without actually measuring, you can get a rough idea of your speaking pace by enunciating your words carefully and pausing to take breaths without gasping for air. Proceed as you would in normal conversation. You can determine your rate by speaking into a recorder for exactly 1 minute, then counting the words.

Perhaps nowhere is the partnership of visual aids and delivery more apparent than in Pecha Kucha presentations. Pecha Kucha is a storytelling platform that originated in Japan in 2003. The goal with this speech format is to make your point using exactly 20 slides, spending only 20 seconds on each slide. You have 400 seconds to tell your story. According to the official Pecha Kucha website, businesses around the world embrace this simple way to connect employees with subjects ranging from corporate updates to new-hire onboarding (PechaKucha.com). The nature of this format builds momentum and anticipation, instead of a presentation where the audience is bombarded with information overload and the presenter drones on and on.

Like most presentations, successful Pecha Kucha rely on a well-chosen topic, audience analysis, powerful visual aids, and careful attention to content and organization. Slide design favors impactful images over verbose text. You are the conveyor of the information. Your slides visually reinforce the feelings and words you express. Aim for one point per slide.

All slides are automatically set to advance every 20 seconds, so practice is essential; your timing must be impeccable. Practice many times, adjusting your story and slides to match the time constraints. You will still need to maintain a reasonable speaking rate, so avoid speaking quickly in order to fit 30 seconds of information on one slide. Less is more. Successful Pecha Kuchas require rehearsal, adjustment, and precision. Like a rollercoaster, once your presentation starts, there's no getting off until the end. Go with it! If you make a mistake, stumble over a word, or forget a number, smile and just keep going. It will be over before you know it and the audience will likely appreciate the crisp design.

Articulation and Pronunciation: Striving for Clarity of Speech

Sloppy speech patterns can make comprehending what you are saying tough for listeners When you mumble your words, who can tell what you said? Mispronouncing words and poor articulation are also common issues for speakers. Proper articulation—speaking words clearly and distinctly—and pronunciation—saying words correctly as indicated in any dictionary based on Standard English rules—can become a credibility issue.

Mispronunciations can make a speaker an object of ridicule. The YourDictionary website identifies the 100 most often mispronounced words and phrases in English, and many are comical. Imagine an audience's reaction if a speaker said, "it's a doggy-dog world" instead of the correct "dog-eat-dog world." It is not real-a-tor; it is real-tor. You do not "take for granite" unless you are into geology; you "take for granted." It is "card*sharp*" not "card*shark*." It is not "revelant" but "relevant." If in doubt, practice your speech in front of several people who know

proper pronunciation and can listen for precise articulation. With thanks to the Internet, we have no reason to mispronounce names, countries, or any other words. Websites like howtopronounce.com and numerous YouTube channels provide audio clips with just a click.

Physical Delivery: Finding the Right Balance Nonverbally

Aim to work the room. Strive for a balance between excessive and insufficient body movement. The general guideline is "everything in moderation." An animated, lively delivery can excite an audience to pay attention, but you do not want to seem out of control. Posture should be erect without looking like a soldier standing at attention. Gestures can enhance perceptions by listeners of a speaker's composure and confidence, and can increase speaker persuasiveness (Maricchiolo et al., 2009). There is no need to plan gestures. As Motley (1995) explains, gestures "are supposed to be non-conscious. That is to say, in natural conversation we use gestures every day without thinking about them. And when we do consciously think about gestures, they become uncomfortable and inhibited" (p. 99). Choreographing your gestures will make them appear awkward and artificial, thereby distracting audience attention. Focus on your message and your audience, and the gestures will follow.

Distracting Behaviors: Avoiding Interference

This is a catch-all category. There are numerous quirky behaviors that speakers can exhibit, often without realizing it. Playing with your pen or pencil while speaking is one example. Fiddling with change in your pocket, tapping fingers on the podium, and shifting your weight from right to left and back like a ship being tossed on the high seas are other distracters.

Distracting behaviors can easily be eliminated. If you do not hold a pen or pencil in your hand, you cannot click it, tap the podium with it, or wave it around while speaking. Take change out of your pocket before speaking if you tend to jiggle coins when you put your hand in your pocket. Move away from the podium so you cannot tap your fingers. Practice standing erect, balanced on both feet, when rehearsing your speech, and you will eliminate the shifting weight problem. Distracting behaviors will not destroy a quality speech unless the behavior is beyond weird. Nevertheless, eliminating them makes your presentation more effective.

A comprehensive list of dos and don'ts when speaking in virtual meetings is in Chapter 12.

Audience-Centered Delivery: Matching the Context   Finally, delivery should match the context for your speech. Like every other aspect of public speaking, delivery is audience centered. The appropriateness of your delivery is dependent on certain expectations inherent to the occasion and purpose of your speech. A eulogy calls for a dignified, formal delivery. The speaker usually limits body movements and keeps his or her voice toned down as a sign of respect. A motivational speech, however, requires a lively, enthusiastic delivery, especially if you are speaking to a large audience. Your voice may be loud, pace fairly rapid, body movements dramatic, eye contact intense and direct, and facial movements expressive. During a motivational speech, the podium is usually moved aside or ignored, and the speaker moves back and forth across a stage, sometimes even moving into the audience. An after-dinner speech or "roast" calls for a lively, comic delivery. Facial expressions consist mostly of smiles or gestures; they may be gross or exaggerated, and a speaker's voice may be loud, even abrasive, for effect. There is no one correct way to deliver a speech but many effective ways. Match your delivery to the speech context and audience expectations.

Delivery of Visual Aids

Poorly designed and clumsily presented visual aids will detract, not aid, your speech. Here are some general guidelines for the competent delivery of visual aids.

Make Aids Visible   Though mentioned in the section about graphs, it bears repeating: The general rule for visual aids is that people in the back of the room or auditorium should be able to see your visual aid easily. If they cannot, it is not large enough to be effective. Effective font size depends on the size of the screen and the room. A huge screen in a large auditorium requires a larger font size for PowerPoint presentations than for a regular-sized conference room. A small object can be enhanced with magnifying equipment or enlarged screenshots of it.

Quality Over Quantity   Do not embarrass yourself by showing a visual aid of poor quality. In a world on content creators and consumers, people expect worthy visuals. Make visual aids neat and attractive. Proofread your aids before showing them. Misspelled words or grammatical mistakes on slides, charts, or tables might signal that you are careless, ignorant, or just don't care—all of which detract from your credibility.

Get Out of the Way   A very common mistake made even by professional speakers is that they block the audience's view of the visual aid. Standing in front of your poster, graph, drawing, table, or PowerPoint slide while you talk to the visual aid, not to your audience, is awkward and self-defeating. Simply stand beside your visual aid if you are using

Standing in front of a visual aid and talking to it, not to your audience, are two common mistakes. Speakers need to get their planet-size heads out of the way, stand beside their visual aid, and speak directly to their audience.

a whiteboard or flip chart, for example, while you explain it to the audience. The touch-turn-talk method is favored when advancing slides on a computer or when using a remote control. Silently *touch* the computer or remote, *turn* to the screen and silently take in what is on the slide, *turn* back to your audience, and *start talking*. The bottom line is *talk to your audience, not to your visual aid*.

Put the Aid Out of Sight When Not in Use
Cover your graph, object, or photo when not actually referring to it. Simply leaving it open to view when you no longer make reference to it or showing it before you actually use it distracts an audience. When using PowerPoint, a quick tap of the B on the keyboard will make the screen go black, and similarly, a tap of the W makes the screen turn white. These are quick shortcuts for hiding a slide until it is needed. Simple tapping the space bar brings the slide forward.

Practice With Aids   Using visual aids competently requires practice. At first, using a visual aid may seem awkward, even unnatural. Once you have practiced your speech using a visual aid, however, it will seem more natural and less awkward. Practice will also help you work out any problems that might occur before actually giving your speech for real.

SUMMARY

Visual aids must be both visually interesting and an actual aid to your speech. Sloppy, poorly prepared, and poorly selected visual aids can bring you ridicule and embarrassment. Always choose and prepare your visual aids carefully. Visual aids can clarify complicated points, gain and maintain audience attention, enhance your credibility, improve your delivery, and make your information memorable. You have many types of visual aids to choose from, but make sure that you do not become enamored with the technologically sophisticated and glitzy aids when you are not well versed in their use and your speech would be diminished by too much flash and not enough substance.

General guidelines for effective delivery are these: use direct eye contact, vocal variety, and few if any vocal fillers; moderate pace and body movement; and eliminate distracting mannerisms. Defer using manuscript and memorized speeches until you become an experienced public speaker. Extemporaneous speaking is the type of delivery to master for most occasions.

Film School Case Studies

Don't Look Up (2021) Comedy/Disaster; rated R

Kate Dibiasky (Jennifer Lawrence) passionately presents the danger of the comet that will hit Earth. What could she have done differently with her vocal and physical delivery to effectively convey such an important message on the *Daily Rip*?

TED Talks and YouTube Videos

These TED Talks and YouTube videos can be accessed by going to the Oxford Learning Link for It's All of Our Business *or by typing the title of the video into a Google search window.*

"Life After Death by PowerPoint 2012" Don McMillan

"How to Embed a Video on PowerPoint" (tutorial) M. D'Angelo

"How to Use PowerPoint Effectively" (tutorial)

"How to Use a Smartboard"; and "Get to Know Your SMART Board 800 Series" (tutorial)

"Statistics at Google" Hal Varian at RSS 2012 Conference

A Pecha Kucha About Pecha Kucha Sumeet Moghe

Glossary

Accommodating style Conflict approach that yields to the concerns and desires of others.

Acquired credibility The care you show for your audience and their concerns, the competence you display in your delivery, and the authenticity of your evidence that likely bolsters your believability and trustworthiness as you give your presentation.

Ad hominem fallacy A personal attack on the messenger to avoid the message; a diversionary tactic that is irrelevant to the primary message.

Ad populum fallacy Basing a claim on popular opinion alone.

Aggregation Collection of unrelated individuals in proximity to each other.

Ambushing When a listener is ready to pounce on a point made by a speaker.

Amplification Echoing and supporting one another's [women's] points and publicly giving one another credit.

Appropriateness Behavior that meets expectations dictated by the rules of a particular context.

Articulation Speaking words clearly and distinctly.

Assertiveness The ability to communicate the full range of your thoughts and emotions with confidence and skill.

Asymmetrical In reacting to the anger of others do the opposite by countering the anger with absolute calm.

Asynchronous Conversations through email, text, and messaging that are out of synch, and not in "real time."

Autocratic leadership style Highly directive and does not encourage member participation.

Autonomy The degree to which team members experience substantial freedom, independence, and discretion in their work.

Avoiding style Communication style of withdrawing from potentially contentious and unpleasant struggles in a conflict situation.

Bad apples Disruptive members who poison the group.

Bar graphs They compare and contrast two or more items or show variation over a period of time.

Behavioral ground rule Rules that assist in managing contributions and communication during discussion in groups.

Behavioral interview questions Queries that focus on past behaviors during an interview.

Belief What a person thinks is true or probable.

Bridging A conflict strategy that looks for overarching goals that find common ground to move beyond conflicts of interest toward mutual interests.

Captive audience Listeners are required to be present for a speech.

Casual audience Composed of individuals who become listeners because they stumble upon a presentation, stop out of curiosity or casual interest, and remain until bored or sated.

Catastrophizing A person sees only failure, not an opportunity for exhilarating success that comes from embracing challenges.

Charge The team task.

Charisma Qualities that some individuals are perceived to possess that draw others to them and provide influence.

Civility Treating people with respect.

Co-culture Any group that is part of a dominant culture yet often has a common history and shares some differences in values, beliefs, and practices from the dominant culture.

Code switching Adjusting one's language to the professional work environment.

Cognitive empathy The ability to understand how a person feels and what they might be thinking.

Cohesiveness The output of the social dimension of groups.

Collaborating style A win-win, cooperative approach to conflict that attempts to satisfy all parties.

Collaboration The cooperative process by all parties involved in decision making and problem solving of working together to achieve a common goal.

Collective effort model (CEM) Suggests that social loafing can be mostly prevented if group members are convinced that their individual effort will likely help in attaining valued results.

Collectivist culture Individuals see themselves as closely linked to one or more groups.

Commitment A passion for excellence to gain knowledge and hone our skills by hard work.

Committed audience Listeners voluntarily assemble to invest time and energy hearing and being inspired by a speaker.

Communication A transactional process of sharing meaning with others.

Communication climate The emotional atmosphere, the enveloping tone that is created by the way we communicate in the workplace.

Communication competence Engaging in communication with others that is perceived to be both appropriate and effective in a given context.

Communication orientation An anxiety reducing strategy that focuses on making the speaker's message clear and interesting to listeners.

Communication skill The ability to perform a communication behavior effectively and repeatedly.

Communication style of conflict management A tendency to manage conflict in a certain way.

Compassionate empathy (do) Empathy that moves us to action.

Competing/Power-Forcing style Approaching conflict as a win-lose contest characterized by threats, criticism, contempt, intimidation, and other combative tactics.

Compromising style Choosing a middle ground in a conflict by giving up something to get something.

Concerned audience Listeners gather voluntarily to hear a speaker because they care about issues being discussed.

Confirmation bias Listening only for information that supports your beliefs and ignoring contrary information.

Conflict The expressed struggle of interconnected parties who perceive incompatible goals and interference from each other in attaining those goals.

Conformity The inclination of group members to think and behave in ways that are consistent with group norms.

Confrontation The overt recognition that conflict exists in the workplace and the direct effort to manage it effectively.

Consensus A state of mutual agreement among members of a group where all legitimate concerns of individuals have been addressed to the satisfaction of the group.

Constructive conflict Characterized by We-oriented, de-escalating, cooperative, supportive, and flexible communication patterns.

Contranyms Words that can have contradictory meanings.

Contrary audience Listeners are initially resistant to a speaker's position on a topic.

Conversational narcissism The tendency of listeners to turn the topics of ordinary conversation to themselves without showing sustained interest in others' topics.

Correlation A consistent relationship between two variables.

Credibility Reliability and validity of supporting materials.

Criteria Standards used to evaluate decisions and solutions to problems.

Critical listening The rational process of analyzing and evaluating others' claims.

Criticism sandwich Offering praise then criticism then praise again.

Culture A learned set of enduring values, beliefs, and practices that are shared by an identifiable, large group of people with a common history.

Curse of knowledge An error in thinking, or a cognitive bias, when we know something so well and we erroneously assume others know it too.

Cyberbullying Online bullying.

Cyberloafing Using the Internet and social media for purposes unrelated to work when in a work situation.

Cynicism Nay-saying, fault-finding, and ridiculing; a jeerleader not a cheerleader.

Deep diversity Substantial variation among group members in task-relevant skills, knowledge, abilities, beliefs, values, experiences, perspectives, and problem-solving strategies.

Defensive communication Patterns of communication characterized by evaluation, control, indifference, manipulation, superiority, certainty, and incivility.

Defensiveness A reaction to a perceive attack on one's self-concept and self-esteem.

Defiance Unambiguous, purposeful noncompliance.

Democratic leadership style Encourages participation and responsibility from group members.

Demographics Characteristics such as age, gender, culture, and ethnicity, and group affiliations.

Designated leaders Individuals appointed through formal processes to positions of authority.

Destructive conflict Characterized by communication that is dominating, escalating, retaliating, competing, and exhibits defensiveness and inflexibility.

Digital body language The myriad signals our digital world presents that heightens our awareness of how a message is presented online but can cause confusion, even calamity.

Discriminative listening The ability to distinguish sound and the basis for all other types of listening.

Disinhibition effect The tendency to say online what you wouldn't normally say in person.

Disruptive roles Behavior patterns that focus attention on the individual at the expense of group needs and goals.

Dominance The communication power over others.

Downward communication Messages that flow from superordinates to subordinates in an organization.

Dunning-Kruger effect Incompetence prevents accurate self-assessments of one's limitations.

Duration of anger How long the anger lasts.

Dyad Two people interacting together.

Dysfunctional anxiety the fear of public speaking that reaches an intensity that interferes with giving effective presentations.

Effectiveness The degree to which you have progressed toward the achievement of your goals.

Electronic brainstorming Group members sit at computer terminals and brainstorm ideas using a computer-based, file-sharing procedure.

Emergent leaders Group members who significantly influence other group members even though they have not been assigned formal authority.

Emotional Appeals Emotions such as happiness, hope, excitement, anger, and determination can be very motivating when trying to persuade, when expressed appropriately and to the right degree.

Emotional empathy The ability to share the feelings of another person.

Emotional intelligence The ability to perceive, glean information from, and manage one's own and others' emotions.

Empathic listening Seeking emotional comprehension of a message commonly used in interpersonal situations.

Empathy Thinking and feeling what you perceive another to be thinking and feeling.

Empathy for others Listening to others' needs and feelings and reflecting them to the speaker for verification and understanding.

Empowerment Power derived from enhancing the capabilities, choices, and influence of individuals and groups.

Ethics A system for judging moral correctness by using a set of standards to determine what constitutes right and wrong behavior.

Ethnocentrism Exalting one's own culture while disparaging other cultures. This is prejudice on a grand scale.

Ethos Aristotle's name for what is now called speaker or source credibility.

Expanding the pie Increasing resources as a solution to a problem that triggers conflict.

Explicit norms Rules in groups that specifically and overtly identify acceptable and unacceptable behavior.

Extemporaneous speech A presentation delivered from a prepared outline or notes.

Extrinsic reward An external inducement, such as money, recognition, praise, awards, or prestige.

Factionalism Members of like mind may splinter into smaller, competing subgroups to withstand pressure from other group members to conform to the majority opinion on an issue.

Fantasies Dramatic stories that provide a shared interpretation of events that bind group members and offer them a shared identity.

Fantasy chains A string of connected stories that dramatize and amplify a group theme.

Fantasy theme A consistent thread that runs through the stories told by group members.

Formal roles An assigned position.

Frame of reference A mindset that can lock group members into a rigid way of thinking.

Framestorming Changing the framework for brainstorming before actually engaging in a brainstorming session by asking different questions.

Functional leadership Shared leadership that recognizes that "it is all of our business."

General purpose Identifies the overall goal of your presentation, and it tells the audience why you are giving the presentation (to inform, persuade, entertain/eulogize).

Glazing over Occurs when listeners attention wanders and daydreaming happens.

Graph A diagram that plots the variance between variables.

Group Composed of three or more individuals, interacting for the achievement of some common purpose(s), who influence and are influenced by one another.

Group potency A team's generalized confidence in its ability to perform across a variety of situations.

Grouphate The view that the group experience is troublesome and to be avoided if possible.

Groupthink A mode of thinking that people engage in when they are deeply involved in a cohesive in-group, when the members' strivings for unanimity override their motivation to realistically appraise alternative courses of action.

Hasty generalization When individuals jump to conclusions based on one or only a handful of examples, especially vivid ones.

Hidden agendas Personal goals of group members that are not revealed openly and that can interfere with group accomplishment.

Hierarchy Members of an organization are rank ordered.

High-context communication style A style that uses indirect verbal expression; you are expected to "read between the lines" for meaning.

High-PD cultures Cultures that have a relatively strong emphasis on maintaining power differences.

Horizontal communication Messages between individuals with equal power.

Hostile environment harassment Employment discrimination based on unwelcome sexual conduct that creates an intimidating, hostile, or offensive work environment characterized by such offensive communication as sexual comments, jokes, and discussions about sex.

HURIER model An acronym for the six stages of the listening process: hearing, understanding, remembering, interpreting, evaluating, and responding.

Illusion of transparency The overestimation of the extent to which audience members detect a speaker's nervousness.

Immediacy The perception of closeness and involvement with others

Impact The degree of significance given by those outside of the team to the work produced by the team.

Implicit norms Observable patterns of behavior exhibited by group members that identify acceptable and unacceptable conduct.

Implicit theories of leadership Individuals' expectations, beliefs, and assumptions about what constitutes an effective leader.

Impromptu speech An address delivered without preparation, or so it seems.

Incivility Commonplace acts of rudeness and disrespect communicated both verbally and nonverbally.

Indicators of power The ways in which relative degrees of power are communicated.

Individual accountability Establishes a minimum standard of effort and performance for each team member to share the fruits of team success.

Individualist culture Individuals see themselves as loosely linked to each other and largely independent of group identification.

Inflection Vocal variety while giving a presentation.

Informal roles Identified functions, not positions in groups.

Informational listening Listening geared toward learning something new.

Integration A creative approach to conflicts of interest that searches for solutions that benefit everyone.

Intensity of anger Varies from mild irritation to outright rage.

Intrinsic reward Enjoying what one does for its own sake and because it gives you pleasure.

Jargon Terms, expressions, or acronyms that are specific to a particular industry or professional group.

Laissez-faire leadership style The avoidance of leadership. Not real leadership.

Language A structured system of symbols for sharing meaning.

Leadership A leader–follower social influence process, directed toward positive change that reflects mutual purposes of group members and is largely accomplished through competent communication.

Logic/Evidence Most persuasion requires laying out logical arguments supported by strong evidence.

Legitimate authority Someone perceived to have a right to direct others' behavior because of his or her position, title, role, experience, or knowledge.

Line graph Shows a trend or change over a period of time.

Listening The process of receiving, constructing meaning from and responding to spoken and/or nonverbal messages.

Logos Aristotle's term for reasoning and evidence used to support claims.

Low-context communication style A style that is verbally precise, direct, assertive, self-enhancing, and explicit.

Low-PD culture A culture that values relatively equal power sharing and discourages attention to status differences and ranking in society.

Maintenance roles Those behavior patterns that address the social dimension of small groups.

Manuscript speech One in which the speaker reads from prepared text.

Mastermind pod A group that assembles to mentor, learn, and hold each other accountable and meets to brainstorm approaches or share strategies on a compelling project.

Meaning The conscious pattern humans create out of their interpretation of experience.

Meaningfulness A team's perception that its tasks are important, valuable, and worthwhile.

Memorized speech A presentation in which the speaker commits to memory the text of the speech.

Mentor Someone knowledgeable and experienced who can help you advance your career.

Microaggressions Seemingly innocuous comments that are subtle put-downs not always intended as such.

Mindfulness When we think about our communication and continually work at changing what we do in order to become more effective.

Mindlessness When we pay little attention to our communication with others and put little or no effort into improving it.

Mission statement Defines why an organization exists by announcing its primary objectives.

Mixed messages Positive verbal and negative nonverbal communication, or vice versa.

Murphy's Law Anything that can go wrong likely will go wrong, somehow, somewhere, sometime.

Myth A belief contradicted by fact.

Narcissists Those who exhibit a grandiose sense of self-importance; arrogant behavior or attitudes; a lack of empathy for others; a preoccupation with fantasies of unlimited success or power; . . . [and] a desire for excessive admiration from others (Pfeffer, 2015).

Negative communication climate When employees do not feel valued, supported, and respected; when trust is minimal; and when workers perceive that they are not treated well.

Negativity bias The strong tendency to be influenced more heavily by negative than by positive information.

Nominal group technique An alternative to brainstorming technique. Individuals work by themselves generating lists of ideas on a problem, then convene in a group where they merely post their ideas.

Nonroutine task One that requires problem solving, has only a few set procedures, and has a high level of uncertainty, even risk.

Nonverbal communication Wordless communication.

Norms Rules applied specifically to groups.

Panel interview Three or more hiring managers interview a prospective candidate at once.

Paraphrasing Restating in your own words the concise essence of a message that you heard.

Parking lot Posting for questions and topics that are worthy of discussion but are not on the agenda.

Parkinson's Law Work expands to fill the time available for its completion.

Pathos Aristotle's term for emotional appeals.

Perception checking Neutral description of an observable fact, two possible interpretations of the aforementioned fact, and a request for clarification.

Phonemes The sounds of a language that we hear.

Physical noise External, environmental distractions, such as startling sounds, poorly heated rooms, etc.

Physiological noise Biological interferences such as sweaty palms, pounding heart, etc.

Pie graph Depicts a proportion or percentage for each part of a whole.

Platinum rule Treat others as *they* want to be treated.

Positive communication climate When individuals perceive that they are valued, supported, and treated well by the group.

Power The ability to influence the attainment of goals sought by you or others.

Power resource Anything that enables individuals to achieve their goals, assists others to achieve their goals, or interferes with the goal attainment of others.

Power-distance dimension The extent to which members of a culture endorse the society's overall level of inequality.

PREP method Used as a model for organizing thoughts into responses consisting of a point, reason supporting the point, an example to support the point, and a restatement of the original point.

Prevention Power used to thwart those with greater influence.

Probing Seeking additional information from a speaker by asking questions.

Procedural ground rules Rules that help the meeting process.

Productivity The output of the task dimension in groups.

Pronunciation Saying words correctly as indicated in any dictionary based on Standard English rules.

Provisionalism Qualifying your statements by avoiding absolutes such as never and always.

Pseudolistening Pretending to listen.

Psychological noise Preconceptions, biases, and assumptions that interfere with effective transmission and reception of messages.

Psychological reactance The more someone tries to control you by telling you what to do, the more you are inclined to resist such efforts or even to do the opposite.

Psychological safety The communication climate that encourages open expression of ideas and opinions, and fosters the freedom to make mistakes, ask questions, and take risks without reprisals or concerns for job security.

Psychopaths Someone who has no conscience and feels no remorse or empathy.

Purpose impact statement Serves to guide the development of your presentation, enabling you to focus on what to include and exclude.

Quid pro quo sexual harassment A more powerful person requires sexual favors from the less powerful person in exchange for keeping a job, landing an employment promotion, or job perks, and avoiding punishment.

Random sample Portion of the population chosen in such a manner that every member of the entire population has an equal chance of being selected.

Readiness The ability (competence) and willingness (commitment) to accomplish a specific task.

Reflective thinking A set of logical steps that incorporate the scientific method of defining, analyzing, and solving problems.

Reframing The creative process of breaking a mindset by describing the problem from a different frame of reference.

Reliability Consistency when citing facts and interpreting data.

Resistance Covert, ambiguous noncompliance.

Robert's Rules of Order Parliamentary procedure composed of numerous formal rules for group interaction and discussion.

Role ambiguity Team members are unsure of the parts they are expected to play in a team.

Roles Patterns of expected behavior associated with parts that you play in groups.

Routine task In a conflict situation, this is when a group performs processes and procedures that have little variability and little likelihood of change.

Rule A prescription that indicates what behavior is obligated, prohibited, or preferred in a given context.

Rule of seven Each member added to a decision-making group that starts with seven members reduces decision effectiveness by 10%.

Screening interview Identifying candidates who are qualified to make it to the next level of interviews.

Self-deprecating humor Humor that makes fun of oneself.

Self-effacement Individuals downplay their performance and exhibit modest talk and self-deprecating messages.

Self-efficacy One's personal assessment as to whether you can execute courses of action required to deal with prospective situations.

Self-empathy Empathy that reflects a deep awareness of one's own experience when communicating.

Self-enhancement Individuals are expected to initiate job searches and engage in personal promotion.

Self-managing work teams Teams that regulate their own performance free from outside interference while completing an entire task.

Self-selected sample Portion of a sample that choose themselves because they are the most committed, aroused, or motivated to fill out surveys on their own and answer polling questions.

Semantic noise Confusing, incomprehensible, or distracting word choice that interferes with accurate transmission and reception of messages.

Semantic satiation Our brain's way of decreasing meaningfulness of oft-repeated words.

Sensitivity Receptive accuracy—the ability to detect, decode, and comprehend signals from others.

Servant leadership Places the good of followers over their own self-interests and emphasizes follower development (empowerment) with strong moral behavior toward followers.

Sexual harassment Verbal, visual, nonverbal or physical conduct of a sexual nature or based on someone's sex that is severe or pervasive and affects working conditions.

Shift response Listener's attempt to shift focus of attention from others to oneself by changing the topic of discussion.

Situational interview questions Queries during an interview that focus on future possibility given certain circumstances.

Skepticism The process of listening to claims, evaluating evidence and reasoning supporting those claims, and drawing conclusions based on probabilities.

Smoothing The act of calming the agitated feelings of group members during a conflict episode.

Social Compensation Taking on more than your share in a group.

Social Dimension Social dimension consists of relationships between group members and the impact of these relationships on the group

Social loafing The tendency of an individual to exert less effort on a task when working in a group than when working alone.

Status equalization effect Blurring the power differences between people, especially in group transactions.

Stratified Cultures divided into various levels of power that put distance between the haves and the have-nots.

Structure A form or shape characterized by an interrelationship among its parts.

Superordinate goal A specific kind of cooperative goal that overrides differences that members may have because it supersedes less important competitive goals.

Supportive communication Patterns of communication characterized by description, problem orientation, empathy, assertiveness, equality, provisionalism, and civility.

Support response An attention-giving effort by a listener to focus attention on the other person, not on oneself.

Supporting materials Examples, statistics, and testimony used to bolster your theme or viewpoint.

Symbolic convergence theory Group members sharing stories create a convergence, a group identity that is larger and more coherent than the isolated experiences of individual group members.

Synergy Group genius, or "wisdom of the crowd." The whole is not equal to but is greater than the sum of its parts.

Table An orderly depiction of statistics, words, or symbols in columns or rows.

Task dimension The work performed by the group and its impact on the group.

Task roles Patterns of expected behavior that advance the attainment of group goals.

Team A constellation of members with complementary skills who act as an interdependent unit, are equally committed to a common mission, subscribe to a cooperative approach to accomplish that mission, and hold themselves accountable for team performance.

Team identity The sense members feel that they are a part of a group, that they belong.

Tone The mood, voice, style, and cadence of business written messages.

Traits Relatively enduring characteristics of an individual that highlight differences between people and that are displayed in most situations.

Transactional process The speaker is both a sender and a receiver, not merely a sender or a receiver.

Transformational leadership Leadership that deals with change, inspiration, motivation, and influence.

Transitions Serve to connect one point to a next point in a speech or written message.

True consensus Requires unanimous agreement, commitment and satisfaction with a decision.

Uncertainty reduction theory When strangers meet, the principal goal is to reduce uncertainty and increase predictability.

Upward communication Messages that flow from subordinates to superordinates in an organization.

Validity Accuracy of asserted facts and interpreting data.

Value The most deeply felt, generally shared view of what is deemed good, right, or worthwhile thinking or behavior.

Value dimensions Varying degrees of importance placed on those deeply felt views of what is right, good, and worthwhile; the deep structure that serves as the bedrock of a culture.

Virtual teams Teams whose members are connected by electronic technology.

Vision statement A statement that reflects a company's brand and overall strategic intent.

Vocal fillers The insertion of um, uh, like, you know, know what I mean, whatever, and other variants that substitute for pauses and often draw attention to themselves as distractions during a speech.

WAIT Why Am I Talking.

Workplace bullying Repeated mistreatment of an employee by one or more employees by abusive conduct that is threatening, humiliating, or intimidating.

Zoom performance anxiety The added fear of presenting speeches in the somewhat uncomfortable and awkward online platform.

References

Abbamonte, K. (2022, May 23). The best presentation software in 2022. Zapier. https://zapier.com/blog/best-powerpoint-alternatives/

Abilities: Written expression. O*NET OnLine. (2022, March 29). https://www.onetonline.org/find/descriptor/result/1.A.1.a.4?a=1

Ackrill, C. (2012, October 5). 6 thought patterns of the stressed: No. 3—catastrophizing. . . . "Lions, and Tigers, and Bears, Oh My!." *American Institute of Stress.* http://www.cynthiaackrill.com/6-thought-patterns-of-the-stressed-no-3-catastrophizing-lions-and-tigers-and-bears-oh-my/

Adam, H., & Brett, J. M. (2018, May). Everything in moderation: The social effects of anger depend on its perceived intensity. *Journal of Experimental Social Psychology, 76*, 12–18. https://www.sciencedirect.com/science/article/abs/pii/S0022103117304638?via%3Dihub

Adler, R. (1977). *Confidence in communication: A guide to assertive and social skills.* Holt, Rinehart & Winston.

Age-related hearing loss. (2018, July 17). *National Institute on Deafness and Other Communication Disorders.* https://www.nidcd.nih.gov/health/age-related-hearing-loss

Agerholm, H. (2016, September 15). 1 in 5 CEOs are psychopaths according to a new study: Here's why. *Business Insider.* https://www.businessinsider.com/1-in-5-ceos-are-psychopaths-according-to-a-new-study-2016-9

Alessandra, T. (2020). The platinum rule: What it is and how does it apply to you? *C-Suite Network.* https://c-suitenetwork.com/news/the-platinum-rule-what-is-it-and-how-does-it-apply-to-you-2/

Alexander, T. (2018, November 6). How to work best with the 4 different types of learners. https://www.atlassian.com/blog/teamwork/how-to-work-4-different-learning-types

Alidina, S. (2018, November 7). 10 ways to be more MINDFUL at work. *Mindful.org.* https://www.mindful.org/10-ways-mindful-work/

Allen, N. (2018, May 22). Why teams fail, according to MBAs. *Poets and Quants.* https://poetsandquants.com/2018/05/22/why-teams-fail-according-to-mbas/?pq-category=business-school-news/

Allen, J. J., & Anderson, C. A. (2017, January). Aggression and violence: Definitions and distinctions. *ResearchGate.* https://www.researchgate.net/publication/323784533_Aggression_and_Violence_Definitions_and_Distinctions

Amanatullah, E. T., & Morris, M. W. (2019). Negotiating gender roles: Gender differences in assertive negotiating are mediated by women's fear of backlash and attenuated when negotiating on behalf of others. *Harvard Kennedy School.* http://gap.hks.harvard.edu/negotiating-gender-roles-gender-differences-assertive-negotiating-are-mediated-women%E2%80%99s-fear-backlash

Ames, D. R., & Wazlawek, A. S. (2014). Pushing in the dark: Causes and consequences of limited self-awareness for interpersonal assertiveness. *Personality and Social Psychology Bulletin, 40*(6), 775–790. https://journals.sagepub.com/doi/abs/10.1177/0146167214525474

Ammerman, C., & Groysberg, B. (2021, May–June). How to close the gender gap. *Harvard Business Review.* https://hbr.org/2021/05/how-to-close-the-gender-gap

Ancona, D., & Isaacs, K. (2019, July 11). How to give your team the right amount of autonomy. *Harvard Business Review.* https://hbr.org/2019/07/how-to-give-your-team-the-right-amount-of-autonomy

Andersen, M. K. (2018, May 7). Why are women better leaders than men? *Linkedin.* https://www.linkedin.com/pulse/why-women-better-leaders-than-men-morten-kamp-andersen

Anderson, D. (2021, May 16). The average American utters 80 to 90 curse words every day. Here's why it's good for you. *Business Insider.* https://www.businessinsider.com/swearing-good-for-workouts-work-life-health-2018-12

Anderson, R., & Ross, V. (1994). *Questions of communication: A practical introduction to theory*. St. Martin's Press.

Antoci, A., Boneli, L., Paglieri, F., Reggiani, T. G., & Sabatini, F. (2018). Civility and trust in social media. *IZA Institute of Labor Economics*. http://ftp.iza.org/dp11290.pdf

Anwar, K. (2016). Working with group tasks and group cohesiveness. *International Education Studies, 9*(8), 105–111.

Apple Park. (2020, March 23). *9to5Mac*. https://9to5mac.com/guides/apple-park/

Aritz, J., & Walker, R. C. (2014). Leadership styles in multicultural groups: Americans and East Asians working together. *Journal of Business Communication, 51*(1), 72–92.

Aronson, E., Wilson, T. D., & Akert, R. M. (2016). *Social psychology*. Pearson.

Arruda, W. (2018, March 18). 8 things teenagers (and their parents) need to know about LinkedIn. *LinkedIn*. https://www.linkedin.com/pulse/8-things-teenagers-parents-need-know-linkedin-william-arruda

Ashe, S. (2018, June 18). 19 things you never knew about McDonald's. *Insider*. https://www.insider.com/facts-you-never-knew-about-mcdonalds-2018-6

ASPCA Mission. (n.d.). https://www.aspca.org/about-us/aspca-policy-and-position-statements/mission

Atlassian Infographic (2019) You Waste a Lot of Time at Work. Retrieved July 09, 2019 from https://www.atlassian.com/time-wasting-at-work-infographic

Aubin, R. M., Amiot, C. E., & Fontaine-Boyte, C. (2016). The impact of group power and its perceived stability on hope and collective action: Applying the concept of hopelessness at the collective level of analysis. *Group Dynamics: Theory, Research, and Practice, 20*(2), 105–119. https://psycnet.apa.org/doi/10.1037/gdn0000045

Aune, K. S., Kim, M., & Hu, A. (2000). *"Well I've been talking long enough about me. . . . What do you think of my accomplishments?" The relationship between self-construals, narcissism, compulsive talking, and bragging*. Paper presented at the meeting of the National Communication Association, Seattle, WA.

Avolio, B. J. (2007). Promoting more integrative strategies for leadership theory-building. *American Psychologist, 62*(1), 25–33.

Axtell, P. (2015, July 14). 5 Ways to improve employee engagement in meetings . . . and why it matters. https://blog.lucidmeetings.com/blog/5-ways-to-improve-employee-engagement-in-meetings-and-why-it-matters

Axtell, R. E. (1998). *Gestures: The do's and taboos of body language around the world*. Wiley.

Aycan, D., Duffy, M. W., & Hale, A. (2020, April 30). Building empowered teams is good for business. *IDEO Creative Difference*. https://medium.com/@ideoCD/building-empowered-teams-is-good-for-business-4e578c010d77

Babiak, P., & Hare, R. D. (2006). *Snakes in suits: When psychopaths go to work*. HarperCollins.

Baghai, M. & Quigley, J. (2011). *As one: Individual action, collective power*. Portfolio.

Bajaj, G. (2020, July 31). 30 million PowerPoint presentations? *Indezine*. https://blog.indezine.com/2013/02/30-million-powerpoint-presentations.html

Baker, G. (2015, July 31). Five top causes of "business communication problems." *Advance Consulting Inc*. http://www.advanceconsulting.com/blog/five-top-causes-of-business-communication-problems/

Bakken, R. (2019). Challenges to managing virtual teams and how to overcome them. Professional Development, *Harvard Division of Continuing Education*. https://professional.dce.harvard.edu/blog/challenges-to-managing-virtual-teams-and-how-to-overcome-them/

Balch, H. (2022, February 22). 5 stats you need to know about LinkedIn in 2022. *LinkedIn*. https://www.linkedin.com/pulse/5-stats-you-need-know-linkedin-2022-sterileprocessing-hank-balch?trk=articles_directory

Baldoni, J. (2012, May 4). Give a great speech: 3 tips from Aristotle. *Inc.com*. https://www.inc.com/john-baldoni/deliver-a-great-speech-aristotle-three-tips.html#:~:text=%22Tell%20them%20what%20you%20are,master%20of%20rhetoric%20himself%2C%20Aristotle

Balliett, A. (2020). Killer Visual Strategies: Engage any audience, improve comprehension, and get amazing results using visual communication. John Wiley & Sons, Inc.

Balsamo, M., & Hays, T. (2021, April 15). Ponzi schemer Bernie Madoff dies in prison at 82. *AP News*. https://apnews.com/article/bernie-madoff-dead-9d9bd8065708384e0bf0c840b-d1ae711

Barrett, J (2018, April 19). The U.S. is facing a critical skills shortage, reskilling can be part of the solution. *LinkedIn*. https://blog.linkedin.com/2018/april/19/the-u-s-is-facing-a-critical-skills-shortage-reskilling-can-be-part-of-the-solution

Baruah, J., & Paulus, P. B. (2008). Effects of training on idea generation in groups. *Small Group Research*, 39(5), 523–541.

Baruah, J., & Paulus, P. B. (2016). The role of time and category relatedness in electronic brainstorming. *Small Group Research*, 47(3), 333–342.

Bary, Emily. (2020, April 1). Zoom, Microsoft teams usage are rocketing during coronavirus pandemic, new data show. *Market Watch*. https://www.marketwatch.com/story/zoom-microsoft-cloud-usage-are-rocketing-during-coronavirus-pandemic-new-data-show-2020-03-30

Bass, B. M., & Bass, R. (2008). *The Bass handbook of leadership: Theory, research, and managerial applications*. Free Press.

Battilana, J., & Casciaro, T. (2021). *Power, for all: How it really works and why it's everyone's business*. Simon & Schuster.

Bauer-Wolf, J. (2018, February 23). Overconfident students, dubious employers. *Inside Higher Ed*. https://www.insidehighered.com/news/2018/02/23/study-students-believe-they-are-prepared-workplace-employers-disagree

Bauer-Wolf, J. (2019, January 17). Survey: Employers want "soft skills" from graduates. *Inside Higher Ed*. https://www.insidehighered.com/quicktakes/2019/01/17/survey-employers-want-soft-skills-graduates

Bear, J. B., Cushenberry, L., London, M., & Sherman, G. D. 2017). Performance feedback, power retention, and the gender gap in leadership. *The Leadership Quarterly*, 28(6), 721–740. http://dx.doi.org/10.1016/j.leaqua.2017.02.003

Bearak, S. D. (2017, May). Protecting what matters most: Insights, trends, and perspectives on protecting your digital world. *Identity Force*. https://www.lsu.edu/hrm/employees/benefits/health_insurance/pdfs/IdentityForce_Newsletter.pdf

Becker, J. A. H., Halbesleben, J. R. B., & O'Hair, H. D. (2005). Defensive communication and burnout in the workplace: The mediating role of leader-member exchange. *Communication Research Reports*, 22(2), 143–150.

Belbin, R. (1996). *Team roles at work*. Butterworth-Heinemann.

Bell, J. (2015, June 23). Knowledge is power. *Data isn't. Human Synergistics*. https://www.humansynergistics.com/blog/culture-university/details/culture-university/2015/06/23/knowledge-is-power.-data-isn-t

Benne, K., & Sheats, P. (1948). Functional roles of group members. *Journal of Social Issues*, 4(2), 41–49.

Bennis, W. (2007). The challenges of leadership in the modern world: Introduction to the special issue. *American Psychologist*, 62(1), 2–5.

Bennis, W., & Biederman, P. (1997). *Organizing genius: The secrets of creative collaboration*. Addison-Wesley.

Benson, K. (2017, October 4). The magic relationship ratio, according to science. *The Gottman Institute*. https://www.gottman.com/blog/the-magic-relationship-ratio-according-science/

Beras, E. (2018, March 9). Poll: Nearly half of the women who experienced sexual harassment leave their jobs or switch careers. *Marketplace*. https://www.marketplace.org/2018/03/09/new-numbers-reflect-lasting-effects-workplace-harassment-women/

Berlin, R. (2017). Sexual harassment in the workplace. *AllLaw*. http://www.alllaw.com/articles/employment/article37.asp

Bernhoff, J. (September 6, 2016). https://hbr.org/2016/09/bad-writing-is-destroying-your-companys-productivity

Bernieri, F. J. (2001). Toward a taxonomy of interpersonal sensitivity. In J. A. Hall & F. J. Bernieri (Eds.), *Interpersonal sensitivity: Theory and measurement*. Erlbaum.

Bernoff, J. (2016, September 6). Bad writing is destroying your company's productivity. *Harvard Business Review*. https://hbr.org/2016/09/bad-writing-is-destroying-your-companys-productivity

Berry, P. S., Gillespie, G. L., Fisher, B. S., Gormley, D., & Haynes, J. T. (2016). Psychological distress and workplace bullying among registered nurses. *Journal of Issues in Nursing*. http://ojin.nursingworld.org/MainMenuCategories/ANAMarketplace/ANAPeriodicals/OJIN/TableofContents/Vol-21-2016/No3-Sept-2016/Articles-Previous-Topics/Psychological-Distress-and-Workplace-Bullying.html

Beugelsdijk, S., Maseland, R., & van Hoorn, A. (2015). Are scores on Hofstede's dimensions of national culture stable over time? A cohort analysis. *Global Strategy Journal*, *5*(3), 223–240. https://onlinelibrary.wiley.com/doi/full/10.1002/gsj.1098

Beugelsdijk, S. & Welzel, C. (2018). Dimensions and dynamics of national culture: Synthesizing Hofstede with Inglehart. *Journal of Cross-Cultural Psychology*, *49*(10), 1469–1505.

Bhatt, J. & Swick, M. (2017, March 15). Focusing on teamwork and communication to improve patient safety. *American Hospital Association*. https://www.aha.org/news/blog/2017-03-15-focusing-teamwork-and-communication-improve-patient-safety

Biddlestone, M., Green, R., & Douglas, K. M. (2020). Cultural orientation, power, belief in conspiracy theories, and intentions to reduce the spread of COVID-19. *British Journal of Social Psychology*, *59*(3), 663–673. https://onlinelibrary.wiley.com/doi/full/10.1111/bjso.12397

Bilandzic, H., Kalch, A., & Soentgen, J. (2017). Effects of goal framing and emotions on perceived threat and willingness to sacrifice for climate change. *Science Communication*, *39*(4), 466–491. https://doi.org/10.1177%2F1075547017718553

Binetti N, Harrison C, Coutrot A, Johnston A, Mareschal I. (2016). Pupil dilation as an index of preferred mutual gazeduration. *R. Soc. open sci. 3*: 160086.http://dx.doi.org/10.1098/rsos.160086

Black, R. (2019, September 12). Glossophobia (fear of public speaking): Are you glossophobic? *Psycom*. https://www.psycom.net/glossophobia-fear-of-public-speaking

Blader, S. (2018). Fairness. *Ethical Systems*. https://www.ethicalsystems.org/content/fairness

Blenko, M. W., Mankins, M. C., & Rogers, P. (2010). *Decide & deliver: 5 steps to breakthrough performance in your organization*. Harvard Business Review Press.

Blom, M., & Alvesson, M. (2014). Leadership on demand: Followers as initiators and inhibitors of managerial leadership. *Scandinavian Journal of Management*, *30*(3), 344–367.

Blom, M., & Alvesson, M. (2015). Less followership, less leadership? An inquiry into the basic but seemingly forgotten downsides of leadership. *Management*, *18*(3), 266–282.

Boateng, D. D. K. (2021). Effect of bias on selection and recruitment. *Academia Letters*. https://www.academia.edu/50949907/Effect_of_Bias_on_Selection_and_Recruitment?email_work_card=title

Bocchiaro, P., & Zimbardo, P. (2017). On the dynamics of disobedience: Experimental investigations of defying unjust authority. *Psychology Research and Behavioral Management*, 10, 219–229.

Bodie, G. D. (2010). A racing heart, rattling knees, and ruminative thoughts: Defining, explaining, and treating public speaking anxiety. *Communication Education*, *59*(1), 70–105. https://doi.org/10.1080/03634520903443849

Bodie, G. D., Worthington, D., Imhof, M., & Cooper, L. O. (2008). What would a unified field of listening look like? A proposal linking past perspectives and future endeavors. *International Journal of Listening*, *22*(2), 103–122.

Bolden-Barrett, V. (2019, August 16). Most people have cried at work at least once, survey says. *HRDive*. https://www.hrdive.com/news/most-people-have-cried-at-work-at-least-once-survey-says/560940/

Bolduc, B. (2020, October 29). Truth decay: A conversation with Michael Rich of the RAND Corporation. *Freefacts*. https://www.freefacts.org/ftf-blog/truth-decay-a-conversation-with-michael-rich-of-the-rand-corporation

Bolman, L. G., & Deal, T. E. (1992). What makes a team? *Organizational Dynamics*, *21*(2), 34–44. https://www.sciencedirect.com/science/article/abs/pii/009026169290062R

Bolton, R. (1979). *People skills: How to assert yourself, listen to others, and resolve conflicts*. New York: Simon & Schuster.

Bonchek, M., & Gonzalez, M. (2018, February 23). 5 ways to get over your fear of public speaking. *Harvard Business Review*. https://hbr.org/2018/02/5-ways-to-get-over-your-fear-of-public-speaking

Bormann, E. G. (1986). Symbolic convergence theory and group decision making. In R. Y. Hirokawa & M. S. Poole (Eds.), *Communication and group decision making* (pp. 81–114). SAGE.

Bormann, E. G. (1990). *Small group communication: Theory and practice*. Harper & Row.

Bortz, D. (2021). Workplace bullying: What can you do? *Monster*. https://www.monster.com/career-advice/article/workplace-bullying-what-can-you-do

Bostrom, R. (1970). Patterns of communicative interaction in small groups. *Speech Monographs, 37*(4), 257–263.

Boudreau, J. (2007, August 21). China prepares to welcome world to 2008 Olympics. *San Jose Mercury News.* https://www.mercurynews.com/2007/08/12/china-prepares-to-welcome-world-to-2008-olympics/

Boughton, M. (2011). *Power, influence tactics, and influence processes in virtual teams.* Unpublished doctoral dissertation, University of North Carolina. http://libres.uncg.edu/ir/uncc/f/Boughton_uncc_0694D_10213.pdf

Bower, S., & Bower, G. (1976). *Asserting yourself.* Addison-Wesley.

Bradberry, T. (2019). How successful people overcome toxic bosses. *TalentSmart.* https://www.talentsmart.com/articles/How-Successful-People-Overcome-Toxic-Bosses-779784437-p-1.html

Bragg, D., Bennett, C., Reinecke, K., & Ladner, R. (2018). A large inclusive study of human listening rates. *Proceedings of the 2018 CHI Conference on Human Factors in Computing Systems.* https://doi.org/10.1145/3173574.3174018

Brainstorming rules. (2021). Innovation Training.org. https://www.innovationtraining.org/brainstorming-rules/

Brannigan, M. (1997, May 30). Why Delta Air Lines decided it was time for CEO to take off. *Wall Street Journal,* pp. A1, A8.

Braun, S. (2017, May 19). Leader narcissism and outcomes in organizations: A review at multiple levels of analysis and implications for future research. *Frontiers of Psychology.* https://www.ncbi.nlm.nih.gov/pmc/articles/PMC5437163/

Brehm, J. (1972). *Responses to loss of freedom: A theory of psychological resistance.* General Learning Press.

Brodie, I. (2021). Debunking the myths of nonverbal communication. *Ianbrodie.com.* https://www.ianbrodie.com/debunking-the-myths-of-non-verbal-communication/

Brown, D. (2013, December 29). Living in a digital minefield. *San Jose Mercury News,* pp. A1 & A16.

Brown, L. (2019, April 26). Does business writing matter anymore? The answer seems to be "yes." *Forbes.* https://www.forbes.com/sites/laurambrown/2019/04/26/does-business-writing-matter-anymore-the-answer-seems-to-be-yes/?sh=1a0243d53284

Brown, S., & Bryant, P (2015). Getting to know the elephant: A call to advance servant leadership through construct consensus, empirical evidence, and multilevel theoretical development. *Servant Leadership: Theory and Practice, 2*(1), 10–35.

Brown, Z. C., Anicich, E. M., & Galinisky, A. D. (2021, March 19). Does your office have a jargon problem? *Harvard Business Review.* https://hbr.org/2021/03/do-you-have-a-jargon-problem

Brownell, J. (2008). Exploring the strategic ground for listening and organizational effectiveness. *Scandinavian Journal of Hospitality and Tourism, 8*(3), 211–229. https://doi.org/10.1080/15022250802305295

Brownell, J. (2019). *The listening advantage: Outcomes and applications.* Routledge.

Bruk, D. (2017, November 2). The 30 biggest cultural mistakes Americans make abroad. *BestLife.* https://bestlifeonline.com/major-cultural-mistakes/

Brunell, A. B., Gentry, W. A., Campbell, W. K., Hoffman, B. J., Kuhnert, K. W., & DeMarree, K. G. (2008). Leader emergence: The case of the narcissistic leader. *Personality and Social Psychology Bulletin, 34*(12), 1663–1676.

Bryant, A. (2013, June 19). In head-hunting, big data may not be such a big deal. *New York Times.* https://www.nytimes.com/2013/06/20/business/in-head-hunting-big-data-may-not-be-such-a-big-deal.html

Bryant, M., & Higgins, V. (2010). Self-confessed troublemakers: An interactionist view of deviance during organizational change. *Human Relations, 63*(2), 249–277.

Buckingham, M., & Coffman, C. (1999). *First, break all the rules: What the world's greatest managers do differently.* Simon & Schuster.

Burger, J. M. (2009). Replicating Milgram: Would people still obey today? *American Psychologist, 64*(1), 1–11.

Burkus, D. (2013, September 10). Brainstorming is dead; long live brainstorming. *Forbes.* https://www.forbes.com/sites/davidburkus/2013/09/10/brainstorming-is-dead-long-live-brainstorming/#6ead496e307b

Burn-Callender, R. (2015, August 12). Beware of business consultant charlatans. *The Telegraph.* http://www.telegraph.co.uk/business/sme-home/beware-of-business-consultant-charlatans/

Callahan, S. (2018, December 28).Picture perfect: Make a great first impression with your LinkedIn profile photo. *Linked In*. https://www.linkedin.com/business/sales/blog/b2b-sales/picture-perfect--make-a-great-first-impression-with-your-linkedi

Canary, D. J., & Lakey, S. (2013). *Strategic conflict*. New York: Routledge.

Carey, H. R., & Laughlin, P. R. (2012). Groups perform better than the best individuals on letters-to-numbers problems: Effects of induced strategies. *Group Processes and Intergroup Relations*, *15*(2), 231–242.

Carleton, R. N. (2016). Fear of the unknown: One fear to rule them all? *Journal of Anxiety Disorders*, *41*, 5–21. https://www.sciencedirect.com/science/article/pii/S0887618516300469

Carnevale, P., & Probst, T. (1998). Social values and social conflict in creative problem solving. *Journal of Personality and Social Psychology*, *74*(5), 1300–1309.

Carr, A. (2010, May 18). The most important leadership quality for CEOs? Creativity. *Fast Company*. http://www.fastcompany.com/1648943/most-important-leadership-quality-ceos-creativity

Carr, C. (2017, August 22). Social media and intergroup communication. *Oxford Research Encyclopedia*. https://oxfordre.com/communication/view/10.1093/acrefore/9780190228613.001.0001/acrefore-9780190228613-e-460

Carton, A. (2017a). "I'm not mopping floors, I'm putting a man on the moon": How NASA leaders enhanced the meaningfulness of work by changing the meaning of work. *Administrative Science Quarterly*, *63*(2), 323–369. https://doi.org/10.1177%2F0001839217713748

Carton, A. (2017b, March 16). Meaningful work: What leaders can learn from NASA and the space race. *Knowledge@Wharton*. http://knowledge.wharton.upenn.edu/article/what-leaders-can-learn-from-nasa

Cash, R., Varker, T., McHugh, T., Metcalf, O., Howard, A., Lloyd, D., Costello, J., Said, D., & Forbes, D. (2018). Effectiveness of an anger intervention for military members with PTSD: A clinical case series. *Military Medicine*, *183*(9–10), e286–e290. https://academic.oup.com/milmed/article/183/9-10/e286/4922538

Castles, A. (2017, October 5). Why Atlassian is using a rubber chicken named Helmut to run more effective meetings. *Smart Company*. https://www.smartcompany.com.au/startupsmart/advice/atlassian-using-rubber-chicken-called-helmut-run-effective-meetings/

Castrillon, C. (2020, December 27). This is the future of remote work in 2021. https://www.forbes.com/sites/carolinecastrillon/2021/12/27/this-is-the-future-of-remote-work-in-2021/?sh=58baea6d1e1d%22+https%3A%2F%2Fwww.forbes.com%2Fsites%2Fcarolinecastrillon%2F2021%2F12%2F27%2Fthis-is-the-future-of-remote-work-in-2021%2F%3Fsh

Caulderwood, K. (2013, October 8). Delta Airlines (DAL) CEO Richard Allen charts independent course: Buying a refinery, half of a rival, and avoiding gas guzzlers. *International Business Times*.

Chaker, A. M. (2021, December 20). We're cursing more. Blame the #%$ pandemic. *The Wall Street Journal*. https://www.wsj.com/articles/were-cursing-more-blame-the-pandemic-11640008801

Chambers, J. (2020, August 11). Top 9 spam filters available in the market. *Astra*. https://www.getastra.com/blog/knowledge-base/best-spam-filters-for-emails/

Chamorro-Premuzic, T. (2019). *Why do so many incompetent men become leaders?* Harvard Business Review Press.

Chamorro-Premuzic, T., & Akhtar, R. (2021, August 3). 3 traits you need to thrive in a hybrid work environment. *Harvard Business Review*. https://hbr.org/2021/08/3-traits-you-need-to-thrive-in-a-hybrid-work-environment

Chan, M. S., Jones, C. R., & Jamieson, K. H. (2017). Debunking: A meta-analysis of the psychological efficacy of messages countering misinformation. *Psychological Science*, *28*(11), 1531–1546. https://doi.org/10.1177%2F0956797617714579

Charges alleging sex-based harassment FY 2010—FY 2020 (Charges file with EEOC). (2021). *U.S. Equal Employment Opportunity Commission*. https://www.eeoc.gov/statistics/charges-alleging-sex-based-harassment-charges-filed-eeoc-fy-2010-fy-2020

Chen, G.-M. (2011). An introduction to key concepts in understanding the Chinese: Harmony as the foundation of Chinese communication. *China Media Research*, *7*(4), 1–12. https://core.ac.uk/download/pdf/56694323.pdf

Chen, S., Geluykens, R., & Chong, J. C. (2006). The importance of language in global teams: A linguistic perspective. *Management International Review*, *46*(6), 679–696.

Cherry, K. (2019, September 30). 11 methods for improving your memory. *VeryWellMind*. https://www.verywellmind.com/great-ways-to-improve-your-memory-2795356

Cherry, K. (2021, July 30). How multitasking affects productivity and brain health. *VeryWellMind*. https://www.verywellmind.com/multitasking-2795003

Cherry, K., & Morin, A. (2019, September 18). What is passive-aggressive behavior? *VeryWell Mind*. https://www.verywellmind.com/what-is-passive-aggressive-behavior-2795481

Chion, J. (2013, October 24). What it's like to work at IDEO. *The Future of Work*. https://medium.com/future-of-work/what-its-like-to-work-at-ideo-6ca2c961aae4

Chira, S. (2017, June 14). The universal phenomenon of men interrupting women. *The New York Times*. https://www.nytimes.com/2017/06/14/business/women-sexism-work-huffington-kamala-harris.html

Cho, M., & Keltner, D. (2020). Power, approach, and inhibition: Empirical advances of a theory. *Current Opinion in Psychology, 33*, 196–200. https://doi.org/10.1016/j.copsyc.2019.08.013

Christensen, C. M., & Raynor, M. E. (2003, September). Why hard-nosed executives should care about management theory. *Harvard Business Review*. https://hbr.org/2003/09/why-hard-nosed-executives-should-care-about-management-theory

Cirque du Soleil on teamwork and creativity. (2011, June 28). *Business Banter*. http://businessbanter.wordpress.com/2011/06/28/cirque-du-soleil-on-teamwork-and-creativity

Clawson, L. (2014, July 11). Company tracks worker bathroom visits so it can punish people who need to pee too much. *Daily Kos*. https://www.dailykos.com/stories/2014/7/11/1313307/-Company-tracks-worker-bathroom-visits-so-it-can-punish-people-who-need-to-pee-too-much

Clifford, C. (2017, July 27). What young Jeff Bezos wanted to be when he grew up—It had nothing to do with e-commerce. *CNBC*. https://www.cnbc.com/2017/07/27/what-jeff-bezos-wanted-to-be-when-he-grew-up.html

Clouse, C. J. (2018, January 10). It's lonely at the top for people of color in corporate America—and CEOs know it. *Huffington Post*. https://www.huffingtonpost.com/entry/corporate-america-is-lonely-at-the-top-for-people-of-color_us_5a552b29e4b003133ecd51c8

Cohen, A. (2020, November 18). How to have difficult conversations. *Psyche*. https://psyche.co/guides/use-mediation-techniques-to-overcome-the-muck-of-blame-and-anger?utm_source=Aeon+Newsletter&utm_campaign=09dc819d49-EMAIL_CAMPAIGN_2021_08_10_01_03&utm_medium=email&utm_term=0_411a82e59d-09dc819d49-70832891

Cole, M. (2016, March 21). What makes a good manager: The case for listening and assessing skills. *Association for Talent Development*. https://www.td.org/Publications/Blogs/Management-Blog/2016/03/Makes-a-Good-Manager-the-Case-for-Listening-and-Assessing-Skills

Cole, S. (2015, February 26). New research shows we're all bad listeners who think we work too much. *Fast Company*. https://www.fastcompany.com/3042863/new-research-shows-were-all-bad-listeners-who-think-we-work-too-much

Conflict is destructive in the workplace, but it can be addressed. (2018, April 9). *Harvard Business Review*. https://www.physicianleaders.org/news/conflict-is-destructive-in-the-workplace-but-it-can-be-addressed

Connely, C. (2018, April 30). Jeff Bezos' 'two pizza rule' can help you hold more productive meetings. https://www.cnbc.com/2018/04/30/jeff-bezos-2-pizza-rule-can-help-you-hold-more-productive-meetings.html

Connley, C. (2020, May 19). The number of women running Fortune 500 companies hits a new high. *CNBC*. https://www.cnbc.com/2020/05/19/the-number-of-women-running-fortune-500-companies-hits-a-new-high.html

Cook, G. (2015, March–April). All together now. *Scientific American Mind*, p. 5457.

Cote, S., Lopes, P. N., Salovey, P., & Miners, C. T. H. (2010). Emotional intelligence and leadership emergence in small groups. *The Leadership Quarterly, 21*(3), 496–508.

Cotton, G. (2013, August 13). Gestures to avoid in cross-cultural business: In other words, "Keep your fingers to yourself." *Huffington Post*. http://www.huffingtonpost.com/gayle-cotton/cross-cultural-gestures_b_3437653.html

Covey, S. (2008). *The speed of trust: The one thing that changes everything*. Free Press.

Coyle, D. (2018). *The culture code: The secrets of highly successful groups*. Bantam Books.

Create your own chat room in 4 steps in 1 minute. (2020, May 29). *Y99.in*. https://y99.in/posts/create-your-own-chat-room/

Creating value in integrative negotiations: Myth of the fixed-pie of resources. (2022, April 11). *Program on Negotiation/Harvard Law School*. https://www.pon.harvard.edu/daily/negotiation-skills-daily/when-the-pie-seems-too-small/?utm_source=WhatCountsEmail&utm_medium=daily&utm_date=2020-09-24-13-30-00&mqsc=E4120720

Critical leadership skills. (2014, March). The Everest Leadership Academy: *The Ken Blanchard Companies* [slides]. http://www.everestla.org/images/pdfs/4_3%20Critical%20Leadership%20Skills%20-%20Ken%20Blanchard.pdf

Cross, R., Rebele, R., & Grant, A. M. (2016, January 1). Collaborative overload. *Harvard Business Review*. https://hbr.org/product/collaborative-overload/R1601E-HCB-ENG?referral=03069

Crowdfunding. (2021, August 11). *Business.gov*. https://business.gov.au/finance/seeking-finance/crowdfunding

Cuddy, A. (2015). *Presence: Bringing your boldest self to your biggest challenges*. Little, Brown and Company.

Curseu, P. L., & Schruijer, S. G. L. (2010). Does conflict shatter trust or does trust obliterate conflict? Revisiting the relationships between team diversity, conflict, and trust. *Group Dynamics: Theory, Research, and Practice, 14*(1), 66–79.

D'Angelo, M. (2018, November 4). How to find a mentor. *Business News Daily*. https://www.businessnewsdaily.com/6248-how-to-find-mentor.html

Daimler, M. (2016, May 25). Listening is an overlooked leadership tool. *Harvard Business Review*. https://hbr.org/2016/05/listening-is-an-overlooked-leadership-tool

Data creation and replication will grow at a faster rate than installed storage capacity, according to the IDC GlobalDatasphere and StorageSphere forecasts. (2021, March 24). International Data Corporation. https://www.idc.com/getdoc.jsp?containerId=prUS47560321

Datz. L. (2020, October 17). "America is experiencing 'truth decay' at an alarming rate, experts warn." *Syracuse University News*. https://news.syr.edu/blog/2020/10/17/america-is-experiencing-truth-decay-at-an-alarming-rate-experts-warn/

Davis, J., Frechette, H. M., & Boswell, E. H. (2010). *Strategic speed: Mobilize people, accelerate execution*. Harvard Business Press.

De Dreu, C. K. W., & Van Vianen, A. E. M. (2001). Responses to relationship conflict and team effectiveness. *Journal of Organizational Behavior, 22*, 309–328.

De Rose, B. (2018, April 3). Cry me a river: How emotions are perceived in the workplace. *Robert Half*. http://rh-us.mediaroom.com/2018-04-03-Cry-Me-A-River-How-Emotions-Are-Perceived-In-The-Workplace

Dean, J. (2021, June). Social loafing: When groups are bad for productivity. *Psyblog*. https://www.spring.org.uk/2021/06/social-loafing.php

Debies-Carl, J. S. (2017, November/December). Pizzagate and beyond: Using social research to understand conspiracy legends. *Skeptical Inquirer, 41*(6), 34–37.

Deggans, E. (2012). *Race-baiter: How the media wields dangerous words to divide a nation*. Palgrave Macmillan.

Delbecq, A., Van de Ven, A. H., & Gustafson, D. H. (1975). *Group techniques for program planning*. Scott, Foresman.

Derber, C. (1979). *The pursuit of attention: Power and individualism in everyday life*. Oxford University Press.

DeRuy, E. (2018). The old college try. *Mercury News*, pp. 1A, 6A.

DeStephen, R., & Hirokawa, R. (1988). Small group consensus: Stability of group support of the decision, task process, and group relationships. *Small Group Research, 19*(2), 227–239.

DeVries, D. (2019, May 23). Successful innovation labs have these four things in common. *IDEO*. https://www.ideo.com/journal/successful-innovation-labs-have-these-four-things-in-common

DeWees, B. (2016, May 19). Want to build an effective team? Check your ego at the door. *Task & Purpose*. https://taskandpurpose.com/want-build-effective-team-check-ego-door

Dewey, J. (1910). *How we think*. Heath.

Dhawan, E. (2021a, May 7). Did you get my slack/email/text? *Harvard Business Review*. https://hbr.org/2021/05/did-you-get-my-slack-email-text

Dhawan, E. (2021b). *Digital body language: How to build trust & connection, no matter the distance.* St. Martin's Press.

Digital, D. J. (2020, May 23). Weight Watchers slammed for firing 4,000 employees on a Zoom call. *HOT 107.9.* https://1079ishot.com/weight-watchers-fire-employees-on-zoom-call/

Dildar, S., & Amjad, N. (2017). Gender differences in conflict resolution styles (CRS) in different roles: A systematic review. *Pakistan Journal of Social and Clinical Psychology, 15*(2), 37–41. https://gcu.edu.pk/wp-content/uploads/2020/04/pjscp20172-6.pdf

Dinh, J. V., Traylor, A. M., Kilcullen, M. P., Perez, J. A., Schweissing, E. J., Venkatesh, A., & Salas, E. (2020). Cross-disciplinary care: A systematic review on teamwork processes in health care. *Small Group Research, 51*(1), 125–166. https://doi.org/10.1177%2F1046496419872002

Dishman, L. (2015, June 11). The science of why we talk too much (and how to shut up). *Fast Company.* https://www.fastcompany.com/3047285/the-science-of-why-we-talk-too-much-and-how-to-shut-up

Diversity at IDEO. (2019). *IDEO.* https://www.comparably.com/companies/ideo/diversity

Dixon-Fyle, S., Dolan, K., Hunt, V., & Prince, S. (2020, May 19). Diversity wins: How inclusion matters. *McKinsey & Company.* https://www.mckinsey.com/featured-insights/diversity-and-inclusion/diversity-wins-how-inclusion-matters

Dol, Q. (2020, February 5). Inside HQ1: The coolest features at Amazon's Seattle headquarters. *Built in Seattle.* https://www.builtinseattle.com/2019/03/08/coolest-features-amazon-seattle-headquarters

Dominant leaders are bad for groups. Why do they succeed? (2018, January 8). *Association for Psychological Science.* https://www.psychologicalscience.org/news/minds-business/dominant-leaders-are-bad-for-groups.html

Donohue, W., & Kolt, R. (1992). *Managing interpersonal conflict.* Sage.

Doodle. The state of meetings report. (2019). https://meeting-report.com/

Dorfman, P. W., Hanges, P. J., & Brodbeck, F. C. (2004). Leadership and cultural variation: The identification of culturally endorsed leadership profiles. In R. J. House, P. J. Hanges, M. Javidan, P. W. Dorfman, & V. Gupta (Eds.), *Culture, leadership, and organizations: The GLOBE study of 62 societies.* SAGE.

Dorfman, P. W. (2004). International and cross-cultural leadership research. In B. J. Punnett & O. Shenkar (Eds.), *Handbook for international management research* (pp. 265–355). University of Michigan Press.

Dotan-Eliaz, O., Sommer, K. L., & Rubin, Y. S. (2009). Multilingual groups: Effects of linguistic ostracism on felt rejection and anger, coworker attraction, perceived team potency, and creative performance. *Basic and Applied Social Psychology, 31*(4), 363–375.

Dougherty, K. M., & Sutton, R. M. (1994). Conforming first impressions in the employment interview. *Journal of Applied Psychology, 79,* 659–665.

Dovidio, J. F., Saguy, T., & Shnabel, N. (2009). Cooperation and conflict within groups: Bridging intragroup and intergroup processes. *Journal of Social Issues, 65*(2), 429–449.

Driskell, J., Radtke, P., & Salas, E. (2003). Virtual teams: Effects of technological mediation on team performance. *Group Dynamics: Theory, Research, and Practice, 7*(4), 297–323. https://doi.apa.org/doi/10.1037/1089-2699.7.4.297

Druskat, V. U., & Wolff, S. B. (1999). Effects and timing of developmental peer appraisals in self-managing work groups. *Journal of Applied Psychology, 84*(1), 58–74.

Duarte, N. (2012, October 22). Do your slides pass the glance test? *Harvard Business Review.* https://hbr.org/2012/10/do-your-slides-pass-the-glance-test

Dubrin, A. J. (2019). *Leadership: Research findings, practice, and skills.* Cengage.

Duhigg, C. (2016, February 25). What Google learned from its quest to build the perfect team. *The New York Times.* https://www.nytimes.com/2016/02/28/magazine/what-google-learned-from-its-quest-to-build-the-perfect-team.html

Duncan, P., & Topping, A. (2018, December 6). Men underestimate level of sexual harassment against women—survey. *The Guardian.* https://www.theguardian.com/world/2018/dec/06/men-underestimate-level-of-sexual-harassment-against-women-survey

Dunning, D. (2017, June 14). We are all confident idiots. *Pacific Standard.* https://psmag.com/social-justice/confident-idiots-92793

Dutton, K. (2016, September/October). Would you vote for a psychopath? *Scientific American Mind, 27*(5), 50–55.

Ebert, R. J. & Griffin, R. W. (2011). *Leadership and decision making*. Pearson.

Ebrahim, N. A., Ahmed, S., & Taha, Z. (2009). Virtual teams: A literature review. *Australian Journal of Basic and Applied Sciences, 3*(3), 2653–2669.

Economy, P. (2019, January 11). A new study of 19 million meetings reveals that meetings waste more time than ever (but there is a solution). https://www.inc.com/peter-economy/a-new-study-of-19000000-meetings-reveals-that-meetings-waste-more-time-than-ever-but-there-is-a-solution.html

Edelman Trust Barometer. (2019). *Edelman.com*. https://www.edelman.com/trust-barometer

Edelman, R. (2019, January 21). Trust at work. *Edelman.com*. https://www.edelman.com/insights/trust-at-work

Edinger, S. (2018, June 29). Stop scheduling conference calls and finally commit to videoconferencing. *Harvard Business Review*. https://hbr.org/2018/06/stop-scheduling-conference-calls-and-finally-commit-to-videoconferencing

Edmondson, A. C., & Mortensen, M. (2021, April 19). What psychological safety looks like in a hybrid workplace. *Harvard Business Review*. https://hbr.org/2021/04/what-psychological-safety-looks-like-in-a-hybrid-workplace?utm_medium=email&utm_source=newsletter_weekly&utm_campaign=insider_activesubs&utm_content=signinnudge&deliveryName=DM129267

Elgoibar, P., Euweman, M., & Munduate, L. (2017, June 28). Conflict management. *Oxford Research Encyclopedia*. https://oxfordre.com/psychology/view/10.1093/acrefore/9780190236557.001.0001/acrefore-9780190236557-e-5

Eligon, J. (2020, June 26). A debate over identity and race asks, are African-Americans "Black" or "black"? *New York Times*. https://www.nytimes.com/2020/06/26/us/black-african-american-style-debate.html

Elliott, M. (2017, June 29). 11 job skills employers wished young people had (and how to get them). *CheatSheet*. http://www.cheatsheet.com/money-career/job-skills-employers-wished-young-people-had-how-get-them.html/?a=viewall

Ellison, S. (2009). *Taking the war out of words*. Deadwood, OR: Wyatt-MacKenzie Publishing.

Elsesser, K. (2019, March 15). Women can use humor at work, but they should follow this advice. *Forbes*. https://www.forbes.com/sites/kimelsesser/2019/03/15/women-can-use-humor-at-work-but-they-should-follow-this-advice/#73830d2d3625

Email subject lines: 5 tips to attract readers. (2022). *Nielsen Norman Group*. https://www.nngroup.com/articles/email-subject-lines/

Enders, A., König, A., & Barsoux, J.-L. (2016, June 13). Stop jumping to solutions. *MIT Sloan Management Review*. https://sloanreview.mit.edu/article/stop-jumping-to-solutions/

Eseryel, U. Y., Crowston, K., & Heckman, R. (2021). Functional and visionary leadership in self-managing virtual teams. *Group & Organization Management, 46*(2), 424–460. https://journals.sagepub.com/doi/full/10.1177/1059601120955034

Evans, C. R., & Dion, K. L. (2012). Group cohesion and performance: A meta-analysis. *Small Group Research, 43*(6), 690–701.

Fadiman, C. (1985). *The Little, Brown Book of anecdotes*. Little Brown & Company.

Fairhurst, G. (2011). *The power of framing: Creating the language of leadership*. Jossey-Bass.

Fancher, L. (2016, June 17). Dacher Keltner's "The Paradox of Power" dishes the details on its uses and abuses. *Mercury News*. https://www.mercurynews.com/2016/06/17/dacher-keltners-the-power-paradox-dishes-the-details-on-its-uses-and-abuses

FAQ. Twitter, Inc.—Contact—FAQ. (n.d.). https://investor.twitterinc.com/contact/faq

Farwell, S (2017). Managing in a multicultural workplace. *The Ayers Group*. http://www.ayers.com/uploadedFiles/Ayers/6-About_Us/News_and_Articles/Consultants_Corner/managinginamulticulturalworkplacellnew.pdf

Felmlee, D., Rodis, P. I., & Zhang, A. (2019). Sexist slurs: Reinforcing feminine stereotypes. *Sex Roles: A Journal of Research, 83*(1–2), 16–28.

Felps, W., Mitchell, T. R., & Byington, E. (2006). How, when, and why bad apples spoil the barrel: Negative group members and dysfunctional groups. *Research in Organizational Behavior, 27*(3), 175–222.

Ferenczi, N., Marshall, T. C., & Bejanyan, K. (2017). Are sex differences in antisocial and prosocial Facebook use explained by narcissism and relational self-construal? *Computers in Human Behavior, 77*, 25–31.

Ferrazzi, K. (2014, December). Getting virtual teams right. *Harvard Business Review.* https://hbr.org/2014/12/getting-virtual-teams-right

Ferrazzi, K. (2017, March 27). How to run a great virtual meeting. *Harvard Business Review.* https://hbr.org/2015/03/how-to-run-a-great-virtual-meeting

Ferrazzi, K., Race, M-C, & Vincent, A. (2021, January 21). 7 strategies to build a more resilient team. *Harvard Business Review.* https://hbr.org/2021/01/7-strategies-to-build-a-more-resilient-team

Fidler, J. (2022, January 27). New data: How the amount of text and images impact email click-through rates. *Constant Contact.* https://blogs.constantcontact.com/email-images/

Fiedler, F., & House, R. (1988). Leadership theory and research: A report of progress. In C. Cooper & I. Robertson (Eds.), *International review of industrial and organizational psychology.* John Wiley & Sons.

Finn, A. N., Sawyer, C. R., & Schrodt, P. (2009). Examining the effect of exposure therapy on public speaking state anxiety. *Communication Education, 58*(1), 92–109. https://doi.org/10.1080/03634520802450549

Fisher, R., & Brown, S. (1988). *Getting together: Building a relationship that gets to yes.* Houghton Mifflin.

Fisher, R., & Shapiro, D. (2005). *Beyond reason: Using emotions as you negotiate.* Penguin Books.

Fleming, N. (2020, June 17). Coronavirus misinformation, and how scientists can help to fight it. *Nature.* https://www.nature.com/articles/d41586-020-01834-3

Folger, J., Poole, M., & Stutman, R. (1993). *Working through conflict: Strategies for relationships, groups, and organizations.* HarperCollins.

Fong, K., & Mar, R. A. (2015). What does my avatar say about me? inferring personality from avatars. *Personality and Social Psychology Bulletin, 41*(2), 237–249. https://doi.org/10.1177/0146167214562761

Ford, H. (2003). *My life and work.* Kessinger Publishing.

Forsyth, D. (2014). *Group dynamics.* Wadsworth, Cengage Learning.

Fostering constructive conflict in team negotiation. (2020, December 3). *Program on Negotiation/Harvard Law School.* https://www.pon.harvard.edu/daily/conflict-resolution/fostering-constructive-conflict-in-teams-nb/

Four conflict negotiation strategies for resolving value-based disputes. (2020, June 16). *Program on Negotiation/Harvard Law School.* https://www.pon.harvard.edu/daily/dispute-resolution/four-negotiation-strategies-for-resolving-values-based-disputes/

Foulke, E. (2006). Listening comprehension as a function of word rate. *Journal of Communication, 18,* 198–206.

Foust, D. (2009, May 14). How Delta climbed out of bankruptcy. *Bloomberg Businessweek.* https://www.bloomberg.com/news/articles/2009-05-14/how-delta-climbed-out-of-bankruptcy

Fragale, A. R. (2006). The power of powerless speech: The effects of speech style and task interdependence on status control. *Organizational Behavior and Human Decision Processes, 101*(2), 243–261.

Franganillo, J. (2017, May). Information overload, why it matters and how to combat it. *Interaction Design Foundation.* https://www.interaction-design.org/literature/article/information-overload-why-it-matters-and-how-to-combat-it

Fredrickson, B. L. (2010). *Positivity: Top-notch research reveals the 3-to-1 ratio that will change your life.* Three Rivers Press.

Friedman, R., Anderson, C., Brett, J., Olekalns, M., Goates, N., & Lisco, C. C. (2004). The positive and negative effects of anger in dispute resolution: Evidence from electronically mediated disputes. *Journal of Applied Psychology, 89*(2), 369–376.

Frisch, B., & Greene, C. (2016, April 8). The right way to cut people off in meetings. *Harvard Business Review.* https://hbr.org/2016/04/the-right-way-to-cut-people-off-in-meetings

Fry, R. (2019, June 20). U.S. women near milestone in the college-educated labor force. *Pew Research.* https://www.pewresearch.org/fact-tank/2019/06/20/u-s-women-near-milestone-in-the-college-educated-labor-force/?

Fulwiler, M. (2018). Managing conflict: Solvable vs. perpetual problems. *The Gottman Institute.* https://www.gottman.com/blog/managing-conflict-solvable-vs-perpetual-problems/

Galimberti, A. (2018, January 30). Lives on the line: The human cost of cheap chicken. *Oxfam America.* https://www.iatp.org/sites/default/files/2018-02/Oxfam%20Poultry%20Webinar%20with%20IATP.pdf

Gallo, C. (2018, January 12). *Steve Jobs practiced 1 habit that turned good presentations into Great Ones*. Inc.com. https://www.inc.com/carmine-gallo/steve-jobs-practiced-1-habit-that-turned-good-presentations-into-great-ones.html#:~:text=The%20answer%3A%2020%20for%2020

Gallo, C. (2019, April 24). *There was a brilliant strategy behind Steve Jobs' penchant for using huge, 190-point text on his presentation slides*. Business Insider. https://www.businessinsider.com/steve-jobs-used-190-point-text-on-presentation-slides-2019-4

Gallo, C. (2019, November 13). *How to look and sound confident during a presentation*. Harvard Business Review. https://hbr.org/2019/10/how-to-look-and-sound-confident-during-a-presentation

Gallo, C. (2021). Public speaking is no longer a "soft skill". It's your key to success in any field. *Inc.* https://www.inc.com/carmine-gallo/public-speaking-is-no-longer-a-soft-skill-its-your-key-to-success-in-any-field.html

Gandhi, Rujuta. (2019, February 4). How to lead a meeting people want to attend. https://www.gallup.com/workplace/246314/lead-meeting-people-attend.aspx

Garber, M. (2016, May 25). Casual Friday and the "end of the office dress code." *The Atlantic*. https://www.theatlantic.com/entertainment/archive/2016/05/casual-friday-and-the-end-of-the-office-dress-code/484334/

Garner, B. A. (2013, March 21). A Bizspeak Blacklist. *Harvard Business Review*. https://hbr.org/2013/03/a-bizspeak-blacklist

Garner, B. A. (2013). *HBR Guide to better business writing*. Harvard Business Review

Garrett, R. K., Weeks, B. E., & Neo, R. L. (2016). Driving a wedge between evidence and beliefs: How online ideological news exposure promotes political misperceptions. *Journal of Computer-Mediated Communication*, 21(5), 331–348. https://doi.org/10.1111/jcc4.12164

Garton, E. (2017, April 25). How to be an inspiring leader. *Harvard Business Review*. https://hbr.org/2017/04/how-to-be-an-inspiring-leader

Gastil, J., Burkhalter, S., & Black, L. W. (2007). Do juries deliberate? A study of deliberation, individual difference, and group member satisfaction at a municipal courthouse. *Small Group Research*, 38(3), 337–359.

Gavin, M. (2019, October 31). Leadership vs. management: What's the difference? *Harvard Business School Online*. https://online.hbs.edu/blog/post/leadership-vs-management

Gaynor, J. (n.d.). 3 Social media red flags recruiters notice. *p.* https://www.monster.com/career-advice/article/3-social-media-red-flags-recruiters-notice-1016

Gelles, D. (2021, April 25). CEO pay remains stratospheric, even at companies battered by pandemic. *The Mercury News*, p. A6.

Gen Z & Millennials' 5 favorite social media platforms now (2020, May 6). *YPulse*. https://www.ypulse.com/article/2020/05/06/gen-z-millennials-5-favorite-social-media-platforms-now/

Gentry, W. A., Weber, T. J., & Sadri, G. (2016). Empathy in the workplace: A tool for effective leadership. Center for Creative Leadership. http://www.ccl.org/wp-content/uploads/2015/04/EmpathyInTheWorkplace.pdf

Gettler, L. (2016, March 4). Three common business mistakes made in Asia (and how to avoid them). *Bluenotes*. https://bluenotes.anz.com/posts/2016/03/three-common-business-mistakes-made-in-asia-and-how-to-avoid-them

Geyser, W. (2022, February 15). TikTok statistics—revenue, Users & Engagement Stats (2022). *p.* https://influencermarketinghub.com/tiktok-stats/

Giang, V. (2015, May 19). What kind of leadership is needed in flat hierarchies? *Fast Company*. https://www.fastcompany.com/3046371/what-kind-of-leadership-is-needed-in-flat-hierarchies

Gibb, J. (1961). Defensive communication. *Journal of Communication*, 11(3), 141–148.

Gilani, P., Bolat, E., Nordberg, D., & Wilkin, C. (2019). Mirror, mirror on the wall: Shifting leader-follower power dynamics in a social media context. *Leadership*, 16(3), 343–363. https://doi.org/10.1177%2F1742715019889817

Giles, S. (2016, March 15). The most important leadership competencies, according to leaders around the world. *Harvard Business Review*.

Glikson, E., Cheshin, A., & van Kleef, G. A. (2017). The dark side of a smiley: Effects of smiling emoticons on virtual first impressions. *Social Psychological and Personality Science*, 9(5), 614–625. https://doi.org/10.1177%2F1948550617720269

Glomb, T. M. (2002). Workplace anger and aggression: Informing conceptual models with data from specific encounters. *Journal of Occupational Health Psychology, 7*(1), 20–36.

Glynn, M. A., & DeJordy, R. (2010). Leadership through an organizational behavior lens: A look at the last half-century of research. In N. Nohria & R. Khurana (Eds.), *Handbook of leadership and practice* (pp. 119–158). Harvard Business Press.

Godin, S. (2007, January 29). Really bad powerpoint. *Seth's Blog.* https://seths.blog/2007/01/really_bad_powe

Godwin, C. A., Hunter, M. A., Bezdek, M. A., Lieberman, G., Elkin-Frankston, S., Romero, V. L., Witkiewitz, K., Clark, V. P., & Schumacher, E. H. (2017, July 10). *Functional connectivity within and between intrinsic brain networks correlates with Trait mind wandering.* Neuropsychologia. https://pubmed.ncbi.nlm.nih.gov/28705691/

Goff-Dupont, S. (2019, February 27). 6 types of meetings that are worthwhile. https://www.atlassian.com/blog/teamwork/types-of-meetings

Goldenberg, O., Larson, J. R., & Wiley, J. (2013). Goal instructions, response formats, and idea generation in groups. *Small Group Research, 44*(3), 227–256.

Goleman, D. (1995). *Emotional intelligence: Why it can matter more than I.Q.* Bantam Books.

Goleman, D. (2013). *Focus: The hidden driver of excellence.* HarperCollins.

Gomez, K., Mawhinney, T., & Betts, K. (2019). Welcome to Generation Z. *Deloitte.* https://www2.deloitte.com/content/dam/Deloitte/us/Documents/consumer-business/welcome-to-gen-z.pdf

Goodreau, J (2016, January 16). A Harvard psychologist says people judge you based on 2 criteria when they first meet you. *Business Insider.* http://www.businessinsider.com/harvard-psychologist-amy-cuddy-how-people-judge-you-2016-1

Gosnell, K. (2018, September 28). How to respond to a leadership attack. *Linkedin.* https://www.linkedin.com/pulse/how-respond-leadership-attack-ken-gosnell

Gottman, J. M., & Gottman, J. S. (2006). *10 lessons to transform your marriage.* Crown.

Gottman, J. M., & Silver, N. (1999). *The seven principles for making marriage work.* Crown.

Goudreau, J. (2012, November 16). The 10 worst communication mistakes for your career. *Forbes.* https://www.forbes.com/sites/jennagoudreau/2012/11/16/the-10-worst-communication-mistakes-for-your-career/#431084e67562

Govier, T. (2010). *A practical study of argument.* Wadsworth.

Grace, D. M., & Platow, M. J. (2015). Showing leadership by not showing your face: An anonymous leadership effect. *SageOpen, 5*(1), 1–10.

Graduate Management Admission Council. (2017). Corporate recruiters survey report 2017. https://www.gmac.com/market-intelligence-and-research/research-library/employment-outlook/2017-corporate-recruiters-survey-report

Grant, A. (2016). *Originals: How non-conformists move the world.* Penguin Books.

Grant, A. (2021, February 18). Who won't shut up in meetings? Men say it's women. It's not. *The Washington Post.* https://www.washingtonpost.com/outlook/2021/02/18/men-interrupt-women-tokyo-olympics/

Grant, M. (2021, Spring). Words matter: Guidelines for pronoun usage. *The Academic Author.*

Gray, K. (2021, April 19). The attributes employers seek on students' resumes. *National Association of Colleges and Employers.* https://www.naceweb.org/talent-acquisition/candidate-selection/the-attributes-employers-seek-on-students-resumes/?utm_source=spotlight-college

Green, A. (2018, February 1). A university negotiates accusations of autocratic leadership. *Program on Negotiation/Harvard Law School.* https://www.pon.harvard.edu/daily/leadership-skills-daily/a-university-negotiates-accusations-of-autocratic-leadership/?utm_source=WhatCountsEmail&utm_medium=daily&utm_date=2018-02-01-13-55-00&mqsc=E3933802

Greengross, G., & Miller, G. F. (2008). Dissing oneself versus dissing rivals: Effects of status, personality, and sex on the short-term and long-term attractiveness of self-deprecating and other-deprecating humor. *Evolutionary Psychology Journal, 6*(3), 393–408.

Greenleaf, R. K. (1977). *Servant leadership: A journey into the nature of legitimate power and greatness.* Paulist.

Greer, L. L., De Jong, B., Schouten, M., & Dannals, J. (2018). Why and when hierarchy impacts team effectiveness: A meta-analytic examination. *Journal of Applied Psychology, 103*(6), 591–613. https://doi.apa.org/doi/10.1037/apl0000291

Greer, L. L., Jehn, K. A., & Manniz, E. A. (2008). Conflict transformation: A longitudinal investigation of the relationship between different types of intragroup conflict and the moderating role of conflict resolution. *Small Group Research, 39*, 278–302.

Grenny, J. (2009). Crucial conversations: The most potent force for eliminating disruptive behavior. *Physician Executive Journal, 35*(6), 30–33.

Grenny, J. (2019, June 17). How to be resilient in the face of harsh criticism. *Harvard Business Review.* https://hbr.org/2019/06/how-to-be-resilient-in-the-face-of-harsh-criticism

Grenny, J., & Maxfield, D. (2017a, January 27). 9 ways to stop a workplace bully. *Leaderonomics.* https://leaderonomics.com/leadership/ways-to-stop-workplace-bullying

Grenny, J., & Maxfield, D. (2017b, November 2). A study of 1,100 employees found that remote workers feel shunned and left out. *Harvard Business Review.* https://hbr.org/2017/11/a-study-of-1100-employees-found-that-remote-workers-feel-shunned-and-left-out

Griffin, E., Ledbetter, A., & Sparks, G. (2019). *A first look at communication theory.* McGraw-Hill.

Griffith, E. (2018, April 17). 19 massive corporate social media horror stories. *PC Magazine.* https://www.pcmag.com/feature/335422/19-massive-corporate-social-media-horror-stories

Grohol, J. M. (2018). What is catastrophizing? *Psych Central.* https://psychcentral.com/lib/what-is-catastrophizing/

Guenter, H., Emmerik, I. H., Schreurs, B., Kuypers, T. (2016). When task conflict becomes personal: The impact of perceived team performance. *Small Group Research, 47*(5): 569–604. https://www.researchgate.net/publication/308191206_When_Task_Conflict_Becomes_Personal_The_Impact_of_Perceived_Team_Performance

Gundemir, S., Homan, A. C., de Dreu, C. K. W., & van Vugt, M. (2014). Think leader, think white? Capturing and weakening an implicit pro-White leadership bias. *PLOSOne, 9*(1). https://www.ncbi.nlm.nih.gov/pmc/articles/PMC3885528/

Gunkel, M., Schlaegel, C., & Taras, V. (2016). Cultural values, emotional intelligence, and conflict handling styles: A global study. *Journal of World Business, 51*(4), 568–585.

Habel, M. (2015, July 1). Building collegial nurse-physician relationships. *OT Today.* http://ortoday.com/building-collegial-nurse-physician-relationships/

Hacker, J. V., Johnson, M., Saunders, C., & Thayer, A. L. (2019). Trust in virtual teams: A multidisciplinary review and integration. *Australasian Journal of Information Systems, 23.* https://doi.org/10.3127/ajis.v23i0.1757

Hackman, M., & Johnson, C. (2018). *Leadership: A communication perspective.* Waveland Press.

Haden, J. (2013, March 14). 8 most common complaints about the boss. *Inc.* https://www.inc.com/jeff-haden/8-most-common-complaints-employees-have-about-their-boss.html

Hadley, C. N., & Mortensen, M. (2022, April 26). Do we still need Teams? *Harvard Business Review.* https://hbr.org/2022/04/do-we-still-need-teams?utm_medium=email&utm_source=newsletter_weekly&utm_campaign=insider_activesubs&utm_content=signinnudge&deliveryName=DM190227

Hall, E. (1981). *Beyond culture.* Doubleday.

Hall, G. C. N. (2017, February 7). The platinum rule. *Psychology Today.* https://www.psychologytoday.com/blog/life-in-the-intersection/201702/the-platinum-rule

Hall, J. A., & Bernieri, F. J. (2001). *Interpersonal sensitivity: Theory and measurement.* Lawrence Erlbaum.

Hambley, C. (2020, February 3). Five strategies for building a better medical team. *Physicians Practice.* https://www.physicianspractice.com/view/five-strategies-building-better-medical-team

Hannah, R. (2019, March 20). Dynamic Signal's annual state of employee communication and engagement study—the 2019 findings are in! *Dynamic Signal.* https://resources.dynamicsignal.com/news-room/dynamic-signal-study-finds-u-s-workforce-stressed-and-ready-to-quit

Hansen, B. (2021, May 16). 7 techniques for more effective brainstorming. *Wrike.* https://www.wrike.com/blog/techniques-effective-brainstorming/

Hanson, R. (2016, October 26). Confronting the negativity bias. *Rickhanson.net.* http://www.rickhanson.net/how-your-brain-makes-you-easily-intimidated/

Harrison, D. A., Price, K. H., Gavin, J. H., & Florey, A. T. (2002). Time, teams, and task performance: Changing attitudes of surface and deep-level diversity on group functioning. *Academy of Management Journal, 45*(5), 1029–1045.

Harrison, L. E. (2000). Introduction. In L. E. Harrison & S. P. Huntington (Eds.), pp. 296-308.

Culture matters: How values shape human progress. Basic Books.

Hart, J. W., Bridgett, D. J., & Karau, S. J. (2001). Coworker ability and effort as determinants of individual effort on a collective task. *Group Dynamics: Theory, Research, and Practice, 5*(3), 181–190.

Hashish, E. A., Hamouda, G. H., & Taha, E. E. (2015). Nursing students' perception of conflict management styles of their nursing educators. *Journal of Education and Practice, 6*(21), 21–31.

Haslam, S. A., & Knight, C. (2010, September/October). Cubicle, sweet cubicle. *Scientific American Mind*, pp. 31–35.

Haslam, S. A., & Reicher, S. D. (2012, July/August). In search of charisma. *Scientific American Mind, 23*(3) pp. 42–49.

Haslam, S. A., Reicher, S. D., & Platow, M. J. (2011). *The new psychology of leadership: Identity, influence and power*. Psychology Press.

Hastie, R., & Kameda, T. (2005). The robust beauty of majority rules in group decision. *Psychological Review, 112*(2), 494–508.

Hastings, R. R. (2012, August 17). Bosses seen as ineffective conflict managers. *SHRM*. https://www.shrm.org/resourcesandtools/hr-topics/employee-relations/pages/bosses-seen-as-ineffective-conflict-managers.aspx

Hayes, J. (2008, July). Workplace conflict and how business can harness it to thrive. *CPP Global Human Capital Report*. https://shop.cpp.com/Pdfs/CPP_Global_Human_Capital_Report_Workplace_Conflict.pdf

Hayes, L. N. (2018, August 9). More than half of employers have found content on social media that caused them NOT to hire a candidate, according to recent CareerBuilder survey. *CareerBuilder*. http://press.careerbuilder.com/2018-08-09-More-Than-Half-of-Employers-Have-Found-Content-on-Social-Media-That-Caused-Them-NOT-to-Hire-a-Candidate-According-to-Recent-CareerBuilder-Survey

Haynie, D. (2016, May 10). Millennial leaders around the world. *U.S. News & World Report*. https://www.usnews.com/news/best-countries/slideshows/10-millennial-leaders-around-the-globe

Heneghan, S., & Mahtani, K. R. (2020, May 26). Leadership in COVID-19: The dangers of groupthink in crisis leadership. *Centre for Evidence-Based Medicine*. https://www.cebm.net/covid-19/leadership-in-covid-19-the-dangers-of-groupthink-in-crisis-leadership/

Henricks, M. (2018, October 30). "The mantle of leadership isn't held only by one pay grade. *Provoke Media*. https://www.holmesreport.com/latest/article/the-mantle-of-leadership-isn-t-held-only-by-one-pay-grade

Henry, C. Y., & Yeung, D. Y. (2020). Conflict between younger and older workers: An identity-based approach. *International Journal of Conflict Management, 32*(1), 102–125. https://doi.org/10.1108/IJCMA-08-2019-0124

Hershey, T. (2021). Living spiritual teachers project. *Spirituality & Practice*. https://www.spiritualityandpractice.com/explorations/teachers/terry-hershey/quotes

Higginbottom, K. (2018, May 31). Why empathy matters in the workplace. *Forbes*. https://www.inkl.com/news/why-empathy-matters-in-the-workplace

Hiring Managers "Spell Out" the Biggest Deal-Breakers Regarding Job Candidates' Resumes. (2018, February 2). *Talent Inc* https://www.talentinc.com/press-2018-02-14

Hodge, N. (2020, April 1). Fake facts: What the rise of disinformation campaigns means for businesses. *Risk Management*. http://www.rmmagazine.com/2020/04/01/fake-facts-what-the-rise-of-disinformation-campaigns-means-for-businesses/

Hoffeld, D. (2015, April). The science of effective PowerPoint presentations. *Hoffeld Group*. https://www.hoffeldgroup.com/wp-content/uploads/2015/04/Science-of-Effective-PowerPoint-Presentations.pdf

Hofherr, J. (2016, March 17). You're "cyberloafing" right now. Here's how your employer might stop that one day. *Boston.com*. https://www.boston.com/jobs/jobs-news/2016/03/17/youre-cyberloafing-right-now-heres-employer-might-stop-one-day

Hofstede, G (2012). Dimensionalizing cultures: The Hostede model in context. In S. A. Samovar, R. E. Porter, & E. R. McDaniel (Eds.), *Intercultural communication: A reader*. Wadsworth/Cengage.

Hofstede, G., & Hofstede, G. J. (2010). *Cultures and organizations: Software of the mind*. McGraw-Hill.

Hollander, E., & Offerman, L. (1990, February). Power and leadership in organizations. *American Psychologist, 45*(2), 179–189.

Holohan, M. (2020, May 15). Masks make communicating hard—here's how to help. *TODAY.com*. https://www.today.com/health/how-communicate-mask-people-who-are-deaf-or-hard-hearing-t181586

Hoption, C., Barling, J., & Turner, N. (2013). "It's not you, it's me": Transformational leadership and self-deprecating humor. *Leadership & Organizational Development Journal, 34*(1), 4–19.

Horila, T., & Siitonen, M. (2020). A time to lead: Changes in relational leadership processes over time. *Management Communication Quarterly, 34*(4), 558–584. https://journals.sagepub.com/doi/full/10.1177/0893318920949700

Hornsey, M. J., Robson, E., Smith, J., Esposo, S., & Sutton, R. M. (2008). Sugaring the pill: Assessing rhetorical strategies designed to minimize defensive reactions to group criticism. *Human Communication Research, 34*(1), 70–98.

Hosman, L. A., & Siltanen, S. A. (2006). Powerful and powerless language forms: Their consequences for impression formation, attributions of control of self and control of others, cognitive responses, and message memory. *Journal of Language and Social Psychology, 25*(1), 33–46.

House, R. J. (2004). Illustrative examples of GLOBE findings. In R. J. House, P. J. Hanges, M. Javidan, P. W. Dorfman, & V. Gupta (Eds.), *Culture, leadership, and organizations: The GLOBE study of 62 societies* (pp. 3–8). Sage.

House, R. J., & Aditya, R. N. (1997). The social scientific study of leadership: Quo vadis? *Journal of Management, 23*(3), 409–473.

Howard, J. W. (2008). "Tower, am I cleared to land?": Problematic communication in aviation discourse. *Human Communication Research, 34*, 370–391. https://doi.org/10.1111/j.1468-2958.2008.00325.x

How we got from 1 to 162 million websites on the internet. (2008, April 4). *Solarwinds Pingdom*. https://www.pingdom.com/blog/how-we-got-from-1-to-162-million-websites-on-the-internet/

Howell, E. & Hickok, K. (2022, March 31). Apollo 13: Facts about NASA's near-disaster moon mission. *Space.com*. https://www.space.com/17250-apollo-13-facts.html

Howell, S. E. (2014, September/October). Conflict management: A literature review and study. *Radiology Management*. http://www.ahra.org/AM/Downloads/OI/qc/RM365_p14-23_Features.pdf

Howell, W. S. (1982). *The empathic communicator*. Wadsworth.

Hughes, A., Gregory, M., Joseph, D., & Sonesh, S. C. (2016). Saving lives: A meta-analysis of team training in healthcare. *Journal of Applied Psychology, 101*(9). https://www.researchgate.net/publication/304032216_Saving_Lives_A_Meta-Analysis_of_Team_Training_in_Healthcare

Hung, K.-P., & Lin, C.-K. (2013). More communication is not always better? The interplay between effective communication and interpersonal conflict in influencing satisfaction. *Industrial Marketing Management, 42*(8), 1223–1232.

Hunt, V., Layton, D. & Prince, S. (2015, February 2). Diversity matters. *McKinsey & Company*. https://www.mckinsey.com/business-functions/people-and-organizational-performance/our-insights/~/media/2497d4ae4b534ee89d929cc6e3aea485.ashx

Husband, R. (1992). Leading in organizational groups. In R. Cathcart & L. Samovar (Eds.), *Small group communication* (pp. 464–476). Wm. C. Brown & Company.

Huss, N. (2021, March 19). How many websites are there around the world? [2010]. *Siteefy*. https://siteefy.com/how-many-websites-are-there/#How-many-websites-are-there-in-the-World?

Hutchinson, A. (2021, March 30). LinkedIn adds new profile features, including video cover stories and "creator mode". *Social Media Today*. https://www.socialmediatoday.com/news/linkedin-adds-new-profile-features-including-video-cover-stories-and-crea/597578/

Hyun, J. (2020, April 1). American innovation challenge: Embracing other cultures' values to fight COVID-19. *Fast Company*. https://www.fastcompany.com/90485082/american-innovation-challenge-embracing-other-cultures-values-to-fight-covid-19

Iglesias, M. E. L., & Vallejo, R. B. (2012). Conflict resolution styles in nursing profession. *Contemporary Nurse, 43*(1), 73–80.

Integrative negotiation examples: MESOs and expanding the pie. (2017, May 18). *Program on Negotiation/Harvard Law School*. https://www.pon.harvard.edu/daily/dealmaking-daily/limit-their-options%E2%80%94and-expand-the-pie/

Intel code of conduct. (2020). *Intel*. https://www.intel.com/content/www/us/en/policy/policy-code-conduct-corporate-information.html

Internet world users by language. (2020, March 31). *Internet World Stats.* https://www.internet-worldstats.com/stats7.htm

Interview: Clifford Nass. (2010, February 2). *Frontline.* http://www.pbs.org/wgbh/pages/frontline/digitalnation/interviews/nass.html

Isaac, M. L. (2012). "I hate group work!" Social loafers, indignant peers, and the drama of the classroom. *The English Journal, 101*(4), 83–89. https://www.jstor.org/stable/41415478

Isaksen, S. G., & Gaulin, J. P. (2005). A reexamination of brainstorming research: Implications for research and practice. *Gifted Child Quarterly, 49*(4), 315–329.

Jacobs, J., & Harrison, C. (2019, April 9). Doctor dragged off United Airlines flight after watching viral video of himself: "I just cried." *ABC News.* https://abcnews.go.com/US/doctor-dragged-off-united-airlines-flight-watching-viral/story?id=62250271

Jaffe, E. (2012). Give and take: Empirical strategies for compromise. *Observer, 25,* 9–11.

Jaksa, J., & Pritchard, M. (1994). *Communication ethics: Methods of analysis.* Wadsworth.

Janis, I. (1982). *Groupthink: Psychological studies of policy decisions and fiascoes.* Houghton Mifflin.

Janusik, L. (2020, July). *Research findings on Listening—Global Listening Centre.* https://www.globallisteningcentre.org/wp-content/uploads/2020/07/research-findings-on-listening-laura-janusik.pdf

Jargon. JARGON | definition in the Cambridge English Dictionary. (n.d.). https://dictionary.cambridge.org/us/dictionary/english/jargon

Jaworski, M. (2019, May 23). The negativity bias: Why the bad stuff sticks. *Psycom.* https://www.psycom.net/negativity-bias

Jehn, K. A. (1995). A multimethod examination of the benefits and detriments of intragroup conflict. *Administrative Science Quarterly, 40*(2), 256–282.

Jenkins, S., & Delbridge, R. (2016). Trusted to deceive: A case study of "strategic deception" and the normalization of lying at work. *Organizational Studies, 38*(1), 53–76.

Jerabek, I., & Muoio, D. (2017, October). Lone wolf, lone sheep: Why some of the best-and worst employees hate teamwork. *ResearchGate.* Jerabek/publication/320456667_Lone_Wolf_Lone_Sheep_Why_Some_Of_The_Best-And_Worst-Employees_Hate_Teamwork/links/59e661650f7e9b13aca3c53b/Lone-Wolf-Lone-Sheep-Why-Some-Of-The-Best-And-Worst-Employees-Hate-Teamwork.pdf

Jiang, J., Chen, C., Dai, B., Shi, G., Ding, G., Liu, L., & Lu, C. (2015). Leader emergence through interpersonal neural synchronization. *Proceedings of the National Academy of Sciences of the United States of America, 112*(14), 4274–4279.

Jiang, M. (2020, April 22). The reason Zoom calls drain your energy. *BBC.* https://www.bbc.com/worklife/article/20200421-why-zoom-video-chats-are-so-exhausting

Johnson, C. (2009). Bad blood: Doctor-nurse behavior problems impact patient care. *Physician Executive Journal, 35*(6), 6–11.

Johnson, D. W. (2003). Social interdependence: Interrelationships among theory, research, and practice. *American Psychologist, 58*(11), 934–945. https://doi.apa.org/doi/10.1037/0003-066X.58.11.934

Johnson, C., & Hackman, M. Z. (2019). *Leadership: A communication perspective.* Waveland Press.

Johnson, D. W., & Johnson, R. T. (2000, June). Teaching students to be peacemakers; Results of twelve years of research. https://www.ojp.gov/ncjrs/virtual-library/abstracts/teaching-students-be-peacemakers-results-twelve-years-research

Johnson, D. W., Johnson, R. T., & Smith, K. A. (2014). Cooperative learning: Improving university instruction by basing practice on validated theory. *Journal of Excellence in College Teaching, 25*(3–4), 85–118.

Jones, E. E., & Kelly, J. R. (2007). Contributions to a group discussion and perceptions of leadership: Does quantity always count more than quality? *Group Dynamics: Theory, Research, and Practice, 11*(1), 15–30.

Jordan, M. H., Feild, H. S., & Armenakis, A. A. (2002). The relationships of group process variables and team performance. *Small Group Research, 33*(1), 121–150.

Josephson, M. (2002). *Making ethical decisions.* Josephson Institute of Ethics.

Judge, T. A., & Piccolo, R. F. (2004). Transformational and transactional leadership: A meta-analytic test of their relative validity. *Journal of Applied Psychology, 89*(5), 755–768.

Kafle, H. R. (2014). Symbolic convergence theory: Revisiting its relevance to team communication. *International Journal of Communication*, *24*(1), 16–29.

Kahlow, J., Klecka, H., & Ruppel, E. (2020). What the differences in conflict between online and face-to-face work groups mean for hybrid groups: A state-of-the-art review. *Review of Communication Research*, 8, 50–77. https://www.rcommunicationr.org/index.php/rcr/article/view/53/61

Kameda, N. (2007). Communicative challenges for Japanese companies: Strategies in the global marketplace. In *Proceedings of the Association for Business Communication 7th Asia-Pacific Conference*. Association for Business Communication.

Kameda, N. (2014). Japanese business discourse of oneness: A personal perspective. *International Journal of Business Communication, 51*(1), 93–113.

Karau, S. J., & Elsaid, A. M. M. K. (2009). Individual differences in beliefs about groups. *Group Dynamics: Theory, Research, and Practice, 13*(1), 1–13.

Karpowitz, C. F., Mendelberg, T., & Shaker, L. (2012). Gender inequality in deliberative participation. *American Political Science Review, 106*(3), 533–547.

Kaspersky. (2021, May 26). Americans face digital amnesia as connected devices are increasingly trusted to recall memories. usa.kaspersky.com. https://usa.kaspersky.com/about/press-releases/2015_americans-face-digital-amnesia-as-connected-devices-are-increasingly-trusted-to-recall-memories

Kavanagh, J., & Rich, M. D. (2018). *Truth decay: A threat to policymaking and democracy*. Rand.

Kavanagh, K. T., Saman, D., Bartel, R., & Westerman, K. (2017). Estimating hospital-related deaths due to medical error: A perspective from patient advocates. *Journal of Patient Safety, 13*(1), 1–5.

Keashly, L., & Neuman, J. H. (2009). Building a constructive communication climate: the workplace stress and aggression project. In P. Lutgen-Sandvik and B. D. Sypher (Eds.), *Destructive organizational communication: Processes, consequences, & constructive ways of organizing* (pp. 339–362). Routledge.

Keating, E. (2020, October 20). Why do virtual meetings feel so weird? *Sapiens*. https://www.sapiens.org/language/nonverbal-communication-online/

Kelakos, E. (2020, June 29). 5 ways to beat zoom performance anxiety (ZPA). *The Eleni Group*. https://theelenigroup.com/2020/06/5-ways-to-beat-zoom-performance-anxiety-zpa/

Keller, S., & Meaney, M. (2017, June 28). High-performing teams: A timeless leadership topic. *McKinsey & Company*. https://www.mckinsey.com/business-functions/organization/our-insights/high-performing-teams-a-timeless-leadership-topic

Kelley, T., & Littman, J. (2001). *The art of innovation*. Doubleday.

Kelley, T., & Littman, J. (2005). *The ten faces of innovation*. Doubleday.

Kelly, L., & Keaten, J. A. (2000). Treating communication anxiety: Implications of the communibiological paradigm. *Communication Education, 49*(1), 45–57. https://doi.org/10.1080/03634520009379192

Keltner, D. (2007, December 1). The power paradox. *Greater Good Magazine*. https://greatergood.berkeley.edu/article/item/power_paradox

Keltner, D. (2016a). *The power paradox*. Penguin Press.

Keltner, D. (2016b, May 18). Why leaders must give away power in order to keep influence. *Fortune*. https://fortune.com/2016/05/18/power-paradox-influence/

Kenski, K., Coe, K., & Rains, S. A. (2020). Perceptions of uncivil discourse online: An examination of types and predictors. *Communication Research, 47*(6), 795–814. https://doi.org/10.1177%2F0093650217699933

Kerwin, S., Doherty, A., & Harman, A. (2011). "It's not conflict, it's differences of opinion": An in-depth examination of conflict in nonprofit boards. *Small Group Research, 42*(5), 562–594.

Khademi, M., Schmidt-Mast, M., & Frauendorfer, D. (2020). From hierarchical to egalitarian: Hierarchy steepness depends on speaking time feedback and task interdependence. *Group Dynamics: Theory, Research, and Practice, 24*(4), 261–275. https://psycnet.apa.org/doi/10.1037/gdn0000114

Khan, A. K., Moss, S., Quratulain, S., & Hameed, I. (2016). When and how subordinate performance leads to abusive supervision: A social dominance perspective. *Journal of Management, 44*(7), 2801–2826. https://doi.org/10.1177%2F0149206316653930

Kim, K., Kim, J., Antonio, J., & Laws, J. (2021, September 7). Emotional intelligence, trust, and functional behavior: Longitudinal study of achievement approach to leadership emergence. *Journal of Organizational Psychology*, *21*(4), 181–192. https://articlegateway.com/index.php/JOP/article/view/4552

Kingsford-Smith, A. (2017, July 12). Cirque du Soleil: The circus that took over the world. *The Culture Trip*. https://theculturetrip.com/north-america/canada/quebec/articles/cirque-du-soleil-the-circus-that-took-over-the-world

Kirkman, B., & Rosen, B. (1999). Beyond self-management: Antecedents and consequences of team empowerment. *Academy of Management Journal*, *42*(1), 58–74.

Kirkman, B. L., Rosen, B., Tesluk, P. E., & Gibson, C. B. (2004). Team empowerment on virtual team performance: The moderating role of face-to-face interaction. *Academy of Management Journal*, *47*(2), 175–192.

Klein, C., DiazGranados, D., Salas, E., Le, H., Burke, C. S., & Goodwin, G. F. (2009). Does teambuilding work? *Small Group Research*, *40*(2), 181–222.

Kluger, J. (2009, March 2). Why bosses tend to be blowhards. *Time*, *173*(8), 48.

Knapp, M. L., Hall, J. A., & Horgan, T. G. (2014). *Nonverbal communication in human interaction*. Cengage.

Knight, R. (2015, August 21). How to stop micromanaging your team. *Harvard Business Review*. https://hbr.org/2015/08/how-to-stop-micromanaging-your-team

Knights, J. (2017). *How to develop ethical leaders*. Routledge. https://www.routledge.com/posts/9951

Knight, R. (2020, January 10). *How to work with a bad listener*. Harvard Business Review. https://hbr.org/2017/08/how-to-work-with-a-bad-listener

Knutson, T. J., & Posirisuk, S. (2006). Thai relational development and rhetorical sensitivity as potential contributors to intercultural communication effectiveness. JAI YEN YEN. *Journal of Intercultural Communication Research*, *35*(3), 205–217.

Knutson, T. J., Komolsevin, R., Chatiketu, P., & Smith, V. R. (2003). A cross-cultural comparison of Thai and U.S. American rhetorical sensitivity: Implications for intercultural communication effectiveness. *International Journal of Intercultural Relations*, *27*(1), 63–78.

Ko, V. (2013, April 14). Can you cope with criticism at work? *CNN*. http://www.cnn.com/2013/04/14/business/criticism-praise-feedback-work-life/index.html

Koenig, A. M., Eagly, A. H., Mitchell, A. A., & Ristikari, T. (2011). Are leader stereotypes masculine? A meta-analysis of three research paradigms. *Psychological Bulletin*, *137*(4), 616–642.

Koirala, B. (2020, March 19). 10 pros and cons of LinkedIn for professional profile. *HPC*. https://honestproscons.com/pros-and-cons-of-linkedin/

Kolmar, C. (2022, April 5). Average number of jobs in a lifetime [2022]: All statistics. *Zippia*. https://www.zippia.com/advice/average-number-ber-jobs-in-lifetime/

Konstantinova, M., & Astakhova, K. (2018, November 16). Experts say . . . Is communication really only 7% verbal? Truth vs. marketing. *Medium Marketing*. https://medium.com/@neurodatalab/experts-say-is-communication-really-only-7-verbal-truth-vs-marketing-9a8e7428fd0f

Korde, R. M., & Paulus, P. (2017). Alternating individual and group idea generation: Finding the elusive synergy. *Journal of Experimental Social Psychology*, *70*(5), 177–190. https://doi.org/10.1016/j.jesp.2016.11.002

Korman, J. (2020, December 1). Why employee surveys, like political polls, are misleading. *Strategy+Business*. https://www.strategy-business.com/blog/Why-employee-surveys-like-political-polls-are-misleading?gko=6a04e

Kossovsky, N. (2017, September 13). CEOs' personal reputations at risk as corporate attacks mount. *Industry Week*. https://www.industryweek.com/leadership/article/22024175/ceos-personal-reputations-at-risk-as-corporate-attacks-mount

Kowalski, S. W. J. (2018). Enhancing the effectiveness of work groups and teams: A reflection. *Perspectives on Psychological Science*, *13*(2), 205–212.

Kozlowski, W. J., & Ilgen, D. R. (2006). Enhancing the effectiveness of work groups and teams. *Psychological Science in the Public Interest*, *7*(3), 77–124.

Kozusznik, M. W., Aaldering, H., & Euwema, M. C. (2020). Star(tup) wars: Decoupling task from relationship conflict. *International Journal of*

Conflict Management, 31(3), 393–415. https://doi.org/10.1108/IJCMA-09-2019-0167

Kraft, R. N. (2017, June 23). Why we forget: The benefits of not remembering. *Psychologytoday.com.* https://www.psychologytoday.com/us/blog/defining-memories/201706/why-we-forget

Krauss, R. M., Freyberg, R., & Morsella, E. (2002). Inferring speakers' physical attributes from their voices. *Journal of Experimental Social Psychology, 38*(6), 618–625.

Kristinsson, K., Jonsdottir, I. J., & Snorrason, S. K. (2019). Employees' perceptions of supervisors' listening skills and their work-related quality of life. *Communication Reports, 32*(3), 137–147. https://doi.org/10.1080/08934215.2019.1634748

Kruger, J., Epley, N., Parker, J., & Ng, Z.-W. (2005). Egocentrism over e-mail: Can we communicate as well as we think? *Journal of Personality and Social Psychology, 89*(6), 925–936.

LaFasto, F., & Larson, C. (2001). *When teams work best: 6,000 team members and leaders tell what it takes to succeed.* Sage.

Lam, C. (2015). The role of communication and cohesion in reducing social loafing in group projects. *Business and Professional Communication Quarterly, 78*(4), 454–475. https://journals.sagepub.com/doi/abs/10.1177/2329490615596417

Lamptey, E. J. (2021, September). Earning their trust: Getting your people to trust your leadership. *Academia/Letters.* https://www.academia.edu/55574045/EARNING_THEIR_TRUST_GETTING_YOUR_PEOPLE_TO_TRUST_YOUR_LEADERSHIP

Lapakko, D. (2007). Communication is 93% nonverbal: An urban legend proliferates. *Communication and Theater Association of Minnesota Journal, 34,* 7–19.

Larcker, D. F., Donatiello, N. E., & Tayan, B. (2016, February). Americans and CEO pay: 2016 public perception survey on CEO compensation. *Stanford Business.* https://www.gsb.stanford.edu/faculty-research/publications/americans-ceo-pay-2016-public-perception-survey-ceo-compensation

Lashbrook, A. (2020, July 22). Remote work can actually flip the power dynamic with your boss. *OneZero.* https://onezero.medium.com/remote-work-can-actually-flip-the-power-dynamic-with-your-boss-c6d232fbcbf

Lauby, S. (2015, March 31). The only 3 reasons to hold a business meeting. *Harvard Business Review.* https://www.hrbartender.com/2015/training/the-only-3-reasons-to-hold-a-business-meeting/

Laughlin, P. R., Hatch, E. C., Silver, J. S., & Boh, L. (2006). Groups perform better than the best individuals on letter-to-numbers problems: Effects of group size. *Journal of Personality and Social Psychology, 90*(4), 644–651.

Leaper, C., & Robnett, R. D. (2011). Women are more likely than men to use tentative language, aren't they? A meta-analysis testing gender differences and moderators. *Psychology of Women Quarterly, 35*(1), 129–142.

Lease, S. H. (2018). Assertive behavior: A double-edged sword for women at work. *Clinical Psychology: Science and Practice, 25*(1). https://onlinelibrary.wiley.com/doi/full/10.1111/cpsp.12226

Lee, C. (2014). Employee job satisfaction and engagement. *Society for Human Resource Management.* https://www.shrm.org/resourcesandtools/business-solutions/documents/2015-job-satisfaction-and-engagement-report.pdf

Lee, M. D., & Paradowski, M. J. (2007). Group decision-making on an optimal stopping problem. *The Journal of Problem Solving, 1*(2), 53–73.

Legg, T. J. (2019, February 01). What is catastrophizing? 6 ways to stop it. https://www.healthline.com/health/anxiety/catastrophizing

Lehr, S. (2020, June 11). How face masks impair communication for people who are deaf, hard of hearing. *Lansing State Journal.* https://www.lansingstatejournal.com/story/news/2020/06/11/covid-19-face-masks-creating-challenges-people-who-deaf/5309411002/

Leimbach, M. (2018). 2018 Leadership development survey: Are your next-gen leaders on track? *Training Magazine.* https://trainingmag.com/trgmag-article/2018-leadership-development-survey-are-your-next-gen-leaders-track/

Leiter, M. P., & Maslach, C. (2015, January/February). Conquering burnout. *Scientific American Mind, 26*(1), 30–35.

Leland, K. T. (2017, June 8). *New research shows that cursing can help you be a better public speaker.* Inc.com. https://www.inc.com/karen-tiber-leland/new-research-shows-that-cursing-can-help-you-be-a-better-public-speaker.html#:~:text=A%20new%20research%20paper%20published,between%20 swearing%20and%20emotional%20 arousal.&text=These%20psychology%20stud ies%20demonstrate%20that,a%20lack%20 of%20linguistic%20hygiene.

Lempp, F., Blackwood, K., & Gordon, M. (2020). Exploring the efficacy of mediation in cases of workplace bullying. *International Journal of Conflict Management, 31*(5), 665–685. https://doi .org/10.1108/IJCMA-09-2019-0145

Lencioni, P. (2004). *Death by meeting: A leadership fable about solving the most painful problem in business.* Wiley.

Lepsinger, R (2020, February 17). Virtual team failure: Six common reasons why virtual teams do not succeed. *Business Know-How.* https://www. businessknowhow.com/manage/virtualteam. htm

Lewin, K., Lippitt, R., & White, R. (1939). Patterns of aggressive behavior in experimentally created social climates. *Journal of Social Psychology, 10*(2), 271–299.

LGBT people's experiences of workplace discrimination and harassment. (2021, September). *UCLA School of Law Williams Institute.* https:// williamsinstitute.law.ucla.edu/publications/ lgbt-workplace-discrimination/

Liao, A. (2017, May 25). What's the most complicated word in English? *Bookstr.* https://www. bookstr.com/most-complicated-word-english

Lickerman, A. (2013, November 10). Dealing with anger. *Psychology Today.* https://www.psychologytoday.com/blog/happiness-in-world/201311/ dealing-anger

Lickermann, A. (2009, November 16). Eight ways to remember anything. *Psychology Today.* https:// www.psychologytoday.com/intl/blog/happiness-in-world/200911/eight-ways-remember-anything

Lilienfeld, S., Ammirati, R., & Landfield, K. (2009, July 1). *Giving debiasing away: Can Psychological Research on Correcting Cognitive Errors Promote Human Welfare?* https://www3. nd.edu/~ghaeffel/Lilienfeld2009%20Perspectives%20on%20Psychological%20Science.pdf

Linebaugh, K., & Knuston, R. (2020, April 7). Dr. Anthony Fauci on how life returns to normal— the journal.—WSJ podcasts. *The Wall Street Journal.* https://www.wsj.com/podcasts/the-journal/ dr-anthony-fauci-on-how-life-returns-to-normal/d5754969-7027-431e-89fa-e12788ed9879

LinkedIn: About Us. (n.d.). https://news.linkedin .com/about-us#Statistics

LinkedIn adds new profile features, including video cover stories and 'creator mode'. JMRConnect press room. (n.d.). https://press.jmrconnect.net/linkedin-adds-new-profile-features-including-video-cover-stories-and-creator-mode

Lipman, V. (2017, May 9). Why confidence is always a leader's best friend. *Forbes.* https://www .forbes.com/sites/victorlipman/2017/05/09/ why-confidence-is-always-a-leaders-best-friend/#6a2199d747be

Littlejohn, S. W., Foss, K. A., & Oetzel, J. G. (2021). *Theories of human communication.* Waveland Press.

Lopez, C., & Ward, M. (2020, June 5). 12 things you should never say to your LGBTQ coworkers. *Business Insider.* https://www.businessinsider.com/lgbtq-workers-discrimination-things-not-to-say-2019-9

Lopez-Garrido, G. (2020, August 9). Self-efficacy theory. *SimplyPsychology.* https://www.simply-psychology.org/self-efficacy.html

Lovett, M. (2016, August 14). Exploring the Mehrabian myth. *Storytelling with Impact.* https:// www.storytellingwithimpact.com/exploring-the-mehrabian-myth/

Lowry, P. B., Roberts, T. L., Romano, N. C., Cheney, P. D., & Hightower, R. T. (2006). The impact of group size and social presence on small-group communication: Does computer-mediated communication make a difference? *Small Group Research, 37*(6), 631–661.

Lublin, J. S. (2017, December 13). Talkaholics sink partnerships, presentations—and careers. *Wall Street Journal.* https://www.wsj.com/articles/ talkaholics-sink-partnerships-presentation-sand-careers-1513173600

Lugris, M. (2021, May 12). Advantages of using email in business communication. *Ueni.* https://ueni.com/blog/advantages-using-email-business-communication/

Lutgen-Sandvik, P. (2006). Take this job and . . .: Quitting and other forms of resistance to workplace bullying. *Communication Monographs, 73,* 406–433.

Lutgen-Sandvik, P., & Sypher, B. D. (2009). Workplace bullying: Causes, consequences, and corrections. In P. Lutgen-Sandvik & B. D. Sypher (Eds.), *Destructive organizational communication.* Routledge.

Lyubomirsky, S., King, L., & Diener, E. (2005). The benefits of frequent positive affect: Does happiness lead to success? *Psychological Bulletin*, *131*(6), 803–855.

MacDonald, L. (2019, March 7). What is a self-managed team? *Chron*. https://smallbusiness.chron.com/selfmanaged-team-18236.html

MacInnis, C. C., MacKinnon, S. P., & MacIntyre, P. D. (2010). The illusion of transparency and normative beliefs about anxiety during public speaking. *Current Research in Social Psychology*, *15*, Article 4. https://psycnet.apa.org/record/2010-15914-001

MacKay, J. (2018, July 10). Communication overload: Research shows most workers can't go 6 minutes without checking email or IM. *Medium: The Startup*. https://medium.com/swlh/communication-overload-research-shows-most-workers-cant-go-6-minutes-without-checking-email-or-im-8ef4392a7159

MacLennan, H. L. (2015). Incivility by degree: The influence of educational attainment on workplace civility. *Journal of Conflict Management*, *3*(1), 35–51.

Macrae, F. (2015, March 11). Twitter anger "is road rage": Psychologist says distance from victim and having vast platform to vent irritation encourages users to be more aggressive. *Daily Mail*. http://www.dailymail.co.uk/sciencetech/article-2989040/Twitter-anger-like-road-rage-Psychologist-says-distance-victim-having-vast-platform-vent-irritation-encourages-users-aggressive.html

Makela, L., Tanskanen, J., & De Cieri, H. (2020). Do relationships matter? Investigating the link between supervisor and subordinate dedication and cynicism via the quality of leader-member exchange. *Journal of Leadership & Organizational Studies*, *28*(1), 76–90. https://doi.org/10.1177%2F1548051820967010

Management consulting in the US. (2021, January 14). *IBIS World*. https://www.ibisworld.com/industry-statistics/market-size/management-consulting-united-states/

Maner, J. K. (2017). Dominance and prestige: A tale of two hierarchies. *Current Directions in Psychological Science*, *26*(6), 526–531.

Manolaki, A. (2016, August 30). Translating body language signs in different cultures. *Terminology Coordination: European Parliament*. http://termcoord.eu/2016/08/translating-body-language-signs-in-different-cultures/

March 2010 web server survey. (2010, March 17). *Netcraft*. https://news.netcraft.com/archives/2010/03/17/march_2010_web_server_survey.html

Maricchiolo, Fridanna & Gnisci, Augusto & Bonaiuto, Marino & Ficca, Gianluca. (2009). Effects of different types of hand gestures in persuasive speech on receivers' evaluations. *Language and Cognitive Processes*, 24. 239-266. 10.1080/01690960802159929.

Marinho, A.C.F., Medeiros, A. M., Gama, A.C.C., & Teixeira, L. C. (2017). Fear of public speaking: Perception of college students and correlates. *Journal of Voice*. https://www.researchgate.net/profile/Anna-Ferreira

Markham, A. (2022, February 14). 4 ways to follow up after a job interview. *Harvard Business Review*. https://hbr.org/2020/11/4-ways-to-follow-up-after-a-job-interview

Marsh, J. (2019). Why say it that way? Evasive answers and politeness theory. *Journal of Politeness Research, Language, Behaviour, Culture*, *15*(1), 55–75.

Martin, R. (2015, June 9). 5 ways to deal with angry people. *Psychology Today*. https://www.psychologytoday.com/us/blog/all-the-rage/201506/5-ways-deal-angry-people

Martin, R. C., Coyier, K. R., VanSistine, L. M., & Schroeder, K. L. (2013). Anger on the Internet: The perceived value of rant-sites. *Cyberpsychology, Behavior, and Social Networking*, *16*(2), 119–122.

Marvin, R. (2019, July 03). The weirdest, most obscure online courses you can take. *PCMag*. https://www.pcmag.com/picks/the-weirdest-most-obscure-online-courses-you-can-take

Matyszczyk, C. (2016, April 26). *This is the magic hour to schedule a presentation, according to science*. *Inc.com*. https://www.inc.com/chris-matyszczyk/this-is-the-best-time-of-day-to-schedule-a-big-presentation-according-to-science.html

Maxfield, D., Grenny, J., McMillan, R., Patterson, K., & Switzler, A. (2005). Silence kills: The seven crucial conversations in healthcare. *VitalSmarts*. https://org-fitness.blogs.com/SilenceKillsExecSummary.pdf

Maxwell, J. C. (2001). *The 17 indisputable laws of teamwork: Embrace them and empower your team*. Thomas Nelson.

May, P. (2007, May 26). Governor salutes rapid repair of Maze. *San Jose Mercury News*, pp. 1B, 6B.

Mayall, T. (n.d.). Weaknesses of Behavioural Interview Questions. https://recruitshop.com.au/blog/2015/12/27/weaknesses-of-behavioural-interview-questions/

Mayo, A. T., & Woolley, A. W. (2016). Teamwork in health care: Maximizing collective intelligence via inclusive collaboration and open communication. *AMA Journal of Ethics*, 18(9), 933–940. http://journalofethics.ama-assn.org/2016/09/stas2-1609.html

Mazarakis, A., & Shontell, A. (2017, November 25). 10 CEOs and top executives reveal their best leadership secrets. *Business Insider*. https://www.businessinsider.com/top-execs-tech-ceos-reveal-secrets-to-being-a-successful-leader-2017-11

McCluney, C. L., Robotham, K., Lee, S., Smith, R., & Durkee, M. (2019, November 15). The costs of code-switching. *Harvard Business Review*. https://hbr.org/2019/11/the-costs-of-codeswitching

McCoy, S. L., Tun, P. A., Cox, L. C., & Wingfield, A. (2005, July 1). Aging in a fast-paced world: Rapid speech and its effect on understanding. *The ASHA Leader*, 10(9), pp. 12, 30–31. https://doi.org/10.1044/leader.FTR7.10092005.12

McCracken, H. (2017, October). Microsoft rewrites the code. *Fast Company*, pp. 50–58.

McCue, T. J. (2020, February 5). The state of online video for 2020. *Forbes*. https://www.forbes.com/sites/tjmccue/2020/02/05/looking-deep-into-the-state-of-online-video-for-2020/?sh=ff07b162eac5

McCusker, B. (2019, May 15). Why you'll never see a Disney employee point with their index finger. *Reader's Digest*. https://www.yahoo.com/lifestyle/why-apos-ll-never-see-012749053.html?guccounter=1&guce_referrer=aHR0cHM6Ly93d3cuZ29vZ2xlLmNvbS8&guce_referrer_sig=AQAAALwlKwK2EL-PlP-Cyse9BSiCqCYFZ35KFiHJ9wsP4Qkaagq3a3c-1xVJ4_3_7uHSTWNQHF5Czfb62Blpk0ui5IaAsxc49_IkPr6bDC5DTtdNAZbbOjZ4IzRTyomMS-uk88_1jeTH3AlFl4GVElz9GwW7843GxHNLnETzqbLuCIopr

McEwan, D., Ruissen, G. R., Eys, M. A., Zumbo, B. D., & Beauchamp, M. R. (2017, January 13). The effectiveness of teamwork training on teamwork behaviors and team performance: A systematic review and meta-analysis of controlled interventions. *PLOS/One*. http://journals.plos.org/plosone/article?id=10.1371/journal.pone.0169604

McFadden, C., & Whitman, J. (2014, March 10). Sheryl Sandberg launches "Ban Bossy" campaign to empower girls to lead. *ABC News*. http://abcnews.go.com/US/sheryl-sandberg-launches-ban-bossy-campaign-empower-girls/story?id=22819181

McGregor, L., & Doshi, N. (2020, April 9). How to keep your team motivated, remotely. *Harvard Business Review*. https://hbr.org/2020/04/how-to-keep-your-team-motivated-remotely

McKay, B., & McKay, K. (2021, September 25). How to avoid conversational narcissism. The *Art of Manliness*. https://www.artofmanliness.com/character/etiquette/the-art-of-conversation-how-to-avoid-conversational-narcissism/

McKay, M., Rogers, P. D., & McKay, J. (2018, October 8). Anger triggers behaviors. *PsychCentral*. https://psychcentral.com/lib/anger-trigger-behaviors/

McKee, A. (2015, July 16). The emotional impulses that poison healthy teams. *Harvard Business Review*. https://hbr.org/2015/07/the-emotional-impulses-that-poison-healthy-teams

McMillan, D. (2009). Life after death by PowerPoint (corporate comedy video)—*YouTube*. https://www.youtube.com/watch?v=KbSPPFYxx3o

McQuaid, M. (2015, March 6). The strengths revolution transforming our workplaces. *Psychology Today*. https://www.huffingtonpost.com/michelle-mcquaid/the-strengths-revolution-transforming-our-workplace_b_6810192.html

McQueen, N. (2018, June 26). Workplace culture trends: The key to hiring (and keeping) top talent in 2018. *LinkedIn*. https://blog.linkedin.com/2018/june/26/workplace-culture-trends-the-key-to-hiring-and-keeping-top-talent

Medina, E. (2021, June 26). Fight and flight: T.S.A. to resume self-defense classes for airline crews. *The New York Times*. https://www.nytimes.com/2021/06/26/business/self-defense-course-tsa.html

Meetings: The good, the bad, and the ugly. (2015, September 16). *Wharton*. http://knowledge.wharton.upenn.edu/article/meetings-the-good-the-bad-and-the-ugly

Meet the anti-LGBT hate group that filed an amicus brief with the Alabama Supreme Court. (2015, November 13). *Southern Poverty Law Center*. https://www.splcenter.org/hatewatch/2015/11/13/meet-anti-lgbt-hate-group-filed-amicus-brief-alabama-supreme-court

Mehrabian, A. (1971). *Silent messages*. Wadsworth.

Melaku, T. M., Beeman, A., Smith, D. G., & Johnson, W. B. (2020, November–December). Be a better ally. *Harvard Business Review*. https://hbr.org/2020/11/be-a-better-ally

Meluso, J., Johnson, S., & Bagrow, J. (2020). Making virtual teams work: Redesigning collaboration for the future. *SocArXiv Papers*. https://bagrow.com/pdf/making-virtual-work-meluso-2020v1.pdf

Mendoza, N. F. (2020, *April 15)*. How too many virtual meetings can cause employee productivity to plummet. *Tech Republic*. https://www.techrepublic.com/article/how-too-many-virtual-meetings-cause-employee-productivity-to-plummet/

Meng, Y., He, J., & Luo, C. (2014). Science research group leader's power and members' compliance and satisfaction with supervision. *Research Management Review*, *20*(1), 1–15. https://files.eric.ed.gov/fulltext/EJ1022035.pdf

Merkin, R. (2015, November). The relationship between individualism/collectivism: Consultation and harmony needs. *Journal of Intercultural Communication*, *39*. https://www.researchgate.net/publication/272747249_The_Relationship_between_IndividualismCollectivism_Consultation_and_Harmony_Needs

Merriam-Webster. (n.d.). Amazing definition & meaning. *Merriam-Webster*. https://www.merriam-webster.com/dictionary/amazing

Michel, A. (2017, January). Harnessing the wisdom of crowds to improve hiring. *Observer*, pp. 14–16.

Microsoft. (2020, October 27). https://www.microsoft.com/en-us/Investor/earnings/FY-2021-Q1/press-release-webcast

Middleton, T. (2019, *May 15)*. The importance of teamwork (as proven by science). *Work Life*. https://www.atlassian.com/blog/teamwork/the-importance-of-teamwork

Milgram, S. (1974). *Obedience to authority*. Harper & Row.

Millennial survey 2020—Deloitte. (2021). https://www2.deloitte.com/content/dam/Deloitte/se/Documents/about-deloitte/deloitte-2020-millennial-survey.pdf

Miller, J. (2018, May 16). Building a LinkedIn profile—Project management institute (PMI)® video tutorial: *LinkedIn learning, formerly Lynda.com*. https://www.linkedin.com/learning/finding-a-job/building-a-linkedin-profile

Miller, M. (2017a) Survey insights part 1—communication in the workplace. *Emergenetics International*. https://www.emergenetics.com/blog/survey-insights-part-1-communication-in-the-workplace/

Miller, M. (2017b). Survey insights part 2—organizational communication as a competitive advantage. *Emergenetics International*. https://www.emergenetics.com/blog/survey-insights-part-2-organizational-communication/

Milosevic, I., Maric, S., & Loncar, D. (2019). Defeating the toxic boss: The nature of toxic leadership and the role of followers. *Journal of Leadership & Organizational Studies*, *27*(2), 117–137. https://doi.org/10.1177%2F1548051819833374

Mission and vision statements. (2018, April 2). *Bain & Company*. https://www.bain.com/insights/management-tools-mission-and-vision-statements/

Mitchell, R., Giles, P. V., & Boyle, B. (2014). The ABC of health care team dynamics: Understanding complex affective, behavioral, and cognitive dynamics in interprofessional teams. *Health Care Management Review*, *39*(1), 1–9. https://doi.org/10.1097/hcm.0b013e3182766504

Mohsin, M. (2022, January 3). 10 YouTube statistics that you need to know in 2021. *Oberlo*. https://www.oberlo.com/blog/youtube-statistics

Montopoli, J. (2021, January 31). Public speaking anxiety and fear of brain freezes. *National Social Anxiety Center*. https://nationalsocialanxietycenter.com/2017/02/20/public-speaking-and-fear-of-brain-freezes/

Moore, A. (2016, February 12). 7 tips for getting more responses to your emails (with data!). *Boomerang*. https://blog.boomerangapp.com/2016/02/7-tips-for-getting-more-responses-to-your-emails-with-data/

Moore, C. (2021, April 26). What is the negativity bias and how can it be overcome? *Positive Psychology*. https://positivepsychology.com/3-steps-negativity-bias/

Moore, D. A., & Bazerman, M. H. (2021). Decision leadership: Empowering others to make better choices. Yale University Press.

Moore, N.-J., Hickson, M., & Stacks, D. W. (2014). *Nonverbal communication: Studies and applications*. Oxford University Press.

Moore, S. (2019). Reactance theory & employee performance. *Chron.* https://smallbusiness. chron.com/reactance-theory-employee-performance-34456.html

Moran, G. (2021, April 13). These 7 phrases can help you sound more powerful at work. *Fast Company.* https://www.fastcompany. com/90623381/these-7-phrases-can-help-you-sound-more-powerful-at-work

Morelli, B. (2017, March 28). Why companies have failed to end harassment in the workplace. *Huffington Post.* http://www.huffingtonpost.com/ entry/why-companies-have-failed-to-end-sexual-harassment_us_58da66c5e4b0ef7ce8c5c1a6

Morgan, K. (2020, December 9). Professional communication has traditionally been buttoned up. But a new generation entering the workforce may help us relax—at least a little. *BBC.* https:// www.bbc.com/worklife/article/20201204-how-young-workers-are-changing-the-rules-of-business-speak?ocid=ww.social.link.email

Morgan, M. (2020, May 26). How to improve collaboration in the remote workplace with whole brain thinking. *Hermann.* https://herrmann. com.au/blog/2020/05/improve-collaboration-remote-workplace-whole-brain-thinki

Morley, L., & Cashell, A. (2017). Collaboration in health care. *Journal of Medical Imaging and Radiation Sciences, 48*(2), 207–216.

Morrison-Smith, S., & Ruiz, J. (2020, May 20). Challenges and barriers in virtual teams: A literature review. *SN Applied Sciences, 2,* Article 1096. https://link.springer.com/article/10.1007/ s42452-020-2801-5

Moss, S. (2016, June 7). Why some bosses bully their best employees. *Harvard Business Review.* https://hbr.org/2016/06/why-some-bosses-bully-their-best-employees

Motley, M. T. (1995). *Overcoming your fear of public speaking: A proven method.* McGraw–Hill.

Motley, M. T. (2011, *January 18).* Reducing public speaking anxiety: The communication orientation. *YouTube.* https://www.youtube.com/ watch?v=GYfHQvi2NAg

Mouawad, J. (2016, February 3). Richard Anderson, Delta chief who led airline's rebound, will retire. *The New York Times.* https://www. nytimes.com/2016/02/04/business/delta-chief-who-led-airlines-rebound-will-retire.html

Mudrack, P., & Farrell, G. (1995). An examination of functional role behavior and its consequenc-es for individuals in group settings. *Small Group Research, 26*(4), 542–571.

Muir, T. (2019). *The collaborative classroom: Teaching students how to work together now and for the rest of their lives.* Dave Burgess Consulting, Inc.

Munim, A. (2017, August 29). 18 of the best code of conduct examples. *I-Sight.* https://i-sight. com/resources/18-of-the-best-code-of-conduct-examples/

Murcott, M. (2016). The customer rage study. *Dialog Direct.* https://epicconnections.com/wp-content/uploads/2016/04/DialogDirect_CustRage_Guide_v5_0.pdf

Murphy, H. (2018, March 16). Picture a leader: Is she a woman? *New York Times.* https://www.ny-times.com/2018/03/16/health/women-leader-ship-workplace.html?&moduleDetail=section-news-2&action=click&contentCollection=He alth&region=Footer&module=MoreInSectio n&version=WhatsNext&contentID=WhatsNe xt&pgtype=Blogs

Murphy, K. (2020, January 09). Talk less. listen more. here's how. *New York Times.* https://www. nytimes.com/2020/01/09/opinion/listening-tips.html

Myers, C. (2017, April 28). How to become a more decisive leader. *Forbes.* https://www.forbes.com/ sites/chrismyers/2017/04/28/how-to-become-a-more-decisive-leader/#62d5fd974336

Naragon, K. (2018, August 21). *We still love email, but we're spreading the love with other channels.* https://blog.adobe.com/en/2018/08/21/love-email-but-spreading-the-love-other-channels. html?ref=emailmarketingtipps.de

Nass, C. (2010). *The man who lied to his laptop: What machines teach us about human relationships. Your Coach in a Box* [CD]. Penguin.

Nauen, R. (2017, October 19). Two in five LGBT workers feel bullied at work, according to recent CareerBuilder survey. *CareerBuilder.* https:// press.careerbuilder.com/2017-10-19-Two-in-Five-LGBT-Workers-Feel-Bullied-at-Work-According-to-Recent-CareerBuilder-Survey

Neily, J., Mills, P. D., Young-Xu, Y., Carney B. T., West, P., Berger, D. H.,. . . Bagian, J. P. (2010). Association between implementation of a medical team training program and surgical mortality. *Journal of the American Medical Association, 304*(15), 1693–1700.

Nawaz, S. (2020, February 7). Don't just memorize your next presentation—know it cold. *Harvard*

Business Review. https://hbr.org/2020/02/dont-just-memorize-your-next-presentation-know-it-cold

Neuliep, J. W. (2014). *Intercultural communication: A contextual approach*. SAGE.

Nevicka, B., De Hoogh, A. H. B., Hartog, D. N. D., Belschak, F. D. (2018). Narcissistic leaders and their victims: Followers low on self-esteem and low on core self-evaluations suffer most. *Frontiers in Psychology*, 9, 422. https://www.frontiersin.org/articles/10.3389/fpsyg.2018.00422/full#B40

Nevicka, B., Ten Velden, F. S., De Hoogh, A. H. B., & Van Vianen, A. E. M. (2011). Reality at odds with perceptions: Narcissistic leaders and group performance. *Psychological Science*, *22*(10), 1259–1264.

Newberry, C. (2021, January 12). 38 LinkedIn statistics marketers should know in 2021. *Hootsuite*. https://blog.hootsuite.com/linkedin-statistics-business/

Nichols, T. (2017). *The death of expertise: The campaign against established knowledge and why it matters*. Oxford University Press.

Nink, M., & Robison, J. (2021, February 9). Add team praise to your employee recognition toolkit. *Workplace*. https://www.gallup.com/workplace/329351/add-team-praise-employee-recognition-toolkit.aspx

Noar, A. (2018, May 22). New survey results on presentations . . . #2 will shock you! *PresentationPanda*. https://presentationpanda.com/blog/new-presentation-statistics/

Noe-Bustamante, Mora, L., & Lopez, M. H. (2020, August 11). About one-in-four U.S. Hispanics have heard of Latinx, but just 3% use it. *Pew Research*. https://www.pewresearch.org/hispanic/2020/08/11/about-one-in-four-u-s-hispanics-have-heard-of-latinx-but-just-3-use-it/

No relief: Denial of Bathroom breaks in the poultry industry. (2016). *Oxfam America*. https://www.oxfamamerica.org/static/media/files/No_Relief_Embargo.pdf

Nordin, S. M., Sivapalan, S., Bhattacharyya, E., Ahmad, H. H. W. F. W., & Abdullah, A. (2014). Organizational communication climate and conflict management: Communications management in an oil and gas company. *Procedia—Social and Behavioral Sciences*, 109, 1046–1058.

Norquay, J. (2021, April 16). How many emails are sent per day in 2022? *Prosperity Media*. https://prosperitymedia.com.au/how-many-emails-are-sent-per-day-in-2021/

Northouse, P. (2021). *Theory and practice*. Sage.

O'Malley, M. (2019, December 12). What the "best companies to work for" do differently. *Harvard Business Review*. https://hbr.org/2019/12/what-the-best-companies-to-work-for-do-differently

Ockey, G. J., Papageorgiou, S., & French, R. (2016). Effects of strength of accent on an L2 interactive lecture listening comprehension test. *International Journal of Listening*, *30*(1–2), 84–98.

Odine, M. (2015). Communication problems in management. *Journal of Emerging Issues in Economics, Finance and Banking Granthaalayah*, *4*(2) 1615–1630.

Omisore, B. O., & Abiodun, A. R. (2014). Organizational conflicts: Causes, effects and remedies. *International Journal of Academic Research in Economics and Management Sciences*, *3*(6), 118–137. https://pdfs.semanticscholar.org/dc47/343acf285d3c6e7af9d5bb935981ac251c02.pdf

Only 9 Hispanic CEOs at top 500 companies. (2020, September 10). *Mexican American Professional Archives*. https://mexican-american-pro-archive.com/2020/09/only-9-hispanic-ceos-at-top-500-companies/

Organizational dynamics survey: Most businesses have a teamwork problem. (2016, December 8). *5 Dynamics*. https://www.simpli5.com/organizational-dynamics-survey-most-businesses-have-a-teamwork-problem/

Osman, M. (2021, March 18). Mind-blowing LinkedIn statistics and facts (2021). *Kinsta*. https://kinsta.com/blog/linkedin-statistics/

Ospina, N. S., Phillips, K. A., Rodriguez-Gutierrez, R., Castaneda-Guarderas, A., Gionfriddo, M. R., Branda, M. E., & Montori, B. M. (2019). Eliciting the patient's agenda—secondary analysis of recorded clinical encounters. *Journal of General Internal Medicine*, 34, 36–40.

Packer, D. J., & Van Bavel, J. J. (2021, October 31). Much of what you know about groupthink is wrong. *The Wall Street Journal*. https://www.wsj.com/articles/much-of-what-you-know-about-groupthink-is-wrong-11635604446

Padavic, I., Ely, R. J., & Reid, E. M. (2019). Explaining the persistence of gender inequality: The work-family narrative as a social defense against the 24/7 work culture. *Administrative Science Quarterly*, *65*(1), 61–111. https://journals.sagepub.com/doi/full/10.1177/0001839219832310

Paradi, D. (n.d.). Choosing Colors for Your Presentation Slides. Think Outside The Slide. https://www.thinkoutsidetheslide.com/choosing-colors-for-your-presentation-slides/

Paradi, D. (n.d.). Selecting the correct font size. Think Outside The Slide. https://www.thinkoutsidetheslide.com/selecting-the-correct-font-size/

Park, D. C., & Huang, C.-M. (2010). Culture wires the brain: A cognitive neuroscience perspective. *Perspectives on Psychological Science*, 5, 391–400.

Patel, J. K., Griggs, T., & Miller, C. C. (2017, December 28). We asked 615 men about how they conduct themselves at work. *The New York Times*. https://www.nytimes.com/interactive/2017/12/28/upshot/sexual-harassment-survey-600-men.html

Patenall, E. (2021, April 21). Five reasons why every student should be on LinkedIn. *TopUniversities*. https://www.topuniversities.com/student-info/careers-advice/five-reasons-why-every-student-should-be-linkedin

Patrnchak, J. M. (2015). Implementing servant leadership at Cleveland Clinic: A case study in organizational change. *Servant Leadership: Theory and Practice*, 2(1), 36–48.

Patroe, P. (2019, March 04). The 29 new skills you can now learn on linkedin learning. https://www.linkedin.com/business/learning/blog/new-courses/the-29-new-skills-you-can-now-learn-on-linkedin-learning-march

Paul, S., Seetharaman, P., Samarah, I., & Mykytyn, P. (2005, February). Understanding conflict in virtual teams: An experimental investigation using content analysis. In R. H. Sprague (Ed.), *Proceedings of the 38th Hawaii International Conference on Systems Sciences*. Los Alamitos, CA: IEEE Computer Society.

Pentland, A. S. (2012, April). The new science of building great teams. *Harvard Business Review*. https://hbr.org/2012/04/the-new-science-of-building-great-teams

Pentland, A. S. (2015, March 27). Alex "Sandy" Pentland (Harvard Business Review): The new science of building great teams. *Emergent Cognition Project*. https://emergentcognition.com/2015/03/27/alex-sandy-pentland-harvard-business-review-the-new-science-of-building-great-teams

Pentland, A. S. (2016, September/October). Betting on people power. *Scientific American Mind*, 27(5), 32–37.

People and environment in our supply chain. (2022. *Apple*. https://www.apple.com/supplier-responsibility/pdf/Apple_SR_2022_Progress_Report.pdf.

People hate being managed—What organizations (and managers) need to do instead. (2021, July 16). *Betterworks*. https://blog.betterworks.com/people-hate-being-managed-what-organizations-and-managers-need-to-do-instead/

Perman, C. (2011, September 2). Think your boss is a psychopath? That may be true. *CNBC*. http://www.cnbc.com//id/44376401

Persun, N. (2018, July 8). How to switch off an angry person. *PsychCentral*. https://psychcentral.com/blog/how-to-switch-off-an-angry-person/

Peshawaria, R. (2017). *Open source leadership: Reinventing management when there's no more business as usual*. McGraw-Hill Education.

Petch, N. (2016, July 26). Why a big ego reduces your business success. *Entrepeneur*. https://www.entrepreneur.com/article/279633

Petras, K., & Petras, R. (2021, December 26). Want to sound less annoying? Avoid these 15 words and phrases that are 'embarrassingly clichéd,' say grammar experts. *CNBC*. https://www.cnbc.com/2021/12/26/most-embarrassingly-outdated-words-and-phrases-to-stop-using-right-now-according-to-grammar-experts.html

Petrone, P. (2018, October 22). The "most frustrating" thing a boss can do is . . . *LinkedIn*. https://learning.linkedin.com/blog/learning-tips/the-single-biggest-complaint-employees-have-about-their-bosses-i

Petrone, P. (2019, March 4). *The 29 new skills you can now learn on LinkedIn learning*. LinkedIn.

Pew Research Center. (2018, March 1). *The Generation Gap in American politics*. Pew Research Center - U.S. Politics & Policy. https://www.pewresearch.org/politics/2018/03/01/the-generation-gap-in-american-politics/

Pewsey, R. (2020, January 21). Does group brainstorming really work? *Ayoa*. https://www.ayoa.com/ourblog/does-group-brainstorming-really-work/

Pfeffer, J. (2015). *Leadership BS: Fixing workplaces and careers one truth at a time*. HarperCollins.

Pham, H. (2019, April 2). "How we culture" with Michelle Lee and Jenny Gottstein of IDEO. *Culture Summit*. https://www.culturesummit.co/articles/how-we-culture-michelle-jenny-ideo/

Pieniazek, J. (2021, February 12). The blow-by-blow on remote work conflict [2021 study]. *MyPerfectresume*. https://www.myperfectresume.com/career-center/careers/basics/remote-work-conflict

Plaister-Ten, J. (2017). Leading across cultures: Developing leaders for global organizations. *Routledge*. https://www.crcpress.com/go/white_paper_leading_across_cultures_developing_leaders_for_global_organisat

Plane Business Ron Allen airline management award. (2021, December). PlaneBusiness. https://www.planebusiness.com/ronallen.shtml

Platow, M. J., Haslam, S. A., Reicher, S. D., & Steffens, N. K. (2015). There is no leadership if no-one follows: Why leadership is necessarily a group process. *International Coaching Psychology Review*, *10*(1), 20–37.

Player, A., de Moura, G. R., Leite, A. C., Abrams, D., & Tresh, F. (2019). Overlooked leadership potential: The preference for leadership potential in job candidates who are men vs. women. *Frontiers in Psychology*. https://www.frontiersin.org/articles/10.3389/fpsyg.2019.00755/full

Poppy, C. (2017, January/February). Survey shows Americans fear ghosts, the government, and each other. *Skeptical Inquirer*, *41*(1), pp. 16–18.

Porath, C. (2016). *Mastering civility: A manifesto for the workplace*. Grand Central Publishing.

Post, C., Lokshin, B., & Boone, C. (2021, April 6). Research: Adding women to the C-suite changes how companies think. *Harvard Business Review*. https://hbr.org/2021/04/research-adding-women-to-the-c-suite-changes-how-companies-think

PowerPoint coaching. (2022, February). *The Communication Center*. https://www.thecommunicationcenter.com/services/presentation-coaching/powerpoint-coaching/

Pre-employment drug tests ground almost 20% in state. (1990, May 24). *San Jose Mercury News*, p. 1A.

Price, N. J. (2017, July 28). Are there any safe and secure alternatives to business email? *Diligent Insights*. https://insights.diligent.com/secure-communication/are-there-any-safe-and-secure-alternatives-to-business-email/

Prieto-Remon, T. C., Cobo-Benita, J. R., Ortiz-Marcos, I., & Uruburu, A. (2015). Conflict resolution to project performance. *Procedia—Social and Behavioral Sciences*, *194*, 155–164. https://www.sciencedirect.com/science/article/pii/S1877042815036083

Public speaking anxiety. (2020, December 07). https://nationalsocialanxietycenter.com/social-anxiety/public-speaking-anxiety/#:~:text=The%20National%20Institute%20of%20Mental,considered%20a%20social%20anxiety%20disorder

Puccio, G. J., Murdock, M. C., & Mance, M. (2007). *Creative leadership: Skills that drive change*. Sage.

Purvanova, R. K., Charlier, S. D., Reeves, C. J., & Greco, L. M. (2020). Who emerges into virtual team leadership roles? The role of achievement and ascription antecedents for leadership emergence across the virtuality spectrum. *Journal of Business and Psychology*, *1*, 1–21. https://doi.org/10.1007/s10869-020-09698-0

Quinnell, K. (2020, July 29). Executive Paywatch: 1,000-to-1 pay ratio CEOs furlough workers. *AFL-CIO*. https://aflcio.org/2020/7/29/executive-paywatch-1000-1-pay-ratio-ceos-furlough-workers

Quintero, J. (2019, May 5). All About Recruiting. Personal interview.

Rahim, M. A., & Katz, J. P. (2019). Forty years of conflict: The effects of gender and generation on conflict-management strategies. *International Journal of Conflict Management*, *31*(1), 1–16. https://doi.org/10.1108/IJCMA-03-2019-0045

Rahmani, D. (2017). Apprehension and anxiety in communication. *Oxford Research Encyclopedias*. http://communication.oxfordre.com/view/10.1093/acrefore/9780190228613.001.0001/acrefore-9780190228613-e-414

Rast, D. E., Hogg, M. A., & Giessner, S. R. (2016). Who trusts charismatic leaders who champion change? The role of group identification, membership centrality, and self-uncertainty. *Group Dynamics: Theory, Research, and Practice*, *20*(4), 259–275. https://psycnet.apa.org/doi/10.1037/gdn0000053

Rathe, C. (2017, July 25). Could Millennials reshape global supply chains. *21st Century Global Dynamics, Global-e journal*, *10*(48). https://www.21global.ucsb.edu/global-e/july-2017/could-millennials-reshape-global-supply-chains

Reed, L. (2013, October 23). UNL study shows college students are digitally distracted in class. http://newsroom.unl.edu/releases/2013/10/23/UNL+study+shows+college+students+are+digitally+distracted+in+class

Reinsel, D., & Shirer, M. (2020, May 8). IDC's global datasphere forecast shows continued steady growth in the creation and consumption of data. *Yahoo Finance*. https://finance.yahoo.com/news/idcs-global-datasphere-forecast-shows-123000572.html

Reisinger, H., & Fetterer, D. (2021, October 29). Forget flexibility: Your employees want autonomy. *Harvard Business Review*. https://hbr.org/2021/10/forget-flexibility-your-employees-want-autonomy?utm_medium=email&utm_source=newsletter_weekly&utm_campaign=insider_activesubs&utm_content=signinnudge&deliveryName=DM159222

Reuell, P. (2017, May 12). Visual images often intrude on verbal thinking, study says. *Harvard Gazette*. https://news.harvard.edu/gazette/story/2017/05/visual-images-often-intrude-on-verbal-thinking-study-says/

Revenga, A. L., & Boudet, A. M. M. (2017, September). Women's work. *Scientific American*, *317*(3), 72–77.

Reynolds, A., & Lewis, D. (2017, March 30). Teams solve problems faster when they're more cognitively diverse. *Harvard Business Review*. https://hbr.org/2017/03/teams-solve-problems-faster-when-theyre-more-cognitively-diverse

Rich, M. D. (2018). *Truth decay: An initial exploration of the diminishing role of facts and analysis in American public life*. Rand. https://www.rand.org/pubs/research_reports/RR2314.html

Rich, M. D., & Kavanaugh, J. (2021, April 8). Truth decay, our new national pastime. *Pittsburg Post-Gazette*. https://www.post-gazette.com/opinion/Op-Ed/2018/07/12/Truth-decay-our-new-national-pastime/stories/201807120026

Riggio, R. E., Riggio, H. R., Salinas, C., & Cole, E. J. (2003). The role of social and emotional communication skills in leader emergence and effectiveness. *Group Dynamics: Theory, Research, and Practice*, *7*(2), 83–103.

Rinne, J. D. (2019, April 25). 16 jaw-dropping facts about Cirque du Soleil. *Mental Floss*. https://mentalfloss.com/article/540342/cirque-du-soleil-facts

Rispens, S., Greer, L., Jehn, K. A., & Thatcher, S. (2011). Not so bad after all: How relational closeness buffers the association between relationship conflict and helpful and deviant group behaviors. *Negotiation and Conflict Management Research*, *4*(4), 277–296. https://onlinelibrary.wiley.com/doi/abs/10.1111/j.1750-4716.2011.00083.x

Robbins, A. (2015). *Unlimited power: The new science of personal achievement*. Simon & Schuster Paperbacks.

Robert, L. P., & You, S. (2018, January 7). Disaggregating the impacts of virtuality on team identification. *Proceedings of the ACM International Conference on Supporting Group Work* (pp. 309–321). https://deepblue.lib.umich.edu/bitstream/handle/2027.42/138817/Old%20Version?sequence=1&isAllowed=y

Rock, D. (2009). *Your brain at work*. HarperCollins.

Rock, J. (2017, March 1). Workplace bullying may be linked to long-term health issues. *Association for Psychological Science*. https://www.psychologicalscience.org/news/minds-business/workplace-bullying-may-be-linked-to-long-term-health-issues.html

Rogelberg, S. G. (2019). *The surprising science of meetings: How you can lead your team to peak performance*. Oxford University Press.

Rogelberg, S. G., Scott, C. W., Agypt, B., Williams, J., Kello, J. E., Mccausland, T., & Olien, J. L. (2013). Lateness to meetings: Examination of an unexplored temporal phenomenon. *European Journal of Work and Organizational Psychology*, *23*(3), 323–341. https://doi.org/10.1080/1359432x.2012.745988

Rogelberg, S. G., Shanock, L. R., & Scott, C. W. (2012). Wasted time and money in meetings: Increasing return on investment. *Small Group Research*, *43*(2), 236–245.

Rogers, K. (2018, July–August). Do your employees feel respected? *Harvard Business Review*. https://hbr.org/2018/07/do-your-employees-feel-respected

Rogers, S. L., Howlieson, J., & Neame, C. (2018). I understand you feel that way, but I feel this way: the benefits of I-language and communicating perspective during conflict. *PeerJ. Peer Reviewed and Open Access*. https://www.ncbi.nlm.nih.gov/pmc/articles/PMC5961625/

Rosen, C. C., Simon, L. S., Gajendran, R. S., Johnson, R. E., Lee, H. W., & Lin, S.-H. (2019). Boxed in by your inbox: Implications of daily e-mail demands for managers' leadership behaviors. *Journal of Applied Psychology*, *104*(1), 19–33. https://doi.org/10.1037/apl0000343

Rosenberg, M. (2019, January 25). Number of McDonald's restaurants worldwide. *ThoughtCo*. https://www.thoughtco.com/number-of-mcdonalds-restaurants-worldwide-1435174

Rosenberg, M. B. (2015). *Nonviolent communication: A language of life: Life-changing tools for healthy relationships* (3rd ed.). PuddleDancer Press.

Ross, M. (2017, April 9). Civility suits the workplace. *San Jose Mercury News*, pp. D1, D8.

Rost, J. C. (1991). *Leadership for the twenty-first century*. Praeger.

Rothwell, J. D. (2022). *In mixed company: Communicating in small groups and teams*. Oxford University Press.

Rousmaniere, D. (2015, March 13). What everyone needs to know about running productive meetings. *Harvard Business Review*. https://hbr.org/2015/03/what-everyone-needs-to-know-about-running-productive-meetings

Ruback, B. R., & Juieng, D. (1997). Territorial defense in parking lots: Retaliation against waiting drivers. *Journal of Applied Social Psychology*, 27(9), 821–834.

Ruggiero, V. R. (1988). *The art of thinking: A guide to critical and creative thought*. Harper & Row.

Ruining it for the rest of us. (2008, December 19). *This American Life*. https://www.thisamericanlife.org/370/ruining-it-for-the-rest-of-us

Ryan, N. (2020, February 19). The four horsemen: Signs your relationship is in trouble. *Sacwellness*. https://sacwellness.com/the-four-horsemen-signs-your-relationship-is-in-trouble/

Sadri, G. (2018). Choosing conflict resolution by culture. *Institute of Industrial & Systems Engineers*. https://www.iise.org/Details.aspx?id=35396

Safian, R. (2017, October). How to lead with empathy. *Fast Company*, p. 12.

Sahni, H. (2021, October 20). 14 fonts that make your PowerPoint presentations stand out. *Piktochart.com*. https://piktochart.com/blog/best-font-for-presentations/

Saint, S., & Lawson, J. (1997). *Rules for reaching consensus*. Pfeiffer.

Sajjadi, A., Karimkhani, M., & Mehrpour, M. (2014). New emerging leadership theories and styles. *Technical Journal of Engineering and Applied Sciences*, 3, 180–188.

Salas, E., Tannenbaum, S. I., Kraiger, K., & Smith-Jentsch, K. A. (2012). The science of training and development in organizations: What matters in practice. *Psychological Science in the Public Interest*, 13(2), 74–101.

Salazar, A. (1995). Understanding the synergistic effects of communication in small groups. *Small Group Research*, 26(2), 169–199.

Salters-Pedneault, K. (2019, July 19). Is venting your anger a good idea? *VeryWellMind*. https://www.verywellmind.com/how-you-vent-anger-may-not-be-good-for-bpd-425393

Samovar, L. A., Porter, R. E., McDaniel, E. R., & Roy, C. S. (2021). *Communication between cultures*. Cengage.

Sanders, G. I. (2020). Employee productivity statistics: Everything you need to know. *Firstup*. https://firstup.io/blog/employee-productivity-statistics/

Santos, H. C., Varnum, M. E. W., & Grossman, I. (2017). Global increases in individualism. *Psychological Science*, 28(9), 1228–1239.

Sao, R., Chandak, S., Patel, B., & Bhadade, P. (2020). Cyberloafing: Effects on employee job performance and behavior. *International Journal of Recent Technology and Engineering*, 8(5), 1509–1515.

Sarokin, D. (2019). What is the meaning of ethical responsibility?. *Chron*. https://smallbusiness.chron.com/meaning-ethical-responsibility-56224.html

Satell, G. (2015, February 6). Why communication is today's most important skill. *Forbes*. https://www.forbes.com/sites/gregsatell/2015/02/06/why-communication-is-todays-most-important-skill/#5f5775841100

Savitsky, K., & Gilovich, T. (2003). The illusion of transparency and the alleviation of speech anxiety. *Journal of Experimental Social Psychology*, 39(6), 618–625.

Sawyer, K. (2017). *Group genius: The creative power of collaboration* (Rev. ed.) Basic Books.

Scandura, R. A., Von Glinow, M. A., & Lowe, K. B. (1999). When East meets West: Leadership "best practices" in the United States and the Middle East. In W. Mobley, M. J. Gessner, & V. Arnold (Eds.), *Advances in global leadership*. JAI.

Schaarschmidt, T. (2017, May/June). Power moves. *Scientific American Mind*, pp. 51–55.

Schlender, B., Tetzeli, R., &; Andreessen, M. (2015). *Becoming Steve Jobs: The evolution of a reckless upstart into a visionary leader*. Crown business.

Schmidt, A. (2020, May 22). Weight Watchers fires thousands of employees over Zoom: Report. *Fox Business*. https://www.foxbusiness.com/lifestyle/weight-watchers-layoffs-zoom

Schmidt, F. (2016, October). The validity and utility of selection methods in personnel psychology: Practical and theoretical implications of 100 years of research findings.

Researchgate. https://www.researchgate.net/publication/309203898_The_Validity_and_Utility_of_Selection_Methods_in_Personnel_Psychology_Practical_and_Theoretical_Implications_of_100_Years_of_Research_Findings

Schneider, M. (2017, July 19). Google spent 2 years studying 180 teams. *Inc.* https://www.inc.com/michael-schneider/google-thought-they-knew-how-to-create-the-perfect.html

Schneider, M. (2018, July 11). Costs of poor communication reaches $37 billion. *Inc.com.* https://www.inc.com/michael-schneider/the-extrovert-vs-introvert-dynamic-could-be-costing-your-organization-millions-heres-how-to-bridge-communication-gap.html

Schroeder, J., & Epley, N. (2015, April 29). The sound of intellect: Speech reveals a thoughtful mind, increasing a job candidate's appeal. *Psychological Science.* https://pubmed.ncbi.nlm.nih.gov/25926479/

Schroth, H. (2019). Are you ready for Gen Z in the workplace? *California Management Review, 61*(3) 5–18. https://cmr.berkeley.edu/assets/documents/sample-articles/61-3-schroth.pdf

Schwantes, M. (2016, September 1). 10 compelling reasons servant leadership may be best, says science. *Inc.* https://www.inc.com/marcel-schwantes/10-convincing-reasons-to-consider-servant-leadership-according-to-research.html

*Schwartz, E. (2020, February 11). The mystery of the disappearing female CEO. *Econlife.* https://econlife.com/2020/02/fewer-female-ceos-2/

Schwartzberg, J. (2020, February 24). Present your data like A pro. *Harvard Business Review.* https://hbr.org/2020/02/present-your-data-like-a-pro

Schwartzberg, J. (2021, August 31). How to respond to "so, tell me about yourself" in a job interview. https://hbr.org/2019/08/how-to-respond-to-so-tell-me-about-yourself-in-a-job-interview?utm_medium=email&utm_source=newsletter_daily&utm_campaign=mtod&referral=00203

Schwarz, R. (2015, March 19). How to design an agenda for an effective meeting. *Harvard Business Review.* https://hbr.org/2015/03/how-to-design-an-agenda-for-an-effective-meeting

Schwarz, R., & Heinecke, S. (2016, June 15v). 8 ground rules for great meetings. *Harvard Business Review.* https://hbr.org/2016/06/8-ground-rules-for-great-meetings

Schyns, B., Felfe, J., & Schilling, J. (2018, July 27). Is it me or you? How reactions to abusive supervision are shaped by leader behavior and fol-lower reactions. *Frontiers in Psychology*, 9, 1309. https://www.ncbi.nlm.nih.gov/pmc/articles/PMC6073698/

Scott, E. (2020, February 12). Learn assertive communication in five simple steps. *Very Well Mind.* https://www.verywellmind.com/learn-assertive-communication-in-five-simple-steps-3144969

Sederino, C. (2019, July 11). The power of public speaking and its impact in the business world. *Illuminated Story.* https://illuminatedstory.com.au/2019/07/11/the-power-of-public-speaking-and-its-impact-in-the-business-world/

Seelig, T. (2015). *Insight Out: Get ideas our of your head and into the world.* HarperOne.

Selvin R. (2017, June 9). I've broken this mortifying office taboo—and I bet I'm not alone. *Refinery29.* https://www.refinery29.com/en-us/is-it-good-to-cry-at-work

Semarjian, M. (2018, June 26). How 10 Famous business leaders, including Musk, *Bezos and Jobs, handle meetings.* https://www.entrepreneur.com/article/315782

Senior, J. (2020, June 16). How layoffs do not ultimately help a company's bottom line. *The Mercury News*, p. A7.

Seppälä, E. (2017, September 28). 6 ways the most emotionally intelligent people handle anger. *Psychology Today.* https://www.psychologytoday.com/us/blog/feeling-it/201709/6-ways-the-most-emotionally-intelligent-people-handle-anger

Sertel, G., Karadag, E., & Ergin-Kocaturk. (2022). Effects of leadership on performance: A cross-cultural meta-analysis. *International Journal of Cross Cultural Management.* https://journals.sagepub.com/doi/abs/10.1177/14705958221076404

Service, C. N. N. W. (2021, January 2). This year's list of 'banished' words and phrases are all about covid-19. *The Mercury News.* https://www.mercurynews.com/2021/01/02/this-years-list-of-banished-words-and-phrases-are-all-about-covid-19/

Service, M. F. (2010, April 28). Afghanistan Power-point Slide: Generals left baffled by PowerPoint slide. *Daily Mail Online.* https://www.dailymail.co.uk/news/article-1269463/Afghanistan-PowerPoint-slide-Generals-left-baffled-PowerPoint-slide.html

Sex discrimination and sexual harassment. (2015, May 25). *Catalyst.* http://www.catalyst.org/knowledge/sex-discrimination-and-sexual-harassment-0

Sexual harassment at work. (2019). *Equal Rights Advocates.* https://www.equalrights.org/legal-help/know-your-rights/sexual-harassment-at-work/

Sexual harassment in the workplace. (2016, November). *National Women's Law Center.* https://nwlc.org/wp-content/uploads/2016/11/Sexual-Harassment-Fact-Sheet.pdf

Sexual harassment: What is it? (2017). *FindLaw.* http://employment.findlaw.com/employment-discrimination/sexual-harassment-what-is-it.html

Shandwick, W., & Tate, P. (2017). *Civility in America VII: The state of civility. Weber Shandwick.* KRC Research. http://www.webershandwick.com/uploads/news/files/Civility_in_America_the_State_of_Civility.pdf

Shapiro, D. (2017). *Negotiating the nonnegotiable: How to resolve your most emotionally charged conflicts.* Penguin.

Shavin, N. (2014, June 25). What workplace bullying looks like in 2014—and how to intervene. *Forbes.* https://www.forbes.com/sites/naomishavin/2014/06/25/what-work-place-bullying-looks-like-in-2014-and-how-to-intervene/2/#3dbabfa0293b

Shaw, E., Hegewisch, A., Phil, M., & Hess, C. (2018, October 15). Sexual harassment and assault at work: Understanding the costs. *Institute for Women's Policy Research.* https://iwpr.org/iwpr-publications/briefing-paper/sexual-harassment-and-assault-at-work-understanding-the-costs/

Sheridan, C., & King, R. (1972). Obedience to authority with an authentic victim. *Proceedings of the 80th Annual Convention,* American Psychological Association, 7, 165–166.

Sherif, M., Harvey, O. J., White, B. J., Hood, W. R., & Sherif, C. W. (1988). *The Robbers Cave Experiment.* Wesleyan University Press.

Shilling, D. (2000, September). How to find and keep top talent in today's tight labor market. *Medical Marketing & Media,* 35, 125.

Shimanoff, S. B. (2009). Rules theory. In S. W. Littlejohn & K. A. Foss (Eds.), pp. 930-935. *Encyclopedia of communication theory.* Sage.

Shin, L. (2014, November 14). 10 steps to conquering information overload. *Forbes.* https://www.forbes.com/sites/laurashin/2014/11/14/10-steps-to-conquering-information-overload/#509cf4bb7b08

Shinn, M. M. (2018). Operation anger management! A guy's guide to understanding his inner hulk. *Psychologically Speaking.* https://www.variationspsychology.com/blogs/operation-anger-man-agement

Shipley, D., & Schwalbe, W. (2010). *Send: Why people email so badly and how to do it better.* Vintage Books.

Shollen, S. L. (2010). The value of collaborative leadership: Leadership approach and leader emergence in virtual work groups. *International Leadership Association Conference.* http://www.ila-net.org/conferences/Program3.asp?ProgramDBID=96

Shonk, K. (2018, January 29). How to resolve cultural conflict: Overcoming cultural barriers at the negotiation table. *Program on Negotiations/Harvard Law School.* https://www.pon.harvard.edu/daily/conflict-resolution/a-cross-cultural-negotiation-example-how-to-overcome-cultural-barriers/

Shonk, K. (2022, May 19). A token concession: In negotiation, the gift that keeps on giving. *Program on Negotiation/Harvard Law School.* https://www.pon.harvard.edu/daily/negotiation-skills-daily/token-concession-negotiation-gift-keeps-giving/

Shonk, K. (2021a, August 30). How an authoritarian leadership style blocks effective negotiation. *Program on Negotiation/Harvard Law School.* https://www.pon.harvard.edu/daily/leadership-skills-daily/how-an-authoritarian-leadership-style-blocks-effective-negotiation/

Shonk, K. (2021b, October 11). 3 types of conflict and how to address them. *Program on Negotiation/Harvard Law School.* https://www.pon.harvard.edu/daily/conflict-resolution/types-conflict/?utm_source=WhatCountsEmail&utm_medium=daily&utm_date=2021-10-11-06-30-00&mqsc=E4137611

Shonk, K. (2021c, October 25). Conflict-managing styles: Pitfalls and best practices. *Program on Negotiation/Harvard Law School.* https://www.pon.harvard.edu/daily/conflict-resolution/conflict-management-styles-pitfalls-and-best-practices/?utm_source=WhatCountsEmail&utm_medium=daily&utm_date=2021-10-25-06-30-00&mqsc=E4138077

Shpitula, N. (2022, February 6). Adding your logo to a PowerPoint presentation. *Logaster.* https://www.logaster.com/blog/how-to-add-logo-in-powerpoint/

Sidky, H. (2018, March/April). The war on science, anti-intellectualism, and "alternative ways of knowing" in 21st-Century America. *Skeptical Inquirer, 42*(2), pp. 38–43.

Silverman, R. E. (2015, September 30). Gender bias at work turns up in feedback. *The Wall Street Journal.* https://www.wsj.com/articles/gender-bias-at-work-turns-up-in-feedback-1443600759

Silverman, S. B., Johnson, R. E., McConnell, N., & Carr, A. (2012). Arrogance: A formula for leadership failure. *The Industrial-Organizational Psychologist, 50*(1), 21–28.

Silverstein, J. (2017, September 3). The running list of typos from President Trump's White House. *Daily News.* http://www.nydailynews.com/news/politics/running-list-typos-president-trump-white-house-article-1.3186396

Sittenthaler, S., Traut-Mattausch, E., & Jonas, E. (2015, October 8). Observing the restriction of another person: Vicarious reactance and the role of self-construal and culture. *Frontiers in Psychology.* https://www.frontiersin.org/articles/10.3389/fpsyg.2015.01052/full

Slack. (2019, January 29). With 10+ million daily active users, slack is where more work happens every day, all over the world. *Slack.* https://slack.com/blog/news/slack-has-10-million-daily-active-users

Sma, S., Schrift, R. Y., & Zauberman, G. (2018). The illusion of multitasking and its positive effect on performance. *Psychological Science, 29,* 1942-1955.

Smedley, T. (2017, March 22). Is public speaking fear limiting your career? *BBC Worklife.* https://www.bbc.com/worklife/article/20170321-is-public-speaking-fear-limiting-your-career

Smith, C. McDonalds statistics, restaurant counts, facts, & news. (2022, March 29). *DMR.* https://expandedramblings.com/index.php/mcdonalds-statistics/

Smith, L. (2018, April 5). Why watching cat videos is totally good for you (because, science). *HealthiNation.* https://www.healthination.com/health/cat-videos-health-benefits/

Smith, M. (2022, March 19). New survey says these are the 3 most annoying co-worker habits—here's how to handle them. *CNBC.* https://www.cnbc.com/2022/03/19/new-survey-says-these-are-the-3-most-annoying-co-worker-habits.html

Smith, S. M., & Shaffer, D. R. (1995). Speed of speech and persuasion: Evidence for multiple effects. *Personality and Social Psychology Bulletin, 21*(10), 1051–1060. https://doi.org/10.1177/01461672952110006

Snyder, K. (2014, August 26). The abrasiveness trap: High-achieving men and women are described differently in reviews. *Fortune.* https://fortune.com/2014/08/26/performance-review-gender-bias/

Solomon, C. (2016). Trends in global virtual teams. *CultureWizard.* http://cdn.culturewizard.com/PDF/Trends_in_VT_Report_4-17-2016.pdf

Solomon, L. (2015, June 24). The top complaints from employees about their leaders. *Harvard Business Review.* https://hbr.org/2015/06/the-top-complaints-from-employees-about-their-leaders

Somech, A., Desivilya, H. S., & Lidogoster, H. (2008). Team conflict management and team effectiveness: The effects of task interdependence and team identification. *Journal of Organizational Behavior, 30*(3), 359–378.

Somvichian-Clausen, 2020, May 19). Female CEOs in the Fortune 500 hit an all-time record high. *Thehill.* https://thehill.com/changing-america/respect/equality/498582-female-ceos-in-the-fortune-500-hit-an-all-time-record-high

Sorensen, S. (1981, May). *Grouphate.* Paper presented at the International Communication Association, Minneapolis, MN.

Sparrow, B., Liu, J., & Wegner, D. M. (2011, July 14). Google effects on memory: Cognitive consequences of having information at our fingertips. *Science, 33*(6043). http://www.sciencemag.org/content/early/2011/07/13/science.1207745

Speagle, A. (2017, May 18). When face-to-face meetings trump virtual meetings software. *PGi.* https://www.pgi.com/resources/articles/when-face-to-face-meetings-trump-virtual-meetings/

Spears, L. C. (2010). Servant leadership and Robert K. Greenleaf's legacy. In D. van Dierendonck & K. Patterson (Eds.), *Servant leadership: Developments in theory and research* (pp. 11–24). Palgrave Macmillan.

Spira, J. B. (2011). *Overload: How too much information is hazardous to your organization.* Wiley.

Spitzberg, B. H. (2015). Intercultural communication competence. In L.A. Samovar, R. E. Porter, E. R. McDaniel, & C. S. Roy (Eds.), *Intercultural communication: A reader.* Cengage.

Stamoulis, D. (2018). Making it to the top: Nine attributes that differentiate CEOs. *Russell Reynolds Associates*. https://www.russellreynolds.com/en/insights/reports-surveys/making-it-to-the-top-nine-attributes-that-differentiate-ceos

Stark, P. B. (2016, June 7). Arrogance is leadership kryptonite. *PeterBarronStark Companies*. https://peterstark.com/arrogance-leadership-kryptonite/

Statistics on remote workers that will surprise you. (2022, January 16). *Apollo Technical LLC*. https://www.apollotechnical.com/statistics-on-remote-workers/

Steffens, N. K., Haslam, S. A., Ryan, M. K., & Kessler, T. (2013). Leader performance and prototypicality: The inter-relationship and impact on leaders' identity entrepreneurship. *European Journal of Social Psychology, 43*(7), 606–613.

Stephens, K. K., Houser, M. L., & Cowan, R. L. (2009). R U able to meat me: The impact of students' overly casual email messages to instructors. *Communication Education, 58*(3), 303–326.

Stewart, M. (2009). *The management myth: Debunking modern business philosophy*. W. W. Norton & Company.

Stogdill, R. M. (1948). Personal factors associated with leadership: A survey of the literature. *Journal of Psychology, 25*(1), 35–71.

Stogdill, R. M. (1974). *Handbook of leadership: A survey of theory and research*. The Free Press.

Stosny, S. (2014, April 18). What's wrong with criticism. *Psychology Today*. https://www.psychologytoday.com/blog/anger-in-the-age-entitlement/201404/whats-wrong-criticism

Strauss, V. (2017, December 20). The surprising thing Google learned about its employees—and what it means for today's students. *Washington Post*. https://www.washingtonpost.com/amphtml/news/answer-sheet/wp/2017/12/20/the-surprising-thing-google-learned-about-its-employees-and-what-it-means-for-todays-students

Striving for a just and safer workplace: Central Minnesota's poultry industry and its disposable workers. (2016, April). *Greater Minnesota Worker Center*. http://www.mygmwc.org/wp-content/uploads/2016/04/Striving-for-a-Just-and-Safer-Workplace-Final-04262016.pdf

Sullivan, B., & Thompson, H. (2013, May 3). Now hear this! Most people stink at listening [excerpt]. *Scientific American*. https://www.scientificamerican.com/article/plateau-effect-digital-gadget-distraction-attention/

Sullivan, B., & Thompson, H. (2013, May 3). *Now hear this! most people stink at listening [excerpt]*. Scientific American. https://www.scientificamerican.com/article/plateau-effect-digital-gadget-distraction-attention/

Supiano, B. (2020, April 23). Why is Zoom so exhausting? *The Chronicle of Higher Education*. https://www.chronicle.com/article/why-is-zoom-so-exhausting/

Survey Reveals: Spelling and Grammatical Errors Top the List of Resume Blunders. February 2, 2018). *Talent Inc*. https://www.talentinc.com/press-2018-02-14

Sutton, R. (2011, October 24). How a few bad apples ruin everything. *The Wall Street Journal*. http://online.wsj.com/news/articles/SB10001424052970203499704576622550325233260

Swann, W. B., Rentfrow, P. J., & Gosling, S. D. (2003). The precarious couple effect: Verbally inhibited men + critical, disinhibited women = bad chemistry. *Journal of Personality and Social Psychology, 85*(6), 1095–1106.

Synnott, C. K. (2016). Guides to reducing social loafing in group projects: Faculty development. *Journal of Higher Education Management, 31*(1), 211–221.

Tafvelin, S., Britt-Inger, K., & Kvist, E. (2019). The prevalence and consequences of intragroup conflicts for employee well-being in women-dominated work. *Human Service Organizations: Management Leadership & Governance, 44*(1), 47–62. https://www.tandfonline.com/doi/full/10.1080/23303131.2019.1661321

Tamir, S. (2020, December 3). The characteristics of virtual teams, when to use them and determinants of their success. *CQ Net*. https://www.ckju.net/en/dossier/characteristics-virtual-teams-when-use-them-and-determinants-their-success

Tankovska, H. (2022, February 9). Distribution of LinkedIn users worldwide as of January 2022, by age group. *Statista*. https://www.statista.com/statistics/273505/global-linkedin-age-group/

Tannen, D. (2003, January 5). Hey, did you catch that? Why they're talking as fast as they can. *The Washington Post*, pp. B1, B4.

Tannen, D. (2017, June 28). The truth about how much women talk—and whether men listen.

Time. https://time.com/4837536/do-women-really-talk-more/

Tannenbaum, S. I., Traylor, A. M., Thomas, E. J., & Salas, E. (2020). Managing teamwork in the face of pandemic: Evidence-based tips. *BMJ Quality & Safety*, *30*(1), 59–63. https://qualitysafety.bmj.com/content/30/1/59

Tanner, R. (2020, November 20). Reframing for innovative and creative problem solving. *Management Is a Journey*. https://managementisajourney.com/reframing-for-innovative-and-creative-problem-solving/

Tanzi, A. (2018, August 6). U.S. women outpacing men in higher education: Demographic trends. *Bloomberg*. https://www.bloomberg.com/news/articles/2018-08-06/u-s-women-outpacing-men-in-higher-education-demographic-trends

Tartakovsky, M. (2017, September 9). Why ruminating becomes a problem. *PsychCentral*. https://psychcentral.com/lib/when-ruminating-becomes-a-problem#1

Taylor, E., Hewitt, K., Reeves, R., Hobbs, S. H., & Lawless, W. F. (2013). Group decision-making: Consensus rule versus majority rule. *Procedia Technology*, 9, 498–504.

http://www.apaexcellence.org/resources/good-company/newsletter/article/481

Tenzer, H., Terjesen, S., & Harzing, A.-W. (2017). Language in international business: A review and agenda for future research. *Management International Review*, *57*(4). https://www.researchgate.net/publication/317253086_Language_in_International_Business_A_Review_and_Agenda_for_Future_Research

Thalheimer, W. (2010, December). How much do people forget? *Will at Work Learning*. http://www.willatworklearning.com/2010/12/how-much-do-people-forget.html

The 7 key trends impacting today's workplace. (2020). *Tinypulse*. https://www.tinypulse.com/2014-employee-engagement-organizational-culture-report

The Chapman University survey on American fears. (2015, May 17). *Chapman University*. http://www.chapman.edu/wilkinson/_files/fear-2015/codebook.pdf

The cost of poor communication: A business rationale for the communication competency. (2019). *SHRM*. https://www.shrm.org/resourcesandtools/hr-topics/behavioral-competencies/communication/pages/the-cost-of-poor-communications.aspx

The Deloitte global Millennial survey. (2020). *Deloitte*. https://www2.deloitte.com/content/dam/Deloitte/global/Documents/About-Deloitte/deloitte-2020-millennial-survey.pdf

The future of jobs report 2020. (2020, October 20). *World Economic Forum*. https://www.weforum.org/reports/the-future-of-jobs-report-2020/

The generation gap in American politics. (2018, March 1). *Pew Research Center*. http://www.people-press.org/2018/03/01/the-generation-gap-in-american-politics/

The hidden pitfalls of video negotiation. (2021, March 11). *Program on Negotiation/Harvard Law School*. https://www.pon.harvard.edu/daily/negotiation-skills-daily/before-negotiating-via-video-consider-the-hidden-pitfalls-nb/?utm_source=WhatCountsEmail&utm_medium=daily&utm_date=2021-03-11-13-30-00&mqsc=E4128143

The power of praise and recognition. (2014, February 18). *Training Journal*. https://www.trainingjournal.com/articles/feature/power-praise-and-recognition

The public and broadcasting. (2019, August 2). *Federal Communications Commission*. https://www.fcc.gov/media/radio/public-and-broadcasting#CRITICISM

The ultimate guide to virtual leadership. (2021). *DDI*. https://lp.ddiworld.com/eg/the-ultimate-guide-to-virtual-leadership?utm_source=google&utm_medium=cpc&utm_campaign=VC&utm_content=300X600&gclid=CjwKCAiAudD_BRBXEiwAudakX2lxbT2Mp-iNFFCLeDAghkCTzW_Uh8QyyPO12JZ-VRjmy-eegc1I_VQxoCHsMQAvD_BwE

The Wall Street Journal. (2020, April 07). Dr. Anthony Fauci on how life returns to normal—the journal.—*WSJ podcasts*. https://www.wsj.com/podcasts/the-journal/dr-anthony-fauci-on-how-life-returns-to-normal/d5754969-7027-431e-89fa-e12788ed9879

Thomas, G., Martin, R., & Riggio, R. E. (2013). Leading groups: Leadership as a group process. *Group Processes & Intergroup Relations*, *16*(1), 3–16.

Thomas-Kilmann conflict mode instrument. (2021). Take the Thomas-Kilmann Conflict Mode Instrument (TKI). *Kilmanndiagnostics*. https://kilmanndiagnostics.com/overview-thomas-kilmann-conflict-mode-instrument-tki/

Thorbecke, C., & Mitropoulos, A. (2020, June 28). "Extreme inequality was the preexisting condition": How COVID-19 widened America's wealth gap. *ABC News.* https://abcnews.go.com/Business/extreme-inequality-preexisting-condition-covid-19-widened-americas/story?id=71401975

Three ways to ensure women in leadership are heard in group negotiations. (2021, October 7). *Program on Negotiation/Harvard Law School.* https://www.pon.harvard.edu/daily/negotiation-skills-daily/in-group-negotiations-make-sure-your-voice-is-heard-nb/?utm_source=WhatCountsEmail&utm_medium=daily&utm_date=2021-10-07-06-30-00&mqsc=E4137483

Tierney, J., & Baumeister, R. F. (2020). *The power of bad: How the negativity effect rules us and how we can rule it.* Penguin Press.

Ting-Toomey, S., & Dorjee, T. (2018). *Communicating across cultures.* Guilford Press.

Tipping. (2022, June 7). *Wikitravel.* http://wikitravel.org/en/Tipping

Tjosvold, D., & Yu, Z. (2004). Goal interdependence and applying abilities for team in-role and extra-role performance in China. *Group Dynamics: Theory, Research, and Practice, 8*(2), 98–111.

Toegel, G., & Barsoux, J.-L. (2016, June 8). 3 situations where cross-cultural communication breaks down. *Harvard Business Review.* https://hbr.org/2016/06/3-situations-where-cross-cultural-communication-breaks-down

Tost, L. P., Gino, F., & Larrick, R. P. (2012). Power, competitiveness, an advice taking: Why the powerful don't listen. *Organizational Behavior and Human Decision Processes, 117*(1), 53–65. https://www.academia.edu/15431294/Power_competitiveness_and_advice_taking_Why_the_powerful_don_t_listen?email_work_card=reading-history

Tousley, S. (2017, January 25). How to be charismatic: The 9 habits of insanely likable people. *HubSpot.* https://blog.hubspot.com/sales/habits-of-likable-people

Trafton, A. (2014, January 16). In the blink of an Eye. MIT News | *Massachusetts Institute of Technology.* https://news.mit.edu/2014/in-the-blink-of-an-eye-0116

Trees, L. (2017, May 26). Why employees hate virtual collaboration and what to do about it. *SmartBrief.* http://www.smartbrief.com/original/2017/05/why-employees-hate-virtual-collaboration-and-what-do-about-it

Triandis, H. C. (1995). *Individualism and collectivism.* Westview Press.

Triandis, H. C. (2009). Ecological determinants of cultural variations. In R. S. Wyer, C. Chiu, Y. Hong, & D. Cohen (Eds.), *Understanding culture: Theory, research and applications.* Psychology Press.

Triandis, H. C. (2012). Culture and conflict. In S. A. Samovar, R. E. Porter, & E. R. McDaniel (Eds.), *Intercultural communication: A reader.* Wadsworth/Cengage.

Tsao, T. (2017, February 22). "Why You Need To Be Rotating Meeting Roles". Meteor.com https://www.meeetor.com/post/rotating-meeting-roles

Tsaousides, T. (2017a, November 27). Why are we scared of public speaking? *Psychology Today.* https://www.psychologytoday.com/gb/blog/smashing-the-brainblocks/201711/why-are-we-scared-public-speaking

Tsaousides, T/(2017b, November 28). How to conquer the fear of public speaking. *Psychology Today.* https://www.psychologytoday.com/us/blog/smashing-the-brainblocks/201711/how-conquer-the-fear-public-speaking

Turman, P. D. (2003). Athletic coaching from an instructional communication perspective: The influence of coach experience on high school wrestlers' preferences and perceptions of coaching behaviors across a season. *Communication Education, 52*(2), 73–86.

Twenge, J. M., VanLandingham, H., & Campbell, W. K. (2017). The seven words you can never say on television: Increases in the use of swear words in American books, 1950–2008. *Sage Journals, 7*(3). http://journals.sagepub.com/doi/abs/10.1177/2158244017723689

U.S. workplace survey. (2019). *Gensler Research Institute.* https://www.gensler.com/uploads/document/614/file/Gensler-US-Workplace-Survey-2019.pdf

Uebergang, J. (2020). The greatest 15 myths of communication. *Tower of Power.* https://www.towerofpower.com.au/the-greatest-15-myths-of-communication

University of Phoenix survey reveals nearly seven-in-ten workers have been part of dysfunctional teams. (2013, January 16). *PhoenixEducation.* https://www.prnewswire.com/news-releases/university-of-phoenix-survey-reveals-nearly-seven-in-ten-workers-have-been-part-of-dysfunctional-teams-187090161.html

Ury, L. (2019, February 11). Want to improve your relationships? Start paying more attention to bids. *The Gottman Institute*. https://www.gottman.com/blog/want-to-improve-your-relationship-start-paying-more-attention-to-bids/

Van der Hoek, M., Groeneveld, S., & Kuipers, B. (2016). Goal setting in teams: Goal clarity and team performance in the public sector. *Review of Public Personnel Administration, 38*(4), 472–493. https://journals.sagepub.com/doi/full/10.1177/0734371X16682815

Van Mierlo, H. & Kleingeld, A. (2010). Goals, strategies, and group performance: Some limits of goal setting in groups. *Small Group Research, 41*(5), 524–555.

Van Quaquebeke, N. & Eckloff, T. (2010). Defining respectful leadership: What it is, how it can be measured, and another glimpse at what it is related to. *Journal of Business Ethics, 91*(3), 343–358.

Van Zandt, D. (2020, October 7). Media Bias/Fact Check. *Harvard Business Review*. https://mediabiasfactcheck.com/harvard-business-review/

Vangelisti, A., Knapp, M., & Daly, J. (1990). Conversational narcissism. *Communication Monographs, 57*(4), 251–274.

Vecchio, R. P., Bullis, R. C., & Brazil, D. M. (2006). The utility of situational leadership theory. *Small Group Research, 37*(5), 407–424.

Verbal and nonverbal communication. (2020). *Sage Publications*. https://us.sagepub.com/sites/default/files/upm-assets/104775_book_item_104775.pdf

Victor, D. A. (2007, March 27–31). What is the language of business? Affecting business outcome before you say a word. *Proceedings of the Association for Business Communication*, 7th Asia-Pacific Conference, City University of Hong Kong.

Vigen, T. (2015). *Spurious correlations*. Hachette.

Vitelli, R. (2015, September 7). Can you change your personality? *Psychology Today*. https://www.psychologytoday.com/us/blog/media-spotlight/201509/can-you-change-your-personality

Voggeser, B. J., Singh, R. K., & Goritz, A. S. (2018, January 11). Self-control in online discussions: Disinhibited online behavior as a failure to recognize social cues. *Frontiers in Psychology*. https://dx.doi.org/10.3389%2Ffpsyg.2017.02372

Vosoughi, S., Roy, D., & Aral, S. (2018, March 9). The spread of true and false news online. *Science, 359*(6380), 1146–1151. https://www.science.org/doi/10.1126/science.aap9559

Vozza, S. (2014, February 25). Personal mission statements of 5 famous CEOs (and why you should write one too). *Fast Company*. https://www.fastcompany.com/3026791/personal-mission-statements-of-5-famous-ceos-and-why-you-should-write-one-too

Vozza, S. (2015, May 15). Seven habits of likable people. *Fast Company*. https://www.fastcompany.com/3046228/seven-habits-of-likable-people

Wahba, P. (2020, June 1). The number of black CEOs in the Fortune 500 remains very low. *Fortune*. https://fortune.com/2020/06/01/black-ceos-fortune-500-2020-african-american-business-leaders/

Wahr, J. A., Prager, R. L., Abernathy, J. H., Martinez, E. A., Salas, E., Seifert, P. C. . . . Nussmeier, N. A. (2013). Patient safety in the cardiac operating room: Human factors and teamwork. *American Heart Association*. http://circ.ahajournals.org/content/early/2013/08/05/CIR.0b013e3182a38efa

Wakefield, N., Abbatiello, A., Agarwal, D., Pastakia, K., & van Berkel, A. (2016). Leadership awakened. In J. Bersin, J. Geller, N. Wakefield, & B. Walsh (Eds.), *Global human capital trends 2016* (pp. 27–35). *Deloitte University Press*. https://www2.deloitte.com/content/dam/Deloitte/global/Documents/HumanCapital/gx-dup-global-human-capital-trends-2016.pdf

Walter, N., & Tukachinsky, R. (2020). A meta-analytic examination of the continued influence of misinformation in the face of correction: How powerful is it, why does it happen, and how to stop it? *Communication Research, 47*(2), 155–177. https://journals.sagepub.com/doi/full/10.1177/0093650219854600

Walumbwa, F. O., Hartnell, C. A., & Oke, A. (2010). Servant leadership, procedural justice climate, service climate, employee attitudes, and organizational citizenship: A cross-level investigation. *Journal of Applied Psychology, 95*(3), 517–529.

Ward, A. F., Duke, K., Gneezy, A., & Bos, M. W. (2017, *April 3*). Brain Drain: The mere presence of one's own smartphone reduces available cognitive capacity. *Journal of the Association of Consumer Research, 2*(2). https://www.journals.uchicago.edu/doi/10.1086/691462?mobileUi=0&

Ward, M., & Premack, R. (2021, March 1). What is a microaggression?14 things people think are fine to say at work—but are actually racist, sexist, or offensive. *Business Insider.* https://www.businessinsider.com/microaggression-unconscious-bias-at-work-2018-6

Ward, M., Akhtar, A., & Lebowitz, S. (2020, March 16). 26 signs you have a terrible boss, and how to stop them from crushing your happiness. *Insider.* https://www.businessinsider.com/signs-you-have-a-bad-boss-2016-2-4

Warden, I. (2021, December 31). Swearing more than usual? Studies show Covid stress is making people swear more. *The Canberra Times.* https://www.canberratimes.com.au/story/7565035/masking-modern-anxieties-with-the-classics/

Wartham, A. (2016, October 14). Four key trends driving the corporate learning and development. *The Evolllution.* https://evolllution.com/revenue-streams/corporate_partnerships/four-key-trends-driving-the-corporate-learning-and-development-market/

Warzel, C., & Petersen, A. H. (2021). *Out of office.* Alfred A. Knopf.

Watts, A., Lilienfeld, S. O., Smith, S. F., Miller, J. D., Campbell, W. K., Waldman, I. D., Rubenzer, S. J., & Faschingbauer, T. J. (October 8, 2013). The double-edged sword of grandiose narcissism: Implications for successful and unsuccessful leadership among U.S. presidents. *Psychological Science OnlineFirst.* http://differentialclub.wdfiles.com/local--files/meetings/2013_Watts%20et%20al._The%20double%20edged%20sword%20of%20grandiose%20narcissism-Implications%20for%20successful%20and%20unsuccessful%20leadership%20among%20US%20presidents.pdf

Watzlawick, P., Bevin, J., & Jackson, D. (1967). *Pragmatics of human communication.* Norton.

Weedmark, D. (2019, June 1). Importance of English in business communication. *Bizfluent.* https://bizfluent.com/about-6710260-importance-english-business-communication.html

Weinrich, M., & Simpson, A. (2014, March). Differences in acoustic vowel space and the perception of speech tempo. *Journal of Phonetics, 43,* 1–10.

Weinrich, M., Simpson, A., Fuchs, S., Winkler, R., & Perrier, P. (2014, May). Mumbling is morphology? *ResearchGate.* http://www.researchgate.net/profile/Susanne_Fuchs2/publication/261322998_Mumbling_is_morphology/links/00b49533dc4e887e33000000.pdf

Weinstein, B. (2020, May 23). Why WW's group firings on Zoom were unethical, terrible PR and bad for business. *Forbes.* https://www.forbes.com/sites/bruceweinstein/2020/05/23/why-wws-group-firings-on-zoom-were-unethical-terrible-pr-and-bad-for-business/#5cde60ff5c0b

Weir, K. (2018). What makes teams work? *Monitor.* https://www.apa.org/monitor/2018/09/cover-teams

Welker, M. (2017, July 27). The future of productivity: Teamwork and collaboration. *Entrepreneur.* https://www.entrepreneur.com/article/295265

Whaley, G. C. (2017, November 13). LGBT workers report bullying at work. *HR Watchdog.* https://hrwatchdog.calchamber.com/2017/11/lgbt-workers-report-bullying/

What are the OSHA restroom break laws? (2021). *OSHAcampus.com.* https://www.360training.com/blog/osha-restroom-break-laws

What makes a good leader, and does gender matter. (2015, January 14). Women and leadership: Chapter 2. *Pew Research Center.* http://www.pewsocialtrends.org/2015/01/14/chapter-2-what-makes-a-good-leader-and-does-gender-matter/

Wheelan, S. A. (2009). Group size, group development, and group productivity. *Small Group Research, 40*(2), 247–262.

Whitmore, J. (2017, February 7). Don't underestimate how much spelling matters in business communications. *Entrepreneur.* https://www.entrepreneur.com/article/288812

Why you need cultural intelligence (and How to Develop it). (2015, March 24). *Forbes.* https://www.forbes.com/sites/iese/2015/03/24/why-you-need-cultural-intelligence-and-how-to-develop-it/#5ed5365217d6

Why you need good business ethics. (2020). *Edward Lowe Foundation.* https://edwardlowe.org/why-you-need-good-business-ethic

Wignall, N. (2020, January 26). How to handle other people's anger like a pro. *NickWignall.com.* https://nickwignall.com/other-peoples-anger/

Williams, M. T. (2020). Microaggressions: Clarification, evidence, and impact. *Perspectives on Psychological Science.* https://journals.sagepub.com/doi/pdf/10.1177/1745691619827499

Wilmot, W., & Hocker, J. (2021). *Interpersonal conflict*. McGraw-Hill.

Wilson, V. (2016, June 9). People of color will be a majority of the American working class in 2031. *Economic Policy Institute*. http://www.epi.org/publication/the-changing-demographics-of-americas-working-class/

Wilstein, M. (2017, April 11). Jimmy Kimmel goes off on United Airlines. *Daily Beast*. http://www.thedailybeast.com/jimmy-kimmel-goes-off-on-united-airlines?source=TDB&via=FB_Page

Wineburg, S., Breakstone, J., Ziv, N., & Smith, M. (2020). Educating for misunderstanding: How approaches to teaching digital literacy make students susceptible to scammers, rogues, bad actors, and hate mongers. *Stanford Digital Repository*. https://purl.stanford.edu/mf412bt5333

Wineburg, S., McGrew, S., Breakstone, J., & Ortega, T. (2016). Evaluating information: The cornerstone of civic online reasoning. *Stanford Digital Repository*. https://cor.stanford.edu/research/evaluating-information-the-cornerstone-of-cor/

Wise, S. (2014). Can a team have too much cohesion? The dark side of network density. *European Management Journal*, *32*(5), 703–711.

Witt, P. L., & Behnke, R. R. (2006). Anticipatory speech anxiety as a function of public speaking assignment type. *Communication Education*, 55, 167–177.

Women in leadership: Why it matters. (2016, May 12). *Rockefeller Foundation*. https://www.rockefellerfoundation.org/report/women-in-leadership-why-it-matters/

Women in the workplace 2021. (2021). *LeanIn.org*. https://womenintheworkplace.com/

Wong, K. (2017, July 27). The case for cursing. *The New York Times*. https://www.nytimes.com/2017/07/27/smarter-living/the-case-for-cursing.html

Woodley, H. J. R., McLarnon, M. J. W., & O'Neill, T. A. (2019). The emergence of group potency and its implications for team effectiveness. *Frontiers of Psychology, 10*. https://www.frontiersin.org/articles/10.3389/fpsyg.2019.00992/full

Words to avoid and include on a resume. (2022, March 10). *Indeed Career Guide*. https://www.indeed.com/career-advice/resumes-cover-letters/words-to-avoid-and-include-on-a-resume

Workplace effectiveness has declined. (2020). *Gensler: US. Workplace Survey 2020*. https://www.gensler.com/uploads/document/677/file/Gensler_US_WPS_Report_2020.pdf

Work shouldn't hurt. (2022, May 21). OSEA. https://www.osea.org/work-shouldnt-hurt/

Wright, L., & McCullough, N. (2018, April 19). New survey explores the changing landscape of teamwork. *Microsoft 365*. https://www.microsoft.com/en-us/microsoft-365/blog/2018/04/19/new-survey-explores-the-changing-landscape-of-teamwork/

Wright, S. A. (2022, May 11). How to talk to someone who is always defensive. *PsychCentral*. https://psychcentral.com/lib/how-to-talk-to-someone-who-always-gets-defensive

Xu, H., & Ruef, M. (2004, November 1). The myth of the risk-tolerant entrepreneur. *Strategic Organization*, *2*(4), 331–355. https://journals.sagepub.com/doi/abs/10.1177/1476127004047617

Yang, J. L. (2006, June 12). The power of number 4.6. *Fortune*, 122.

Yang, Z., Sun, J., Zhang, Y., & Wang, Y. (2018). Virtual collaboration with mobile social media in multiple-organization projects. *Proceeding of the 51st Hawaii International Conference on System Sciences—2018*. https://scholarspace.manoa.hawaii.edu/bitstream/10125/49956/1/paper0069.pdf

Yavorski, K. (2021). Why college students should use LinkedIn. *Collegiate Parent*. https://www.collegiateparent.com/career/why-college-students-should-use-linkedin/

Yavuz, F., & Celik, O. (2017). The importance of listening in communication. *Global Journal of Psychology Research: New Trends and Issues*, *7*(1), 8–11. https://doi.org/10.18844/gjpr.v7i1.2431

Yorke, Z. (2020, April 24). The science of why remote meetings don't feel the same. *Life at Google*. https://www.blog.google/inside-google/working-google/science-why-remote-meetings-dont-feel-same/

Young, G. (2016, August 12). Women, naturally better leaders for the 21st century. *LeaderShape*. https://www.crcpress.com/rsc/downloads/WP-TL2-2016_Transpersonal_Leadership_WP2_FINAL.pdf

Yousaf, A., Shaukat, R., & Umrani, W. A. . . . (2020). Linkages between group level task conflict and individual outcomes in non-routine technical jobs. *International Journal of Conflict Management*, *32*(1), 158–176. https://doi.org/10.1108/IJCMA-08-2019-0128

Yu, R., & Chen, G.-M. (2008). Intercultural sensitivity and conflict management styles in cross-cultural situations. *Intercultural Communication Studies, 17*(2), 149–161.

Yuan, Y. C., Liao, W., & Bazarova, N. N. (2019). Judging expertise through communication styles in intercultural collaboration. *Management Communication Quarterly, 33*(2), 238–271. https://journals.sagepub.com/doi/full/10.1177/0893318918824674

Zak, P. J. (2017, January–February). The neuroscience of trust. *Harvard Business Review*. https://hbr.org/2017/01/the-neuroscience-of-trust

Zara, C. (2018, March 20). People were asked to name women tech leaders: They said "Alexa" and "Siri." *Fast Company*. https://www.fastcompany.com/40547212/people-were-asked-to-name-women-tech-leaders-they-said-alexa-and-siri

Zarankin, T. G. (2008). A new look at conflict styles: Goal orientation and outcome preferences. *International Journal of Conflict Management, 19*(2), 167–184.

Zenger, J. (2015b, November 19). Humble versus egocentric leaders: When lacking self-awareness helps. *Forbes*. https://www.forbes.com/sites/jackzenger/2015/11/19/humble-versus-egocentric-leaders-when-lacking-self-awareness-helps/#3e0be285bf4b

Zenger, J., & Folkman, J. (2012, March 15). Are women better leaders than men? *Harvard Business Review*. https://hbr.org/2012/03/a-study-in-leadership-women-do

Zetlin, M. (2018, April). 54 percent of women report workplace harassment. How is your company responding? *Inc. magazine*. https://www.inc.com/magazine/201804/minda-zetlin/sexual-harassment-workplace-policy-metoo.html

Zimmerman, E. (2010, September 25). Staying professional in virtual meetings. *New York Times*. https://www.nytimes.com/2010/09/26/jobs/26career.html

Zoom sees more growth after 'unprecedented' 2020. (2021, March 01). https://www.bbc.com/news/business-56247489#:~:text=Zoom%20boss%20Eric%20Yuan%2C%20whose,bn%20(%C2%A32.66bn)

Zoonen, W. van, Verhoeven, J. W. M., & Vliegenthart, R. (2015, September 29). How employees use Twitter to talk about work: A typology of work-related tweets. *Computers in Human Behavior*. https://www.sciencedirect.com/science/article/abs/pii/S0747563215301527

12 UK phrases and sayings. (2017, December 21). *Veem*. https://www.veem.com/library/12-uk-business-phrases-and-sayings/

2012 report card on the ethics of American youth. (2012). *Josephson Institute*. https://b3vj2d40qhg-sjw53vra221dq-wpengine.netdna-ssl.com/wp-content/uploads/2014/02/ReportCard-2012-DataTables.pdf

*2017 management consulting outlook. (2017). *Greentarget*. http://greentarget.com/wp-content/uploads/2017/03/Management-Consulting-Outlook-2017-Final.pdf

2018 Student Survey Report. (2019). *National Association of Colleges and Employers*. https://www.naceweb.org/store/2018/2018-nace-student-survey-report/

2020 vision: The future of business information. (2016). *Infodesk*. https://www.readkong.com/page/2020-vision-the-future-of-business-information-7218527

5 reasons why your company needs to embrace video conferencing now. (2017, October 30). *Forbes*. https://www.forbes.com/sites/insights-zoom/2017/10/30/5-reasons-why-your-company-needs-to-embrace-video-conferencing-now/

8 facts from the 2021 Executive Paywatch Report you need to know. (2021, July 14). *AFL-CIO*. https://aflcio.org/2021/7/14/8-facts-2021-executive-paywatch-report-you-need-know

21 collaboration statistics that show the power of teamwork. (2019). *BIT.AI*. https://blog.bit.ai/collaboration-statistics/

25 Mobile Email Statistics & Facts for 2022. *99firms*. (2021, February 2). https://99firms.com/blog/mobile-email-statistics/#gref

25 Mobile Email Statistics & Facts for 2022. *99firms*. (2021, February 2). https://99firms.com/blog/mobile-email-statistics/#gref

54 workplace statistics—What has changed in 2021? (2021, August 20). *What to Become*. https://whattobecome.com/blog/workplace-statistics/

Credits

Photo and Cartoon Credits

Index

Page numbers in *italic* indicate photos and figures.